BLUE-COLLAR MARRIAGE

BLUE-COLLAR

MARRIAGE

Mirra Komarovsky

BARNARD COLLEGE, COLUMBIA UNIVERSITY

With the Collaboration of
JANE H. PHILIPS

Howard University

Vintage Books

A DIVISION OF RANDOM HOUSE · NEW YORK

FOR *Mark*

ACKNOWLEDGMENTS

Associated with the author in the field-work phase of this study, from September 1958 to June 1959, were Dr. Jane H. Philips and Dr. Dorothy Willner. It is with pleasure that the author acknowledges their substantive and methodological contributions to this study, Dr. Philips as anthropologist and Dr. Willner as sociologist. Both collaborated with the author in the preparation of a paper using some of the collected data, read at the meetings of the American Sociological Society in August 1959. Dr. Philips is responsible for the major share of the field work, having completed 35 of the 58 case studies used in the analysis. Although not involved in the analysis of the data, she returned to the project in its final stage, read an early draft of the manuscript, and made useful editorial suggestions.

Mrs. Barbara Eichner and Miss Madeline Engel ably assisted the author with the coding and analysis of the data.

My colleagues, Professors Paul F. Lazarsfeld and Robert K. Merton, read several chapters of the manuscript. As on many previous occasions, I am again indebted to them for their unfailing generosity and their keen criticism. I wish to express my gratitude also to Professors Herbert H. Hyman and Alex Inkeles for their helpful suggestions on several chapters.

The financial support for this study was provided by a grant (M-2604) from the National Institute of Mental Health and supplementary grants from the Barnard Committee on Faculty Research. Millicent C. McIntosh, now President Emeritus of Barnard College, President Rosemary Park and Henry T. Boorse, Dean of the Faculty, have always been understanding and encouraging. I am grateful to the Bureau of Applied Social Research for housing the staff and providing research facilities and wish to thank especially its Administrative Director, Miss Clara Shapiro, for her helpfulness.

To Professor Charles H. Page I owe a great debt of gratitude for his expert and generous editorial aid.

Finally, our major debt is to the families of Glenton who collaborated in this study with such courtesy and patience.

CONTENTS

TABLES

BLUE-COLLAR MARRIAGE

INTRODUCTION

A familiar refrain runs through the writings on the American family—"This is a study of a middle-class and a college-educated segment of the population." As recently as 1957, a specialist in the field of the family could write: "We have almost no research which could be considered representative of the entire population." [1] The existing studies of the working classes give disproportionate attention to dependent, delinquent and generally problem families. The fact that the research worker is usually a college professor contributes to this imbalance, since his most readily accessible subjects are his students and colleagues, who constitute also his audience. Such individuals tend to be more reflective and articulate than less educated respondents. College graduates are also more likely to recognize the value of scientific research. Married couples have an acknowledged right to privacy which the scientist subordinates, under safeguards, to the interests of scientific progress. It was feared that working-class couples would regard research as a violation of privacy. Unlike stable families, the troubled or disorganized working-class couples submitted to investigation either in search of help or in response to pressures of social agencies.

Recent studies cited throughout this book have begun to cor-

[1] Judson T. Landis, 1957. See Bibliography, pp. 377-387, for complete reference.

rect this onesidedness. The gap in our knowledge about stable, as opposed to disorganized, working-class families nevertheless remains wide. The marriage relationship itself has received less attention than child-rearing practices and parent-child relationships. The working-class husband has been neglected. Family studies depend predominantly upon interviews with women. What the husband feels and thinks about marriage reaches us usually only through the report of his wife.

Blue-collar or manual workers (skilled, semi-skilled and unskilled) constituted, in 1963, 48.9 per cent of employed white persons and 79.7 per cent of employed Negroes.[2] The citizen who wants to understand our society, the sociologist concerned with the development of his field and the members of the helping professions—teachers, doctors, lawyers, ministers, social workers, psychiatrists—would all profit from a fuller knowledge of the family patterns of so large a proportion of our population. A recent study of buying habits concludes that the separate identity of the "working class" in the United States is rapidly fading away.[3] This may be an accurate description of changing patterns of consumption. But it does not necessarily follow that with the spread to the wage earners of such visible symbols of middle-class life as cars, television sets, washing machines and other home appliances, there comes also a standardization of marriage patterns throughout our society. Such an assumption remains to be tested.

The concentration of past research upon the better-educated classes has led at least one sociologist to express the hope that this limitation has not vitiated the search for generalizations: "There may be certain universals in human relationships which are true at all socio-economic levels. Some factors may be basic . . . in husband-wife relationships and it may make little difference whether one studies college students, their parents' marriages or the marriages of the non-college population." [4] But the existence of such universals cannot be assumed; it must be discovered

[2] *Statistical Abstract of the United States*, 1963, p. 231.

[3] In the words of the report: "The wage-earner's way of life is well-nigh indistinguishable from that of his salaried co-citizens. Their homes, their cars, their baby-sitters, the style of the clothes their wives and children wear, the food they eat, the bank where they establish credit, their days off, the education of their children, their church—all of these are alike and are becoming more nearly identical." *How American Buying Habits Change*, U.S. Department of Labor, 1959, p. 6.

[4] Judson T. Landis, 1957, p. 104.

through comparative studies. It has been said, for example, that sexual adjustment is a sensitive barometer of marital adjustment. Is this generalization, supported as it is by middle-class data, a "universal" in our society? Chapter 15 summarizes the findings of this study as related to this issue of "universals" in marriage relationships.

Insofar as patterns of marriage vary from class to class, the ignoring of class differences severely handicaps the helping professions. The middle-class or upper-class professional approaches his clients with the values of his own milieu. We have long realized that hidden cultural differences can cause international misunderstandings. But subtler variations within a country, if unrecognized, create similar confusion. To cite but one illustration, a few of the wives in this study, when they first suspected that they were pregnant, spoke to their mothers about it before telling their husbands. This fact, we would claim, is not as symptomatic of immaturity or of marital conflict as it would be if reported by educated, middle-class wives. If cultural differences are not recognized, the clues upon which we depend to make psychological assessments are bound to mislead us.

This is a study of 58 marriages and as such it sacrifices the advantages of a large survey. The scarcity of case studies of stable blue-collar marriages was one factor in our decision to use the case study method. The available research is based largely upon schedules and questionnaires. The flexible case study interview has unique advantages. For example, Chapter 2 describes the ways in which a clique of mutual friends eased for some couples the transition from single to married life. Such facts could be discovered only through interviews or observation. The last chapter contains an inventory of the kinds of results presented in this book which required these qualitative research methods.

Analysis was systematic, within the limits of our sample. A hypothesis suggested by any single observation was checked, whenever possible, by an examination and a count of all the cases. Because the sample is relatively small, our findings remain to be tested with larger numbers. This holds especially when the findings pertain not to the whole sample but to subgroups within it. But many hypotheses of this study are buttressed by, in addition to statistical tables, the internal evidence of case studies—the expressed motivations of the respondents checked by the succession of events.[5] For example, we adduce some quantitative support for the statement that a man's marriage to a better-educated wife tends to be associated with in-law problems. But, in addition, the causal links between educational inferiority and friction with the mother-in-law are examined on the basis of detailed case studies. A statistical correlation that was a mere accident of sampling would not be supported by such further evidence.

The case study method was chosen also for its advantages in conveying to the reader something of the flavor of working-class family life—a major purpose of this book. This is a sociological study, and its job is to dissect, compare, abstract and generalize, rather than to re-create the life of a group in its totality and uniqueness. But, within certain limits, artistic and scientific aims do not prove incompatible. Excerpts from interviews can evoke the flavor of first-hand experience without distorting and indeed enhancing the scientific endeavor. Although the excerpts are generally referred to as "illustrations," they do more than illustrate—they convey additional knowledge. At times they give a more precise meaning to a summary statement couched in abstract language. Consider, for example, the assertion that the "wife's continued dependence upon her mother caused irritation in the early years of marriage." Dependence in what spheres, how manifested, and how strong an irritation? There is no assurance that the generalization carries to the reader the meaning it has for the writer who derived it from a scrutiny of concrete episodes.

At other times the case material conveys to the reader some aspects of a generalization which have not as yet been captured with scientific precision. Asked to comment upon a story about a wife who was dissatisfied because her husband did not talk to her in the evenings, 37 per cent of the respondents took the side of the husband and accused the wife of being spoiled. Following this summary, Chapter 5 records the comments of men and women in their own words. The reader now catches the idiom and the tone of the remarks, the indignation and the humor, the reasons offered for the opinion, the associations of ideas and the depth of expressed convictions. All of these facets may eventually be classified with statistical precision. In the meantime,

[5] See "discerning," in Mirra Komarovsky, 1940, pp. 135-146.

while the study of marital interaction is still in its infancy, to deprive the student of such descriptions is often to leave him with too spotty and arid a portrayal.

A major theoretical concern of the study is with the relationship between the ideal (or at least the acceptable) and the actual. As the discussion turns from one aspect of marriage to another, it poses the same questions: what are the social values and the norms accepted by our respondents, and what is their actual behavior in each particular sphere? If behavior departs from the norms, what accounts for the discrepancy? We shall find many reasons why the desirable may not be the desired goal and why, even when the two do coincide, the goal is out of reach or the norm violated.

The implication of such facts for marital satisfaction is a further concern of our analysis. That a discrepancy between ideals and reality can cause guilt, strain or discontent is a familiar idea. But it will be seen that certain discrepancies are tolerated easily and, conversely, that conformity to norms—the congruence of values and behavior—is occasionally a source of strain. Moreover, the data repeatedly illustrate the role of cultural factors in human reactions to circumstances. Identical objective conditions are cheerfully accepted by some and resented by others depending upon their cultural expectations. But some situations will be shown to be stressful even when they do not violate cultural expectations. This book, in other words, illustrates both the power of cultural norms to modify human experience and the limitations of such power.

⋀⋀⋀

CHAPTER

I

Meeting Glenton's Families

Marriages studied by American sociologists have dealt predominantly with white, Protestant, native-born and college educated couples. In order to isolate the influence of social class upon marriage, we decided to limit the inquiry to a group comparable to the previous samples in race, religion and nativity but differing in occupation, income and education. Our sample was to consist of a homogeneous group sharing a number of characteristics. All were to be white, native born of native parents, Protestant, not over 40 years of age, and parents of at least one child. Only blue-collar workers were to be included. The highest level of education was set at four years of high school. The actual sample corresponds closely to the initial specifications.[1]

The locality in which the study was carried out was chosen through the examination of Census data and after interviews with Protestant church leaders in the state. Our respondents resided in two contiguous, closely interwoven, townships forming a community with a total population of about fifty thousand which we shall name Glenton.[2] Glenton is located less than five miles from a city of about half a million and less than twenty miles from a metropolis.

[1] See appendix, p. 356, for description of sample. The few cases which fall outside our specifications were accepted towards the end of the study to explore a number of hypotheses.

[2] All exact Census figures are omitted to protect the anonymity of the community.

The industrial development of Glenton dates back to the establishment of a mill in the mid-nineteenth century, a forerunner of other similar concerns which brought thousands of Scottish and English immigrants to the region. Members of the third generation of these settlers still retain traces of dialects from various parts of the British Isles. The area subsequently attracted other, heavier, industries, which changed the composition of the original population. White-collar commuters developed suburban areas but there are many neighborhoods of blue-collar workers employed in nearby industries.

The 1960 Census enables us to compare the larger of our two communities with the "urbanized area" in which it is located.[3] It is close to the average for the total region with regard to the median education, the median income, the nativity composition, and certain other characteristics. A somewhat higher proportion of its population is native to the state and a somewhat lower proportion moved into present house since 1958, a difference of two per cent.

The working-class character of Glenton's population is reflected in several facts. White-collar occupations constitute slightly more than one-third of Glenton's labor force as against almost half for the "urbanized area." Only slightly more than one-third of Glenton's residents have completed four years of high school compared to about 40 per cent for the region. Though the median income is similar, Glenton has a lower proportion of family incomes in the $10,000 and over category.

The Selection of the Families

Practical difficulties prohibited the use of a random sample.[*] The main source of respondents was the city directory, which gave name, address and occupation of the head of the family and the name of his wife, if married. Having ascertained from town officials the most likely location of working-class neighborhoods, we listed all who qualified on the basis of their occupations. We then eliminated the names which seemed to be Polish, Jewish, Irish and Italian. Letters on the stationery of Columbia Univer-

---

[3] As defined in the 1960 Census, an urbanized area contains city or cities of 50,000 and more, as well as the surrounding, closely settled area meeting certain criteria.

[*] We were not able to get access to the public school lists originally intended to serve as the frame for the selection of the sample.

sity's Bureau of Applied Research were written to the remaining persons. The letter did not call for a reply. It explained the purpose of the study and stated that an interviewer would soon visit the family. During the first interview the family was screened in the light of our specifications. Large numbers had to be eliminated because they failed to meet our age, ethnic or other requirements. This means that our original deletion of unsuitable names did not result in any considerable loss of qualified prospects.

Of the 58 cases used in this study, 41 came from the city directory. These include several which were recommended to us by the original respondents. The screening proved to be so time-consuming that we decided to supplement the 41 cases by others obtained from Protestant churches. Five churches were approached. In each congregation the names of prospective respondents were secured not on the basis of recommendations of the ministers, but from membership lists, taking in alphabetical order every case which qualified in terms of our criteria.

Of the eligible respondents who were approached, eight couples refused to be interviewed. Among them were two couples whose names had been suggested by those already contacted. Moreover, five husbands whose wives were interviewed refused to see us. We generally asked for an interview with the husband after our second meeting with the wife.

Our purpose was to study "normal" family life. Although ours was not a random sample, there is no reason to suspect that it included an overrepresentation of problem families. If there is any suspected bias in our method it may be a tendency to reduce the variability within the sample because a few of our cases were recommended to us by other interviewed couples and were thus not obtained independently. If this is so, such variation as we report understates rather than exaggerates the range of variation that might exist in a random sample.

The minimum number of hours spent with each family was six, including two interviews of two hours each with the wife and one two-hour interview with the husband. Some persons were seen four and five times, and several additional joint interviews were conducted with husband and wife. In six cases we also interviewed the parents of the wife or the husband to investigate special problems. Chance meetings with relatives were frequent, enriching our understanding of the marriage.

The interviews took place in the homes. Wives were seen during the day, the husbands in the evenings and on week ends. We made it clear that the interviews were to be private, and while young children were sometimes in and out of the room, each adult was seen separately. We occasionally arranged to talk to the men during their wives' "night off." At other times wives would use the occasion to go visiting, or would remain discreetly in another part of the dwelling. The couples were quite conscientious in keeping their appointments. Even so, overtime work, illness or other unforeseen events often necessitated several visits to complete the case.

Only two interviews were recorded on tape, as the recording machine made the respondents uncomfortable. They did not, however, seem to object to detailed note-taking. We began the interview with a schedule and our informant watched us fill it out. Other schedules and check lists followed. The major part of the interview consisted of open-ended questions within a carefully worked out guide, which had been tried out in five pilot interviews. The guide, following a pattern laid out in the author's earlier study,[4] was characterized by an emphasis on concreteness. Direct and general questions followed an inventory of specific situations.

Why They Talked to Us

The motives prompting participation in the study varied. For some it hardly involved a conscious decision. These persons paid no attention to our letter, assuming it to be a scheme to sell books or even to recruit college students. The reassurance and the persuasiveness of the interviewer kept the conversation going and before they knew it they were drawn into an experience they found rewarding.

But even those for whom the interview was merely a conversation with a sympathetic listener had some dim idea of the nature of social surveys. One woman was not sure at first whether she had ever heard of Columbia University, but then exclaimed, "Oh yes, of course, what's the matter with me, of course I have." The interviewer explained that we were not selling anything, but wished rather to learn about her opinion of family life. "That kind of thing is going on more and more all the time," she remarked: "We see it on T.V., we read about it in the papers. I

[4] Mirra Komarovsky, 1940, pp. 17-22.

guess it's sort of a fad now." Another woman compared our study to the divorce court series which she had watched on television. Television, radio and the newspaper paved the way for us. Without the rationale provided by experiences with these media even the most skillful interviewer might have been frequently rebuffed. Some younger women welcomed the interview as an exciting link with the glamorous world of mass media. The late Alfred Kinsey and his colleagues, in some measure, eased our path ("Is this another Kinsey survey?" one young woman asked hopefully), but in the main those studies proved more of a handicap. We gathered from the remarks of the wives that the indignant refusals of several husbands to allow family interviews were caused by suspicions that, despite our disclaimer, we were writing a new Kinsey report.

Some respondents cooperated with us because they shared the values in terms of which we appealed to them. To be sure, they asked for further explanation and reassurance as to the confidential nature of the study. But our letter made sense to them because they believed, as we did, although they phrased it differently, that solutions to many human problems can come through the extension of scientific rationality to human behavior. Moreover, once they had decided that the project was worthwhile they felt some obligation to help us. The prestige of the University and the mention of the minister, in the introduction to the couples who were approached through church rolls, were additional aids in securing cooperation.

Sheer curiosity tipped the scale in our favor in some cases. Still another motive was expressed by an upwardly mobile man: "I'm trying to learn decent grammar and I practice on everybody. I liked the way you talked and wanted to hear you talk some more, which was why I said you can come back."

We were struck with the openness of the women. Obviously not all were equally candid with us, but the great majority— usually during the second interview—were open enough to confide intimate feelings. Although 58 husbands did grant us interviews, more husbands than wives refused to cooperate. In fact, the initial response of many wives to our request for an interview with the husbands was "Oh, he won't be interested," or "I don't think he will talk to you," or "He's tongue-tied, he'll just say yes or no." Some wives who sincerely wanted to help us complete the study were often skeptical about their mates. We always asked for a chance to put our case directly to the husband.

The husbands talked easily enough about their jobs, but when the interviewer turned to the marriage relationship, many became noticeably uncomfortable. They squirmed, perspired or got up and moved about the room. Some men spoke volubly, but craftily parried every personal probe. The reader will be able to judge for himself, as our story unfolds, the extent to which the husbands disclosed their feelings. We do not know whether the husbands would have spoken more freely to a male interviewer. But, in any event, we shall show that the reticence of the men cannot wholly be explained by the sex of the interviewer.[5]

The Interview: First Impressions

The quality of the interviews can perhaps best be captured by relating some personal reactions growing out of the contrasts between the current interviews and the author's earlier studies of college-educated women.

My initial perception of a "difference" had to do, not with clothes, appearance, manners or material surroundings of the women I interviewed, but with their approach to the interview. In general I felt more "at home" with the manners of Glenton families than with their mode of thinking. During my very first interview in this study I suddenly realized that I had no need of the usual parrying devices to deflect the interview from myself to the respondent. College women of my earlier studies had generally interspersed their talk with such questions as "Don't you agree?" or "Don't you think that was unfortunate?" They also exhibited care about my reaction, a concern shown in self-conscious comments such as: "Don't get me wrong"; or "That sounds terrible, I suppose you'll think we are selfish."

But of the 15 women I personally interviewed in this study only 2 exhibited the kind of self-conscious awareness I had observed in college-educated respondents. Both women were high school graduates and among the most "middle-class" of our respondents. One of them interrupted her description of her husband with "Gosh, I make him sound like a dud. He is really a lot of fun"; the other said: "Gee, we sound like a dumb bunch."

[5] For effect of the sex of the interviewer in social surveys see Herbert H. Hyman, 1954, pp. 164-167.

This is not to say that the working-class women opened their hearts to us without guile or reticence. My first interviewee waited till our third meeting before confiding certain experiences. But whatever she was ready to say she told flatly and directly, without self-conscious or clarifying asides.

Were Glenton housewives, perhaps, diffident in the presence of middle-class persons? The interviewers were introduced as "Mrs." rather than as "Doctor" or "Professor," although our affiliation with the university was known to them. Actually they were quite at ease and seemed to be less impressed with academic status than many of the college respondents in my earlier studies. There was barely a trace of defensiveness covering some sense of inferiority: "We don't talk so fancy, just plain, we ain't educated. One couple in our bunch think they're long-hairs. We like to enjoy life and not pretend we're so smart."

The working-class respondents did not carry on the interview with the eye on their "looking-glass" self. One woman, it is true, having blurted out some details about her sex life, gasped in embarrassment at her own disclosure. A husband remarked: "It makes one feel pretty small to tell you this stuff." But, generally speaking, they exhibited much less concern with reactions of the interviewer than did the college respondents. The latter told their story while at the same time taking on the role of the interviewer, imagining her attitude. They were concerned not alone with her moral judgment but the accuracy of her understanding. They would describe someone, realize at once how such a characterization might sound to a stranger, and be quick to correct a possible misunderstanding. All this implies a complex mental organization, including the capacity to be an "object to oneself" and to imagine the attitude of the other. It requires psychological sophistication to realize that some described action may stem from a variety of motives, hence the need to point to the "correct" one and to eliminate the others. The working-class women appear to lack this sophistication.

We considered the possibility that we erred in attributing to Glenton women this unconcern with the interviewer's attitude. Were we, perhaps, merely reacting to the nonchalant manner in which women described some behavior which violated *our* social norms?[6] Observations about the college women, on the other

[6] The main danger in cross-cultural comparisons is that the observer will

hand, may have reflected the common moral values shared with them. But this possibility would not account for the wealth of qualifying and explanatory remarks about morally neutral matters on the part of the college woman. If anything, the latter, perceiving as she did our more similar backgrounds, might have been expected to dispense with her endless clarifications. We have encountered, we believe, a real difference in cognitive styles.

A similar contrast was reported by Leonard Schatzman and Anselm Strauss, who compared the reports about a community disaster, a tornado, given by two groups of respondents. The grammar school graduates gave a straight account of what they saw through their own eyes. They seldom anticipated responses to their statements, nor did they describe events from the standpoint of others. The better-educated respondent on the other hand qualified, illustrated, anticipated doubt and, in general, displayed "a parallel consciousness of the other and himself." [7]

That such cognitive differences may emerge early in life is suggested by Claudia Lewis in a comparative study of children of professional parents in a New York City nursery school and children in the Tennessee mountains. The author claims that the play of the latter group was less imaginative and creative than of the former. The mountain children appeared deficient in their ability to take the role of the other. "They rarely throw themselves into play with the complete immersion that the [New York] children did. Ina Lee, while she rocked her doll, remained Ina Lee. She did not lose her identity in a mother's role and in a mother's tone of voice." [8]

Glenton women differed from college-educated women in yet another respect. The latter sought the interviewer's help with their own psychological problems. In the background of the interview one could sense two questions, "Do you find me typical or different?" And "What can be done about such a problem?"

---

identify some tendency or motive with its specific manifestation in his own group and, conversely, fail to see that an identical tendency may assume an unfamiliar form.

[7] Leonard Schatzman and Anselm Strauss, 1955, pp. 329-338.

[8] Claudia Lewis, 1946, p. 36. Lower-class children were found in another study to have a relatively meager imaginative activity in comparison with middle-class children and to be oriented towards the outside world rather than to their own impulses, handling the latter through introspection and fantasy. Basil Bernstein, 1958, p. 160.

These questions might be asked directly or veiled in more general inquiries. The contrasting stance of the working-class women may be illustrated by a 23-year old wife who found, after five years of marriage, that her husband's interest in "sex" had declined. "I guess," she added sadly, "this is natural as you get older." But there was no question in her voice as she said this and she did not search the interviewer's facial expression for clues. This person did talk to her sister about sexual matters. Neither she nor the others turned to us as to experts. They did not seek our help because, in comparison with the college graduates, they knew less of psychological dynamics, did not recognize the therapeutic value of talk or the existence of expertise in these areas.[9]

Six hours of interviewing should have focused the attention of our respondents upon family *relationships*, but they continued to blur the distinction between situational and relationship features of marriage and to stress the former. "What in your marriage would you change, if you could?" we asked at the end of the interview, having already discussed in detail many specific areas of the marriage relationship. "If I could get a better job," "more money," "move to a larger apartment" were interspersed with criticisms of the mate. Even when allowance is made for deliberate (or unconscious) use of "money" to avoid the more sensitive areas, the impression remains that conceptualization of the marital relationship is primitive. The days may be full of joy and resentment, pity and pride, anger and love, but these emotions are not named, distinguished or reflected upon to anything like the degree characteristic of better-educated respondents. Whatever such lack of reflection portends for marital adjustment, it surely confronted the interviewer with special problems. We often had the feeling that the questions we raised had never been the subject of previous reflection. We were often told exactly that: "Gee, I don't know. I have never thought about it."

Some typical answers of Glenton's couples throw additional light upon the way they think about family relationships. "Does your husband have any favorites among the children?" we asked, and the frequent answer was: "No, if he gets something for one kid, he always brings something for the other." "Think back to

[9] August B. Hollingshead and Frederick C. Redlich, 1958, p. 340, report that lower-class patients express lack of confidence in a "talking treatment."

the past week or two," asked the interviewer, "Has your husband done anything that hurt your feelings, made you mad, surprised you?" The word "surprise" was usually interpreted as referring to an unexpected gift. The word "help" meant money or services even when it was used by the interviewer in a psychological sense. "When you feel that way [low for no apparent reason] can your mother help you?" we inquired. The women might pause for a moment (being herself puzzled by this non sequitur) and say, "No, she doesn't have any cash to spare."

Marriage relationships were discussed by Glenton's couples with few distinctions of kind and degree. A man, speaking about the marriages of his pals, was asked whether any of them were happier than others. Well, he remarked, he does not know anyone who is unhappy: "They have no troubles which cannot be patched up." He apparently recognized only two categories, the happy marriages with their usual troubles and others, near the breaking point. A woman was asked whether her husband was an easy or a difficult person to talk to: "Is there anything you wish you could talk to him about more easily than you do?" She might have asked herself: "If I spend too much money, if the kid is sick, can I tell him?" and then responded, "I can tell him anything I need to say." She did not perceive that the question may lend itself to qualifications as to degree and kind of communication. Such refinements had to be brought out by laborious questioning.

To sum up, for Glenton's couples psychological relationships are not the subject of constant reflection, as they appeared to be for the college women in the previous study. The explanation may lie in a lack of psychological sophistication as well as in poverty, which increases the saliency of economic factors. A similar finding has been reported by Gerald Gurin and his colleagues. In answer to questions about sources of marital happiness and unhappiness, college-educated respondents mentioned some aspects of the marriage relationship (rather than conditions of life) more frequently than the less-educated men and women.[10]

[10] The sources of marital happiness and unhappiness studied by Gurin included relationships, situations and characteristics of the spouse and of self. "The differences among groups of different educational levels are particularly striking in the happiness question: 32 per cent of the grade school group, 41 per cent of the high school group and 55 per cent of the college group saw their marital happiness as deriving from some aspect of the marriage

The women were cordial in manner and observed the familiar amenities, such as asking the interviewer to sit down, offering tea or coffee, apologizing for interruptions by a telephone conversation, scolding a child for whispering in front of the interviewer and so on. Indeed, we were impressed with the degree to which they controlled irritation with us over prolonged questioning or inconvenient visits. Only a minority failed to introduce the husband if he returned home during the interview, in which case the man would sometimes walk awkwardly through the room glancing furtively at the interviewer. We noted that no special thanks were given us when, on occasion, we helped with some household chore while talking to the woman or when we brought a jar of instant coffee or a cake after having been offered some refreshments on a previous visit. This reciprocity obviously was taken for granted.

We were seldom asked personal questions. This may reflect a lack of curiosity, but it is surely also a matter of polite self-restraint. Only when we happened to volunteer some information, a person might say: "I had wondered about it, but I didn't want to ask." Even those who had only a vague idea of social surveys perceived quickly the essence of the interviewer's role. Unlike the reciprocal confidences of friendship, an interview is characterized by one-way disclosure. They respected our privacy and recognized that our probings gave them no corresponding privileges. We believe what explains the reserve was neither awe of the interviewer nor lack of curiosity about us as persons, but rather the norm of discretion.

We recognized early in the study that some words had different meanings for our respondents and for us. The word "quarrel" carried the connotation of such a major and violent conflict that we had to add "spat," "disagreement" and other terms to convey a variety of marital clashes. To "confide" often meant to seek advice rather than share for its own sake. "Talk" to a few implied a prolonged discussion ("telling each other news isn't talking"). "Intelligent" and "smart" were the terms used, not "bright";

relationship. Although not so striking, the question on sources of marital distress yielded similar results, with college-educated respondents again mentioning more relationship aspects of marriage. 15 per cent of the latter, compared to 8 per cent of the grade school group and 9 per cent of the high school group." Gerald Gurin *et al.*, 1960, p. 105.

"unfair"—not "unjust." "What kinds of things make you feel pleased or satisfied with yourself?" we asked. "When I get my work done," "When I get a bargain" and similar responses were given by some. But to a large proportion of men and women the phrase "pleased with yourself" carried the unfavorable meaning of "being stuck on yourself." These tended to answer the question in the manner of one confessing moral defects.

The unintended consequences of pure research for the participants raise some moral problems for the researcher. The interviews stimulated self-analysis. For example, we were told that subsequent to the interviews the role of in-laws in marriage was the subject of heated discussions in a tavern. One husband reported having kidded a friend: "Now who will you confide this to?" Another man, having described his job and prospects, got, as he put it, "all stirred up" by the picture he gave of his frustrations. After the interview he went to the union to demand that they at long last act on their promises to upgrade him. A woman realized, she said, in depicting leisure-time interests, how lazy the couple had become about doing things and seeing people and reported that they had started bowling again. Still another couple asked the interviewer for a referral to a marriage counselor. We hoped that such clarification of experience played a constructive role in their lives, and we doubted that an interview such as ours could break down psychological defenses in any dangerous way. But whether or not our optimism was warranted in this particular instance, the larger problem of the human costs of scientific progress remains unsolved. The social scientist is now beginning to face the moral issues long familiar to medical science, where long-range progress frequently requires experiments which carry no benefit—and occasionally even bring risks—for their subjects. Incidentally, the fact that this brief encounter with the interviewer could so stimulate even a few individuals suggests that the lack of reflectiveness shown by our respondents does not necessarily betoken limited mental capacity.

A Preview of a Finding: Educational Differences

We set out to study the married life of what was intended to be a homogeneous group of blue-collar workers: all currently employed, Protestant, native-born of native parents, with high school education or less, parents of at least one child, and not over

40 years of age. But this restricted sample turned out to be far from homogeneous with respect to the characteristics of their marriages. We refer not to the expected individual variations from family to family but to socially structured differences in ethical values and in actual behavior. Distinctive patterns of marriage can be discerned among the many individual variations.

The patterns are associated with differences in the level of education. Occasionally our data permitted a comparison by occupation (unskilled, semi-skilled and skilled) and by income. But the major contrast discovered in the study was between high school graduates and those who had not completed high school.

It would be naive to attribute the differences found between the two educational categories to their schooling as such, because formal education is linked with other circumstances. For example, in comparison with the fathers of the less-educated husbands and wives, the fathers of high school graduates had more skilled occupations and, conversely, a smaller proportion were unskilled laborers. More skilled jobs, we can reasonably assume, also meant higher wages. Several of our less-educated respondents found it necessary to leave school to help support their families. Case histories abound in instances of other differences. One high school graduate married to a man who dropped out of high school commented upon the home-centered life of her in-laws. Her father, on the other hand, belonged to a lodge, her mother to a lodge auxiliary and both enjoyed an active social life. We interviewed both parental families of another couple in which the wife was also better educated than her husband. The husband's mother expressed the view that a husband's job and his home should be kept apart: "When the hours is done, that's the end." The wife's mother on the other hand, expected her husband to share with her the news of his job.

The high school graduates and the less well-educated had spent their pre-marriage years in different types of environment. The parents of the high school graduates have, we believe, given their children a head start towards middle-class patterns of family life. Moreover, whether because of this initial advantage or possibly because they were more able, emotionally stable or ambitious,[11] the high school graduates in our sample have a somewhat higher average income, and a higher rate of church and

[11] See Solomon Lichter *et al.*, 1962.

club affiliation. The high school couples have, on the average, a smaller number of children than the less-educated. Higher education does not increase the extent of newspaper reading on the part of women but it does raise the proportion of daily readers among the men. The two educational groups, however, do not differ in extent of magazine reading. Books are mentioned only very rarely by either group.

Clearly, we are dealing here with a whole complex of factors each of which may contribute to differences in married life. We have occasionally been successful in disentangling these causal connections. But our main concern throughout has been to discern the common and the divergent patterns of belief and of marital behavior and to consider their further *consequences* for marriage and its problems.

If it is important to realize that the designation "the stable blue-collar class" does not describe a uniform subculture of family life, we must, however, also guard against the opposite danger. It was tempting to speak of distinctive patterns of marriage, but this should not create a stereotype of discrete subgroups with sharply contrasting types of marriage. The differences indicated between the educational groups are differences of degree, with considerable overlapping between them. Income, occupation, education and family background are in themselves imperfectly correlated and, moreover, these are not the only factors affecting married life. The result is a complex, criss-crossing pattern of differences rather than two distinct types.[12]

---

[12] Our finding of intra-group differences is another reminder of the lack of precision in the concept of the "blue-collar worker." S. M. Miller and Frank Reisman, 1961, urge that a distinction be made between the "lower class" (the unskilled, disorganized, the disadvantaged Negro and ethnic minorities), on the one hand, and the "stable working class" on the other. But even the latter turns out to embrace variations in mode of life and in values. The "stable working class" might be, in turn, divided into "high" and "low" subgroups.

CHAPTER
2

Learning Conjugal Roles

The Glenton study was limited to families with children. Excluded, therefore, were the newly married couples who might have described their problems in learning conjugal roles in the first year or two of marriage. Even though we did not set out to investigate these problems we found many references to them, especially in the interviews with couples married less than seven years. This chapter examines the influences that eased and hindered the transition from single to married life.

Brides and bridegrooms in all social classes must reconcile their new marital relationships with former attachments to relatives and friends. Problems arise when a person finds it difficult to give up the rewards of the old ties. Parents (or more generally, any former "role partners") may contribute to the difficulty if they refuse to modify their claims despite the change in the status of the newly married person. Psychoanalysts and novelists have had much to tell us about "silver cords"—the strong ties to a parent that persist through life, impairing the capacity to love a mate.

It is not known whether the incidence of such excessive bonds to parents varies from class to class. We did find other conditions related to this problem that are likely to be class-linked. Within our sample of working-class families, the better-educated, as we shall see, emphasize the priority of marriage and demand a more complete transfer of loyalties to the mate, while the less-educated tolerate continuing ties to parents and friends.[1] All newly married persons must unlearn some old habits, but some groups require more drastic changes than others.

Norms, or accepted rules of conduct, are not the only factors affecting ease of transition. The following pages show how the modes of life—residential, occupational and leisure-time patterns —tend either to exacerbate the conflict between prior attachments and the demands of marriage or to minimize it. For example, the likelihood that the bride and the bridegroom will reside in the same community with their parents depends upon patterns of mobility characteristic of men and women in a given segment of the population.

Marriage as Liberation

The relative ease of rechanneling one's primary loyalty from parents to mate is obviously affected by the strength of the former ties. When a person is unhappy in the parental home, marriage may bring a welcome escape. This was brought out by the replies to the question: "How does marriage change a man's life?" [2] We had expected that, whatever else the husbands might say, they would feel that marriage put an end to the freedom and irresponsibility of bachelorhood. And, indeed, one-half of the men[3] did respond to this question with such replies as "He's got to settle down" and "A husband has more responsibility." Yet, 10 per cent of the men emphasized the freedom they acquired with marriage. "Your wife can't boss you around the way your parents can," said a 32-year-old factory worker who married at age 23. A 25-year-old park employee (married three years) answered: "He's got his own place and he's boss. With my mother, I had to come home when she said or I wouldn't get anything to eat. Now I can come and go whenever I like." A 26-year-old bus driver, after three years of marriage, admitted that he married to escape an unhappy home. "I didn't get along with my step-father, and Mother was always in the middle of it." It was only later that

---

[1] Similar findings about the strength of kinship ties are reported in a study of English working classes. See Michael Young and Peter Willmott, 1957.

[2] The author is indebted for this question to Gerald Gurin *et al.*, 1960, p. 412.

[3] Twenty-five out of the 50 men who answered this question.

he recognized that marriage "wasn't just an out," that it was "something good in itself." The same thought was expressed by another respondent: "Your parents think they are cock of the walk. They don't let you do what you want to. When you have your own home, you can free-wheel around."

Considering the responsibility that a man assumes with marriage, such a sense of liberation and escape is noteworthy. The working-class youth generally resides with his parents up to the time of his marriage. Aside from a complete break with the family, marriage is the usual means of release from oppressive parental control. An out-of-town college or an independent residence is available to middle-class youth but for the young men in the present study military service generally constitutes the only period of separation from the parental home. Excluding those who married while in service, the one orphan, and four previously married men, 97 per cent of the men had lived in the parental home until they married. Two-thirds of the men were over 20 years of age at the time of marriage to their present mates. That this may be a fairly common pattern is suggested by the fact that an English study reports that it is rare for a working-class child to leave home before marriage unless he takes a non-manual job.[4]

Marriage provides the most acceptable escape from an unhappy home. Moreover, marriage in itself is less restrictive because the working-class bridegroom enjoys some privileges not granted the middle-class husband. Only a minority of Glenton's husbands, it is true, feel free to come and go as they please, but such a minority does exist.

The greater control which the family exercises over the adolescent daughter in comparison with the son no doubt largely explains the greater frequency with which women listed escape from home as one of the benefits of marriage. Almost three times as many women as men when asked "How does marriage change a woman's life?" spontaneously mentioned the escape from the parental home as a blessing.[5] "One reason I got married at sixteen," explained a 23-year-old wife, "was to get away from home." She told of constant squabbles, fights and "hollering" during childhood. Although her parents finally separated, she com-

---

[4] Peter Townsend, 1957, p. 79.
[5] Twenty-seven per cent of the 43 who answered this question.

mented bitterly, "They would tell us kids that they stayed together for our sakes—that made us feel real good!" She said she
dreaded the Sunday outings to the shore supposedly intended to
give the children a good time; no sooner did they leave home
than "the hollering would start." She never had a room of her
own. Her bed was in the parlor, and she always had to wait till
her brothers' friends would go home before she could go to
sleep. She concluded: "I got married to get away from it all, but
I got out of the frying pan into the fire."

The following remarks made by other women also stress escape as a motivation: "If my mother had been more free and
easy I might not have married him." "It's regular to be married.
It's a lot of headaches too but I'd hate being in prison with my
family. You get all cooped up and you don't know which way to
bust out." "I got out from under" was the way still another wife
described the advantages of marriage.

However, while the young people sometimes sought in marriage an escape from an unhappy home, lack of means for establishing a separate household frequently delayed their liberation.
Thus, nearly 40 per cent of the couples in this study began their
married life in the home of parents of either the bridegroom or
the bride.[6] The joint household with parents did not invariably
cause marital strains, but it frequently did have unfavorable consequences. (See Chapter 12.) The accepted norm is the establishment of a separate household upon marriage. This is felt to be
especially important precisely during the initial period of adjustment. Working-class couples share with the middle classes, then,
the ideal of a separate establishment at marriage, but economic
obstacles frequently render this ideal unattainable.

"Silver Cords"

For the husband, prior attachments occasionally creating
strain in the first year of marriage are to the mother and to a
clique of buddies. For the wife, the competing relationships are
those with her mother and, in two exceptional cases, those with
father and sister. The following case illustrates such attachment to the mother:

[6] In the country as a whole about 20 per cent of married couples in the
early 1950's postponed setting up a separate home during the first year of
marriage. Paul C. Glick, 1957, p. 60.

"Our biggest problem when we were first married was my husband's fight to break me away from my mother. I can see now that he was right in trying to cut the apron strings, but I couldn't see it then. I used to take the bus home from work, and it stopped right in front of my mother's. I'd visit with her for a while before going home. But Jim got home an hour before I did and when I came in he'd say: 'I suppose you stopped at your mother's again today.' Then one time I got sick and I went to stay with my mother. That made him sore and he said: 'Next time you are sick, you stay home.' "

The attachment of the young wives to their mothers is reflected in the frequency of their contacts. The young wives see their mothers frequently. Ninety-two per cent of wives married less than seven years whose mothers live in the community see their mothers several times a week or daily. But contacts decline with the duration of marriage. Only 59 per cent of the wives married seven years and over see their mothers several times a week or daily. The corresponding figures for the husband's contacts with his mother are 60 per cent for the husbands married under seven years, and 48 per cent for the older men. (See Chapter 11.)

The men have fewer contacts with their mothers, but in a number of cases it is the husband's ties to his mother that caused marital conflict. A young wife bemoans such a relationship:

"He works for his dad, and the shop is right in front of their house, so he has lunch at his mother's every day. It's handy and saves money. And when he's mad at me he goes to his mother's and simply stuffs himself, the way he might have done when he was a little boy. . . . When we were first married he never wanted to do jobs around the house for me, but he did plenty when his mother sent for him to help at home. He was confused about being a loyal son and being a husband. . . . It burned me up and I raised Cain about it. . . . When he was living at home, his mother would sometimes bring his breakfast to him in bed. He knows now that when the alarm goes off I get up, and if he comes down late he has to eat his eggs cold. . . . He tells me he wishes I appreciated his mother more and could fit in better with his family."

A 19-year-old woman married her 21-year-old husband while he was in the army in the South. Back in Glenton, his home town, she became disturbed that they never went anywhere without his mother and his sister. But she did not know how to tell her husband that this upset her. She soon became pregnant and complained to her doctor about her depressions. The doctor told her that this was a natural reaction in pregnancy, and the young wife, using pregnancy as an excuse, asked her husband whether they could do a few things as a couple without his mother. "He didn't know at first how to say no to his family, how to accommodate both them and his wife," she explained.

Since attachments to parents continue to play an important role in many older marriages, they will be considered more fully in Chapter 11.

The task of integrating the pre-marriage friends into a new social circle is another common problem of newly married couples. A most biting analysis of the loss of friends by marriage comes to us from another country and another century, in Charles Lamb's "A Bachelor Complaint on the Behavior of Married People." [7] But the mode of life characteristic of a given social class shapes this common problem in distinctive ways.

The Pull of the Male Clique

Many Glenton families do not entertain friends at home and, in fact, the pattern of entertaining does not exist among these couples. (See Chapter 14.) Consequently, if the young husband wants to maintain association with old friends, he has to do so outside the home. It is thus more difficult for the working husband to continue old friendships than for the housekeeping wife. The women frequently see old girl friends during the day. Although the husbands have evenings and week ends when they might have contacts with male friends, such leisure hours are to some extent claimed by the family. Meetings at lunch are feasible in rare situations, such as when an old friend is also a workmate.

A middle-class wife, if she dislikes her husband's friends, may subtly and gradually maneuver to alienate them. In the working class, however, there is no contact between the wife and the male clique. Any conflict over the husband's absence from home in order to be with his friends is quickly forced into the open.

The conflict is not so sharp as a middle-class observer might expect because some social life for husbands with friends outside of the home is accepted in Glenton. (See Chapter 14.) In transi-

[7] See Willard Waller and Reuben Hill, 1951, pp. 264-266.

tional families, however—those with both working and middle-class norms—inconsistencies arise that work to the disadvantage now of one sex, now of the other. For example, a 27-year-old husband confesses that he feels hampered by marriage. He would like to go out with the boys but "it just isn't done." The disapproval of the practice in this case may reflect the influence of the church (he is an active member) or the middle-class ideals of his wife. This couple, however, remains true to the working-class pattern in another respect. They do not entertain friends at home. This combination of patterns prevents the husband from maintaining any contact with male friends.

Fourteen per cent of the total group reported having had conflicts over the husband's friends in the early years of marriage. Had we interviewed more couples soon after marriage, the percentage reported might have been higher.

The male clique retards the domestication or the marital socialization of the husband. The marriage of a member threatens the others with loneliness and the breakdown of their social world. They are quick to seize upon the concessions that a young husband has to make to his wife and are apt to taunt him for his "weakness." Fighting for its very existence, the clique rewards resistance to the new role, and it mocks capitulation to what the wife claims as her due.

Marriage at a young age was anticipated by clique members. The feeling of betrayal occasioned by the marriage of a buddy, mingled with his expectation of it, is revealed in the bitterness of a young husband: "They razzed me plenty, 'Now you are married, you have to go home.' That's how they are, and as soon as they get a girl, they'd drop you like a hot potato." One 19-year-old wife described how her husband's buddies used to call him up in the first year of her marriage and ". . . invite him to come along as if he had no wife. They would make wisecracks about his being henpecked." She decided to take things into her own hands and tell them that she and her husband had plans to go somewhere together. Marriage conflict was avoided mainly because the young husband shifted to night work and had less opportunity for evenings with his friends.

The pull of the male clique can exceed the accepted limits of tolerance in a variety of situations. Psychiatrists might suggest latent homosexual attachments as one explanation. But social conditions play their part. For one thing, the cliques often consist of men who had been friends as boys in school. Patterns of residential mobility will determine the chances for such persistence of school associations. In Glenton, the attraction of the clique was especially strong in those cases in which the circumstances of marriage were unfavorable. In two of the most extreme cases, a young husband had no regular employment, and a couple lived with parents. In such cases, acquisition of marriage roles was slow because marriage offered few rewards for severing old ties.

The circumstances involved in the tug-of-war between the clique and the wife are illustrated in the case of the 25-year-old wife of a truck driver, who married at the age of 17. She described a stormy first year of marriage. No sooner did they marry, the wife stated, than "he started going out with his four buddies almost every evening just as if he was still single. Sometimes if he drank too much he would go to his mother's house to sleep it off and not even come home at all." At one point she packed her husband's bag and told him that she was through with him. He moved back to his parents' home and started calling her up and courting her again. They became reconciled and, she says, "We get along good now."

The wife in this case is a Protestant who married a Catholic against her mother's wishes. We interviewed her mother and the opposition turned out to be less on grounds of religion than because of the young man's somewhat lower social status. The young couple did not have any furniture or any savings, and had to move in with the girl's parents. Both went to work.

In his own interview, the husband made it clear that *the conflict was not caused by any differences in normative expectations:*

"I was a louse, it was all my fault. She is easy-going." But he tried to explain his side of the story. "I was broke and we moved in with her parents and had an audience whenever we had a fight. I was disgusted with my in-laws. There was a slump in the trucking business, and I'd ride around all day looking for work and getting very few jobs." His wife worked and saved her wages to buy the furniture. After some months, they moved into two furnished rooms in his friend's house but this didn't improve matters. "My wife got pregnant, I had no work and no money and was so disgusted with all this trouble that I'd say to hell with it and walk away from it all and go out with my buddies."

He was then just 20 and the first of his four buddies to marry. So he would go out four or five nights a week, drink and gamble, "just like I was single."

His mother used to say to him, "You got a wife now and you gotta treat her right." His father talked to him: "Are you going to stay with her or aren't you? Make up your mind." His married older brother (as we learned from the interview with the parents of this young husband) was "even wilder than he was." Our respondent explained that he himself was drinking and gambling and not running around with girls.

The husband attributed the alleviation of this problem to job security and to parenthood. When asked to explain the improvement in his behavior, his answer was: "Steadier work. I began to earn good money. The baby was born. My wife stopped working. We moved into a better apartment. We moved back into my in-law's house, but now we had a separate apartment on the top floor, we didn't have our meals with them and had more privacy." In another part of the interview he was asked: "How does marriage change a man's life?" Significantly his answer was: "I don't think it is marriage that does it. When I got married I worked, my wife worked. It was still like being single. But having children sure makes a difference; then you have responsibility."

Eight years later, at the time of the interview, the major marriage problems have been "ironed out." The mother-in-law is resigned. "Half of the time," said the wife: "he is down with them [her parents] drinking coffee." The husband still has his Friday nights and Saturday afternoons playing pool or cards with the fellows. There still is some residue of conflict. "What is your husband's idea of a good time?" his wife was asked. "To come and go as he pleases. . . . Over the week end he stays home for an hour, and then goes out to see who he can find to talk to." But "We get along good" is the couple's own estimate of their present relationship.

The marital socialization of this young husband was hindered in several ways. His limited occupational skills and the lull in the trucking business made it difficult for him to assume the role of provider and establish a separate home. Frustrated in his efforts to enact the expected role, and finding few rewards in the new relationship, he was tempted to "walk away from it all." He credits parenthood with his domestication. The very unambiguous and inescapable nature of parental responsibility helped to control his behavior, whereas while his wife worked "it was still like being single." He had apparently internalized the sense of parental responsibility sufficiently to respond to its challenge. Paradoxically, then, the very magnitude of the responsibility of parenthood made it easier for him to accept it than the lesser demands of marriage as such.

The idea that the greater change in life comes not with marriage but with parenthood is likewise expressed by others. "There are two categories," remarked another husband, "marriage and family life. When married people don't have children they are still babies. The two of us worked before the children came. She worked for about four years and it was very different. It's having kids that makes for responsibility. You cannot go on doing what you like." Parenthood did not always have so beneficial an effect upon the marriage as in the case just cited. For some couples it created new problems. In other studies of parenthood as a crisis it was noted that couples in which the husband was not a college graduate experienced greater strains of transition to parenthood.[8]

The male clique created difficulties for another young marriage described by the wife:

"We got married when I was sixteen and he was twenty. We moved in with his parents. They were nice to me—they even took my side against him but it was awful living with them. Our bedroom was right next to theirs, you'd turn over in bed, they'd hear you. He didn't have any job; he'd work for awhile and then quit. He used to go out every single night after supper, just as if he was single. His parents tried to shame him about leaving me to be with the fellows. I tried every trick in the pack. I cried and I cursed. I would have gone back home but by that time my parents were separated and there was no place to go. I don't think I would have split up, I would have gone home just to scare him, but I just had to stick it out."

When asked how her marriage improved this wife explained that other fellows in the clique married too. In time the couple found an apartment of their own and he settled down to a steady job.

The Separate Worlds of the Sexes

Men and women live in different psychological worlds whatever their class position. Much of the zest and the exasperation of the early years of marriage results from each partner's intro-

[8] See, for example, Everett D. Dyer, 1963, and E. E. LeMasters, 1957.

duction into the mental world of the opposite sex. For many Glenton couples the confrontation brought more exasperation than delight.

Chapter 5 indicates that the gulf between the sexes in interests and attitudes may be wider in the working classes than among the educated middle classes. A number of our couples found the gulf so wide that neither could serve as a satisfying audience to the other. They repeatedly missed the cues and, when they did understand the other's concerns, found them trivial and boring. "When I was first married, half of the time I didn't know what she was driving at, what it was all about," confessed a 23-year-old grade school graduate. "Sometimes I'd think I'd got her all figured out and then I don't make her out at all. The women in her bunch understood her pretty well though," he added. "They seemed to understand her better than I did sometimes. They'd tell their husbands about her and the fellows would tell me." His 22-year-old wife remarked, "Men are different. They don't feel the same as us."

This husband was not the only person who sought the help of his own sex to translate incomprehensible ways of the spouse. A young wife, for example, perplexed about her husband's refusal to explain his low spirits, turned to her mother-in-law for guidance. The latter in turn asked her husband and then passed along his suggestion to the young wife.

Several newly married men and women still exhibited watchful caution because they did not know, as one put it, "which way the other will jump."

"You're supposed to tell your husband everything," said one young wife, "but you don't. Nobody can tell you what you ought to tell him. Sometimes you tell him just the little old nothings and it is just as wrong as it can be. And sometimes you tell him something you think will bring the roof down and he won't even bat an eyelash."

Sharp sex differences in interests and attitudes continued to affect marriage beyond its initial period and will be discussed in subsequent chapters. (See especially pp. 148-156.)

The Parental Family as a Major Agent of Socialization

Much has been written about the wide gap between generations allegedly so characteristic of rapidly changing societies.[9]

[9] See, for example, Karl Mannheim, 1952, and Kingsley Davis, 1940.

The impressive fact about Glenton, however, was the narrow generational cleavage. The parental family within which our men and women consciously or unconsciously acquired their conception of marriage roles remains their major reference group after marriage. The mother, for example, may be considered old-fashioned about sex and religion but in most respects the married woman's guide is still her mother and certainly not Dr. Spock nor even her own peer group. This conclusion was reached on the basis of the evidence to be presented in chapters on contacts with relatives and on confidants.

The importance of the family is also revealed in our rough inventory of agents of socialization. All references to a discussion of marriage roles with a person (other than one's mate) were culled from the interviews with 46 persons, married for less than seven years. Any mention of personal or impersonal sources of information about marriage roles was recorded. For example:

"When something goes wrong, like when he [her husband] is sick and when I don't know what to do with the baby, it's only a couple of steps around to Mom's and I talk to her."

Of sex relations in early marriage a wife said: "When him and me couldn't figure things out, he'd ask his brother and I'd ask Jane [her sister]."

"I read an article on young married couples in a magazine and I brought it home for my wife to see."

"I had to teach him to be more interested in the children, to spend more time with them, and to give more of himself which he didn't know how to do. I read parent magazines and watched T.V. and I would tell him about it, and he asked around, and we talked to his family, and now he's doing it systematically."

"Women do strange things," remarked a young husband. He talked to his married friends, who seemed to have had the same experiences.

"When I was first married," said a wife, "I couldn't make a move without asking my sister's advice."

The resulting summary of agents of socialization includes relatives, friends, in-laws, doctors, ministers, books, magazines and television. The relative frequency with which any one of these categories is mentioned by the group as a whole is reported in Table A.

We did not attempt to rate the relative importance of these categories for any single person, noting only the fact that a given category was mentioned. Chapter 9 will evaluate the depth of personal relationships and show who are the significant others in the lives of every husband and wife.

TABLE A

SOCIALIZATION INTO MARRIAGE ROLES
(exclusive of housekeeping and home maintenance)

	Per cent of 46 young husbands and wives (married under 7 years) referring to a specified agent
Books	9
Magazines	15
Television	4
Relatives of same sex	56
Relatives of opposite sex	13
In-laws of same sex	24
In-laws of opposite sex	11
Friends of same sex	54
The "crowd"	6
Experts	9

Such an inventory of sources of information includes, of course, only those of which the person is aware. With this limitation, the list may be relatively representative in view of our systematic questions about sharing marriage experiences with others and about reading.

The printed word plays an exceedingly small part as a model or a source of information about marriage roles. "I read this in a book," "It says in the Bible," "I saw this in a magazine," were mentioned by only 24 per cent of the group. Even television, despite extensive viewing, is rarely mentioned. Possibly the models presented on the screen are so at variance with the accepted practices of some couples that to imitate them is to risk instant recognition and teasing. "Sometimes he'll talk real soft to me, kind of mushy-like," said a 25-year-old wife (with ten years of schooling), married six years, "I kid him and tell him he's got romantic ideas from the movies. He said he learned it from the T.V. It was good for a laugh."

Studies of the effects of mass media repeatedly show what has been termed the two-step process of influence. To a large extent mass media reach the public through the mediation of "opinion leaders." [10] We came across such leaders and we understand, in at least two or three cases, the sources of their leadership. One woman, unhappily married and reticent, plays the role of a confidante and marriage counselor to a clique of friends. Although not superior to them in education or social background, she is the only one in her group to read the marriage columns in the newspapers and to quote them to her friends. The motivation which made her reach out for vicarious experience of other women and to assume the role of a marriage counselor also created an interest in reading newspaper columns on marriage.[11]

In the content analysis of the interviews the overwhelming bulk of references are to personal interactions, especially to relatives. For these working-class couples parental families emerge as the major agent of socialization in the early years of marriage, for the husbands as well as for the wives. Sixty-nine per cent of the group made some reference to parents and siblings. But this, in fact, grossly underestimates the importance of relatives when compared with the mass media. Phrases such as "I always ask my mother" and "I saw this in a newspaper," in this particular count are given equal weight even when the first may be a weekly occurrence and the second a single episode. Thirty-five per cent of the group mentioned in-laws.

Next to relatives, friends form the most important category, with 60 per cent of the group making some reference to discussing marriage roles with friends. The professionals trail, with only 9 per cent of respondents mentioning ministers and doctors.

It is generally held that the influence of parents over adult offspring increases with socio-economic status. The higher classes have a greater stake in the maintenance of family property and prestige, and they command greater resources to enforce control.[12] But such a view must be qualified. Glenton's parents (and

---

10 See, for example, Elihu Katz and Paul F. Lazarsfeld, 1955.
11 Another opinion leader is described on p. 76.
12 William J. Goode, 1963, p. 12, and William J. Goode, February 1959, pp. 38-47.

relatives in general) may not have the motivation or the resources to regulate the lives of the young couples, but they do influence them. Their continuing impact stems from the lack of competing pressures. It is power by default because the relative insulation of the young couples from other social influences, heightens the importance of relatives and, in turn, strengthens continuity of traditional patterns.

This situation suggests the need to distinguish between what might be called the absolute and the relative role of kin. In one study the higher-class respondents cited reliance upon relatives in case of an emergency somewhat more frequently than the lower classes. This fact led to the assertion that relatives play a greater part in the aid pattern of the higher classes. But the upper class also relies more on friends. In fact, kin as a source of aid are *relatively less* important for the top socio-economic group than for the lower ones.[13]

Moreover, the relative influence of kin may differ with the spheres of life. In respect to norms of marriage and of child-rearing, stable working-class couples may continue to be influenced by their relatives to a greater extent than the educated middle classes (though not, perhaps, the "upper-upper" classes). The upwardly mobile working-class persons, on the other hand, may reject parental models even more frequently than do the better-educated middle classes.

Support for this hypothesis comes from an investigation of child-rearing practices which concludes that "middle-class mothers often mention experts, other mothers and friends as their sources of ideas about child-rearing. If they mention their own parents, it is usually as a negative reference. Lower-class mothers, on the other hand, use their parents as a positive reference group."[14] Similarly, a study of political socialization reports that among the college graduates in the sample, 58 per cent changed to some degree from the political position of their parents while only 28 per cent of those who did not graduate from high school did.[15]

The relatives and friends with whom Glenton's couples discuss marriage roles, in the case of the wives, are almost exclusively other women. Fathers, brothers, male in-laws or men friends

---

13 Wendell Bell and Marion D. Boat, 1957, p. 396.
14 Martha Sturm White, 1957.
15 Herbert H. Hyman, 1959, pp. 144-145.

are mentioned very rarely. The husbands are relatively more exposed than the wives to the influences of the opposite sex, consulting their mothers or being instructed by them without any solicitation. Sometimes mothers-in-law are consulted: "The old girl really understands her brat." Excluding the experts, of all the persons who figured in the socialization of the women only 4 per cent are men. But mothers, sisters and mothers-in-law constituted 38 per cent of all persons listed by the husbands. The mother apparently occupies a pivotal position for both sexes. The job and finances are occasionally discussed with fathers, but the figure of the father remains shadowy. The low occupational position of the father does not generally make him a valued model for the blue-collar worker.[16] But for the wife, her mother continues to be the principal source of information on domestic and household problems. Relatively fewer husbands, it would appear, found satisfactory role models in their fathers than did the wives in their mothers.

Even though the persons involved in the continued education for marriage are all close associates, we found some tendency toward specialization. (See Chapter 9.) The wives confide intimacies of their sex lives to sisters and girl friends more frequently than to their mothers. The mother-in-law is consulted on child rearing more frequently than on marriage, whereas both these roles are discussed equally with one's own mother. Sex matters are discussed with friends, but financial affairs are thought to be too private for anyone outside the kin group and frequently even for the relatives themselves.

When relations with in-laws are friendly, women frequently express solidarity across kinship lines. For the wife, one danger in antagonizing her mother- and sisters-in-law is the risk of losing allies in socializing her husband. A 25-year-old husband, a grammar school graduate (married three years), describes a recent marriage quarrel. The husband wanted to work on his car on Saturday, but his wife wanted him to join in the regular Saturday marketing trip with his sister and her husband. The wife telephoned his mother and his sister and told them he was going on strike. They came down, he told us, and "put a squeeze on

---

[16] Though all seniors studied by Empey hoped to improve their occupational position over that of their father, the lower-class boy aspired to a higher relative improvement. La Mar T. Empey, 1956.

him." His mother "jumped in on her side." He thought he had better agree just to keep out of trouble but he wasn't going to do it every week—"I'd show 'em!" We asked him how he would do this. He said he would go out Saturday morning and not come back.

A 22-year-old husband (with ten years of schooling) who had been married three and one-half years explained why he did not "blow off steam" about marriage problems to his mother. "She is more or less on my wife's side about helping my wife with the babies, getting up earlier and looking for another job. It seems that women stick together. I get the short end of it."

But the image of the powerful female group "putting a squeeze" on the young husband must be qualified. The older women may strengthen the wife's hand when it comes to major demands but, quite as frequently, their influence is to lower her expectations and to counsel resignation. A young wife is speaking: "My mother would listen to my gripes and calm me down. She'd hand me the line about a woman's place, and after a while I got to seeing that maybe that was right." One of the few "great arguments" they had after marriage, reports another wife, was over her husband's loss of chivalry. He no longer moved chairs, lighted cigarettes or helped her into a car. Her sister told her that all men change after marriage and that she was silly to expect the same manners as in courtship. She realized that he wasn't going to keep up his attentive ways and she reconciled herself to the change. A woman who had been married three years was told by her older sister that she could not expect her honeymoon to last. Her sister gave the young couple at most another year before "they begin petering out." The wife was told that her husband would stop being so generous in giving her everything she wants.

The young husbands also receive counsels of resignation from their relatives. One man dissatisfied with his wife's poor housekeeping asked his brother about it and was told that all woman have "fits of letting things go."

The lessening of romantic idealization of marriage may have promoted marriage adjustment, but the tendency of the relatives to quell discontent seemed to us excessive. This may merely reflect the feelings of a middle-class observer as to where the limits of tolerance should lie. It also reflected our judgment that the counsel to bear and forbear drove underground problems which might have had a chance of more constructive solutions.

Although female relatives sometimes take the side of the husband, there are certain disadvantages for the wife in the fact that socialization is controlled so exclusively by members of her own sex. Fathers, brothers and brothers-in-law might have given the young wife some insight into the masculine world had channels of communication across sex lines been freer. One fundamental fact offsets this one-sidedness: Of all those involved in the socialization of a person during the first years of marriage, the most important, beyond a doubt, is the marriage partner.

The Marriage Partner as a Socializing Agent

No one has a more vital stake in getting a married person to fulfill his obligations than his spouse. Hardly any aspect of marriage is exempt from mutual instruction and pressures to change. If the peer group plays an important role in the emancipation of the adolescent from parental control,[17] the spouse carries on the process after marriage. The relatively young age at which working-class persons marry is no doubt one relevant factor in this situation. Thus, a 19-year-old high school graduate was irritated by the way in which her husband's older brother was always "dishing out free advice." She told her 23-year-old husband that as a married man he should make his own decisions. "You tell him," she said, "that if we want his advice we'll ask for it." Her husband did not want to hurt his brother's feelings, so this continued to be a source of friction for the couple. Finally he did tell his brother "very nicely" and, "though the problem still comes up once in a while, it is better than it used to be." Husbands often express the expectation: "You are a married woman now and you have to stand on your own two feet." We shall say more on this point in Chapter 12 on in-law relations.

A 23-year-old grade school graduate illustrates the role of a husband in the sex education of his wife. He married a sheltered girl brought up in a religious home. "I don't see," he told us, "how kids could be kept so innocent. I had to teach her almost everything when we were married." Another wife, a high school graduate, received her sex education from her future husband, who, after their engagement, discovered her ignorance and brought her some books to study. Just before marriage, her

[17] See Talcott Parsons, 1959, p. 209.

mother asked her whether she had any idea about sex and was shocked to hear that she had been instructed by her fiancé.[18]

The immaturity of a person, or his lower-class background, sometimes resulted in a Pygmalion-like pattern of socialization by his spouse. One such case is especially instructive. Differences in class origins are generally found to be unfavorable to marital adjustment, but this intermarriage was one of the happiest in our group, despite the determined efforts of the husband to reshape much of his wife's behavior. The following depiction of the case is focused upon the factors which offset the expected strains of such a marriage.

"My family," explained the 32-year-old husband in a quiet, self-restrained manner, "is a cut or two above hers." His people were respectable, churchgoing Scottish Presbyterians. His father was a textile worker who read books and listened to good music on the radio. They had high hopes for their son, but the father's illness forced the husband to leave school at 15 and to get a special work permit to help the family. Later, having spent two years in the army, he took a job as a bricklayer.

The wife's parents were separated, and she was brought up by her paternal grandparents, who were strict and unloving. They always complained to her father that he didn't give them enough money for her upkeep. She ran away from home several times, did poorly in school and "flunked out the first year of high school." She then located her mother, ran away to her, and took a job as a waitress. She was glad, she said, that she "had the guts to get the hell out of there and shake my ass loose from those people who were pounding me to death." She soon realized that her "mother was having a pretty gay time of it with boy friends."

The couple met in the company cafeteria where she worked as a waitress. "Men were around her like a honey pot," he said, and he thought she was too beautiful to make a good wife. He asked her to go out with him one Sunday and he admitted that he had some rather dishonorable designs. But to his great amazement he found that this glamor girl was a very innocent child. He learned about her unhappy life and began to have a deep feeling for her and wanted to take care of her.

During the six years of their marriage the husband has

---

[18] In a few cases men in the armed services acquired new standards of orderliness and learned methods of cleaning, cooking, bedmaking, etc., which they later taught their wives.

played the role of a teacher and a mentor. He has taught her about sex and housekeeping, and has tried to improve her grammar and her taste in clothes and to develop in her a liking for good music. He still works hard to break her habit of swearing, especially within the hearing of their 5-year-old son. He reads to her. She is a hot-tempered and spirited girl and yet this effort to improve her has not jeopardized their happiness.

The wife's emotional gratification in this case is apparent. Having felt rejected and inferior all her life ("The funny part of it," said the husband in speaking of her appearance, "is that she doesn't know she's such a knockout"), the wife found in this man a tender, loving father-husband. To be loved by this superior man and to be warmly accepted by his family whom she longed to resemble was "the most wonderful thing that could have happened to me."

A similar expansion of the ego is experienced by the husband, for different reasons. He said that marriage has "made me stretch myself" and he liked the change. He had "never pictured myself getting anything as knockout as my wife." He referred to her as a "surprise package." We suspect he referred to the innocence of this sexually exciting woman. A certain unpredictability added zest to his life. If he had married a girl from his own church congregation, he said, he would know exactly what to expect, but his wife was an unknown quantity, and "it has worked out very well."

"She couldn't be any more interested" in the kind of things he liked to talk about, said the husband in answer to our question. It was much more fun than bringing up a child because she was grown up and could grasp things at once.

His compassion and self-restraint were amply manifested in his relationship to his mother-in-law, who tried at first to disrupt his marriage. He knew his wife was loyal to her mother, and he did not want to disillusion her. He waited until his wife began to see the truth herself before criticizing his mother-in-law.

With all that, the wife sometimes finds the re-education tiresome. He can be "too serious," going into things so deeply that she gets bored. The role of an inferior can become oppressive. Whenever she does not understand something she sees on T.V., she asks him, but, she added with glee, "Sometimes he don't know either and then I have a good laugh." Sometimes she feels so "cooped up" that she wants to "let out a yell or something."

The husband, however, understands and tolerates her restlessness. Far from feeling threatened by it he helps her find relief. The couple arranged to have the wife work part-time at her old job in the cafeteria, with an elderly friend taking care of the two children. She doesn't earn much money but the husband thinks it is good for her to get out and do the work she enjoys. The cafeteria is that of the firm where the husband is employed.

Several factors appear to explain the happy outcome of this effort on the part of one spouse to re-educate the other. This husband's endeavor to lift his wife to his level is being carried out under conditions deeply gratifying to each. Moreover, his tact and compassion help him to pace the rate of socialization. Finally, he is able to accept and to handle the occasional backwash of this educational campaign, that is, the restlessness and resentment the wife does sometimes experience. The case also illustrates the reciprocal character of such relationships. Although on the face of it the husband is molding his wife, he is changed in the process. He confessed that her bad language had bothered him a lot. He added, "The trouble is that I no longer notice it and I swear more than I used to. Mother is very unhappy when she hears me swear." When his wife teases him about swearing, he tells her that it sounds dreadful in a woman but not so bad in a man.

The Socializing Role of the "Crowd"

The male clique can survive only if it defends itself against the claims of the wives. But a "bunch" or a "crowd" composed of couples acquires a stake in enforcing marriage solidarity. Its social activities require that both husband and wife be present and that centrifugal interests be curbed. In our sample, however, only one-fifth of the young couples "go with a crowd," which usually consists of some three or four couples. A wife may see another woman by herself during the day, but the couples engage in many activities together.

The crowd serves as a *reference group enforcing common definitions of marriage roles*. A member of the group tests the legitimacy of his marital claims by asking the others or observing their behavior. In intimate matters the comparative evaluations are made tentatively, through trial and error. Thus, one bride troubled by a vulgar habit of her husband tested the reaction of a woman friend by attributing the habit to "a couple she heard about." When her friend remarked that the behavior is not unusual in husbands, the young wife divulged that she was describing her own experience.

The crowd enforces common definitions through direct pressure upon deviants. Thus in the case of one husband who was known for his excessive jealousy the crowd "teased him about it and kidded his wife along." Once they were dancing around in one of the houses, and all the fellows when dancing with this particular woman held her at a great distance and teased her husband. "He got sore about it at first, but then he got over it and we think he's better."

Another function of the crowd is to *drain off resentment against the mate for the common frustrations of marriage.* "I talked to the fellows and I found out that it is this way all around," remarked one husband. A wife said, "He needs sex a lot more than I do. I guess it's that way with everybody, at least that's what it seems like from what my girl friends tell me." The realization that the grievance or worry is a common one tends to take the sting out of it—to reassure and to promote resignation.

The line dividing permissible griping from the violation of marriage confidences is quite tightly drawn. When assembled, the sexes exchange accusations only about stereotyped shortcomings of husbands and wives. *This ritualized criticism serves not so much to release irritation as to strengthen the self-image as a "wife" or a "husband."* In joking about the extravagance of women, husbands experience the fellowship of married men. Wives similarly exchange knowing looks about the awkwardness of men in the kitchen.

The crowd sometimes promotes marital communication. Under the guise of a joke and under the protective cover of the group, a person expresses a sentiment he had concealed from his spouse out of pride or caution. Perhaps a similar sentiment or criticism was expressed by another and he followed suit. The presence of others, he senses, will keep the expressed feeling from developing into a quarrel or will mute its deeper overtones (since the deeply troubling sentiments are supposedly reserved for private occasions).

Conclusion: Aids and Hindrances to Socialization

The phrase "our rapidly changing and heterogeneous society" is a familiar one. In such a society, marriage roles are ambiguous. Men and women tend to enter marriage with different scripts, misunderstanding each other's cues and playing discordant roles. Moreover, each is torn between alternative versions of his or her own role. This confusion is often said to be a major stumbling block to marital socialization in the first years of marriage.

Glenton's families present a contrasting picture. It is apparently possible to live in a rapidly changing society and to be relatively insulated from both the changes and the cultural diversity. This fact is all the more striking since these families reside within 15 miles of a metropolis. One reason is that the socialization of the young couples takes place in a culturally homogeneous milieu. The early years of these marriages were certainly not free of conflicts, but these were not conflicts over norms. Husbands and wives knew what was expected of them and generally agreed about marital ideals. Such consensus reflects a sheltered existence, although in a few cases religious intermarriage, minor differences in the class backgrounds of the mates, or regional mobility exposed couples to somewhat different conceptions of marriage. Television brings new ideas, but these seemingly have little influence. Generational differences, as we have pointed out, are relatively narrow. And the same small circle of associates sets one's standards in many areas of living, from food and house furnishings to politics, sex, family life and religion.

It is said the middle-class girl has a more sheltered upbringing than the girl in a working-class family. This may well be true in some respects. But the author has observed extensive "culture shock" in undergraduate college women confronted with diverse ideas through books, teachers and classmates. In contrast, the Glenton women lead a protected intellectual existence. The difference may be illustrated by quoting from an autobiographical paper of a college senior who was anticipating marriage and full-time homemaking. (and students with career drives are even more ambivalent). The college woman writes:

"When I get married, I want to be a homemaker and raise a family. I feel that this role can offer me a life of satisfaction, and I see no necessity to seek any outside job.

"But I already foresee some possible conflicts. First I may feel guilty because, having had the privilege of a college education, I do not use it in some occupation. This privilege involves also an obligation that I continue to be an intellectually stimulating companion to my husband. This may require activities other than just children and housework. I wonder also, whether it will be difficult to adjust one's ego to what society classifies as 'just a housewife.' I expect it would be a considerable comedown from the status I enjoy now as a student. There might even be the problem of not enjoying the full respect of one's husband because one is not living up to one's fullest potential.

"I have learned from the unfortunate experience of my mother that a woman should be equipped to go out and work. When my father died, she had no occupation to which to return. She is bored and lacks direction now that her children are grown. I am very much afraid of something like this happening to me. I want to devote myself entirely to my family, but I also want to be capable of going out and earning a comfortable living in an interesting job in case of an emergency. . . ."

As the following chapter, describing how Glenton homemakers feel about their roles, makes clear, there are few traces of the conflicts cited in the above autobiography. The somewhat puzzled response of one working-class woman to our questions conveys the prevalent attitude towards the status of the housewife: "It's regular, isn't it? It can't be anything else." Spared the soul-searching and mental conflict over diverse patterns, less-educated persons can more easily make the transition to a new status.

But there is another side to the picture. The very conditions which make marriage roles so unambiguous have other—and less favorable—consequences. Roles may be clearly defined but yet be unsuitable under given conditions of life. Glenton's families, after all, do live in industrial society. Largely isolated from this society's intellectual mainstreams, however, they are slow, as we shall show, to modify their conceptions of marriage in ways which would prove more conducive to happiness under changing conditions.

The similarity and consistency of norms facilitate the socialization of our young couples, but many other circumstances of working-class existence are less favorable. It is not enough for a young husband to have a clear idea of his role in marriage: conditions of life must enable him to act it out. Transition to new roles is hindered by circumstances such as the poverty of some young couples, the poor occupational adjustment of the young unskilled workers, and the need to reside in the parental home after marriage. The young man whose marriage was almost destroyed by his loyalty to a clique diagnosed his difficulty correctly when he remarked that he hardly felt married, with his wife working, and the couple living as they did with her parents. The self-image as responsible family provider does not come full-blown at marriage. Even when the youth is mentally prepared to assume this role, it has to be played out in the concrete context of paying for the living room set, establishing a home, and supporting or sharing in the support of the family. The reminiscences of a 32-year-old husband, a grammar school graduate, illustrate how unfavorable these circumstances can be:

"You keep thinking you can do almost anything and get away with anything when you're still young. There had been a couple of big layoffs when we got married, but work was still pretty good and I thought I could do anything and that I was going places and I was going to be somebody. Nothing was good enough for my wife, and we didn't think nothing of charge accounts and buying things. We hadn't been married long when I got my first layoff, they said I was young. They laid off others and said they was old. We couldn't keep up our payments on the furniture, and we lost every stick of it, and she was pregnant. And I mean to tell you. We went and stayed at her ma's for a few days, and then up to my ma's for a while. There wasn't no room for us at her ma's and my ma had a spare room, and we must have stayed there about a month while I was looking for work and then I got it, and then we moved out again. And then this time, we got one thing by paying the whole money on it that we borrowed the money for. We borrowed it from people, and not the bank. And we bought a bed. We figured we could sit on that, and we had our cooking pots and could eat out of them. But we didn't want to think of sleeping on the floor anymore. It would have been all right if it was summer and she wasn't pregnant."

Among our families not only the husband but the wife too was occasionally blocked from performing her role because of crowded living quarters, or poverty or too many infants too soon after marriage. One striking instance is that of a Catholic woman:

A 21-year-old woman, married three years, is the mother of a 2-year-old, a 1-year-old and a month-old baby. She stated: "I wanted to have more children, but I thought maybe they would be a couple of years apart." Her husband works from four to midnight. Her family resides in a neighboring town but neither her parents nor the young couple owns a car, so that frequent visits are impossible. She does not know her neighbors; her sole visitor during the day is her mother-in-law. The loneliness of this young mother is brought out by her remark that if a child wakes up at night "he's company. You'd be surprised." She has pleaded with her husband to give up the evening shift and to look for a job with regular hours. She often cries when he leaves for work, but "not always, it's just when I'm up to my neck with the children and feel bad." The husband said that his wife seems to cry for no reason at all. "She picks a bad time, just when I'm ready to go to work. She shouldn't foul me up like this. She acts as if I go out to have a good time. My work isn't easy." The husband stated that the nicest treat that he can give his wife is to take a day off: "She talks me into it and then I just kick myself for losing a day's pay. Where does it get you? It is just like any other day."

Hardships of this kind greatly handicap socialization because they rob life of pleasures. They prevent either partner from rewarding the other for fulfilling role obligations. The depression and apathy of some young mothers and the resentment of others result from the scarcity of present rewards and the uncertainty of future ones. Husbands cannot always say to their wives after a rainy day at home with the infants, "Come—I'll take you to a movie." And wives cannot always create pleasant and serene homes that might tempt young husbands to forsake their cliques.[19]

Such external difficulties are particularly disruptive because some couples are not able to turn towards one another for companionship and emotional support. We refer here not to the clashes of personalities in unhappy marriages but to certain shared difficulties rooted in a shared culture. What these difficulties are will be shown in subsequent chapters.

[19] We do not know the frequency of these economic hardships at the outset of the marriage. For the present economic status of the families, see Chapter 13.

CHAPTER
3

The Homemaker
and the Working Wife

The discontent of the housewife is often attributed to contemporary values. She chafes, it is said, because of the low prestige society attaches to her role. She no longer receives recognition for her skills as a housekeeper. Whatever lip service is paid to the importance of the home, the housewife herself notes that social esteem and economic rewards go to women who achieve success in careers outside the home.

Such an explanation of discontent may perhaps apply to educated, middle-class housewives, but we find little evidence of status frustrations among working-class wives. They accept housewifery. There is hardly a trace in the interviews of the low prestige that educated housewives sometimes attach to their role, as reflected in the familiar phrase, "I am just a housewife." This is not to say that Glenton women are all satisfied homemakers. But their discontent is not caused by the low evaluation they place upon domesticity, stemming rather from other frustrations of housewifery. The esteem they attach to their role does not, then, ensure their contentment in it.

Our findings in this chapter temper still another current generalization about prevalence of role conflicts. We have already noted that we found less ambiguity about mutual obligations than the emphasis upon conflicting roles would have led us to expect. But the large degree of "moral consensus," for all the allure the phrase may have in our changing society, does not necessarily ensure happiness.

Division of Labor in the Home

Every housewife in this study was asked to describe her activities on the day before the interview from the time of awakening till bedtime, and to give her schedule for a "typical" weekday and week end. In the course of these descriptions, the interviewer raised questions concerning the allocation of tasks within the home. This section of the interview revealed the extent of the husband's participation in traditionally feminine tasks. Table B summarizes the results.

TABLE B

HUSBANDS' PARTICIPATION IN DOMESTIC ACTIVITIES
(*per cent of husbands performing specified tasks*)

Activity	Never or Hardly ever	Occasionally	Frequently or Regularly	Total No. of Cases for Whom This Information Is Available
Cooking	88	8	4	60
Laundry	83	13	4	60
Cleaning	75	21	4	57
Doing dishes	63	30	7	55
Grocery shopping	46	18	36	55
Care of infants	31	33	36	43
Planning Christmas gifts	19	6	75	58
Buying home furnishings	18	33	49	57
Care of older children	10	34	56	51

Cooking, laundry and cleaning emerge as exclusively feminine activities in about four-fifths of the families. Almost two-thirds of the husbands hardly ever help with the dishes. Shopping for groceries, however, is "frequently" a joint enterprise for nearly two-fifths of the couples, and as many as 75 per cent plan Christmas gifts together.

Least institutionalized is the husband's share in the care of infants. The father's involvement in child care was assessed on the basis of criteria such as feeding, bathing the children, taking care of them when sick, taking an interest and helping in school work, disciplining them or playing with them, making their toys, teaching them various skills, and similar activities. The fathers are divided into three nearly equal groups: one-third "hardly ever helps [or helped]" with the babies, another third helps "occasionally" and the rest help "frequently or regularly." As children grow older, the fathers become more active in child care and child rearing, with only 10 per cent of the fathers quite uninvolved.

An illustration of the wide contrasts in the role of the father is seen in the comparison between two cases. Note first the well-established schedule of cooperation of one couple, married five years, with three children aged 4 years, 16 months and 3 months. The husband is a packager of soap. He shaves every other day, when his wife gets up to make coffee and prepare his lunch, while on other days he attends to these chores. She does not ordinarily wake him at night to help with the children unless she has been up several nights in succession. As soon as he comes home after work, he takes over the children and she starts supper. He washes the dishes and she dries them. He plays with the children, helps to bathe them, and they both put them to bed every night. On week ends they work even more closely together.

The contrasting case is a family with four children under 8. The wife was pregnant at the time of the interview. The wife reports that her husband never touches the dishes and expects her to get his breakfast. He leaves the younger children entirely to her but occasionally plays with the older ones. Asked whether he ever took care of the children, the husband replied that he did so when his wife was confined: he had helped with the older children even though his sister-in-law always stayed with the family when his wife was having a new baby. This father's help was limited to such exceptional times.

During an era of changing attitudes the question of the husband's responsibilities might be expected to cause some conflict in marriage. Should a husband be expected to help with the dishes, to scrub the kitchen floor occasionally or to take turns during the night with the baby's bottle? For eight out of every ten of these working-class couples "who does what around the house" does not constitute a troublesome issue. When the wives were asked to rank qualities which characterize a good husband, "willing to help wife with housework" was low on the list, the 18th among the 21 qualities presented for rating. Only 4 per cent of women considered "helps with the housework" as "very imporant." Even "helps with care of babies" was evaluated as "very important" by only 12 per cent of the women. On the other hand, 64 per cent gave this higher rating to "helps children with their school problems." The husbands were asked whether they thought that wives nowadays (in comparison with their mothers' generation) demanded too much help with housework and care of children. Three-fourths of the men answered negatively, again indicating that this was not a sensitive issue.

Division of labor in the home presents few problems because not only the men but the women accept the traditional segregation of masculine and feminine tasks. The wives do not normally expect assistance from their husbands.

The couples are "traditional" in both ideology and in practice, but their traditionalism has a new flavor. Only a handful of men and women feel very strongly about task segregation. "No son of mine will wash dishes," thundered one father when his wife asked their boy to help with the dinner dishes. "My mother had done everything with all of us. After that, I wouldn't have much patience with a complaining wife." Another man was vexed indeed: "I see husbands in this housing development carrying out the garbage and I say this is garbage!"

Such emotional outbursts are rare. Moreover, the majority do not feel that certain household tasks are inherently unmanly. On the contrary, when circumstances require it, the husband expects and is expected to pitch in without worrying about doing "woman's work." It is recognized that some men "feel funny" about particular jobs: it may be hanging out the wash in the sight of the neighbors, or making beds or washing out a diaper. Allowances might be made for such sensibilities but generally nothing that clearly needs to be done is viewed as beneath masculine dignity.

One-fourth of the husbands think that modern wives in general demand more help with housework than was the case a generation ago. Even these men criticize wives less for emasculating their husbands than for exploiting them. They belabor the wife who idles away hours in gossip and is then too tired to wait upon her hard-working husband. If the picture of a husband with a dishtowel perhaps still appears ridiculous, it is no longer because dishwashing is inherently unmanly but because of the implication that the husband is too weak to resist exploitation. It is thus a violation of the norm of reciprocity rather than of "natural" sex roles.

This new spirit is conveyed in a letter written to a girl friend by a woman in the last month of her second pregnancy: "I'm getting so lazy and clumsy and miserable, it is pitiful. John has been doing just about everything around the house for me, besides working all day. Saturdays, he did the wash and scrubbed the floors; he even did the supper dishes for me. *What a man.*" A 33-year-old woman, a mother of four sons, asserted: "If a man likes to take care of children, it is all right; if he doesn't, he shouldn't be expected to do it unless his wife is sick."

The change from extreme traditionalism about the division of labor does not cause a radical shift in practice because only exceptional circumstances are held to warrant extensive help from the husband. Such help is considered a favor, not an obligation. A 21-year-old husband says: "I can't push it all on her [the housework]. I'd be glad to help but when she insisted it was my job to do it—well, I didn't like it." A 26-year-old freight-handler, a father of five children, said that he would probably be angry with his wife if she asked him to do housework, and she never does—but if he should "find her snowed under, I might pitch in." In her own interview, however, his wife stated that he helped with housework only when she was ill. The one high school graduate who complained that her husband sat around all day Sunday, with the result that Sunday was just another working day for her, was an exception. More typical is the wistful remark of another woman that it is nice when a fellow does give his wife a hand, indicating that such help is an extra concession and not a legitimate right. "When he is in a good mood, I'll ask him sometimes to help out with something."

The two out of every ten couples who fight over the division of labor do so over the failure of the husband to help with the feminine tasks and not the reverse. The masculine chores are thought to require physical strength or skills no woman is expected to possess. The husband consequently may delay fixing the screen door or repairing the lamp, but he does not say, "Why don't you do it yourself?" If women in the future receive better technical education and the home becomes increasingly mechanized, "Why don't you do it yourself?" may well also become the husband's rejoinder.

The conflict over the husband's help, when it does exist, very rarely reflects a disagreement about norms. The wife who thought she was entitled to a day of rest is one such case. Another instance is seen in the husband who insists: "I don't ask her to wash my car, why should I wash the dishes?" Generally, however, the conflict erupts because one or the other tries to receive some unearned increment in the accepted exchange of services. A 21-year-old mother of three infants (aged 2 years, 1 year, and 3 weeks) complains that her husband won't get up at night to help with the crying baby. He confesses guiltily that he likes to sleep, although he adds with a sheepish smile that even his mother warned him that his exhausted wife might drop the baby out of sheer fatigue unless he relieved her occasionally.

Sometimes it is the wife who asks too much. The motivation may be quite complex. One young wife remarked that she didn't like to ask her husband to do the dishes because of the cartoons of henpecked husbands washing dishes. Yet, we noted, she did ask him. Her mother, she said, called her son-in-law lazy when he did not help and a ninny when he did. We suspect that the young wife herself is equally ambivalent. A wife who made futile efforts to get her husband to help her spoke with envy of her mother: "My mother always said that a husband shouldn't have to do anything, if his wife is in good health. But I notice," she added wryly, "my father always does a lot of work around the house." Still another man, determined to make a go of his second marriage, made a number of concessions to his wife; for example, he washed the evening dishes until skin trouble gave him a welcome excuse to stop—since neither partner made any reference to psychosomatic medicine, the issue of the dishes was thus solved.

Even if in principle the husband is prepared to help, the couple may disagree about the importance of a particular task.

Acting only in the role of a helper, the husband is not subject to the sanctions surrounding an institutionalized role. He will not be criticized if visiting relatives find the beds unmade, nor will he be praised for a meticulous home. Consequently he may dismiss a request for some chore that his wife deems important.

General agreement about the allocation of work does not mean that peace reigns over home maintenance. Dissatisfactions with each other's role performance are more frequent than disputes over the boundary lines of responsibilities. Of the 58 husbands, 6 were strongly dissatisfied with their wives' housekeeping and 12 others expressed fairly strong dissatisfactions. Almost the same proportion of the wives expressed similar grievances about the failure of their husbands to perform the "masculine" tasks in the upkeep of the home.

The poor housekeepers do not even attempt to defend themselves. One or two claimed that their husbands were spoiled by over-meticulous mothers; another, that keeping children out-of-doors in the fresh air was more important than having a spotless house. But generally they accept housework as their share of the marriage bargain and feel guilty about their poor performance.

The one-fifth of the women who express a strong dislike for housework often feel guilty about their dislike of this normal feminine responsibility. Unlike some college-educated housewives who detest housework, our respondents never say that they are too good for it, that housework is unchallenging manual labor.

The high school graduates appear to have a slightly less favorable attitude toward housework than the less-educated wives. Twenty-four per cent of them, against only 18 per cent of the latter, expressed strong dislike of housework. Moreover, housework figures more prominently as a source of "bad" moods among the high school graduates than among the less educated; the former listed 0.6 such items per person and the latter only 0.2 items.[1] The less favorable attitudes towards domestic activities of educated women have been reported by other writers. One study, for example, found that upper-class homemakers, consisting largely of college-educated women, had less favorable attitudes

[1] Aspects of housework as sources of bad moods mentioned by a given subgroup divided by the number of respondents in the subgroup.

towards housekeeping activities than the lower-class women (largely high school graduates). Both groups preferred food preparation and supervision to house care.[2] A psychologist studying 8- and 11-year-old girls, reports that "in comparison with girls from lower middle-class homes, the girls from upper middle-class homes were especially apt to perceive women as disliking domestic activities." Since these girls have not yet been exposed to the influence of high schools or colleges their attitudes, the author infers, must reflect differences of their social milieux.[3]

The high school men help their wives with shopping and with infant care more than do the less-educated, and this difference persists when the duration of marriage is taken into account. Forty per cent of the less-educated "never or hardly ever help with the babies," against only 10 per cent of the high school graduates. A previous investigation found that home responsibilities taken by husbands are greatest in middle status families and less in high and low status homes.[4] The few helpful fathers among the less-educated men include husbands of working wives, a husband of a depressed and inefficient woman, a man who "just loves doing everything for the babies" and a poor provider of whom his wife said, "When he does not bring in enough money he feels he should help more."

The high school graduates, however, help their wives also for other reasons. One husband confessed that he felt guilty "to be sitting down when my wife has a lot of work to finish." Several men care for the children on their wives' night off; two have dominant wives who demand and get help. The marriages of the high school graduates tend to be happier, and the warmer the relationship, the more likely the husband is to help with the infants.[5] A happily married man tends to be less calculating about the balance of services.

How Content Are the Homemakers?

Glenton women regard homemaking as a respected role for women. Even those who speak wistfully of the job they held

2 Dorothy Greey Van Bortel and Irma H. Gross, 1954, pp. 34-35.
3 Ruth E. Hartley, 1962, p. 212.
4 Marvin E. Olsen, 1960, pp. 60-65. See also Rachel Ann Elder, 1949.
5 Of 12 unhappy husbands, 5 never help with infants. In the 24 average or happy marriages, there are only 7 such inactive fathers.

prior to marriage and expect to hold again when the children are older, give no indication that the transition from work to housewifery entails any loss of prestige.

Such untroubled acceptance of housewifery stems from the lack of exposure to certain values. For one thing, attitudes towards occupation and occupational success differ from those characterizing the college-educated population; here the worth of a person is not measured so predominantly by his competence in a specialized vocation. A good provider, a man who is not afraid of hard work and is ambitious enough to take a better job if one is available, is of course admired. But women sometimes do not even know the specific occupations of their close relatives —just the name of the firm for which they work. A good job is a means to a good living, but achievement in a specialized vocation is not the measure of a person's worth, not even for a man, much less for a woman.

We asked for examples of women's conversation about husbands so as to discover the particular qualities that evoked envy or commiseration. We also asked for ratings of qualities desirable in a husband. The wife is little concerned with the kind of a figure her husband cuts in the outside world. Only 19 per cent of the women rate as "very important" the quality "successful in his job so that his wife can be proud of him." This contrasts with the 48 per cent who assign this high rating to "tells his wife exactly what he earns" and the 52 per cent who cite "affectionate enough to satisfy wife" as "very important."

The sharp distinction between brain and brawn that makes the college-educated wife occasionally feel that she is too good for housework is absent among these blue-collar families. Women express admiration for their husbands' manual skills. Much respectful reference to expertise in carpentry, painting, repairing and the like appeared in response to our question: "Can you think of any qualities of your husband's which you discovered after you were married?" Of 58 women, only 2 referred to the fear of "mental stagnation" which college-educated women frequently list among the frustrations of housewifery.[6]

There is still another basis for the conclusion that housewifery is not only positively evaluated in principle but is in fact a source of satisfaction. One section of the interview dealt with

[6] Mirra Komarovsky, 1953, pp. 112-113.

sources of pleasant and unpleasant feelings. "What makes you feel happy, good, satisfied with self or low, mad, hurt, worried and dissatisfied with self?" Housewifery (as distinct from family relationships) figures more prominently among the "good" than the "bad" moods. References to some household activity constitute 8.4 per cent of all the "good" moods and only 3.7 per cent of all the "bad" moods. In contrast, relations with husband constitute 19 per cent of all the good moods but 20 per cent of all the bad ones. Housewifery as a source of pleasure or self-satisfaction sometimes involves a particular skill—cooking, sewing, managing money well. At other times it is simply the relief of "getting my work done." (We do not include in housewifery "getting a bargain," a frequent source of self-satisfaction—shopping is a separate category.)

Despite the fact that most of these homemakers receive little help from their husbands with housework and infant care, they do not appear harried. Overburdened and harassed women are in the minority: a mother of ten children with an alcoholic husband, in and out of work; a mother of seven who takes in piece work to help pay the grocery bills; women with five or more young children whose day is one hopeless effort to "get caught up with my work"; and the mothers who hold outside jobs. We asked the housewives: "If there were two more hours every day, how would you like most to spend them?" "Get caught up with my work" or a curt "Sleep!" are the answers of this overburdened minority. There are a few high school graduates caught up in a busy schedule generally associated with suburbia. But the majority of Glenton housewives show a decided lack of interest in this gift of two hours a day. "Gee, I don't really know. What can you do for free?" Time is apparently not the scarce commodity that college-educated housewives report it to be. "Time too interrupted, with no blocks of free time for hobbies, study or recreation" was checked as a major frustration of housewifery by 40 per cent of college-educated mothers in one study.[7] In contrast, the day and the week of our housewives appear to have a more relaxed, if also a more monotonous, rhythm. Their daily schedules show a full day's work with constant responsibility for young children. Following a fairly early rising, they serve breakfast to their husbands and try to finish housecleaning before

[7] Mirra Komarovsky, 1953, p. 112.

lunch. Their standards of cleanliness are generally high—children's clothes are frequently changed and there is daily laundry and ironing. Weather permitting, young children are taken to the main shopping street or to the park. Some make weekly expeditions to the supermarket with the assistance of their husbands, but even these do supplementary shopping during the week. Supper is served soon after the husband's return from work, about 5:00 or 5:30. There is a steady flow of demands on a mother of young children, but her eye is not constantly on the clock.

The greater sense of pressure experienced by the college-educated mother is not due to the time spent on housework and care of young children.[8] The fact is that working-class life is more restricted. There is no chauffeuring of children to and from art or dancing classes, no rushing with the children's dinner before the baby-sitter takes over for the parents' night out. There are no books to be finished or current magazines to be read. There is very little club work and little social life with other couples. Visiting with relatives is informal, and meals away from home are usually at the home of one of the couple's parents. Women friends and relatives occasionally drop in for coffee and then continue visiting as their hostesses iron or mend. In comparison with college-educated women, then, the lives of these homemakers are narrow in range of activities and interests. For educated women, a sense of pressure is generated by the sheer volume of the stimuli to which they respond and by their consequent awareness of the many uses to which they might put free time.

In spite of this contrast, an impression of serenity and contentment on the part of the working-class homemaker would be misleading. Housewifery may be a respected role and still entail frustrations. One index of discontent, the full measure of which will emerge as we consider the various facets of marriage, is found in the answer of the less-educated women to the question: "Who has it harder in marriage, a man or a woman?" Of the 26 less-educated women to whom we put this question, 16 replied, "A woman"—"She is more tied down"; "She is practically in jail"; "More heartache about the kids and less fun"; "Takes care of the kids around the clock." Only 4 women declared that

[8] Dorothy Greey Van Bortel and Irma H. Gross, 1954, p. 11.

the man "has it harder" in marriage, and the remaining 6 indicated that marital burdens are about equally divided between spouses.

Unrelieved responsibility for young children and a feeling of being tied down creates discontent. It is thus not surprising that fully one-third of our 58 women expressed a strong desire to work, preferably part-time, often simply "to get out of the house."

The homemaker herself attributes her major problem to the lack of sufficient money for necessities of life, for pleasanter living arrangements, for baby-sitters and fun. But the sharp segregation of the roles of the sexes, despite her acceptance of it, adds to her sense of restriction and isolation. The contrast between the less-educated women and the high school graduates supports such an impression. The 25 high school graduates receive more assistance with child care and with shopping from their husbands, and more of them enjoy a "night off" while their husband serves as baby-sitter. And more of them, as will be shown in Chapter 6, share their problems with their husbands. When the high school graduates were asked, "Who has it harder in marriage, a man or a woman?" only 5 cited their own sex. The grievance "she's tied down" was listed three times more frequently by the less-educated than by the high school graduates. The latter may have a less favorable view of housework but they are more satisfied with their total position as homemakers.

The husband of the less-educated wife tends to leave child care and housework entirely to his wife. He enjoys greater freedom to spend occasional evenings away from home, as will be shown in Chapter 14. His wife regards these privileges as his due. But an important effect of these accepted patterns is to make her feel "cooped up" and lonely. She rarely enjoys relief from her duties and misses the emotional support the high school wife receives from the greater involvement of her husband in her world.

The loneliness of the less-educated wife is intensified if she is a newcomer to the community, separated from her relatives, or if she lives in a neighborhood with very little neighborliness. Under such circumstances the remark of some women that they are "practically in jail" is understandable.

Working Wives

The majority of the men and women interviewed believed that the wife's place is "in the home," but this generally held view obscures the great distance that they have traveled from the traditional attitude. The questions that in the past aroused indignation—"Should a married woman work?" or "Should a mother of teenagers work?"—are now discussed calmly. The current debate about the employment of wives centers on the children, and it is the working mother of younger children who is attacked. This emphasis upon the effect of the wife's employment upon children leaves the husband in a vulnerable position. Unless he can prove that his wife's employment will harm their children, he is in danger of seeing his own motivations and acknowledging the self-interest and insecurities that may lie at the root of his objections. The following case illustrates such a situation.

A 39-year-old high school graduate, vegetable-grader for a grocery chain, invoked the support of his 11-year-old son to dissuade his wife from taking a job. The wife's mother lives with the family and the husband has a late shift at work.

> "My son and I don't want her to work. We're spoiled. She does everything for us. I like her to prepare lunch for me. I don't like it when her mother prepares lunch. I said to her, 'What is the matter with you? Do you have a guilt complex about staying home? If I were after you to work, that would be different, but I am not.' Oh, I may be old-fashioned, my mother never worked. Of course, most of the time I didn't need her, but when I needed her, she was right there. So I think it's all wrong for her to work, unless it's really necessary. I think during the last year or so she began to see things our way and is satisfied to stay home."

Note this husband's reference to his being "spoiled" and "old-fashioned" and his lack of moral condemnation of his wife's employment. His reference to the "guilt complex" is the only instance of its kind in the interviews. College-educated husbands in a similar struggle would frequently employ the new weapons supplied by psychoanalysis. But "rejection of femininity" or "the masculine protest" are not as yet part of the workingman's weapons.

Another evidence of changing attitudes is acceptance of

other than strictly economic motives for working. The most acceptable reason for working is still the economic one—to pay a debt, to buy lamps, slip covers, children's clothes and the like. Nevertheless, the desire to work "just to get out of the house" is readily admitted. And one young husband with ten years of schooling remarked, "If a woman works, she keeps up with things, meets more people, and has something interesting to talk about."

In one earlier study, college-educated mothers appeared more defensive and guilt-ridden about their desire to work.[9] This was substantiated in another investigation of middle-class working mothers who "insist to their children that they work only because they need the money, a statement they acknowledge to be untrue. 'Otherwise what excuse could I give . . . for working?' "[10] The self-doubts raised by the spread of psychoanalytic theory ("What is wrong with me that motherhood and homemaking do not suffice?") do not plague our respondents. The desire to work "for a change of atmosphere" was expressed by them without any embarrassment or defensiveness. The working-class housewife is so tied down that to work in order to "get out of the house" is an acceptable motive even when it may occasionally disguise a wish for independence or adventure. But the prosperous housewife who wants to work can hardly claim that this is her only way to get "out of the house." She must acknowledge that she wants to "realize her potentialities" or be a "person in her own right." Such individualistic drives have however been made suspect by the doctrine that the truly feminine woman finds ample rewards in her familial roles and does not crave individual achievement. In comparison with college-educated homemakers, these respondents felt more guilt about detesting housework and less guilt about a desire for a job.

Two stories were used to tap attitudes towards women's employment outside the home. The first of these follows:

Mr. and Mrs. Allen have two young children. Mrs. Allen heard of a part-time job and would like to take it. Her mother is willing to stay with the children in the afternoons and Mrs. Allen would be back at five o'clock to take over. Mrs. Allen wants the job for the extra money and also to get out of the

[9] Mirra Komarovsky, 1953, Chapters 4 and 5.
[10] Ruth E. Hartley, 1962, p. 214.

house, but her husband doesn't like the idea. He has nothing against his mother-in-law and her ways with the children, but he thinks that a mother's place is in the home and they should get along on what he earns.[11]

There is general agreement in the responses to this story that Mrs. Allen should not work if her husband cannot be persuaded to give his consent. Even the woman who called Mr. Allen "real crabby" counseled resignation. But apart from the agreement, attitudes vary. About one-half of the husbands take a strong and inflexible stand against Mrs. Allen's taking the part-time job, citing juvenile delinquency and other dire consequences of the mother's absence. The rest of the men raise further questions. How old are the children? Can the mother-in-law be trusted? Does the couple want to buy a home, is that why the wife wants to work? How good a mother is Mrs. Allen? One 28-year-old husband (a high school graduate) declared, "Mr. Allen ought to be glad to have a wife with that much get up and go."

The wives are even less inclined to give an outright "no" to Mrs. Allen's desire to work. Only one-third of the wives, as compared with one-half of the husbands, express an unconditional opposition. Two-thirds, on the other hand, qualify their answers much in the same manner as the husbands just cited.

The second story was intended to discover whether with increased working opportunities the wives are subjected to pressures to contribute to family support.

The Bakers have two children, 12 and 14. Their icebox is small and Mrs. Baker wants a new Frigidaire. Mr. Baker doesn't think they need one. He says, "If you are set on having a new Frigidaire, take a part-time job."

The responses to this story made clear that the husbands do not shift the responsibility for family support to their wives. Mr. Baker is condemned: "It isn't up to him to tell her to work for it. That's out altogether. A Frigidaire is a necessity and it is up to the husband to provide it." A few younger husbands added, "Let

[11] According to the arbitrary system adopted for designating families discussed in this book, fictitious names have been assigned in alphabetical sequence by order of appearance; Allen being the first family, Baker the second, etc. All the names used are among those having the highest frequencies for the ethnic group studied.

her work and find out how hard money comes." In the opinion of the great majority, Mr. Baker would be justified in telling his wife to "work for it" if she asked for a luxury instead of a Frigidaire. In any case, the wife's employment should ideally be a joint decision of the couple when circumstances dictate it.

The possibility of earning money was used by some wives as a power device. For example, one wife wanted a new washing machine while her husband thought that the old machine was adequate. The wife took a job as a checker in a store and bought a new machine with her own earnings. She obviously relished the memory of this coup: "It was a kind of a lesson to him." "I'll get it myself," can be used as blackmail only because the husband treasures the role of being the sole provider. This leverage is not available to the mother of young children, who is no longer free to take a job. (This may in part explain the decline in the power of the wife at this stage of the family cycle.[12])

Does the wife's employment reflect adversely upon her husband's social status? The words of one woman convey what appears to be the general attitude: "If a woman has very young children and goes to work, then that's for bread and butter and people might feel sorry for her. But if the children are older, say in the fifth grade or so, and she works part-time, they know it is just for the extras, and that's nothing against her husband."

As to personal preferences, about a third of the woman disclose decidedly favorable attitudes towards working. They are either currently working and enjoying it or have a strong desire to work, as shown by such statements as "If my mother wasn't working [and could baby-sit] you can bet your boots, I'd be working" or "I wouldn't leave the children with a stranger but if he [respondent's husband] was willing to baby-sit when he gets home from work, I'd take a job in a minute." The largest proportion, about one-half of the group, have no interest in working. Eighteen per cent qualify their answers in various ways.

Turning from the women's attitudes to their experience, 17 per cent of the interviewed women earn some money in part-time jobs—in restaurants, cafeterias, department stores, factories, or by baby-sitting, office cleaning and piece work at home. Typing is the most skilled of represented occupations. There are no career women among our respondents. One could hardly so

12 See Robert O. Blood, Jr., and Donald M. Wolfe, 1960, pp. 41-44.

designate a 26-year-old mother of two children who has had a few vaudeville song-and-dance engagements before marriage and now dreams of returning to the stage. Our study, however, understates the extent of employment in a comparable group in the community at large because our original plan was to eliminate the employed housewives and the decision to include them was made later in the study. In the community at large, according to the United States Census of 1960, 34.7 per cent of all women (with husband present) and 17.2 per cent of mothers with children under 6 were in the labor force.

CONTRASTING TYPES OF WORKING WIVES

Studies of the effects of maternal employment upon the mother herself and her family have in general yielded negative results. The mere fact of working is not apparently associated with consistent or striking differences between working mothers and homemakers.[13] Our interviews give a clue to these negative findings because even within this homogeneous and restricted group, the working mothers differ sharply from one another in motivations for work and in modes of life, and represent not one but a variety of patterns.

Some of the working women illustrate only too vividly the familiar image of the overburdened working-class mother. A 37-year-old woman, a mother of seven, is forced to do piece work at home. Her sickly mother-in-law lives with the family and is a heavy liability. Even with occasional overtime, the husband, a maintenance man, cannot provide the necessities of life for his large family. This woman's day begins at 6:00 A.M. and by 8:30 P.M. she hopes that "it might let up a little so that I could put my feet up. I try to see that my husband and kids have enough to eat. Sometimes he yells at me when I ain't got enough and I tell him I do the best I can." She gets very little help with housework from her husband and her life is grim and exhausting. Equally trying is the double job of the 30-year-old wife of a hospital attendant, a mother of two children. She cleans offices at night after a full day of work at home.

In the small group of working mothers there are others, however, who do not fit such a stereotype. They may be under some pressure during part of the day, but they are not overworked.

[13] See, for example, Lois M. Stolz, 1960, pp. 749-782.

The job provides a welcome and refreshing change of activities. The following case is an illustration:

"I guess we want to get things in a hurry," confessed a 19-year-old wife of a factory worker and a mother of a 2-year-old child. She works in a plastics factory, clearing $30 a week. She and her husband came from poor Southern families. When they married three years ago, they "had to start from scratch." They "didn't get a single wedding gift," and didn't have a dish or a fork or a chair. "You go into a store and you nearly go crazy with all the things you want to buy." They had to buy everything "on time," the living room set, the beds, the dinette set, the baby's crib and the car. In addition, they have had doctor's bills. The little girl needed braces on her legs, costing $50. The husband did not want her to work, but they realized that they needed her $30 a week to pay the bills.

This woman gets up at 6:00 A.M. to make breakfast for her husband and to put up his lunch. She wakes him up at 6:15. Then she goes back to sleep because their little girl stays up late at night and sleeps late in the morning. Getting up again at 8:00, she rushes through her housework, cleaning, washing and ironing; then she prepares dinner and leaves it to be warmed by her husband at night. At 3:30 she leaves for work. A neighbor looks after the little girl for half an hour or so before her husband returns to take over. He takes care of the child, giving her her bath and her supper. The wife returns home at 10:30. Her husband calls for her in the car, with the neighbor looking after the child. They go to sleep at about 11:00; once in a while they watch a late T.V. show and are sleepy the next morning.

The best time of the week is Saturday. They take the child along and spend the day in the stores. Her husband "isn't the kind who enjoys going out with the fellows . . . he is a homebody." Apart from her sister's family they know no couples in the community. Shopping appears to be their main recreation. "We have never seen such beautiful things as we see here in the stores. One time we had two hundred dollars and spent it like crazy. We got a bedspread and curtains for the living room and a tricycle for the girl. It's all the things that we need, but I guess we are in too great a hurry to get them." She expects to stop working when they get what they need and can live on her husband's salary, but she will miss work: "There is so much commotion and yelling in the house in the morning. When I get to the factory I work alone in the room and it's restful. It's the only time I get a chance to think straight. Then during the breaks and at lunch I talk to the girls and I like that too."

The couple just described have the week end for joint activities. In another case, the 23-year-old mother of two children also enjoys her job, but the penalty for her working is an almost complete separation of the spouses.

The husband, a cook in a large concern, gets up at 5:00 A.M. and returns at 2:30. The couple and their children have their dinner at 4:00 and remain together until 5:30 when she leaves for her job as a cashier. Her husband takes over the supervision of the children and puts them to bed and the wife returns home at 10:30. On Saturdays and Sundays she works eight hours a day, with the husband in charge of the children. The couple view this as a temporary arrangement although it has already lasted over a year.

This dovetailing of work shifts by husband and wife is made possible by the shorter work week for the husbands and the availability of part-time work in the evenings and on week ends for the wives. Fitting into such work necessitates the couple's acceptance of a partial reversal of their normal roles. But not every husband is temperamentally capable of supervising the children. One husband offered to give his wife an afternoon off. Upon her return she found him so cross and helpless with the children that she never tried it again. Her husband's irritability with the children rules out work despite this woman's strong desire to take a job.

The net balance of advantages and disadvantages of working is affected by still other conditions. The husband of the cashier who works an eight-hour shift on Saturdays and Sundays complains of his lonesomeness during the week ends. But lonesome as he is he cannot claim that his wife's job disorganizes their social life, because the couple never had any joint social life. In contrast, another husband, in opposing a pre-Christmas job his wife wants to take, cites the following objection:

"This is exactly the time when we ought to be together. We are very lucky because we have a built-in baby-sitter [his father lives with them], and we have quite a few invitations— to a church gathering, to her sister's, and to a couple of other social occasions just around Christmas."

WHY DO THEY WANT TO WORK?

The economic motive for taking a job is universally acknowledged, but it turns out to be not one but a cluster of motives. The women work, of course, because they desire what money can buy—but the sheer pride of earning is itself another reward. "I like to think that I am bringing in some money too," said one working wife. This pride, however, cannot be fully expressed. In reporting about her husband's hurt feelings, one wife cited an episode with the car. Her husband had wanted to buy a small car but she persuaded him to buy the Super-Buick. She was working at the time and she contributed to the purchase of the car. "He gets hurt," she confided, "when I say something terrible to him, like when I told him later that we got the Super-Buick being as I was working." And another woman speaks indignantly of her own sister, "My sister comes right out in front of the family and says, 'If it weren't for what I bring in we couldn't have a vacation.' I think that is an awful way of tearing down her own husband." Thus, although the wife's role of a secondary provider is accepted, she cannot fully savor all its rewards. This illustrates anew the ethical inconsistencies arising when some elements of interlocking roles undergo change while other aspects persist.

Money is a source of self-esteem and of power. Even in happy marriages in which earnings are pooled, many working wives feel entitled to more control over the expenditures. This becomes apparent when husband and wife disagree about expenditures: "When I have my bridge club to entertain, that adds three or four dollars to the food bill. If I tell my husband that I'm running short of food money he says, 'Well, don't entertain so much,' or he may tell me that I don't need to give somebody a gift. When I work and have my own money, I do as I please." This woman had worked in the early years of her marriage and is eager to return to work.

In only one case does the disposition of the wife's earnings cause a conflict. The wife in this case maintains that as long as she fulfills all the obligations of a full-time homemaker, she is entitled to full use of the money she makes as a waitress. Her husband is resentful. This ethical disagreement is accentuated, or perhaps even precipitated, by other marriage problems.

Apart from money, the working wives mentioned other rewards of working: the enjoyment of social life on the job, the pleasures of workmanship, the bracing effect of having to get dressed up in the morning, some relief from constant association with young children, and "having something interesting to tell my husband." A job apparently need not be a highly skilled one to yield the worker some satisfaction from its effective execution. A 27-year-old woman (with eight years of schooling) works in a cafeteria: "I'm strong and I do a good job. They like the way I put the food on plates without slopping it over. I know I am good. They tell me I help digestion because I make cracks and laugh, and they like it."

Another woman has recently left her part-time job in a real estate office for reasons of health. Her children are in school and the house is too quiet for her. "I've got to get a bird or a dog. I used to talk to people in the office. Now I have no one to talk to; I feel like I'm no use to anyone."

The desire to escape housework appears to be the decisive motive for working in only a few cases. It is even possible that the women with a strong interest in a job are among the most, not the least, efficient housekeepers. Unfavorable attitudes to housewifery are symptomatic in some of Glenton's women of a generally low vitality and inability to cope with life. It is not surprising that the depressed Mrs. Clark[14] does not want to work although she sometimes wonders whether she ought to help pay the bills. On the other hand, another woman who works part-time and enjoys it, has this to say:

"Some women really do take it [housework] very hard. They don't like sitting around the house and they hate doing things like this [making a quilt]. I get a big kick out of working in my garden and sewing and taking care of the kids. I really like taking care of the kids. A lot of women get so griped, I can't understand them. It isn't so bad washing out the diapers. Sure it stinks, but kids are a hell of a lot of fun to watch—you never know what they are going to do or to say next."

These contrasting cases suggest that the rejection of housewifery may not be the dominant motive for working that it is sometimes alleged to be.[15]

[14] See pp. 95-98.
[15] For similar conclusions, see Robert R. Sears *et al.*, 1957, pp. 44-50.

Contacts with working women arouse longings for a job in some homemakers. Possibly the advantages of working are more visible than its costs. One woman plays bridge with her employed sister and two friends, one of whom is also working. This woman expressed the view that women who work look trimmer and more up-to-date than housewives. She once suggested to the bridge club that they sell dishrags and get a little money and her sister said, "Gee, you sound poor." This made her realize "that a dollar means a lot more to me than to my sister and it reminded me that maybe I ought to take a job. My mother-in-law is after me to get a job. She would like us to get a new tiled bathroom, and we really have to fix the porch. We'll have to borrow to do it. If I worked I don't think we would live a lot different. We just wouldn't wait so long to get the things we want."

This woman is the president of the P.T.A. and this activity is a source of pride to her and her family. Nevertheless, her mother and her sister both think that what she does is not as important as a paid job. Once her mother agreed to baby-sit for her to enable her to go to a very important meeting of the P.T.A. But her sister called to say that she had a couple of hours of overtime— "so Mother backed down at the last minute. . . . They feel that if you don't get paid for it, it isn't important."

The new role of supplementary earner has created problems for women. If the family needs her earnings and she does not want to work, she may experience feelings of guilt. If she does work, the double burden is often a drain on her energy. The effects of such new developments upon the men have received little attention. But in Glenton, the men's dilemmas are found to be as poignant as those of their wives. This is one aspect in which recent social changes do create the familiar dislocations.

THE HUSBAND'S DILEMMA

Circumstances forced some reluctant wives into the labor market, but there are only one or two husbands who had urged their wives to work, for the men take too great a pride in their role of provider to demand such assistance. But the husbands are ambivalent. They have many objections to their wives' employment —and yet the women's earnings can add a substantial increment to income. The wife who wants to work dangles the over-due bill for the living room chair or the T.V. set before her husband. "He wants me to stop working," said a 32-year-old woman, mother of two children, who enjoyed her evening job as a waitress. "But he doesn't believe in bills," she added slyly. "We don't buy anything on time. I paid cash for the parlor set with the money I saved up from working. He sure liked that part of it." Women use a similar argument with children; "Do you want me to quit work?" a mother asked her 10-year-old girl. "But then I couldn't get you the Bermuda shorts."

In higher economic classes, at a comparable stage of life, the husband is spared this particular mental conflict because he need only remind himself how expensive it would be to engage a nurse or a maid in order to enable his wife to work.

Even if the husband is prepared to sacrifice the additional income, his wife may feel differently. The standard of living is not fixed and there is no traditional yardstick to which the husband can refer his claim that his earnings are adequate. "I just as soon get along with what we have, but she wants a new living room," said a 26-year-old high school graduate, a garage mechanic. "She isn't the kind who wants to keep up with the Joneses, she gets disgusted with the women who have to have anything they see in a friend's house. But she thinks we need a new living room. She is talking about taking a job before Christmas in the department store. She wants to make a bigger splash around Christmas time, but I am going to talk her out of it."

The following conversation between a 28-year-old taxi driver and his 26-year-old wife took place in the presence of the interviewer. It is typical of the men's attitudes. This marriage of seven years is one of the happiest in the whole group. There are three children. The husband had nine years of schooling, and the wife, seven. She works part-time.

"He doesn't want me to work at all," said the wife. Her husband nodded. "He's against it, but I got to do it because we got to have enough money to eat and dress and it isn't just the rent and the food we have to have. It's to keep on going and to get places. He works harder than most people and I work real hard too. But we still have to have more money coming in. We want to have another baby in a year or two and we have to save up for that too. We want to start him in his business and not be stuck this way for the rest of our lives. But he doesn't like me to work at all. He thinks kids should have their own mothers around. He thinks nobody can love them the way we can. He ain't proud about my working like some men are, no sirree. It's just that he thinks the kids really need us." At that the husband said firmly: "That's right. It's just like she says. If I can get the work the way I've been doing, you'll never have to go out and work again." "But, hon, I like to go out and do some work sometimes. It's nice for a change, and I like to think I'm bringing in some money too. We could buy our house sooner and get you set up sooner if we could just get some more money quicker." "If you feel that way about it," said the man, "We'll borrow money." But the wife countered that she doesn't believe in borrowing if they can possibly make it themselves. She was then told by her husband that their plan to use his friend's capital was after all a form of borrowing.

Opposition to the wife's employment may be partly rooted in the husband's jealousy, as was stated explicitly in four cases and suggested indirectly in others. "He won't hear of my taking this restaurant job," said one wife in her husband's presence. Her husband then said to the interviewer, "The men get fresh with waitresses. I see it myself all the time." Another husband forced his wife to give up her factory job because he feared that a fellow worker was getting "familiar" with her. Still another, an older man, refuses to allow his wife to resume her eight-to-midnight job as a waitress. Although the husband did not admit this to the interviewer, his sister-in-law told us that his wife's infidelities were common knowledge. A truck driver remarked:

"A woman will work with a fellow and before you know it, she'll be seeing him day in and day out. He might say, 'Let's go and have a drink together,' and that's how things start. A couple of dollars extra ain't worth it. Before you know it the woman will be running out on him. I don't say that every working girl does it, but it happens. I've seen it myself."

In the absence of paid help in the home, part-time jobs often require a dovetailing of work shifts with the result that they increase the husband's duties around the house. But even apart from such practical disadvantages, the working wife still violates an emotionally charged image: "It just doesn't seem like home to me when I know that my wife is out working."

Desire for additional income conflicts with the husband's

jealousy, his anxiety over the loss of power, and other objections to his wife's employment. Such emotions are all the more stressful because they can no longer be fused with moral indignation. The men have been influenced by the growing acceptance of working wives, so they have to cope with emotions which they themselves can no longer consider wholly justified. The shift in social norms has not modified the sentiments of the men as they relate to the gainful employment of their wives.

Parental Roles

The image of the working-class father as the stricter disciplinarian and the court of last resort fits only four out of every ten fathers.[16] In these cases the fathers are acknowledged by both parents to have firmer control over the children. The mothers are said to have superior control in three out of every ten families. In the remaining three, the parents feel they have equal control, occasionally claiming that each succeeds better with a particular child.

Such data as we have do not uphold the idea that the mother is generally the indulgent and supportive parent and the father the disciplinarian. For one thing, the non-involvement of some fathers forces both roles upon the mother. But there are fathers who also perform the double function. "They like him a lot," said one wife of her three children, aged 4, 2 and 1. The father is 27 years old, with seven years of schooling. "They like him better than they like me." She explained that this was natural because she was always having to shoo the kids out of the way to do her housework "but when their father comes home he can play with them. It's really funny to see them all on the floor." "No," she answered the interviewer, "he don't have to spank them. They listen to him. He makes them get in line. He is very good about teaching them things too."

The father is the indulgent and supportive parent in the following case. "He is too easygoing," complains the wife, "I don't like it because he is the great guy and I am the tough one. He thinks I hound the boy too much. I tell the boy to stay in the room and after a while my husband will say, 'Oh, let him go out.'"

Another fact makes it difficult to assign a specialized function

[16] Thirty-seven per cent of the 51 fathers (with at least one child over 2 years of age) for whom this information was available.

to each parent. Impartiality towards children is an important value. For instance, equal treatment is scrupulously observed with respect to gifts. But special fondness for a particular child is often admitted, usually somewhat apologetically, "I guess I am a little soft on the boy," or "She is his pet." Favoritism is acknowledged by the parents (or observed by the interviewers) in nearly 30 per cent of the families. In such families, one parent may be so indulgent to the favored child that the other is forced to be the disciplinarian. In a few unhappy marriages, coalitions of a parent with a child divide families into warring camps. Punitiveness towards the spouse's pet can be a weapon in marital warfare.[17]

Finally, parents may differ as to the importance of some phase of discipline. "Each one of us will think," reports one happily married wife, "that the children ought to snap into it at a different time. Sometimes we let out about it right in front of the kids. I think that's a terrible thing." A united front of parents is felt to be important but is not always realized in practice. The parent with a low tolerance for a particular activity presses for harsher discipline while the other defends the child. Parental roles may be reversed with regard to another activity.

A more intensive study might have revealed greater specialization. But another item of information argues against this: the complaints expressed by each parent about the other are very similar. In speaking about the spouse's shortcomings, 16 per cent of the wives and 14 per cent of the husbands accuse the other of being too lenient; some husbands fear that wives are making "sissies" out of the boys. Were the mother generally the supportive and the father the disciplining parent, one would hardly expect this symmetrical pattern of accusations.[18] Sixteen per cent of the wives feel that their husbands are too harsh with the boys. Ten per cent of the husbands complain that their wives punish the children excessively and are too harsh generally.

[17] Ezra F. Vogel and Norman W. Bell, 1960. See also our case on pp. 164-170.

[18] The following questions at the end of the interview afforded our respondents an opportunity to sum up parental roles: "Would you wish that your husband (wife) were more of a help to you in the upbringing of your children: In what ways?"; "What are his (her) shortcomings and strong points as a parent?"; "What can a wife rightfully expect from a husband in the care and upbringing of the children?"; "How well does your husband (wife) understand your children?"

In addition to the specific criticisms that the wife is too lax or too harsh with the children, one out of every five husbands has other complaints such as that she "hollers too much," is inconsistent or impatient with the children. Child rearing is one of the few areas of family life in which husbands list more grievances than wives. The major responsibility for child rearing falls upon the mother, so if "things go wrong" even she accepts the major share of the blame.

So much for the dissatisfactions. At the other end of the scale, one-third of the couples are quite satisfied. Questions about possible shortcomings here failed to evoke any criticism, and many in this third of the families expressed warm praise of the spouse's parental performance.

Parental Values

The goals of child rearing are generally phrased in moral terms, "to bring up kids in a respectable manner to live a decent life, honest and true" or "to be good Christians." Only a minority departs from this emphasis upon character and respectability to mention happiness, getting along with people, and, very rarely, success or achievement. "I think it is important for them to be happy—and he [respondent's husband] thinks—to be somebody" remarked one woman.

Parents hope that their sons will rise above them. A good report card is commended as a promise of such upward mobility. But in talking about goals of child rearing only very rarely do they say, "I hope he'll be ambitious" (or "successful," or a "go-getter," or "be somebody"). This does not necessarily mean that these parents prize virtue above worldly success. But they define success precisely as a respectable life in a job, a house, a neighborhood a rung or two up the ladder. Many Glenton families have observed at close range, or have actually experienced, such problems as unemployment, partial layoffs, relief during depressions, alcoholism, and minor brushes with the police over children's offenses. We noted the anxiety with which parents spoke of juvenile delinquency. Understandably they want to move their children safely over the dividing line into the world of security and respectability.

If middle-class parents give the higher priority they do to ambition, curiosity, self-reliance, happiness and independence it is because, as Melvin Kohn explained, respectability and decency are no longer problematic for them. They can afford to turn to other goals.[19] Moreover, their level of aspirations is more open-ended, as well as higher. Instead of specifying the end result, middle-class parents point to the kind of qualities that can continue to promote achievement.

Values concerned with personality development are seldom voiced in Glenton. The fullest realization of one's potentialities is not a familiar idea. There are few references, no matter how simply expressed, to creativity, curiosity, independence, self-direction, zest for living or capacity to grow. Such values glorify the process of development without specifying any end result. Our observations confirm an earlier study, which found that working-class parents emphasized what was termed the "traditional" values of obedience, neatness and respect for adults. The middle-class parents in that study, on the other hand, wanted their children to be happy, to confide in them and to be eager to learn.[20]

When one of Glenton's respondents does express a developmental value, he turns out to be atypical in other ways also. One woman, exasperated by her easygoing, dependent husband, admittedly strives to develop independence in her sons. "When the boys ask me, 'What shall I do, Mommy?' I tell them, 'Think about it, maybe you can figure it out yourself.'" This woman is, in her own words, an "avid reader." "My girl friends always kid me because I always say, 'I read somewhere.' . . . They think reading is a waste of time." She is dreaming of writing a newspaper column on child rearing when the children are older. This is, incidentally, the highest occupational aspiration expressed in the study by either women or men. This woman left high school at 16 to get married. She was unhappy at home because her mother was a "cold woman and had no love for me." Perhaps, she added, her mother was too busy with eight children. As an adolescent, the woman used to spend much time in the library. She could not explain the source of her interest in reading, but whatever the original motivation, the printed word played a part in the transmission to her of middle-class ideas. Other wives might have been similarly vexed with a husband's lack of drive.

19 Melvin L. Kohn, January 1959.
20 See Evelyn Millis Duvall, 1946, pp. 193-208.

But her clear diagnosis of the problem and her deliberate attempt to develop independence in her sons bear the imprint of the books and columns on child rearing of which she alone in her circle is "an avid reader."

An interpretation of class differences in parental values is offered by Melvin Kohn. He characterizes the contrast by saying that "working-class parents want the child to conform to externally imposed standards." The middle classes are more concerned with self-direction and internal dynamics of the child. These differences derive, he holds, from the "entire complex of differences in life conditions . . . of the two social classes," but more specifically from the kind of qualities each requires to get along in the world of work. Middle-class occupations require manipulation of interpersonal relations rather than of things. They are more demanding of self-direction and less subject to direct supervision than blue-collar jobs. Getting ahead in middle-class occupations is more dependent upon one's own action than upon the collective action of a union.[21]

Consistent with this interpretation is our observation that the less-educated wives refer to "bad luck" when speaking of the economic failure of their husbands. The better-educated women who are married to poor providers, on the other hand, tend to accuse the latter of lack of drive. It appeared as if the less-educated see themselves at the mercy of unmanageable forces.[22] The high school graduates, closer to the middle classes in many ways, may be less fatalistic. And once economic destiny is held to be affected by one's own effort, the poor providers are more likely to be held responsible for failure. The uneducated blame themselves for failure to complete school but not for lack of ambition. They may be correct in assuming that, given their educational limitations, ambition cannot play a decisive role in their occupational status. The adjective "ambitious" was occasionally used to describe a man willing to take on an evening or a weekend job to raise his income.

Parental values may be influenced by occupational realities, but they have an independent source in culture. The ideology of parenthood is affected by the concept of human nature, by religious beliefs, the state of psychological knowledge and other

[21] Melvin L. Kohn, 1963, pp. 471-480.
[22] See, for example, Lee Rainwater *et al.*, 1959, Chapter 3.

ideational currents. The view that the child is born in original sin, for example, is not consistent with the notion that child rearing consists of drawing out the child's natural qualities. The premium upon originality is not consistent with religious dogmatism.[23]

Glenton families voice ideas reminiscent of the American past. A century or so ago, even middle-class parents, whose occupations required and rewarded self-direction, would have no doubt emphasized good character as an end and discipline as the means of child rearing (and taken it for granted that virtue and worldly success providentially go together). Working-class parents do not mention "self-direction" for the same reason that they do not speak of emotional security or capacity to relate to others. Such concepts are not in their frame of reference. These ideas—which educated middle-class parents get from college courses—and child psychologists, from the novels they read, the doctors and teachers they consult, the plays they see and the social gatherings they attend—have not yet reached the majority of the parents in our study. Orville Brim[24] raises a pertinent question about the effect of education upon what parents actually do, but there can be little doubt that it affects what they say and think. We, the interviewers, felt transported, as if by a Wellsian time machine, into an older era, one of pre-Freudian innocence about human behavior.

An example is found in the case of a 32-year-old woman (with ten years of schooling) who has a daughter of 9 and a son of 6. Her husband, with similar schooling, is a skilled worker earning $135 a week. The daughter is an honor student, but they worry about the boy because he is so slow and so stubborn. The conceptual tools this mother possesses for interpreting her children's behavior are revealed as she talks about them. The interviewer's questions are at once translated into matters of discipline or obedience. "What kind of a father is your husband? Is he good about understanding the differences between the two children?" "No," she answered, "he isn't. He never hits them. I tell him, you've got to punish them, they've been running wild." "Yes," she said, "the kids are different. If I just holler, the girl minds me, but even hitting doesn't help with the boy."

This mother mused about the differences between her two

23 Edmund S. Morgan, 1944, p. 53.
24 Orville G. Brim, Jr., 1959.

children: was she perhaps stricter with the girl and too easy with the boy? If the hypotheses about strictness or spoiling, favoring one child or being impartial, fail, then the explanation falls back upon inherited tendencies: "He is a nervous child," or "He has his father's temper." The concepts she employs to puzzle out the difference between her children are few and simple.

Another mother, a high school graduate of 31, describes the problem she has with her 8-year-old daughter. The little girl starts sobbing and gets a stomach ache and red blotches on her forehead whenever she has to attend a social gathering. She gets these attacks before Sunday school, a birthday party and occasionally even before school. The father thinks that they should force her, "just take her over bodily." But the mother worries that perhaps the girl does have a stomach ache and should lie down. They started quarreling over her once before Sunday school and the little girl came downstairs and "was real cute. She said, 'If you two will only stop arguing, I will go.' " The mother remarked that she had always been worried that something would happen to the girl, that she would become sick: "I don't know why I always had that fear about her. Just after she was born I asked the doctor, 'Is she all right?' " This mother described her fear as a kind of an omen about the girl, not as a possible factor in the child's behavior. Here again, it is not the perplexity of the parents that we are noting but the paucity of ideas in terms of which they speculate about the possible causes of problems.

It is sometimes alleged that whatever their value, the psychological advances of the twentieth century tend to rob parents of self-confidence and spontaneity. The awesome realization of possible effects of parental behavior makes parents fearful of taking some wrong and fateful step. They are burdened with a sense of guilt for every inadequacy of their children. It was hard enough to walk the night with a crying infant when the mothers thought that some infants are just born nervous. But now the psychologist tells the mother that if her baby cries without any apparent cause, it may be reacting to the mother's tension conveyed by touch or gesture. It is not surprising therefore that college-educated parents in one study report more frequent feelings of inadequacy in comparison with less-educated parents. The better-educated show relatively more concern over difficulties in their relationships with children.[25]

[25] Gerald Gurin *et al.*, 1960, pp. 134-135.

The less-educated mothers are nonetheless far from complacent. We estimate that one out of every four Glenton mothers has considerable anxiety over her irritability, "hollering" and impatience with children. "It's real hard to know what to do," sighed one mother: "I know they've got to be spanked sometimes but I spank them when I get mad. I shake and beat them and then I feel lousy." The high school graduates do not differ from the less-educated in this respect. More women than men express feelings of inadequacy in relation to children. Such feelings in fathers center about providing the means of livelihood, not on their personal relationships with their children. Not one father volunteered the typical complaint of the busy professional man that he is unable to spend as much time with his children as he feels he should.[26] In comparison with higher classes, the working-class father actually spends more time in the house with his children. And children are more often taken along on social occasions. Moreover, he feels less guilty than the educated father because he is less exposed to the new cultural demands for closer father-child relationships.

If it is true that educated parents nowadays risk a loss of self-confidence and too anxious a scrutiny of motivations, there is another danger threatening the working-class parents. Ignorance of psychological dynamics allows serious conditions to go unrecognized. When problems become too troublesome to be disregarded, parents feel bewildered and helpless.

We found only a trace of the intellectual issue frequently said to divide middle-class parents. The middle-class wife is more attuned than her husband to the latest teachings of child psychologists. She wants to heed the latest doctrine, whereas her husband clings to the more traditional views. In Glenton, in the three exceptional cases in which parental arguments do reflect such intellectual differences, it is, again, the wife who quotes the expert. For example, a 2-year-old daughter of two grammar-school graduates started to wet her pants after the birth of her brother. The husband insists that the little girl be punished, but the mother quotes a magazine to the effect that such lapses are temporary

26 Gerald Gurin *et al.*, 1960, pp. 130-131, report that 18 per cent of mothers felt inadequate "a lot of times, often." This is close to our figure of 25 per cent with considerable anxieties. These authors also found that more mothers than fathers express feelings of inadequacy as parents.

and should be ignored. "I did what I thought was right and he did what he wanted to do, but he found out that punishing her didn't do any good anyway."

Another couple, both high school graduates, disagree about the eating problems of their 3-year-old daughter. The father wants the child to "clean off her plate" before allowing her to leave the table. When the mother opposed this practice, quoting a book on child raising, he said, "It's my daughter and I'll raise her as I like." The child begins to cry when the two of them quarrel. "If I holler at him, it's bad and if I keep quiet, it's bad," sighed the wife.

But in general both Glenton parents are insulated from modern currents of thought and advice. Husband and wife share similar goals for the children and have similar ideas about human behavior. If Glenton parents argue about discipline, the reason is found in factors of temperament and personality, not in a difference between the sexes in exposure to newer doctrines.

Sex and Marital Happiness

The familiar stereotype of the virile but insensitive working-class husband and his long-suffering wife who grimly performs her sexual duty fits only a small minority of Glenton's families. It is overshadowed by other patterns.

Most of our information about sexual relations was derived from the wives, although the husbands were also asked about their sexual satisfactions and disappointments. The following two stories and one question were presented to the wives for comment:

One woman has been married for three years and she says she gets nothing out of intimate relations with her husband. She can take it or leave it. She could enjoy it more if he knew what she liked and what she didn't. But she said she'd rather die than talk to him about such things.

A couple has been married for a year and the wife is close to her sister. The wife says that her husband is a good man, she has nothing against him, but she doesn't enjoy intimate relations with him. He never pays attention to the way she feels, and he doesn't understand what she likes or doesn't like. Her sister says that he is a good man and she should count her blessings and be content.

Some mothers told us that after they gave birth to their first child, they lost interest in sex for quite a span of time. Have you had this experience?

The great majority of the wives think that men are more highly sexed than women, but there is no mistaking their feeling that ideally wives should also experience sexual enjoyment. For the sister's counsel of resignation in the second story is upheld by only three women who say "the sister is right," and let it go at that. The majority feel that the first story presents a genuine problem indeed: "Rough break"; "They are unlucky." The proposed remedies vary from praying to "She ought to get drunk and let fly everything in her." Only one woman suggested reading a book on sex. Seven recommended seeking advice from a minister, doctor or a marriage counselor.

The ideal of sexual fulfillment for women is sometimes conveyed indirectly, in the wives' criticism of the kind of husband who "takes what he wants and don't try to do anything for his wife." Many wives do not find this fulfillment in life. And those who fail to experience pleasure in sexual relations do not today have the support of the Victorian ideology that sexuality is basically sinful and that "cold" women are thereby "pure."

Agreeing on the ideal of sexual fulfillment, the women nevertheless accept the view that in practice every wife must occasionally submit to intercourse regardless of her inclinations. Some 15 per cent assert that the wife's duty is "to give it to her husband whether she likes it or not" in words reminiscent of the stereotype cited. All the women in this 15 per cent have less than a high school education. The high school graduates, on the other hand, tend to regard such submission less as a moral duty than as a necessary evil, or as an expression of sympathy for their husbands' needs. The husband was described as more passionate than the wife in three-fifths of the 45 cases for whom this information was available, the wife more passionate in one-fifth, while the two were described as equally passionate in the remaining fifth.

Frank discussion of the sexual preferences is generally endorsed. The shy wife in the first story evoked little sympathy: "That's a real dumb babe"; "How will he know if she doesn't talk to him?" One contemptuously remarked, "Oh, one of those prissies. I know two or three of them. Butter wouldn't melt in their mouths." One wife felt that a smart woman finds ways better than words to convey her preferences to her husband. Still another offered the qualification: "I think you can be in-between —not as brassy about sex as some girls around here, and not like this girl [in the story]."

Several women recognized in the words of the shy girl their own embarrassment in the early days of their marriages. "The first year we was married," said one young wife, "before he got wise to the time of the month, things was going awful sometimes. I didn't want to tell him what was the matter when he'd come after me, it embarrassed me terribly—and it made me cross all day." A deeply religious bride startled her young husband with her innocence. He remarked to the interviewer: "I don't see how kids could be kept so innocent."

The majority of the wives, however, not only disapprove of the excessive reserve of the young wife in the story, but are incredulous about it. "Yeah, I heard about some of them dumb babes [who know little about sex prior to marriage and are extremely shy], but I don't see how they could have missed with what goes on in school. All the girls tell each other things before they know what it's all about. I don't care what nobody says about keeping their kids pure. Nah, I think they're making it up when they say they don't know."

Several of the men agreed with one husband who said to the interviewer, "As long as she gives me what I need when I need it, I got no complaints." But a much larger number expressed concern with the sexual responsiveness of their wives and held themselves responsible for it. The fact that three women confessed to simulating sexual enjoyment is a further indication that husbands care about the women's responses. The following excerpts from the interviews convey typical attitudes:

The wife of a taxi driver (the husband had nine years of school): "It is no fun for him unless I come across, so I try."

The wife of a semi-skilled worker (grammar school education): "Sometimes he wants it when I don't and I usually let him have it. But he really don't like it so much, and he wants us to come together. He understands real good too what I need to get me going. Sometimes I don't want to start and he'll fool around until I do."

A pressman's helper (ten years of school): "There is no enjoyment for me if she doesn't."

A semi-skilled factory worker (grammar school graduate): "She gets a bang out of it, I couldn't ask for anything better."

The wife of a stock worker (11 years of school): "It bothers him that I don't feel very much sometimes."

The wife of a plumber (grammar school graduate): "You can't enjoy it all the time. . . . He gets all let down when it is blaa."

A hog-handler in a meat packing concern (ten years of school): "She's real good in bed, but she doesn't always enjoy it." (This bothers him, his wife reported.)

A motel attendant (grammar school graduate): "It doesn't seem to mean anything to her, and that isn't half as much fun."

A construction worker (ten years of school): "She wants it as much and as often as I do—I couldn't ask for anything more."

Although the ideal of mutual sexual gratification appears to be widely accepted, reality falls far short of that ideal. Only 30 per cent of the women express high satisfaction with their sexual relations. Of these, some, like the following, stress the physical experience of intercourse: "Sometimes I just got to have it"; "If you play it right sex is the most!"; and "Sex is about the best time in the world." One woman was asked, "Does it ever leave you feeling nothing?" and answered: "Well, even if I don't work up to going off like a factory whistle, it's still almost always nice."

Included in the highly satisfied group were women who accented the emotional intimacy of intercourse, rather than the physical thrill. Thus: "There is more to sex than just sex. There's being together and knowing you love each other. It doesn't always have to be hot." Again: "I wanted him to take me when I was far gone in pregnancy and you aren't supposed to. It isn't so much that I felt so hot but it's real comfortable and warm and I like it." Another woman said she liked anything that made them feel so near and so good about each other.

At the other extreme, an identical proportion, 30 per cent, voice serious dissatisfactions with their sexual lives. The intermediate group of 40 per cent are moderately satisfied; they express some satisfactions but also disclose some problems.[1]

Varieties of Sexual Problems

Sexual maladjustment may be classified from a variety of perspectives. The following discussion centers upon the role of social factors in sexual difficulties.

Social factors may play an indirect role in sexual maladjustment, insofar as they have shaped the personalities of the partners from infancy on. Even without intensive psychological study it became clear that some respondents suffered from deep-rooted psycho-sexual impairment.

In other cases, however, social factors directly disturb sexual adjustment. This is not to say that social factors, such as fear of pregnancy or a husband's economic failure, produce inimical results invariably and regardless of the personalities involved. But in the absence of such adverse circumstances, sexual adjustment would have no doubt proven better.

In still other cases, sexual maladjustment results from general marital conflict, rather than from a basic sexual impairment. In fact, sexual relations, in a number of cases, had been quite satisfactory in the early years of marriage, but worsened as the total relationship deteriorated. In contrast to the second category there seems to be no major social condition directly disturbing the sexual relationship.

In the cases reported below, we shall first illustrate problems caused by husbands' psycho-sexual impairment. The husbands who are less passionate than their wives do not, of course, invariably suffer from sexual impairment. ("I don't like her build,"

---

[1] One of the problems we did not attempt to analyze is infidelity. But four husbands are definitely known to have been unfaithful and one husband and one wife are currently so.

A reference has been made in the previous chapter to the jealousy of the husbands. Several men spoke of the disadvantages of marrying women who were too good looking. Others told of the misery of some friend whose wife was "running around." All in all, the husbands appear somewhat anxious about the fidelity of their women.

blurted out one husband whose wife had grown thin with age, losing her attraction for him.) But the two men about to be described do appear to lack sexual vitality.

SEXUAL IMPAIRMENT OF ONE OF THE MATES

An attractive 23-year-old high school graduate, married for five years and a mother of three infants, spoke sadly about the declining interest of her 26-year-old husband in sexual relations:

> "You have to go and sit on his lap before he would show any affection. A couple of weeks or more pass before he takes any notice of me. I don't know how long he could stay away. I guess I don't want to wait long enough to find out." She talked to him and he said, "Well, that's just the way I am." The young wife is resigned: "He is just not that much of a lover."

Apart from sexual relations, this couple enjoys a high degree of companionship. They read and share matters of interest and they speak frankly about their in-law problems. Both were direct and open with the interviewer. The young husband participates in the care of the three infants and they work and shop together during the week end.

According to the husband's sister, of all the children he was the closest to their mother. "He often stayed home to keep her company" when his siblings were out dating. His sister thought "it was funny for a boy to give up good times with the girls to stay home with his mother."

In another case, two young high school graduates, married for three years and parents of one child, describe themselves as extremely happy. But the husband often comes home so tired that he can hardly wait to get to sleep. She doesn't "have the heart to ask him to make love when he needs his rest." They talked about this and he said that, being around the house all day, she "worked up a lot of energy," and that they "must do something about it," but so far they have found no solution. This young man is a tense person who describes himself as an "oddball." He "just hates" his father and had tried to be domineering like his mother, but grew to resent her too. Not having had much respect for her husband, his mother had tried too hard to mold her son, he said. It was marriage that brought him happiness. He has to "pinch himself," he said, when he wakes up and finds himself in bed with his wife because he can hardly believe that his happiness is real. But his weak sexual drive does worry him.

In the next case, it is the wife's lack of sexual response that the couple sees as their major problem.

"He says I'm a cold potato." This was said by one of the most troubled women in the group. She is 27 years old, with 10 years of schooling, married six years, and a mother of two. The 30-year-old husband is a factory operative with 11 years of schooling. The couple is so unhappy that they asked the interviewer to direct them to a marriage counselor.

During her last visit, the interviewer observed both husband and wife: The wife appeared tense and tongue-tied in the presence of her husband. "Well, go on, talk," he said, "what have you got to say for yourself?" But she would just shake her head and look down at her tightly clenched hands. He said repeatedly: "There. You see how it is."

In an earlier interview the wife said: "It's like I told you. He don't like it that I'm cold and so I don't like the way things go and the first thing you know, we aren't talking to each other at all. It isn't that we are mad at each other. It isn't that we're embarrassed, it's just that we can't talk. And then he's out every night and how can we get along any better. He claims to be a good father and yet I think he neglects the kids. They'll do what he says and they won't do what I say, if he isn't around. My nerves are shot!"

"I get deeply hurt," said the husband, "I get hurt by my wife and about what there is and isn't between us. She doesn't respond to me and the trouble is she won't talk to me. We seldom talk things out. We just let things fade out. She says I wouldn't understand and she cries if I insist."

The wife started working at the age of nine because her "father was lazy" and her mother was sickly. In the course of her reminiscences she flushed in recounting an incident when she discovered some children indulging in sex play in a storeroom across an alley from where she worked. She called the police to break this up and was criticized for this even by her own family. She asked whether the interviewer thought she had been justified in calling the police.

This wife's frigidity appears to reflect a deeply rooted difficulty and is claimed by both husband and wife to be the initial cause of their unhappiness. The sexual maladjustment, however, is in turn aggravated by many other features of an unhappy relationship.

THE FEAR OF PREGNANCY IN A PATRIARCHAL MARRIAGE

The following case illustrates how a social factor—in this case fear of pregnancy—can affect sexual adjustment.

The grim, overworked 37-year-old mother of seven children takes in piece work to make ends meet. The interviewer, after seeing this woman on three different occasions, noted that she hardly ever smiled during the five hours of interviewing. This woman lives in dread of another pregnancy. Since she and her husband are Protestants, and use contraceptives, we were puzzled by her anxiety and hopelessness. In the third interview we arranged to discuss specifically the couple's sexual relationship and family planning.

The wife herself was one of seven children and she attributed the poverty of her parental home to the large size of the family. After her fourth child was born she told the doctor she simply couldn't stand having any more. The doctor "was afraid to tell her because of all the Catholics in their community," so she had gone to the neighboring town and got fitted out with a pessary.

"We paid eight dollars for all that junk, and a fat lot of good it did us." The interviewer said, "This is what we're interested in. How come it didn't work?" The wife said, "Well, God knows, we might have had ten more if it hadn't been for that. The thing is I'd have to wear it all the time, and I can't. It hurts me. I went back to the doctor about it, and he said it wasn't safe to wear it all the time, I might give myself a cancer. A cancer is worse than a kid. Once you got cancer, you're through. It may be hard to feed a kid, but you're still alive. You never know when the fit is going to come on him. He seems to know when I got it on and not bother me and then the minute I take it off, he seems to know and comes for me." Asked if he wouldn't give her time to take care of this, she said, "Not him." Did she mind it? "Of course, I do." We reproduce the fully recorded interview.

Question: Why do you let him then? / Answer: What else can I do?

Q: Can't you tell him to wait a minute? / A: Yea, but he don't want to.

Q: Does he want the children? / A: He don't care.

Q: What do you think makes him this way? / A: I don't know.

Q: Is he rough with you? / A: No, not exactly. Not like the others I hear about.

Q: Well, why don't you make him wait? / A: I wouldn't feel right about it.

Q: Have you given up wearing it altogether? / A: No, I have it in a lot when I know he's going to be around. I think I'd have a baby every ten months without that. I put it in at night, and sometimes it bothers me and gets sore, and so I get up and take it out. That seems to wake him up and that's it.

Q: Does he come for it a lot in the morning? / A: Sometimes. Not as much as he used to when he was young.

Q: How is he on week ends? / A: He has fits and starts. It depends on what else he's doing and what's on his mind. Sometimes when he's worried about money and work, he wants it more, and sometimes he don't want it at all. When things is going on smooth now, he wants it two or three times a week. Sometimes when he has a fit on the week end, he wants it three or four times. You never know how it's going to be.

Q: Do other women feel this way? / A: Yea, especially the Catholics.

Q: But you're a Protestant, how come you let him get away with it? / A: I don't know quite. He made sure that I knew he was boss when we were first married. I was kind of young, and my ma said I had to give in to him. I didn't like it. He used to hurt me a lot when we first started. But my ma said I had to take it.

Q: Are there a lot of women in the same fix with you around here? / A: Yea, I guess so, most of them, I guess.

Q: Haven't you heard of women who managed to get their

husbands to be more considerate? / Λ: Yea, I guess they're better fixed with money.

Q: What's it got to do with money? / A: Well, I guess when a man's got other pleasures, he ain't so selfish about this one.

Q: Do other women feel that way around here? / A: Yea, a lot of them do. They say they pity the men. That's the only thing they got. Most of the people is Catholics, and they say it goes against God if you don't give into a man and give him his one pleasure.

Q: Well, he does have other pleasures. He smokes cigars and he looks to me like he eats a lot too. / A: Yea, he smokes all the time, and he gets more than he needs to eat.

Q: Does he get more to eat than the children do? / A: I try to see that they get enough to eat, but he says that he's got to eat to keep his strength up so he can work so they can all have something to eat. So he gets the best of it. Sometimes I keeps some back and feed them after he's gone.

Q: But you're not Catholic, and don't you think that it's wrong to have children if you can't bring them up right? / A: Yea, sometimes it bothers me real bad. I get scared if I don't feed them right, like they'll get sick and maybe die. I think maybe that's a sin too.

Q: Do you know other people whose husbands are nice to them, nicer than yours? / A: Yea, but they ain't so busy, they ain't got so many kids to feed.

Q: Well, then why does he keep on making more kids? / A: I don't know. I asked him about it a couple of times and he didn't say nothing.

This woman confessed that she and her husband had sexual relations from the time she was 17, prior to their marriage. He had used a condom in those days, but at one time she thought she was pregnant and so they had married—"He's been takin' it out on me ever since."

Feelings of guilt may have compounded this wife's problem, but her submissiveness also has its roots in her patriarchal conception of marriage. She is bitter, but her bitterness is directed against "fate" even more than against her husband. "We gotta decent family. I always say thank God. He's real steady and good on his job. He don't run around with other women. He ain't so bad about my takin' on work. He knows I gotta do it. I know one man who beats up his wife because she goes to work, but they can't eat without it."

The husband gives no indication whatsoever that he bears his wife a grudge for the forced marriage. He appears to be satisfied with himself and with her and does not feel that their large family is a problem. He is the oldest of five brothers and occupies a position of some authority in relation to them. He appears to be satisfied also with the respect he enjoys in his own family; we sensed that he feels he has earned it by his sense of responsibility, his steady work and his sobriety. He described his ideal of marriage:

> "A man's gotta live his life and do his job. He's gotta be strong. He's gotta think about the whole family and not just himself. Not all the fellows bring home their pay straight to their wives, but I think that makes things a lot simpler. It don't do no good to cut up and drink a lot of beer on payday. You just put off the grief that way. It's better to go out and have a beer when you enjoy it and after you've done the things that have to be done the most. A man shouldn't say one thing one time and another, another. It gets the kids upset. He's gotta be strong and stick to his word. He shouldn't be afraid to put his foot down when it's going to do some good.

> "The wife ought to do her duty and I don't rightly know how to say what her duty is, except that you can tell when she's doin' it. And you want her to do it right, and not be a sourpuss about it. I tell the girls to do their work and keep at it until it's done and not to go poopin' around all over the place but to stick to it and get it over with. After that they can play and they can enjoy it more. I guess that holds true right into married life. Sometimes you get more on your hands than you know how to handle. A good wife has to be able to take it when times like that comes along."

"I like her the way she is," was the man's repeated answer to the interviewer's probings of dissatisfactions. The interviewer asked:

Q: Some of the fellows I've talked to have said that they wished their wives would make more fuss over them. Do you feel that way? / A: No, as long as she does her duty, I ain't got no complaints.

Q: Well, you like her to respond to you, don't you? / A: She does respond to me.

Q: Did you ever meet a woman that you thought you'd rather marry than your wife? / A: No, I looked around a bit when I was in the Army, but she's just fine.

Apart from the fear of pregnancy that so oppressed the woman just described, there are other social factors disturbing sexual adjustment. Chapter 13 shows that some poor providers felt "beat" and that the husband himself or his wife traced the decline in the husband's potency to his sense of economic failure. In other cases it is the wife whose sexual response is affected by her disappointment in her husband as a provider. Some wives are quite explicit in making this connection. A 29-year-old mother of five children, married ten years, expressed disappointment that "sex is wearing off." She is dissatisfied with her economic situation and feels that her husband is not trying hard enough to better himself. She remarked that she might have been more interested in sexual relations if he were "getting along better."

Another mode of sexual maladjustment, one resulting from marital strife, is illustrated at length on pages 164-170. That couple had a satisfying sex life which, however, deteriorated with the growing breakdown of their marriage.

Sexual Behavior and Educational Level

The educational level of the women makes no difference in the strength of their sexual desire. One-third of the women describe themselves as passionate and—at the other extreme—one-fifth say they are "cold." These proportions are identical in the two educational groups. Case histories, however, do reveal some difference in behavior. The sexually cold high school wife, partly no doubt because of her relatively superior position in marriage, resists her husband's advances more frequently than the less educated woman. A 27-year-old high school graduate (married to a high school graduate) feels that she is "getting a little more out of sex now," after the birth of her two children, than at the outset of marriage, when poor sex adjustment "led to a mood and was a problem." She would still often prefer to go to sleep but "you can't always have it your way." If she feels he is in need of sex, she complies. Sometimes "he clowns and pesters" her until she starts laughing about it and there is mutual agreement. In a less satisfactory marriage, the wife, a 31-year-old high school graduate, married to a 37-year-old, less-educated man, says that her interest in sex has declined: "We have fights over it. Sometimes I give in, sometimes he does." She goes to sleep in the living room and he usually promises to leave her alone if only she returns to their bedroom. She tries to reassure him by explaining that she loves him despite her refusal.

Similar efforts to escape sex are described by the less-educated wives, and to that extent the two groups are alike. But some less-educated women not only submit more regularly, but voice the moral principle of the "wife's duty to her husband."

As to relative frequencies of "good," "fair" and "poor" sexual adjustment, the less-educated women report a somewhat higher proportion at both extremes (See table 1).[2] One-third of the less-educated, but only one-fifth of the high school graduates, enjoy good adjustment. The next section will consider the hypothesis that, among the educated women, sexual adjustment may be closely linked to overall satisfaction with marriage, whereas some less-educated women can be sexually adjusted despite unhappiness in marriage.

At the other extreme, the proportion of poorly adjusted is 42 per cent for the less-educated and 36 per cent for the high school graduates. Poverty and the fear of pregnancy, more prevalent among the less-educated, affect their sexual relations adversely. Moreover, a higher proportion of the less-educated are unhappily married. Although some unhappy couples remain well-adjusted sexually, others are so estranged that even among the less-educated, sexual relations do suffer.

Sexual Adjustment and Marital Happiness: Some Deviant Cases

Sexual adjustment is held to be a sensitive index of happiness in marriage. Many studies have found a positive association be-

2 For tables 1 to 31b, see appendix, pp. 354-376.

tween sexual adjustment and general satisfaction with marriage,[3] and a theory has been put forth to explain this association. The theory states that ". . . the sexual harmony of the couple would be influenced by and therefore not endure in a situation in which the marital partners did not love each other, were in conflict on non-sexual issues, or were otherwise dissatisfied with the marriage. This outcome might be expected for the wife, particularly since the female in American society perhaps tends to be more strongly imbued than the male with the idea that sexual intercourse is acceptable and proper only in a context of love and respect." [4]

In the present study sexual and marital adjustment also tend to go together (Table 2), but let us examine the exceptions. Six couples with excellent sexual adjustment are very unhappy in their marriages; on the other hand, nine are happily married despite their unsatisfactory sex life. An analysis of such deviant cases helps to clarify the dissociation of sexuality from the total relationship. Why does not the high sexual enjoyment suffuse the marriage with warmth and mutual consideration? What keeps the hostility of the unhappy couples from disturbing their sexual response? Again, in the sexually maladjusted but happy marriages, why does sexual frustration not destroy the rapport of the couple?

Psychoanalytic literature abounds in case histories of individuals whose peculiar sexual needs frustrate their other wishes or run counter to their moral principles. In such cases sexual gratification is bound to bring some unhappiness. But, as we shall see, ambivalent or morally unacceptable sexual needs are not the only factors producing the dissociation of sex from the total relationship.

SEXUALLY ADJUSTED, BUT UNHAPPY, COUPLES

In the first two cases reported below, good sexual adjustment coexists with marital unhappiness.

Mrs. Clark is a submissive wife, inferior to her husband in social status, education and strength of personality. His periodic depressions trouble and bewilder her. She suspects that he will

---

[3] See, for example, Lewis M. Terman, *et al.*, 1938, pp. 373 ff.; Ernest W. Burgess and Paul Wallin, 1953, pp. 687-697.

[4] Ernest W. Burgess and Paul Wallin, 1953, p. 680.

never realize his grandiose ambitions and is worried about their future. She finds her husband, and her responsibility for the children and housework, so overwhelming that she is often too depressed to be able to tackle her daily tasks. She then worries about her "lack of gumption." The neglected, untidy apartment upsets her husband, who comes and goes without concern for her wishes. Her life is barren of pleasures. Without her mother's constant emotional support it is doubtful that she could maintain her equilibrium. But this is how she describes their sexual relations:

> Mrs. C. said she did not like much sex foreplay and that both she and her husband liked a rather prolonged intercourse. She confided that he had a mistress before they were married who liked him to have two or three ejaculations a night. She, on the other hand, had no particular preference about this. His own preference was to be with her during one, two or three orgasms previous to his own and then to work them both up to a good climax. She said, "But we ain't always got time for that or we are too tired. Saturday night's a good time after he gets his mind off things and relaxes.[5] Sometimes, Monday or Tuesday nights, after things get started at work again, he'll get all worked up and take me in a hurry, and sometimes that'll make him cuss. Other times he don't seem to mind at all, and he'll just sigh and be gone the minute it's over." She volunteered the information that, in spite of their full sex life, he occasionally still has wet dreams. According to her description, whenever this occurs, he is quite chagrined. "I can't figure him out on things like that."
>
> "Sometimes he wants it when I don't and I usually let him have it. But he really don't like that so much, and he wants us to come together. He understands real good what I need to get me going. Sometimes I don't want to start and he'll fool around until I do."

When asked about the effect of pregnancy, she replied: "He always wants it right up until the last minute. Even after the doctor tells him to stop, he's gotta do something about it. Even though he doesn't go all the way, he's gotta do something about it. And it's the same after the kid is born. After a while, I want it, too, and everything's all right. My sister was just like me, and she had a bad time because her man made her take him. She said it hurt like hell. She wanted to do it for him

---

[5] For further description of this marriage, see also pp. 270-274.

outside, but nothing would do for him but the regular way. She left him for a couple of months and stayed up to Ma's. I heard about it then so I weren't surprised. But one of my girl friends thought something awful had happened to her when it hit her. Well, I did ask my ma about it when this thing dragged on four or five months instead of stopping after a couple. She said that I'd feel better soon as I got the curse, but I'd already got the curse. I told J. he could go ahead more'n once, but he said he didn't like it so good that way. He'd try it out every once in a while. A couple of times I even took it in my mouth when he needed it bad, and I simply couldn't stand it. But mostly he would just lie against me and pump any old way."

Her husband at times withdraws from her emotionally and physically. She said: "Sometimes he looks like he hates me. He's terribly cold and he seems to want to kind of get away from me, even though he's here. He'll go out and he won't get in until one or two o'clock or he'll stay up late watching T.V. and not talk much to me. Sometimes he'll sit in his easy chair and put his feet up on the stool there and go to sleep and not want to come to bed at all, all night. I've tried to get him to take off his clothes, at least his belt, and stretch out. And I've tried to take care of him like a kid, just like I told you a wife should. Sometimes he gets mad at me for that and tells me to leave him alone." During such periods of withdrawal on the part of her husband she herself experienced strong sexual desires. The longest such "spell" went on for about three months. At first she thought that maybe he was trying to get even with her for her long loss of interest in sex after the birth of her child. Then she realized: "It was different. It wasn't just that I had the baby and didn't love him any more. I loved him a lot, but my body was all haywire. I suppose he loves me just the same. He says he does, but he just gets terribly cold." She explained that she herself felt very warm and full of affection for the whole world when she had given birth to her oldest daughter, even though she was disinclined towards sex. He, on the other hand, seems at such times to be unhappy about everything, the disenchantment with sex being merely one symptom of the total feeling. She said that she had tried hard but in vain to find out "what was eatin' him" during one of these spells. She grew so irritable at such periods that she once asked the doctor to give her something to quiet her nerves.

Mrs. C. volunteered: "Me and my husband went all the way [sexually] long before we was married. There was a lot of girls

goofy about him, but he picked me and we settled down."
Asked if she thought she was lucky he picked her, she said:
"Maybe sometimes yes and sometimes no."

Mr. C. said he had no disappointments in his sex life: "She is
always there when I want her. She really likes it, as women go;
she gets a tremendous bang out of it. Of course I try to do a
pretty good job at that like everything else."

Mrs. C.'s marital problems do not impair her sexual functioning, because she admires and loves her husband. But her norms of
marriage also play a part in her tolerance of him. His neglect of
her does not violate her moral expectations. (See pp. 270-274.)
In fact, she blames herself for her unhappiness, feeling that she
lacks her mother's skill in handling a husband. Even if she derived no pleasure from sexual relations, she would submit from
expediency and a sense of duty. As it is, sex is not only a physical
pleasure but a factor alleviating her sense of isolation from her
husband.

The next case is more striking in that the glum, discontented
wife does not feel for her husband the admiration and affection
Mrs. C. still exhibits despite her frequent depressions and her admission that she sometimes regrets her marriage. The Daniels
epitomize nearly all the problems which can befall a young
couple unprepared for marriage. Their conception of marriage,
devoid of any expectation of friendship, their shallow personalities, their poverty, their unpreparedness for parenthood, and
their lack of mutual understanding—all combine to create unhappiness. Yet the sexual relationship is highly satisfactory to both.

Mr. and Mrs. D., 25 and 23 years old respectively, are both
grammar school graduates, married for three and one-half years
and parents of two sons, aged 2 and 1. Mr. D. has an unskilled job
and makes about $3000 a year.

Mrs. D. feels trapped. One of the rare compliments Mrs. D.
paid her husband referred to the time they were dating:

"He was fun on a date, he was fun dancing. He can still be
a card and get everybody laughing. The fellows like him and
they like the way he juices up a car. Before we were married,
we used to drive around in a motorcycle so fast that you
couldn't tell whether we were driving or flying. We almost
got caught by the cops a couple of times." Then Mr. D. explained to her: "I have to have a woman regular and I want a

home," and he sold his motorcycle to settle down. So now, she said, they are "settled down and have two children and so what?" She hates housework; she is stuck in the house; they have no money for baby-sitters and she never does anything, goes anywhere or has any fun. "I can't go to work with the brats. They are nice kids," she added guiltily, but she would like "to get out and live." Sometimes she gets "terribly mad about housework. I slam around the house and get into a regular fit. I have to be careful when he is home, because he don't like it." Once he had offered to baby-sit for her, but when she got back, she found him very cross because the baby had been crying and he didn't know what to do. She was worried about the kids and didn't have a good time anyway. Her mother is working, but her sister drops in sometimes during the day. Most of the time she is all alone with the kids, very bored, with the radio blaring all day long as her sole company.

Money is so short that her husband once "got very cross because it was snowing and his shoes had holes in them and he couldn't go out in the evening. Doctor bills get us down." She told of the time she had to go to her mother for some food because she had run out of cash before his payday. She feels she is "good at stretching their money." People tell her not to be impatient, that money will be coming along later. In the meantime, "I am ready for the booby hatch." She would like to go to work and to go out a couple of nights a week. Her husband gets disgusted with her "sloppy housework, but he never does anything around the house; he says the house and the kids is my job."

The marital relationship is shallow and the communication between husband and wife is meager:

Mrs. D. frequently "grouses" and freely expresses her irritation with the children in front of her husband, but much of what matters to her she does not share with him. For example, she told her mother about her pregnancy and waited two months before telling her husband. That was her first pregnancy and she wanted to be completely sure. He does not know how deeply hurt she is by her mother's sarcasm because "he wouldn't hear this sort of thing." She talks about it to her sister. She discusses all of her marital grievances with her mother and sister. Asked if she tells her husband everything and if she believes she should, she said, "Hell, no, I don't tell him nothing." She discusses with her mother and sister the fact that she doesn't know how to act when he leaves home without telling her where he is going and when he will come back. And they tell her that "all men are like that. Men are terribly hot for a year or two after they marry and then they start wandering." Eventually they settle down. Mrs. D. said that she "started looking around and saw there were lots of women sitting around, out-of-doors in the evening, and they didn't know where their husbands were and didn't seem to care much." At one point the interviewer asked Mrs. D. whether her husband had ever been unemployed. She said no, he had a steady job; she doesn't know what they would do if he lost his job. Perhaps, the interviewer tested, he could stay with the children while she went to work. She said, "That's a laugh. If you stuck him with that job, he'd walk out on you."

Is it difficult for women to understand men? Mrs. D. thought that it was difficult because men and women were "so different from each other," and they each had their own things to do. He would go and see the fellows and she can talk more easily to her sister. Do she and her husband ever talk about these things? Mrs. D. was getting annoyed by the interviewer's questions about communication: "What do you think a man and woman get married for? To talk?" A sample of their conversation was given by Mrs. D.: "He'll come in and slam down his cap and say, 'Watcha got to eat?' While he is feeding his face, sometimes he'll tell me a thing or two that happened and if anything is going on, I'll let him know." Asked if they ever "just plain talked to each other," she said, "What's there to talk about? I'll ask him, or he'll ask me what has to be done and sometimes he'll lay down the law and sometimes I'll lay down the law." Then she added, "most of any talking done is done when there is a big bunch of us *together, when the relatives come over*" (italics ours). Asked if she wished he would explain why he was so quiet at times, she merely shrugged her shoulders.

When asked what helped her when she felt low, Mrs. D. replied, "Crying does." Once she got very mad and broke things. Her husband held her tight in his arms and hit her a number of times. "He really socked me. He said we couldn't afford it for me to get mad and go busting things like that and he'd bust me one every time I did it. I know it's an awful funny thing to say, but I felt a lot better after that." Does he slap her often? "Not really as much as other people do around here." He had only done it three or four times since they were married, but he spanked her several times and that makes her mad, "He may look skinny, but he is strong as the devil."

They don't often quarrel, she said because she doesn't believe in nagging and she knows it is "healthier not to bring up certain topics." When they do quarrel they "make up because he has to have me." Sometimes they get to laughing at each other or sit down over cigarettes and coffee. And a couple of times he even apologized. She said the first time he did she "almost dropped dead with surprise." She thought it was so funny that a couple of weeks later she said to him, "I'm sorry, honey," and he turned around and slapped her and said she was phoney.

"The kids sometimes drive us both mad. But he doesn't understand how small the kids are, it isn't that he is so mean, he just wants the boy to be like himself, right away." Once she had to come between her husband and the little boy when he started to spank the child and he "took it out on me. I let him do it because I thought he was mad and it would cool him off. When he said to me, didn't I mind, I said, of course, it hurt terribly. But I'd rather he hurt me than hurt the boy and that sobered him up."

In his interview, Mr. D. voiced a similar complaint. "The boy won't do something she wants and she'll get so mad and she shouldn't at anybody that little. She'll holler at him and he'll cry and then if I cuss her out, she really turns on me. Then she'll cuss twice as bad as I did."

She told of one big "fight" they had because she wanted them to take a bigger apartment and to take in boarders. They couldn't find a couple and she suggested a single man and he said, "Not on your life." He called her a whore and she called him a lot of bad names too. "He went roaring out of the house, saying he would kill me and any other man he would find in the house."

"*I guess you could say sex makes me happy,*" replied Mrs. D. to our question about sources of happiness. She had been surprised at the beginning that sex was as nice as it was and she wondered how she got along without it for so long. It's hard to believe, she remarked, that what her mother and sister tell her "about it wearing off after a while" can be true. He kisses her quite often. For example, "He kissed me this morning and I know I am going to have it when he comes back. We didn't quite get around to it last night and so he was kind of promising me when he left today. We were both too tired last night." The only times she is disappointed is when he comes too fast and she hasn't had any satisfaction. Sure, she tells him, Mrs. D. said in reply to the interviewer. A few times he made it up to her later, but at other times he could not.

As to the effect of pregnancy upon her sexual desire, she remembered that the baby was having a first-month birthday when she got "real interested in sex again." Of course, she added, he was wild after being without. As we learned from Mr. D.'s interview, he went with another woman during her pregnancy. He said that his wife offered to help him out in other ways during her pregnancy, but he told her he'd rather have it the right way and none other.

Mrs. D., asked whether her husband shows his appreciation of her, said: "He appreciates me in bed most of all. Once he whistled when he came home and found things especially fixed up." That was nice but "a lot of times, though I fix things up or cook something, he can't be bothered with it so it ain't worth it."

The central passion of Mr. D's life is a hobby he cannot share with his wife and that causes marriage friction.

The young husband has a swagger about him and talks tough. The interviewer remarked that his words will appear tougher in print than in the interview because he often has a half-amused look that takes much of the violence out of his words. In general, he appears not so harsh as his words would indicate.

To the question on sources of happiness, Mr. D. replied: "A sweet motor job that you've just tuned up. Out of nothing you suddenly get this sweet motor singing." As to sources of self-satisfaction, he mentioned two: being able to fix up a car and "I got a lot of pep and know how to handle women." Of his two skills, the first appears to absorb more of his personality. Before his marriage, he used to belong to a motorcycle club. He gave it up, but has continued working on cars whenever he gets a chance. If he could do what he wanted, he would be a racer. He makes some money on car jobs, but his poetry in describing cars shows that money is not his sole motivation. "Sometimes you feel all hot. You can make a car grow hot. It just kinda gets into you and you know what to do when the car gets sweet." Now and then, Mr. D. admits, "I get into a real jam because I spend a lot of my own money and can't fix a car after promising to."

He does not discuss with his wife the central interest of his life—his work on the cars. She disapproves of his hobby and he is "afraid she may blab and get me into trouble. . . . Besides, she doesn't listen too much." He can talk safely to his brothers and his friends. He turns over his paycheck to his wife but keeps the money he makes on the cars. "She gets burned up if I take the kitty money to get a part for a car. I always pay it back, though. I wish she wouldn't mind my driving. She's afraid I'll get myself killed." She wanted him to take out some insurance for the children's benefit. "She tells me that if I get killed, they'd hit the jackpot. Well, if I get killed, it don't matter. Let it happen. Right now, I need my money if I got any."

Mr. D. spends a great deal of time away from home. He gets restless in the house and goes out to work on a car or to see the fellows. His brother warned him that he "stayed out so much, it would serve him right if his wife ran off with somebody else." This "burned me up and I raised my hand at him and told him to back down, and he said he was sorry." Mr. D. added, "I can settle her hash all right in bed."

Mr. D. is puzzled by his wife. He knows that she would like to have more money and would like to have some fun, but he has very little understanding of how trapped she feels. He does not understand the full extent of her dissatisfaction and certainly does not understand its causes. "She sure is down in the dumps a lot of the time and she don't seem to take much interest in nothing. She just seems to get real moody for no account. I don't know what you can do about it. I asked one of my uncles about it, on account of the woman he married, that's my aunt, was something like this. He told me the name of his doctor, said it was something like neurasthenia. He said she just wasn't exactly sick, but she wasn't exactly interested. I'd like her to have a good time, I'd like her to get a kick out of things, but she don't seem to like nothing that you can do for free. I'll admit that it takes a little jack to get the cars moving around but she don't even like to go out for a spin the way she used to. You can see how it is. It's on account of the children and the money. I don't know what you can do about it. She wants me to buy my own car. That wouldn't do me no good. It's always trying to do better and to set a new record that counts."

Mr. D. manipulates his wife. For example, she leaves the radio on all the time and this annoys him. Instead of telling her to turn it down, he "fixed it so it wouldn't turn up as loud as she wants it. She told me something was wrong with it and I told her, 'I don't want to spend the money to buy the part for it.'" She uses, incidentally, similar techniques of manipulation with him. When she gives him a "wise answer" he beats her.

(He also once did that when he thought she was flirting.) He said, "No, she wasn't hurt, she knew it was coming to her, but she was sore in more ways than one!" As to arguments, he said that his wife "hollers" at him sometimes, but if he does not holler back, he doesn't think it is an argument. Sometimes he'll just go away and leave her there. If he "hollers and she takes it, then again that's no argument."

Speaking of sexual relations Mr. D. reported that the doctor told him "to lay off when my wife was six months pregnant the first time, so I got myself another woman." He did it again during the second pregnancy. He said his friends knew about it and the married ones did the same thing. No, he "didn't tell her. . . . No use making trouble. The woman cost me a lot of money because she wanted all kinds of presents." He found he talked to her a lot about his work on the cars because she had no rights over him but once he told something to his wife "she'd be after me about it all the time, especially about the money." He said his friends knew more about him than anybody else, especially three or four of them who worked with him on racing jobs.

When Mr. D. feels depressed he usually tells his wife that he has to go out and he tries "to get my hands on the wheel of a machine, maybe borrow a friend's motorcycle that will tear up the road." He said, "I think I worry more about getting into a jam than anything else" (spending too much money on a car and not being able to deliver the job). The interviewer asked him if he ever felt he would get into a jam with his family. He said no, he didn't think he would and if it got real bad, he would just "light off or go to sea or turn hobo or go out West where they really know how to race cars." Sickness worries him. He was upset when his boy was sick and when his wife had the flu; he didn't know who was going to take care of the kids, but her sister helped them out. He "feels very low" when his wife runs up some debts and "I guess it's when I feel the world's against me." Does his wife help when he is feeling low? "She doesn't usually know; no good to let her know, she'll just worry for nothing." Does he swear or cuss when he is feeling bad? No, he said, only when he is mad. When asked about his wife's appreciation of him, he smiled broadly: "Oh, she appreciates me all right," referring to sex.

Finally, asked to sum up his marital problems, Mr. D. said that he knew they had a lot of problems but he doesn't "know exactly how to say it. Some things are a little wrong, but not really bad." The main trouble, he thinks, is the lack of money.

He added: "I hadn't counted on what it would be like when the kids came."

Mr. D., for all his perplexity about the mood of discontent pervading his home, is not so unhappy as his wife. He might wish for a higher income or for more appreciation from his wife of his skill with cars—but he has asserted his power and does not feel threatened. Nevertheless, neither partner is content with marriage. Why does not the evident maladjustment of this couple adversely affect their sexual relations? The hint of masochism in the woman and the shallowness of both personalities probably play a part in the explanation, but here, as elsewhere in this book, the focus is on norms and other social variables.

Both are proud of their sexuality and experience in sex almost the sole instance of the partner's approval and appreciation. This comes through even when they are angry with one another. Once after a quarrel, Mrs. D. reported "he took me kinda rough" —and she liked it. Did she let him know? "Not on your life! But he couldn't help knowing that I felt something."

But this very fact, that a man's appreciation of his wife is limited to sex, has led in other cases to the familiar feminine complaint—"That's all you care about." But Mr. D.'s behavior does not outrage his wife's ideal of marriage. She accepted Mr. D.'s almost completely contractual and impersonal proposal of marriage: he "had to have a woman regular and he wanted a home." Her own characterization of marriage is quite similar: "You gotta live with somebody. You expect the two are going to fix each other up when you need it. You know it's going to make you pregnant and so he's the one that's got to go to work."

Even when the attitude towards sexuality is so bare of overtones of romance or even love, and when there is so little expectation of friendship, human needs for fuller emotional response do assert themselves. The attention, appreciation and sense of closeness Mrs. D. misses are reflected in her remarks: "He don't know much about what I feel about anything"; "Nah, I don't tell him nothing"; "He appreciates me in bed most of all." She has observed another marriage—her brother-in-law "makes an awful fuss over my sister and they are real friendly." But she appears to think that such friendliness is not a rightful expectation in marriage, but a surprising boon some are lucky enough to find.

Her discontent lacks focus and a sense of moral outrage because she cannot refer it to any explicit moral yardsticks. Mr. D.'s neglect of her, her relatives assure her, is quite normal. So is his occasional violence. At the end of the final interview, she summed up her marriage problems as financial, since their poverty prevents them from enjoying the life they had before the birth of their children.

Both Mrs. C. and Mrs. D. found in sexual experience the sole relief from the bleakness of life, and some sense of appreciation from otherwise neglectful husbands. The behavior of the husbands, however frustrating, did not arouse either contempt or moral indignation because it did not violate the wives' normative expectations. Women who expect more fusion of sexuality with tenderness and more companionship and consideration in marriage would not be so likely to enjoy such a vigorous sexual life in similar marriages. The happy sex life does improve these marriages, although sex yields no magic to transform them completely.

A SEXUALLY MALADJUSTED, BUT HAPPY, COUPLE

The following case illustrates the reverse side of the problem: Mr. and Mrs. Evans are satisfied with their marriage despite their sexual difficulties. Mrs. E. was the first member of the family to be interviewed. Her description of her husband created an image of the man that the actual meeting with him did not confirm. "Mr. E.," wrote the interviewer, "was less prepossessing and impressive than I expected." This fact reflects the admiration with which Mrs. E. spoke of her husband: "He's so sure of himself, he moves around, quick and sure. I like the way he's put together." He turned out to be a rather dapper man, two or three inches shorter than his large, placid, blonde wife. The interviewer did note an aggressive sureness about his gestures and conversation.

Mr. and Mrs. E., aged 25 and 23, both high school graduates, have been married four years and have two children. Mr. E. is an upwardly mobile stock clerk who changed his $100-a-week job to his present (borderline) white-collar position at a loss in wages "in order to raise my social status." He now earns $3000 a year but has hopes of a promotion. The move was his decision, fully approved by his wife.

The sexual adjustment of the Evans' is not satisfactory. At the end of their separate interviews, Mr. and Mrs. E. together met with the interviewer and talked of their marriage:

"We have problems about sex," said Mrs. E. Her husband agreed with her and said that he was doing the best he could. Mrs. E. went on to repeat (what she had said in her own interview) that he reached a climax first and that he wished they could reach it together and was quite worried about it. "I don't always feel very much and that bothers him too. But as far as I'm concerned it's all very nice. I'd like to learn to do what he wants more though." Mr. E. admitted in his own interview that he was often very disappointed with his wife because she didn't respond as quickly as he wished she might: "I know that I should take more time and talk to her more and get her in the frame of mind, but somehow I don't have a chance to do it. In a way it's my own fault, and in a way it's just a bad break."

In response to the story about the wife who has a good husband but is not adjusted sexually the wife said: "The sister is right. She should count her blessings."

Mr. E. began teaching his wife about sex before they were married because he discovered that she was extremely naive. He brought her some books to study after they became engaged. Just before she was married, her mother asked her if she had any idea about sex and was deeply shocked to hear from her daughter that her fiancé had given her some sex education.

The Evans' have other marital problems.

Mrs. E. isn't as good a housekeeper as Mr. E. would like her to be. She loves taking care of babies, but has always disliked housework. "I'll do things for him that I wouldn't when home with my mother," but he was the only son in a family of meticulous housekeepers (mother and sisters) and has in addition quite traditional views about the division of labor between the sexes. "It is a sore subject and always has been with us," stated Mrs. E. Mr. E. said, "I like the house cleaner than she does. It was the way I was brought up. Next to being in debt, that gets me low." And Mrs. E. countered in the joint interview, "And what gets you feeling high is money, money, and more money." "Well, that's all right," he said. Mrs. E. then added: "He doesn't keep too straight a line on this helping, I am glad; he often says 'That's your job' but helps me just the same."

They disagree also on methods of child rearing. Their 3-year-old boy "is not a good eater and at supper his father wants him to clean up the plate before he can get up." According to a book Mrs. E. once read, this was all wrong. She tried to tell her husband about it and he said: "It's my son and I'll raise him as I like." Mr. E. wishes his wife would be a sterner disciplinarian.

How would he change his wife if he could, asked the interviewer. Mr. E. stated that he would make her more energetic. She is tired a great deal of the time and needs more sleep than he does. On the other hand, he said, "It's natural for her to be happy and smiling when another woman would be a natural sourpuss. She is a very happy woman. She gets awfully mad, though, at me sometimes when I punish the kids. I think I do this for their own good, but she doesn't always agree with me."

Despite these grievances the general tone of the Evans' marriage is quite happy.

Mrs. E. admires her husband's ability and has confidence in his economic future. "He is smart, he will always be able to get work and he will always take care of us. I like the way we live; I've got everything I want and we are going places." The plans for the future of the family—moving to a better neighborhood, home ownership, hopes for the children— are frequent topics of conversation. Though Mr. E. discusses his occupational plans with his wife, the decisions are his. She tries to temper her husband's ambition, so that they can enjoy life in the present. He is a more ambitious and a tenser person. Mrs. E. admires her husband for his other qualities: "I'll ask him about politics and world affairs and he always knows." Another favorable comment of hers was: "He is a real saint with my relatives." Her mother died recently and Mr. E. assumed a lot of responsibility for her adolescent brother and sister. He said in his interview: "Sometimes I wish she could kick through there a little better than she does, but it is simply because she doesn't know how."

Their norms of marriage call for full and frank communication. Dissatisfactions are openly discussed. Each is the other's chief confidant in the most intimate and important spheres, but each also has other important confidants. For the wife, the confidants included her mother when alive and now her sister-in-law and girl friends; for the husband, the confidant is his father. Mrs. E. follows the policy of "taking out petty gripes with my girl friends and getting smoothed down before my husband comes home." However, there are some things that "I'd die rather than talk about to anybody but my husband."

To the question about sources of emotional support, Mr. E. replied, "It depends on what sets off the problems. If they are technical [related to Mr. E.'s work], my father or friends help. If personal, talking them out with my wife helps."

Not only dissatisfaction, but mutual appreciation is freely expressed. "Does he show his appreciation of you?" the wife was asked. "He thanks me so much sometimes I get embarrassed even. He'll put his arms around me and say something like, 'Gee, honey, you are wonderful, thanks a lot,' and then we will go on with whatever we are doing or we'll neck around a little while and it is very nice." When did he last say he loved you? "Gee, I don't remember; he tells me quite often, though. It's nothing so special. He loves me all right, I know that for sure and I love him too." During the first interview with Mrs. E. she received a phone call from Mr. E. and the interviewer noted the wife's apparent pleasure in talking to her husband.

When asked what she would like to do with two extra hours a day, Mrs. E. decided she wanted to have more time with her husband on their free nights together. She likes to sew, and he works around at something, and they can still talk to each other.

Mr. and Mrs. E. not only express their feelings openly to one another but they have enough insight to recognize the true cause of their dissatisfactions. For example, Mrs. E. said: "He usually knows when I am tired or feel blue and if he doesn't, I tell him. I don't complain; I just tell him that I have come to the end of my rope and then he'll do something about it." He usually takes her out. She had been feeling "cooped up" after she had her baby, so they hired a baby sitter because it was important for her to get out. "It is not just the kids, but I think I am a human being and we have to get out sometimes." Again, Mr. E. complained about the high telephone bill. "I tell him," explained Mrs. E., "that I don't smoke and I do enjoy talking to my sister-in-law on the telephone. She is a good friend of mine. I told my husband that he is close to his father and he calls him. He says that's different, because he is calling him about business." She explained to her husband how the companionship of her sister-in-law helps her when she is "cooped up" alone, when the weather is bad. Another example of open communication was reported by Mrs. E. when she had been hurt by her husband's spending too many nights away from home. "He gets so absorbed that he doesn't realize what he is doing. I sit around here and I get bored and I'd like to have him here. He says it's my job to be here and that I can have my fun with my girl friends during the day when he is at his job. So he don't feel too sorry for me. But when I told him about it, he apologized and he cut out staying quite that late." Is your husband an easy or a difficult person to talk to? "He is one of the easiest people in the world to talk to." Does he ever get bored or just not listen? "Sometimes he is a little absent-minded," she admitted.

Mr. E. also speaks out: "If I have problems, I talk them over with my wife." The husband commented on the projective stories: "Why can't they talk things out with each other?" And the wife: "Some men just come home and dump their money into their wives' laps and go off. Whenever we have a problem of any kind, we're likely to tell each other about it."

Some limits to their frankness are indicated by both. The wife shares petty gripes with women. The husband was asked in whom he could confide some instance of lack of appreciation by his wife. "I'd probably be too proud to tell anybody, even to talk to her about it," he answered.

To sum up, sexual adjustment does constitute a problem for Mr. and Mrs. E. Of the two, the husband appears the more disturbed about the problem although the wife's frequent periods of fatigue may be symptomatic of unexpressed frustrations. But the marriage has strong favorable elements compensating the couple for sexual dissatisfactions. Among these are feelings that they are going places, that their economic hardships are only temporary, and that their future is full of promise. In the personal sphere of marriage, each receives esteem and emotional response from the other.

This case also illustrates further factors promoting marital satisfaction: the norm of sharing problems; the norm of selective communication (sparing the other certain "gripes" which can be easily shared with friends); and the norm of talking out difficulties instead of sulking. A high standard for personal relationships is seen in disapproval of manipulation and in the belief that each must be allowed to act voluntarily and that each can be trusted to recognize the legitimate demands of the other. Self-knowledge and the ability to communicate feelings helped the Evans' to solve some of their problems, although their sexual difficulty persists. The case thus illustrates both the values and the limits of full communication as the remedy for marital problems.

Conclusion

The three case studies presented above help to explain why the association between sexual and marital adjustment is not invariably a high one. They raise also a problem of more general significance. The theory that sexual harmony will not endure in the face of unhappiness in other spheres of marriage was derived from a study of middle-class couples.[6] Yet sexual satisfaction may turn out to be a more sensitive barometer of marital happiness in some classes than in others. Mrs. C. and Mrs. D., both grammar school graduates, had a highly satisfactory sex life despite many conflicts in their marriages. Of 14 unhappy women of the less-educated group, 5 testified to complete sexual fulfillment. But of 6 unhappy high school graduates, only 1 was sexually well adjusted. The high school women expect closeness in marriage and may not be able to isolate the sexual response from the total relationship in the way that Mrs. D., the wife of the car enthusiast, can.

The sole high school graduate who is sexually satisfied, though unhappy in marriage, is psychologically deviant. She appears to be engaged in a sado-masochistic struggle with her husband. She takes him to court because he beats her but she obviously provokes his violence by humiliating him. This case suggests the further hypothesis that, among the educated women in our culture, sexual gratification in the face of marital unhappiness carries a greater likelihood of deviant sexual needs than among the less-educated.

The hypothesis arising from our data suggests that the degree of association between sexual and general marital adjustment varies with the educational level of the wives. If confirmed by future studies, this finding will again corroborate the relativity of psychological processes in marriage and their conditioning by social variables.

[6] Ernest W. Burgess and Paul Wallin, 1953, p. 680.

CHAPTER
5

The Marriage Dialogue:
Expectations

"Among the many curious features of modern woman's life," states a recent book on women, "is one that would have thoroughly offended St. Paul, bewildered Tristan, and amused Don Juan—namely, the fact that she is her husband's best friend and he is hers." [1] To the traditional functions of marriage, such as sexual, reproductive, child-rearing and economic, modern society has added that of companionship. We expect that a married person will be his mate's closest confidant, with whom he will share his deepest feelings and thoughts. The romantic ideal calls for completeness of communication—no secrets from the mate. It implies also that the secrets of marriage must not be disclosed to outsiders.

These values of primacy and privacy of marital communication are illustrated in the words of a college senior, recently engaged. The young woman made a deliberate effort, after her engagement, to become more reserved with her mother. "I wanted," she explained, "to feel closer to John than to Mother, so that when we are all together I would exchange a look of understand-

[1] Morton M. Hunt, 1962, p. 199.

ing with him and not with her." The same values are reflected in a remark of a college-educated mother of a recently married daughter. "I wouldn't tell my daughter anything that had to be kept secret from her husband. It is important for a young couple to feel close and united."

These values are often said to be characteristic of our society as a whole.[2] But such a generalization is based upon studies of middle-class couples. Much less is known of the working classes. The ideal of friendship in marriage presupposes a certain equality between the sexes, and is not likely to flourish in a strongly authoritarian family or in a culture that holds women in contempt. Neither will it emerge if the mode of life makes for sharp differences in the interests of men and women. There are other conditions that further and hinder it and we cannot therefore assume that the ideal itself, or its realization in life, is equally characteristic of all segments of our society. Several investigations of the English working classes report considerable psychological distance between husbands and wives. When one married woman in a London study used the word "we," she meant "my mother and I," not "my husband and I."[3]

This chapter and the following one will describe what 58 workingmen and their wives ideally expect, and subsequently, what they actually experience in the sphere of communication in marriage. We will study the sharing of deep emotional concerns with the mate, conversation about matters of mutual interest (which might be termed companionable talk), and finally the mate's role in providing emotional support. Although its primary purpose is to describe certain values held by the families, the discussion has a bearing upon the general problem of the acquisition of values. The "anticipatory socialization" of the upwardly mobile, the catalytic role played by personal misfortune, the socializing role of the mate and the influence of social institutions are some processes to be considered in the following pages.

It became apparent early in the interviewing that a sharp difference in ideals of marriage existed in this group of working-class families. Some couples voiced what has come to be recognized as the dominant modern ideal of friendship. Thus a 27-year-old high school graduate, a truck driver, when asked whether

[2] See, for example, Ernest W. Burgess and Harvey J. Locke, 1953, p. 386.
[3] Michael Young and Peter Willmott, 1957, p. 47.

women in his opinion had more need of heart-to-heart talk than men, said, "They both need each other. That's one of the purposes of marriage." To the question, "What helps you to overcome bad moods?" his answer was, "To talk about it with my wife." They made it a point, he said, when they were first married that if something was wrong, they would speak out. If her behavior puzzles him, "I make her clarify it . . . what goes on between my wife and I stays with us. I never talk to anyone about it. I am supposed to be adult; that is part of adult life." Again, a 33-year-old bottler in a beer company (with ten years of schooling) testified: "I can't think of anything my wife and I wouldn't tell each other that we'd tell someone else. I suppose there are some things one doesn't want to be thinking even, and so a husband wouldn't want to talk about it. But anything a husband can talk about, he can talk about to his wife, *at least I think he should* [italics ours]. If I don't get the drift of what she is saying, I'll ask her again, and perhaps over again, until I do understand." And a 27-year-old high school graduate, the wife of a machinist commented: "If a wife can't talk to her husband [about very personal things], she can't talk to anyone."

Not only are such views not expressed in other interviews, but indeed different attitudes are explicitly stated. For example, asked whether she thought it was in general difficult for a husband to understand his wife, a 28-year-old woman with eight years of schooling, said, "Well, men and women are different. They each go their separate ways. A man does his work and a woman does her work and how can they know what it's all about?" When, after a long series of questions on communication, the interviewer remarked that the wife appeared to talk more easily to her girl friend and to her sister than to her husband, she exclaimed, "But they are girls!" A 21-year-old wife (with ten years of schooling) remarked, "Men are different, they don't feel the same as us. That's the reason men are friends with men, and women have women friends."

We attempted to tap conceptions of marriage by asking for comments on two stories. The first story deals with "companionship talk":

A couple has been married for seven years. The wife says that her husband is a good provider and a good man, but still she complains to her mother about her marriage. She says he comes home, reads the paper, watches T.V., but doesn't talk to her. He says he "doesn't like to gab just for the sake of talking." But she says he is not companionable and has nothing to say to her.—*What do you think of this couple?*

In commenting upon the story, some interviewees referred to their own marriages, identifying with the fictitious couple: "Say, you know, I feel like that guy"; "That's home plate, that's right on the button"; "Why, that's a typical marriage. My husband is a lot like that, so is my cousin's husband and my sister's husband." One man asserted: "If my wife acted like that, I would straighten her out in short order."

Apart from such incidental references to personal experiences, three themes are expressed in the responses to this story. The first theme reflects the view that *the lack of husband-wife conversation in the story presents a genuine problem.* Of the 99 men and women who commented upon this story only 37 per cent took this position (Table 3). Not all of these blamed the husband— "Does *she* have anything interesting to say?" Some expressed resignation, while others proposed remedies. But whether pessimistic or "constructive" about the situation, these individuals share the view that it is deplorable:

A 27-year-old wife: "Maybe he is in a rut and needs her help. This girl would think up things to talk about if she had any sense."

A 40-year-old husband: "Looks like they are incompatible. If he never talks to her, they've got it bad, but if he's just that way once in a while, we all are that way sometimes."

A 31-year-old wife: "She should make it interesting enough around the house to get him away from the T.V. and the newspaper; invite people over or find some things like church work or hobbies that they can work at together."

A 31-year-old husband: "Maybe she should talk to him about subjects he knows about or things they have in common."

A 25-year-old husband: "He should listen to her and talk to her. He can't expect her to sit in the house all day and do her job and not have anyone to talk to at night."

A 31-year-old wife: "There is something wrong if he has nothing to talk about. If something is bothering him, he shouldn't hide behind a paper."

A 25-year-old wife: "If that's the way he is, you've got to live with it."

A 29-year-old wife: "That's something like him and me. There is nothing you can do about it except grin and bear it."

A 29-year-old wife: "He gets mad at me sometimes for wanting to talk. I learned to keep my mouth shut—you do that as you get older."

In contrast with these attitudes, another 37 per cent of the group *categorically denied that the wife in the story presents a legitimate grievance*. It is the wife who is criticized for her immaturity and selfishness—by women as well as their husbands, as illustrated below:

A 28-year-old wife: "Gee, can you tie that? He's generous, don't bother her, he just keeps out of the way, and she's fussing and wants him to sit there and entertain her."

A 40-year-old wife: "She isn't busy enough or she'd be glad to have him quiet. She is in clover and don't know it."

A 32-year-old wife: "That woman would have a lot more to complain about if her husband drank or beat her up. The husband is right."

A 38-year-old construction worker: "If you do right by the woman and your job, they owe you a little rest to yourself."

A 28-year-old butcher's assistant: "I don't know what is the matter with some women. Their husbands will come home and wish they could lie down and just forget everything and a woman will come yakity yak about nothing at all until a guy has to go out and get a drink. I don't know what they think their husbands are made of. They work their guts out making a living, trying to get along, and then they come home and their wives want them to be some kind of fancy pants, say silly things to them."

A 33-year-old metalworker: "Some women ain't satisfied no matter what you do. Ah, she makes me sick. A guy comes home, and wants a little bit of quiet and it's bad enough with the kids making a racket; his wife doesn't have to come and gab at him, too. How about her being companionable and not saying nothing? You should dance like a monkey on a string to keep them amused."

A 38-year-old pipefitter: "Oh, for Christ's sake! He ought to shut her up good and hard. Companionable! Let her work in a factory eight hours and be companionable."

A 25-year-old street cleaner: "That one needs the biggest spanking. Still complaining! What's he going to talk to her about, the price of beans?"

A 33-year-old truck driver: "That woman isn't grown up. Does she have to be entertained like a kid?"

A 20-year-old taxi driver: "Ah, that's a terrible thing. I know a whole lot of husbands who would just like to have a little peace and quiet when they get home, and their wives yammer and yammer."

The apparent assumption underlying these irritated outbursts is that the husband himself has little to gain from such evening talks. To talk is either to entertain the wife or to hear her "yammering." It is a concession to her—and one that no mature woman should demand.

Besides the two main types of responses, 11 per cent of the interviewees read into the story a particular situation that, as a subsequent chapter will show, is a source of great concern to women: "Maybe the husband's got something on his mind. She should leave him alone." When men appear worried, "poking at them only makes it worse. You let them alone and with time they'll come around."

The second story was intended to tap attitudes towards the primacy and privacy of marital communication:

Mrs. Fox is 26 years old. The Foxes live near Mrs. Fox's mother, and the wife sees her mother daily. Mr. Fox says he has nothing against his mother-in-law, but he doesn't see why his wife has to see her daily. He thinks they gab too much and he doesn't see why his mother-in-law should know what they have for dinner every day and everything else that happens to them. Mrs. Fox says it is natural for a woman to be close to her mother—that the husband is unreasonable.

The responses to this story fall into two types. About a third of the group disapproved of Mrs. Fox's daily talks with her mother on the ground that she *violates the privacy of marriage* (Table 4).

> Husband: "It is not natural to discuss intimate things with the mother. What goes on between husband and wife is nobody's business."

> Wife: "You have to draw a line at what you are going to gab about to your mother. You're not going to tell her everything that happens in your married life."

> Husband: "What a couple does is its own business."

In contrast to the above response, 63 per cent of the interviewees did not criticize the wife who talked a lot to her mother —at any rate, not for violating conjugal privacy. Unqualified approval is seen in such comments as these:

> Husband: "Wife is right. She can always learn something about cooking and other things from an older person."

> Husband: "Why shouldn't women talk to their mothers— it would probably do the women good."

> Wife: "It's no skin off his nose, but kind of nice all around if they are friendly."

The qualifications cited by these respondents pertain not to violation of privacy, but, often, to interference with the wife's household responsibilities: "As long as she doesn't neglect her house or the kids, why not?" And husbands enter another qualification— that the mother-in-law not use the information to "tear the husband down" or to make trouble: "If mother-in-law doesn't bother husband, I see no reason why they shouldn't talk all they want to"; "Don't know why he raises Cain about a little thing like that unless his mother-in-law makes him trouble." Several husbands —far from expressing jealousy of the mother-in-law and a wish to share in confidences—want to be protected from them. Thus:

Husband: "As long as he don't have to listen to them, and she don't gossip, I don't see what difference it makes."

Husband: "As long as the man isn't around and doesn't hear them. Maybe the husband is mad at his wife for gossiping and telling him what she and her mother have talked about."

Attitudes of the Two Educational Groups

Responses to the two stories varied with the educational level of the respondents. The high school graduates tended to deplore the lack of conversation described in the first story—this might be termed the "companionable" or "middle-class" response.[4] Those with less than high school education were apt to feel that the wife has no legitimate grievance. Of 34 male and female high school graduates, 59 per cent believed that the lack of conversation is a genuine problem while only 26 per cent of the 65 less-educated respondents expressed a similar attitude. The level of education affects both men's and women's responses similarly (Table 6).

The high school graduates criticized Mrs. Fox because she violates the privacy of marriage—the "middle-class" view. Fifty per cent of the 38 educated men and women voiced this criticism, as compared to only 16 per cent of the 67 less-educated persons. Again, the difference by education holds for both men and women (Table 5).

Considering the fact that in the first story the plaintiff is the wife and in the second, the husband, the sexes are remarkably impartial in their judgments. Educational level clearly is more important than sex in influencing responses to these stories. The less-educated wives, however, differ from both their husbands and the high school men and women in one respect. They often remark: "She should leave him alone when he's like that." They

---

[4] We have no middle-class respondents. We assume on the basis of previous studies and common knowledge that responses to the stories expressing the values of companionship and of primacy of marital communication tend to be typical of middle-class persons. For example, Ernest W. Burgess and Harvey J. Locke claim that "when couples are asked what they have gained from marriage, one of the most frequent answers is companionship, intimate association, sympathetic understanding. . . ." The studies cited in their book involve predominantly middle-class respondents (1953, p. 386). In any event, the comparison between the educational subgroups is not affected by the accuracy of this identification of the value of companionship with middle-class patterns.

obviously sympathize with the lonely wife in the first story and do not criticize her so often as their husbands do, but neither do they invoke the ideal of companionship in her defense. It is the educated men and women who condemn the withdrawal of the husband as a violation of an ideal.

But do the different responses to the two stories really indicate differences in ideas of marriage? The positive expression of a value is more conclusive than its absence. The expression means at the very least that the respondent knows this value and perceives its relevance to the situation. On the other hand, a person may fail to mention a value for a variety of reasons, not merely because he does not recognize it. For example, the wife who is herself a dependent daughter would have a strong motive for exonerating Mrs. Fox, whether or not she is aware of the norm of conjugal privacy. A husband who is especially fond of his mother-in-law can afford to be benevolent. And an unhappily married woman may consistently side with the wife and against the husband.

The responses to the Fox story were considered in relation to the personal situation of each respondent. Personal experiences do tend to color the responses but do not eliminate the differences between the two educational groups. Even in identical personal circumstances, the high school graduates voice middle-class values with greater frequency than the less-educated. For example, the male high school graduates tend to criticize Mrs. Fox even if they are happily married—of 8 happy husbands, 5 objected to Mrs. Fox's violation of marital privacy, but of 16 happy less-educated husbands, only 1 raised this issue. Moreover, the high school husbands prove more critical of Mrs. Fox although at the same time they report *fewer* mother-in-law problems than the less-educated men. The high school graduates, we conclude, disapprove of Mrs. Fox on normative grounds.

Linking the response to the story with the personal situation throws some light upon the acquisition of values. The "middle-class" response on the part of the less-educated husband tends to be associated with mother-in-law problems. The majority of them, as pointed out above, if they disapprove of Mrs. Fox at all, object to neglect of housework or possible interference on the part of the mother-in-law; but 7 less-educated husbands do invoke the norm of conjugal privacy. Of these 7 men, 5 have mother-in-law problems because of the excessive dependency of their wives upon the mothers. But of 28 less-educated men who gave the typical "working-class" responses, only 4 suffer from such mother-in-law problems. This may mean that personal difficulties sharpen the perception of congenial and supportive values present in the general culture although deviant for this educational level.

The different responses to the stories on the part of the two educational groups are not caused by their differences in age or in duration of marriage. Age for age and with the duration of marriage kept constant, the high school graduates still express the more "middle-class" attitudes. For example, only 7 of 13 less-educated men (married under seven years) reported that the lack of evening talk in the first story constitutes a genuine problem. The comparable figure for the high school graduates is 7 of 9. Of 9 less-educated women (married under seven years), only 6 said that the first story presents a real problem, but 9 out of 10 high school graduates (married under seven years) took this view.

In addition to the stories, another attempt was made to assess the importance attached to friendship in marriage. We asked 85 men and women to list the qualities of a good husband and a good wife.

The 563 qualities volunteered by our respondents are classified into three categories. Qualities pertaining to the major institutional roles of provider, homemaker, parent and in-law make up the first class. General human qualities, such as "kind," "doesn't nag," "loyal" or "honest," are in the second class. The third category is divided into sexual responsiveness or attractiveness and what is here termed "psychic compatibility," our principal interest in this chapter. "Psychic compatibility" implies some recognition of the uniqueness of each marriage and a concern with the interplay of personalities in it. Included in this subdivision are "companionship," "common interests," "emotional support," "love" and other expressions, however formulated, which seem to imply psychic compatibility—for example, "Gives husband peace of mind at home"; "Is nice to wife"; "Likes the same T.V. programs"; "Partnership"; "Tries to fit in with husband and his wants." But even with such generous inclusion of items, psychic compatibility does not appear to loom large in the responses given by these couples. Of 563 qualities listed by men and women, only 95, or 17 per cent, are interpreted as belonging in the category of psychic compatibility; the proper performance of institutional roles ranks first and general human qualities, second.

The level of education affects the responses. Of the 361 qualities of a good mate listed by the less-educated, only 15 per cent refer to psychic congeniality, against 20 per cent of such traits of a total of 202 qualities volunteered by high school graduates. The low priority given by these working-class men and women to psychic congeniality (in contrast with general human virtues or effective performance of institutional roles) may not accurately portray their attitudes. The qualities mentioned or omitted in answer to such open questions partly depend upon the respondent's frame of reference at the moment. These questions came at the very end of the interview. On the one hand, the emphasis on communication with the mate should have brought this matter to the forefront of awareness; on the other hand, the section of the interview immediately preceding the questions about what is important in a good husband or a wife dealt with role performance. This may have slanted the answers towards the institutional roles of provider and homemaker. The fact nevertheless remains that in similar circumstances the high school graduates do place a somewhat greater accent upon compatibility.

"Middle-class" responses to the stories, in the case of the men, are associated with mobility aspirations and with marriages to high school graduates. All 5 of the less-educated husbands who are upwardly mobile and married to high school graduates gave middle-class answers to the stories, whereas of 31 less-educated men who lack one or both of these features, only 4 expressed such views. (See Chapter 13 for our definition of upward mobility.) The reaching out for middle-class standards ("anticipatory socialization") on the part of the upwardly mobile husbands is manifested in a number of ways. One man confessed that he consented to the interview in order to hear the interviewer talk—he thought he might learn something from listening to her. Another man wanted to improve his English in order to associate with "people who have class." This orientation of the upwardly mobile men towards middle-class standards helps to explain their middle-class conceptions of marriage. The influence of the educated wives is apparent in two or three cases. Dissatisfied with the lack of companionship, one young high school wife repeatedly told her less-educated husband that that was "not the kind of marriage" she wanted; she felt she had finally succeeded in changing his behavior.

Church membership is also associated with "middle-class" responses. Church members tend to criticize the husband in the first story and the wife in the second. Not a single male grammar-school graduate unaffiliated with a church gave a middle-class answer to the first story, whereas one-third of the male church members with grammar-school education endorsed the value of companionship. Among high school graduates, both male and female, the church members expressed a higher proportion of middle-class views than the non-members. Among the less-educated women, however, the church members offered fewer middle-class answers than the unaffiliated—a finding seemingly inconsistent with the other replies (see Tables 7a and 7b), and one which we will shortly consider.

Is the church a purveyor of middle-class values or do the more middle-class attitudes expressed by church members reflect some selective forces? The evidence mainly points to the latter explanation. Within our sample, the churches attracted the younger, better-educated and more upwardly mobile men, who regard church membership as an attribute of a "respectable" citizen. But the middle-class views of the male church members cannot be attributed wholly to this kind of selection. The church members tend to give a slightly higher proportion of middle-class responses even when we narrow the comparison to men of identical schooling, age and aspirations. Case records show that joining a church can increase the area of common interests and, perhaps, reinforce middle-class conceptions of marriage. For example, a young high school graduate, married to a man with nine years of schooling, had this to say about the first story: "Our marriage used to be that way. But we've been so close since we started church." The husband listed his attendance at church affairs as an activity he enjoys "very much." Since joining the church this couple have enjoyed reading and discussing devotional books in the evenings. The husband said: "That man is wrong. He should mix, and talk to his wife about her day and how the family is." Although this still is an unhappy marriage, the wife attributed to the church their newly found evening companionship. The minister had been consulted about their marital problems. The church has certainly given the couple a common interest, but whether it has also communicated new values to the husband remains uncertain though probable. Another couple also joined the church in a deliberate effort to improve their marriage. Such a move in itself reflects the middle-class view that marriage problems are soluble through increasing common interests and, in general, through some purposive action. Again, this fact does not rule out the possibility that once the husband becomes active in church his endorsement of middle-class values becomes more explicit.

The inconsistent finding noted above is that, among less-educated women, church members gave *fewer* middle-class responses than the unaffiliated. Why should church membership play a different role for men and women? In the first place, the selective forces differ: the older and the less-educated women are overrepresented among church members. Among the less-educated respondents, relatively more women than men are affiliated with a church. The less-educated women, understandably, may attend church services and remain steeped in working-class values—some unhappy wives draw upon religion for psychological strength. The wife's grievance presented in the first story must have appeared trivial to one of these women, a mother of ten, with an alcoholic husband, who remarked (as cited earlier): "She isn't busy enough or she would be glad to have him quiet." In contrast with such church women who maintain their traditional values, upwardly mobile men and women may find in the "couples' club," and in their contacts with the minister, some reinforcement of middle-class conceptions of marriage. This illustrates again that individual responses to external influences are selective and depend upon pre-existing dispositions.[5]

The interview did not explore the influence of formal education per se or of family background upon responses to the stories. It was noted in Chapter 1 that the parents of the high school graduates had higher occupational status than those of

[5] Rebellion against parents appears to explain the middle-class responses of two unaffiliated women. One grade school graduate, an impassioned union member, rejected the church as well as the traditional working-class values of her parents. "We ain't so hipped on church," she said. The couple never attends church. Another, rebelling strongly and resentfully against her religious mother, may have been thus led to acquire deviant values.

the less-educated. The case studies provide many illustrations of other differences in parental attitudes linked with occupational and economic superiority. The current attitudes of the two educational groups in part reflect, no doubt, different family backgrounds.

A final question about the comments upon the two stories is: Have the stories actually elicited different norms of marriage or merely different attitudes toward verbal communication? When the high school graduate endorses the full sharing of concerns with one's mate, it is likely that he expresses a belief in the therapeutic value of "talk," not merely conviction about the importance of friendship in marriage. For the less-educated person, verbal communication may not constitute so significant a feature of any social relationship. The middle-class interviewer runs the danger of identifying friendship with some of its particular manifestations typical of his own social background. For the less complex personality, friendship is construed as being companionable, that is, having an evening snack together, going for a ride, exchanging gifts or giving each other sexual satisfaction.

Different attitudes towards verbal communication are certainly an element in our findings. But more generally, the responses to the stories and fuller analysis of the cases strongly suggest that for some of Glenton's families—albeit a minority —marriage is "not for friendship." It is not merely the meagerness of verbal communication that characterizes these marriages, but the absence of certain norms, especially the norm that the spouse should be one's closest confidant. In interpreting specific cases, such norms were judged very weak or non-existent, not only because they were not voiced, but because emotionally significant experiences were regularly shared with others in preference to one's mate without any perceptible feeling that this reflected upon the quality of the marriage. Moreover, some persons acknowledged their ignorance of the thoughts and feelings of the mate without the apology or defensiveness usually accompanying violations of norms.

The following case will illustrate such a marriage. We have selected a "happy" couple whose meager verbal communication clearly does not result from marital conflict. The detailed summary is intended to illustrate concretely the interpretation offered above and to portray a style of marriage that excludes norms

BLUE-COLLAR MARRIAGE / 126

sometimes taken to be more or less universal in American family life.

Marriage Is Not for Friendship:
The Case of Mr. and Mrs. Green

Mr. and Mrs. G. are a young couple, married for three years, with a 2-year-old son. The 23-year-old husband is a garbage collector, earning $2500 a year. He completed two years of high school; his 22-year-old wife is a high school graduate. But the interviewer commented: "It is hard to believe in view of her poor vocabulary and illiterate handwriting that she had completed high school." The husband said: "She was sort of a dumbbell at school, but people liked her and she got through."

Mr. G. is a slim tall man, slow-moving and soft-spoken. Asked what makes him satisfied with himself, he replied, "People tell me I'm easygoing but not a chump." The interviewer noted his deceptively lazy attitude as the manner of a man who thinks that most people, particularly women, become too excited about things and foolishly so. He "quit school at fourteen because I didn't like it." He has held a number of unskilled jobs, and concerning his present occupation as a garbage collector he stated: "People laugh at you for being in this line of work. I don't know what's so funny about it. It's got to be done. There is no future in it, though, and the pay is terrible. I'm going to make a break for it as soon as I can. Everybody's looking out for me now, and something is bound to turn up pretty soon."

Mr. G. appears to be quietly dominant in the marriage and both he and his wife express satisfaction with their sexual relations and with the marriage in general. A good deal of the communication between them is non-verbal. This had been anticipated during their courtship. When asked whether her husband when he proposed to her had said he loved her, Mrs. G. answered:

"He just got softer and softer on me and I could tell that he did and we got to necking more and more and he wanted to go all the way and I didn't want to unless we were going to get married. So finally we got engaged, so everybody knew about it, so we were going steady together." Prior to their marriage he had said a few times "when we were being mushy" that he loved her. "But we usually just started doing it without saying much." And now "when he'll come up and kiss me in the middle of a T.V. show or after he's going to the icebox for something, I know that he is going to want it later on." Has he ever said out and out that he could go for her or wanted her or anything like that? She said, "No, we don't go in for that kind of stuff." Did he say anything when she told him that she got pregnant? "He looked a little funny when I told him, but he didn't say much. You know that's what's going to happen. After a while, when I began to show a lot, he asked me sometimes how I felt."

Mrs. G. was asked to describe their quarrels. They quarrel little, but when they do, over such things as his failure to help move the furniture or her failure to do something he demands, she said, "We just get over it." He might "crab around and then he would know that he had been mean and make it up" to her. There is no conversation after such quarrels, but Mr. G. helps to dry the dishes or asks her if she likes a T.V. program or wants something else. Mrs. G. felt that it doesn't do any good to talk, it might make things worse.

When asked whether they like to talk about what makes people tick or to discuss the rights and wrongs of things, each said in separate interviews, "No, we don't hash things over." Mr. G.: "It's either right or wrong—what is there to discuss?" Mrs. G. said that they do not talk much about the future of their son: "No matter what plans we make, the times change and the children will have ideas of their own."

This "conversation of gestures" between Mrs. G. and her husband contrasts sharply with the full and open verbal communication characterizing her relationships with female relatives and friends. On many counts Mrs. G. reveals her emotional life more fully to the latter than to her husband. And this extends to spheres of experience beyond the "feminine world" of babies, housework or talk about people:

Mrs. G. sees her sister and her mother daily. "Oh yes," she said about her sister. "We tell each other everything, anything we have on our minds. We don't hold nothing back." But when asked whether she can talk to her husband, she answered: "Sure, I can talk to him about anything that has to be said." Her view is that "men and women do different things; he don't want to be bothered with my job and I don't want to be bothered with his. Sometimes we got to do the same things, something around the house and we have to tell each other."

When asked what helped her when she was "in the dumps," Mrs. G. replied, "Talking to my sister or my mother helps sometimes." She was then asked directly whether conversations with her husband ever have a similar effect. "No," she answered, "when I am in the dumps he can't help me feel any better."

Mrs. G.'s friends are also her neighbors whom she sees several times a day. One friend phoned her six times in one day, and that was unusual, but these women do often telephone one another. She was embarrassed to admit that she discusses her sex life with her friends. "You'd be surprised what they talk about, the things they do in bed. When somebody tells you something, you got to say something back or they think you are a wet fat dishrag and all washed out and they don't talk to you and you got no friends." Mrs. G.'s embarrassment in reference to sex appears to be caused more by the nature of the topic than by any violation of marital confidence. She is still under the domination of her religious and puritanical mother. Mrs. G. finds sexual fulfillment in marriage, but she shares her reflections about her own sexual responses and about the sexual behavior of men more fully with women than with her husband.

An incident reported by Mrs. G. illustrates her intimacy with her sister. During the first year of her marriage, Mrs. G. was troubled by her husband's habit of "walking around the house with his fly open." She remonstrated with him, but he persisted, saying that he can do what he wants in his own house. She then asked her sister's advice and was told to disregard the offensive habit. But her sister reported the conversation to their mother and Mrs. G. suspects that her mother in turn talked to Mr. G.'s mother. Mr. G. now "closes the zipper whenever a stranger comes into the room" and Mrs. G. is inclined to attribute the reform to the intervention of her mother-in-law. She added that she no longer minds this practice of his when they are alone.

Mr. G. enjoys an active social life with male friends and relatives, but it is doubtful whether he shares his emotional experiences with them to the extent that his wife does with her friends. Nevertheless, Mr. G. revealed to his father and his brother his fears that Mrs. G. was making a "sissy" out of their son, and he regularly consults them about his occupational plans. He does not discuss the latter topics with his wife because "there is no need of exciting her for nothing. Wait until it's sure. Women get all excited and talk too much."

Mr. G. "thinks the world" of the fellows in his clique whom he sees after supper several times a week and on Saturday afternoons. Mrs. G. does not always know where he meets his "friends" when he leaves in the evenings. Mr. and Mrs. G. testified independently that having a beer with the fellows is the best cure for Mr. G.'s depressions. When he cannot afford a beer, he can sometimes "sweat it out by working." Asked if his wife could help him when he felt in "the dumps," Mr. G. replied, "Yes, she can. I tell her, 'just keep out of my way,' and she does." Mr. G. appeared to know less about his wife's sources of emotional relief than she knew of his. Asked what helped his wife when she felt low, Mr. G. remarked "Oh, it wears off after a while. Sure I can tell [when she feels low] by the way her shoulders hang down and by her sour puss." He admitted that his wife sulks sometimes, and was asked whether they ever talk this over. "Nah, I don't pay no attention to it," was his reply.

Additional light is shed upon the couple's values by their responses to the projective stories and the schedules on "what makes a good mate." Both Mr. and Mrs. G. criticized the wife in the story who demanded more evening companionship with her husband. They moreover found nothing reprehensible in Mrs. Fox's daily conversations with her mother. "She don't have to aggravate her husband by gabbing about it to him, does she?" was Mrs. G.'s only comment. Presented with the case of a wife who complained about being lonely because her husband went out twice a week, Mrs. G. commented: "Why shouldn't he go out, she shouldn't nag him." And Mr. G. said: "If he can afford it, fine. She has the kids, she ain't alone."

The thesis that the lack of psychological intimacy in this marriage does not violate the ideal expectations of Mr. and Mrs. G. is supported by the satisfaction they express with their marriage.

With the exception of her lack of neatness ("But I guess I am fussier than most husbands," Mr. G. added) Mrs. G. is a good wife—"She suits me fine." Mr. G. described her qualities: she is good-natured ("I just tell her how it's going to be and she doesn't talk back. Of course, I'll ask her what she wants sometimes and we try to work it out. I'll try to satisfy her the best I can"); she never nags him about money and is economical; she doesn't "gripe" about his going out with the fellows, and she never denies him sex. He thinks, moreover, that she is very "cute." Her irritating tendency to gossip Mr. G. accepts as the natural failing of all women.

Mrs. G., on her part, is equally satisfied. She considers her husband a considerate sexual partner by comparison with the selfish men—often described by her friends—who "just take what they want and do nothing for their wives; we have a lot of fun sometimes." Her religious mother was critical of her; marriage brought emancipation from parental control. She hopes for an improvement in their financial status—to have the money for baby-sitters, a bigger television set, a better car and more housekeeping gadgets. But, rating her husband on the schedule of what makes a good mate, Mrs. G. gave him the highest of the three possible marks on the following qualities: "isn't afraid of hard work"; "is always on the lookout for an opportunity to better himself"; "is attractive to wife physically"; "is a considerate lover"; "has an attractive appearance"; "speaks his mind when something is worrying him"; "does the man's job around the house without nagging." And asked if she wished Mr. G. were more open with her, she said, "He crabs around if he wants to, and hollers if he feels like it." Sometimes, it is true, she starts talking to him when he watches T.V. and he tells her to "shut up" but "it usually isn't anything special and I can wait." Similarly, she may occasionally be too busy with the children to pay any attention to what he is saying, but that, again, is to be expected. In answering the interviewer's questions, Mrs. G. claimed that she understood her husband well and is, in turn, understood by him, and that she has "never given up talking to him about something because I felt it was no use."

Although generally happy in her marriage, Mrs. G. did reveal a few dissatisfactions with her husband: "He expects too much of our little boy, and treats him as if he was grown up." Moreover, she confessed that she would like to have her husband "around more" and sometimes when she feels warm towards him, "he brushes me off." Having previously rated these qualities "very important," Mrs. G. gave her husband only an "average" and not a high mark on the following: "is successful in his job so his wife can feel proud of him"; "doesn't chase after women" ("Hasn't yet, I don't think"); "easy to tell one's worries to"; and qualities pertaining to child rearing.

The case of Mr. and Mrs. G. illustrate a certain psychological distance in marriage tolerated because nothing more is expected. The fact that this distance was occasionally frustrating to Mrs. G. may appear to contradict our thesis. But human needs, though molded by culture, are not solely its creation. Needs may emerge in some situations regardless of social expectations. The right of the husband to go out evenings in search of male companionship may be accepted by his wife. But this acceptance does not rule out the possibility that when *she* feels warm towards *him*, he may not be around to satisfy her needs, whereas he can remain at home whenever his feelings dictate it. The significant fact is that these frustrations do not arouse any moral indignation in Mrs. G. She does not feel aggrieved.

A similar relationship is that of a couple, married eight years, who live in the same house with the wife's parents. The early years of marriage were troublesome, but now the wife claims: "We get along good." She appears to be quite satisfied with her economically successful and handsome husband. However, he is "not handy around the house" and is less interested than most Glenton husbands in the women's world of child rearing, interior decoration, housework and shopping. The wife shares such feminine interests with her mother and her girl friends. The impression of a certain distance in the marriage is conveyed by other facts:

> Having checked "confiding worries" and "talking about what makes people tick" as activities she enjoys very much, she named her mother and her girl friends as preferred associates in such discussions. The standard question, "If there were two more hours every day, how would you like most to spend them?" was answered by this woman without hesitation: "Having a longer afternoon, visiting with my girl friends."

This woman, though apparently quite satisfied with her life, admitted feeling depressed periodically: "I feel out of sorts twice a year. It's kind of seasonal, spring and fall. I feel like a fat slob, the house is a mess; I feel depressed. I talk to Mother about it and she tells me she had the same thing!" Has she ever talked to her husband about these moods? the interviewer asked her. She could recall no such conversation and she "couldn't really tell" whether he knew about her moods. Two incidents confirm the impression of meager communication between the spouses. The wife made arrangements for the interviewer's meeting with the husband's parents. A week later the husband was surprised to learn from the interviewer that she had met his parents; the wife never mentioned the incident to him. Moreover, during the first interview, the wife was enthusiastic about the T.V. play which she saw the preceding evening, on her husband's night out. She was subsequently asked whether she mentioned the play to him and the answer was negative.

Additional illustrations of the sharing of confidences with others than the spouse are provided by the women who, suspecting themselves to be pregnant, told their female relatives about it before informing their husbands. One woman first told her mother that she thought she was pregnant. Her mother advised her to wait a month before telling her husband, which the wife did. This procedure was repeated during her second pregnancy. Two other women reported similar incidents: "My sister told me to wait after I skipped my second period before telling him [respondent's husband]."

We estimate that, of 58 marriages, 7 are unmistakably of the type just described. A few others are similar, but do not exhibit so extreme a pattern. Of the 14 persons involved in the 7 marriages only 1 (Mrs. Green), is a high school graduate. This corroborates the evidence obtained by means of the two stories. The less-educated couples tend to be more traditional in their ideas about sex-linked interests and about "rights" of men to silence and protection from tiresome children and women's trivia. They tend to think that friendship is more likely to exist between members of the same sex, whereas they see the principal marital ties as sexual union, complementary tasks and mutual devotion.

ΛΛΛ
CHAPTER
6

The Marriage Dialogue:
Reality

Having considered the attitudes towards marital communication displayed by Glenton couples, we turn to their actual behavior. This chapter deals with friendship in marriage as indicated by the extent of mutual sharing of experiences. How fully a person is going to reveal himself in marriage, what he will withhold and what he will share, would seem to be uniquely determined by the interplay of personalities in each marriage. The results however once again confirm the sociological truth that people sharing similar conditions of life and a similar culture will exhibit some common patterns of behavior even in their most personal and private spheres of existence.

Psychological intimacy is an aspect of marriage which is difficult to assess. How closely we came to the actual facts can be judged only by knowing our methods.

Rating Self-Disclosure

The degree of self-disclosure was assessed by first ascertaining the emotional concerns of each person and only then asking with whom particular concerns were shared.

The emotional concerns were studied through an inventory of major areas of experience: children, job, spouse, relatives, friends, one's own personality, political and civic interests, and so on. With regard to each of these the questioning followed the same pattern. We asked about emotionally significant events (those arousing pleasure, irritation, hurt, anxiety, surprise, pride, guilt) possibly occurring during the week or two before the interview. Having ascertained those events, the interviewer asked with whom, if at all, a particular experience was discussed. Each person was also asked to describe situations in a given area which, not only in the immediate past but in general, stimulated feelings of pleasure or stress. And, again, he was asked to tell with whom, if anyone, he shared a given experience.

In still another part of the interview, a section dealing with marital adjustment, having ascertained the most recent "spat" or quarrel, we asked whether it was discussed with anyone, and then posed general questions about sharing marital satisfactions and dissatisfactions with one's mate and with others.

Finally, whenever the interviewer encountered some experience of apparent significance to the respondent he asked whether the spouse or anyone else knew about it.[1]

The ratings of self-disclosure in marriage about to be presented were based upon the interviews with both the husband and the wife. Both sets of interviews were evaluated in making the final judgment about the ratings to be assigned to each person. The five ratings ranged from "very full" and "full" to "moderate," "meager" and "very meager" self-disclosure. For comparisons between subgroups we used a three-fold classification: "full," "moderate" and "meager." "Very full" self-disclosure was a rating given when the person shared a high proportion of thoughts and feelings that deeply concerned him with his spouse. Even those who were assigned this top rating maintained areas of reserve, but these were fewer and less significant to the individual than in the case of lower grades of disclosure.

The final rating, then, depended not just upon the number of areas of reserve, but on their nature. It involved an assess-

[1] The method of studying self-disclosure is an adaptation of the technique described in a pioneering study by Sidney M. Jourard and Paul Lasakow, 1958. The author wishes to express thanks to Dr. Jourard for other suggestions as to method.

ment on our part of the significance for the respondent of the particular matters revealed or concealed from the mate—a judgment on how close these were to the core of personality and how deeply they were felt. Psychological intimacy, as defined here, depends not alone—or even not so much—upon the extent of overlapping in the inner worlds of two persons, but upon the content of what they habitually share.

To test the reliability of ratings two judges rated 30 cases independently taking every other case of our total sample. They used the three-fold classification of "very full" (or "full"), "moderate" and "meager" (or "very meager"). Out of 60 ratings of wives and husbands, the two judges disagreed in 8 cases and agreed in 52. In every case the disagreement represented only one step of the scale.

Two questions concerning the validity of the ratings require comment. Could we have penalized the frank respondents and rewarded those who concealed the truth? Those who confessed to us areas of reserve in their marriages might have received lower grades than others who, actually more reserved with their mates, were also reserved with us. But a high rating for self-disclosure was never assigned on negative evidence; it required some positive instance of disclosure of significant experiences. In any event, insofar as the families concealed from us areas of reserve in marriage the rating overestimated the fullness of marriage communication.

Another threat to the validity of the ratings derives from variations in the educational level of respondents. People with low verbal skills may talk less in general: a larger segment of their communication is non-verbal—a wife senses her husband's low spirits and cooks him his favorite dish; a husband expresses his apology by turning on his wife's favorite T.V. program. Could we then have mistaken absence of talk for non-disclosure? Of course, we were aware of this problem and used a safeguard: the grade of "meager" disclosure was never given merely because there was little conversation. It required positive evidence that some significant experiences were withheld from the mate. Additional proof was frequently furnished by the fact that these particular experiences were shared with others. Our purpose was to measure not the absolute volume or richness of communication but the extent to which each mate, no matter how simple his inner life, shared it with his spouse. Our attempt here was to measure the closeness of the relationship, not richness of personality.

Finally, the ratings of self-disclosure deal with the conscious segments of personality. However much a person may repress his real feelings, if he fully shares his conscious experiences he receives the rating of "full" disclosure.

The meaning of the ratings will be clarified by discussing individuals with full and meager self-disclosure.

"Very full" and "full" self-disclosure. A 39-year-old woman, who has been married for 17 years, describes her husband and his whole family as warm, outgoing and open about their feelings, much more so than her own mother. It was her husband who taught her over the years not to sulk, and to express her feelings openly.

The husband is the person in whom she confides all the irritations and hurts in her relationship with her own mother who lives with them. Both husband and wife realize that it was a mistake to have asked her mother to live with them, both realize there is no solution but to live with this problem, and they help each other to bear it by sharing their irritations. Mrs. H.'s relationship with her sister is also unsatisfactory. In fact, the person who is closest to her, next to her husband, is her mother-in-law. The husband supports his wife in her P.T.A. work and comes to hear her preside over important meetings of the organization. They talk at length and fully about aspirations for their only son and other plans. She tells him of her feelings of inferiority because she does not express herself well and he tells her, "You do well enough. You make me happy." He himself is a source of some frustration; he doesn't give her a feeling of "being a brain." She starts telling him some story she read in the newspaper, and he tells her he read it already. "Damn it," she exclaims, "why don't you let me finish the story?" They can talk about sex, and he helped her in the early years of marriage to find satisfaction in sex.

There are areas of reserve but we judge them to be much less significant than the shared areas. She doesn't always tell him when she feels self-satisfied, because she doesn't want him to think that she is vain. She knows that he was hurt because his promotion was delayed, but as she does not want to nag him about it she does not know exactly how he feels. She respects his privacy in this connection. She does not admit to him that she would rather not go on certain family excursions that have become a kind of a ritual for him. She prefers to discuss people with her girl friends. She protects some of her friends' confidences and he in turn doesn't tell her everything he knows about his male cousin who is also his good friend. When the interviewer asked her not to discuss the details of the interview with her husband before our interview with him, she said that she understood the purpose of the study and will not feel disloyal about withholding the details of what was, after all, *her* interview, as she put it.

Of course, persons who fully disclose their feelings are not always happy in marriage. The grade of "full" disclosure was given, for example, to one wife who has major dissatisfactions. She appears to have no insight into the real causes of her discontent but she freely expresses her "gripes" and she tells her husband all she knows about herself. There is no one else with whom she is any more open than with him.

As one goes down the scale, there is less sharing and areas of reserve become more significant. For example, the rating of "full," rather than "very full," disclosure was given to one wife despite her abundant and open talk with her husband about children's problems, personalities, her own depressions, her problems with her family, her hopes for the future and so on. But, seriously troubled about her husband's lack of ambition and aggressiveness, she conceals the full extent of her disappointment in him because she feels that complete frankness on her part would damage his self-esteem and make him even more passive. She talks over her worries with her sister who is her close confidante. Another woman pretended during the first two years of marriage that she enjoyed sexual relations with her husband; her real feelings about sex she confided in detail to her girl friend. This and other, less significant concealments, lowered her grade from "very full" to "full."

"Meager" self-disclosure. The ratings of "meager" and "very meager" also describe marriages varying in degrees of happiness. The rating of "meager" was given to Mr. and Mrs. Green, whose marriage was described on pages 126-131. These two persons, it will be remembered, share much of what is most intimate and most stimulating with outsiders rather than with one another.

However, they are quite satisfied, in part, at least, because they do not expect friendship in marriage.

Although some couples whose communication is rated as "meager" are satisfied with their marriages, all those in the "very meager" category turn out to be unhappily married. Apparently so severe a break in communication does not occur, whatever the norms, unless the marriage is very unhappy. Moreover, even if the spouses do not expect friendship in marriage, severe estrangements become stressful. We shall return to this problem later.

Some couples who are rated "very meager" in self-disclosure are locked in intense emotional conflict. (See pp. 164-170 for a description of such a marriage.) For other marriages in this category the accurate adjective is "dead": there is hardly any interaction between the husband and wife except the irreducible minimum for persons inhabiting a common household. Such a marriage is described in the following case study.

"Very meager" self-disclosure. "He's a lot closer to the kids than he is to me. Sometimes I'll come home and find him talking to them in the sweetest way," said a 30-year-old woman about her husband. They have been married for 12 years and have an 8-year-old boy and a 9-month-old girl.

> "I used to talk to him a lot when we were first married, but now I can't talk to him at all. He kinda draws away from me. Sometimes I think that all he wants me around for is to cook for him and the kids and then to leave him alone. I don't know too much about him because he is so close-mouthed. He gets tighter with his money and more close-mouthed every year, especially after his accident."

The husband hurt his hip in an accident, lost his job and now, as he put it, has "to grub around for odd carpentry and painting jobs." His earnings, including accident compensation, do not exceed $2000 a year. The interviewer described him as a bitter man with a poker face and a forbidding manner. He gives his wife money for expenses, but never tells her how much he makes. "I don't like that," she said: "It's not like married life should be. I can tell he is griped about my picking up a couple of dollars table waiting [note that she "can tell" he is griped. They never discussed it] but I gotta scrounge around to make do." Her neighbor looks after the children while she takes these occasional jobs.

When questioned about her husband's feelings, the wife said

that she is not sure just how anxious and worried he is. "He is a hard nut to crack, maybe he talks to the fellows. Sometimes I think he's beat, he is a broken man but he don't want to admit it."

As to their sex relations, her husband is leaving her more and more alone: "It's enough to drive a woman batty." She thinks that he is a very handsome man: "He's got the nicest back and shoulders and hands I ever saw. He looks marvelous in a swimming suit, too." After volunteering the information that during the last two months of her last pregnancy her husband played with her to a successful climax for himself without complete intercourse, she said: "I kinda liked that too," and they have continued this practice.

She knows "when he is mad because he stamps his foot a little bit, clears his throat or knocks things around. He cusses a blue streak when he drops things." She knows that he is mad about something else, though she doesn't always know what it is. They had a big fight after the baby was born about finances and their future. But although *she* still talks to him, he talks less and less.

"Sometimes he treats me as though I was a piece of furniture. He's either doing some work or reading a paper. We do not have a T.V. and I want it more than anything else in the world. I'm sneaking out money and saving it. It's no good making a down payment on it, cause he'll raise hell. I'll get the money all saved and then get my mother to go along with me and say she gave it to me. He'd be mad 'cause he doesn't want me to have a T.V." She added, "I gotta keep cheerful no matter what I feel. If I don't, everything would fall apart. That's the cross I gotta carry."

The husband was noncommittal in his interview. His one problem was, he said, the shortage of money. When worried, "I stop around for a drink but usually I work it off and forget about it." The one time he let his guard down in the course of the interview was in describing the satisfaction he gets having done a good carpentry job—"I like to work with my hands." Asked about his wife's moods, he replied, "God only knows."

This couple is one of three families that we interviewed who live on the same floor of a tenement. The women, very close friends, confirm the picture of the marital estrangement depicted above. The failure of the husband as a provider, the decline in sexual relations, the deviousness of the wife, which she covers up with a flow of words—whatever caused the alienation, the break in communication is severe.

Having illustrated the various grades of self-disclosure, we shall now present their frequencies in the Glenton group.

Are the Husbands and Wives Friends?

For almost one-third of these men and women the answer to this question is clearly in the negative. If it is one of the functions of modern marriage to share one's hurts, worries and dreams with another person—a large number of couples fail to find such fulfillment. Moreover, the breaks in the marriage dialogue are not a matter of preference. They result from abortive attempts at communications; attempts frustrated by what is felt to be the mate's lack of interest or an unsatisfactory response. On the other hand, almost one-half of the respondents share their feelings and thoughts "fully" and even "very fully" with their mates.

One-tenth of all the respondents are rated "very meager" in self-disclosure, with 12 per cent of the husbands and only 6 per cent of the wives in this category. "Meager" disclosure characterizes 21 per cent, and "moderate," 23 per cent, of all the respondents. These proportions are nearly identical for men and women. The two top grades, "full" and "very full," comprise 47 per cent of the total. Twenty-two per cent of the husbands but only 17 per cent of the wives are rated "very full," thus giving the husbands somewhat higher proportions at both extremes (Table 8).

Turning from individuals to married couples, we find a high similarity in the ratings of husbands and wives in 69 per cent of the couples. Apparently, self-disclosure requires some reciprocity, and reserve in one spouse creates reserve in the other. At the same time, however, in almost one-third of the cases, one partner is considerably more expressive than the other; the wife has the higher self-disclosure rating in 21 per cent, and the husband, in 10 per cent, of all the couples (Table 9).

Areas of Reserve Between Husbands and Wives

We culled from the interviews every instance of reserve in marital communication, including both matters concealed and matters not fully disclosed to the mate—434 instances in all.

These subjects, and the reasons given by the respondents to explain the reserve, have been classified and are given below in the order of frequency mentioned. The wives reported the following areas of reserve: (1) "about myself"—worries about health, dissatisfactions with the self, hurts, dreams and aspirations for the self and the family, transgressions, reminiscences; (2) feelings of hurt and irritation in relationships with in-laws, own relatives and friends; (3) confidences entrusted by others— things told in confidence by relatives and friends; (4) dissatisfactions with the husband; (5) worries about the children; (6) worries about bills.

The 264 reasons indicated by the wives for instances of reserve are also listed in their order of frequency: (1) husband not interested or unsatisfactory reactions to such disclosures in the past (by far the most frequently mentioned reason); (2) not to hurt husband's feelings; (3) to protect confidences of others; (4) to protect self; (5) not to worry husband; (6) "hard to talk about such things."

Areas of reserve reported by the husbands, again listed in their order of frequency, are: (1) the job: satisfactions, dissatisfactions, worry about bills and the economic situation in general; (2) feelings of hurt and irritation in relation to in-laws, relatives, co-workers and friends; (3) "about myself": feelings of hurt, dissatisfactions, aspirations, transgressions; (4) dissatisfactions with wife; (5) confidences of others.

Men have also frequently mentioned sports, cars and politics as topics they wouldn't normally discuss with their wives because women are "naturally" not interested in such typically masculine spheres. Apart from this explanation, the classification of the 168 reasons given by the husbands for reserve, in the order of frequency, are: (1) wife not interested, or her reaction not satisfactory in the past; (2) "hard to talk about such things"; (3) self-protection; (4) not to hurt wife's feelings; (5) not to worry wife.

Two differences between men and women deserve emphasis. "Confidences entrusted by others" as an area of reserve is more frequently mentioned by women, no doubt, because the women have a greater number of close relationships with relatives and friends than the men. "Hard to talk about such things" is, for men, the second and, for women, the sixth most frequently mentioned reason for reserve. But for both men and women the primary reason for reserve is that the mate is not interested or does not respond satisfactorily.

The reasons for reserve given by these men and women convey their own perceptions of the problem of communication. Our analysis of what causes the breaks in the marriage dialogue will be presented in the next chapter.

Self-Disclosure and Marital Happiness

Although an attempt was made to assess marital happiness quite apart from the degree of self-disclosure, we suspect that the latter may have affected our appraisals. Such remarks as "Oh, I can talk to him about anything" may in fact have been entered on the credit side of a marriage. Despite this possible "contamination" in the ranking of happiness in marriage, its correlation with the degree of self-disclosure is not perfect (see Tables 10a and 10b). Some unhappy persons disclose their feelings fully to the mate. Conversely, some reticent persons prove satisfied with their marriages. The one consistent finding is that all persons— men *and* women—who rate "very meager" on self-disclosure are unhappy in marriage. As suggested earlier, a nearly complete withdrawal does not occur under normal conditions, and causes unhappiness when it does occur.

The persons who are unhappy despite full disclosure fall into two types. Some suffer from problems that undermine the happiness of marriage without causing a severe break in communication. But others appear unhappy precisely because they communicate all too freely—fully expressing their hostilities. "Why does she have to tell me what her mother said about me?" complains one husband, divining the hostile intent that his wife rationalizes as frankness. Sometimes the unconscious need to punish, or to incur the other's wrath, prompts the person to "spill all."

The reserved but happy persons present another variety. Among these are couples who are satisfied, at least in part, because they do not expect much friendship in marriage. But there are other types. Married partners sometimes achieve a satisfying relationship precisely because they are able to grant one another considerable privacy. These persons either do not need, or are afraid, to share their deeper feelings. A keener sensitivity to the moods of the other, and deeper probings might arouse anxieties; the relationship may be somewhat shallow but is nevertheless a satisfying one.

Still another type is represented by a 38-year-old man and his 31-year-old wife, both with grade school education. He is open with his wife, but the interviewer referred to her as "the silent one." "Golly, she is one interesting woman," this man told the interviewer, "I'll never know the end of her. I never know what she's coming up with next, and I am sure glad I married her." Their mutual sexual satisfaction, his admiration and her appreciation of him, make for a satisfying marriage. Her reserve is in no way punitive in intent or threatening and, in fact, continues to intrigue him.

This marriage illustrates Georg Simmel's observation that reserve can be functional for marriage in the sense that the couples "belong more to one another qualitatively if quantitatively they do so less." [2] A certain indistinctness in the wife's image, and her unpredictability, add to the interest of the marriage. Simmel holds that "only those individuals can give themselves wholly without danger who cannot wholly give themselves, because such individuals contain an inexhaustible reservoir of latent psychological possessions." But less creative persons by their complete psychological abandon run the risk of "coming to face one another with empty hands."

There is another reason why reserve may be compatible with marital happiness and indeed actually enhance it. Some misperceptions of the mate's personality may promote mutual satisfaction. The fictions of marriage may be beneficial, like the reserve that helps to protect those fictions.

The connection between self-disclosure and marital happiness differs for men and women. Unhappy men tend to conceal their feelings, while some unhappy women are "full" disclosers. Furthermore, a higher proportion of men whose disclosure is "meager" can still enjoy moderate happiness in marriage. Women who cannot share their feelings in marriage are somewhat less likely to be content with their marriages. Chapter 9 will reveal a striking tendency on the husbands' part to "clam up" in the face of conflicts. Furthermore, women appear to have a greater desire to share their experiences with their mates than

[2] In Kurt H. Wolff, ed., 1950, pp. 327-330.

do men. The greater reticence of the unhappy men (as compared with unhappy women) would tend to increase, in the case of men, the association between self-disclosure and marital happiness. The other difference between the sexes works in the opposite direction. Men who do not disclose themselves can still be moderately happy, whereas women who cannot share their feelings tend to be less content.

These findings may throw light upon a recent study that reports a positive association between the extent to which the wife gratifies her husband's needs and his self-disclosure to her.[3] "It is not at all clear," write the authors, "why this relationship was not observed in wives." The explanation may lie in the greater tendency of the husband whose needs are not satisfied than of the dissatisfied wife to "clam up." But what of the fact that women tend to be unhappy when they cannot share their feelings in marriage? The authors report that the wives in their study show higher self-disclosure scores than the husbands. Their respondents had all attended college. Possibly the educated wives of educated husbands demand that they be heard— whatever other problems they may have, their need to express their anxieties may not be as thwarted as among the Glenton women. These considerations may explain why the relationship between self-disclosure and need satisfaction was found to exist among the husbands but was absent among the wives.[4]

Educational Level and Self-Disclosure

We had expected the level of education to make a difference in the fullness of self-disclosure, but the extent of this difference was surprising. The high school graduates, both male and female, share their experiences in marriage much more fully than do the less-educated persons. Sixty-five per cent of the former, but only

---

[3] Irwin Katz *et al.*, 1963, pp. 209-214.

[4] The relationship between communication and happiness in marriage was the subject of another investigation in which intimacy of communication was measured by questions about talking things over, kissing, engaging in outside activities together and methods of solving disagreements. The indices of intimate communication were significantly higher for the happily married than for the unhappily married, divorced or separated couples.

The samples used in this study were (1) Harvey J. Locke's Indiana sample of divorced and happily married couples and (2) the Locke-Karlsson Swedish sample of happily married, general population, unhappily married and separated couples. See Harvey J. Locke *et al.*, 1955.

36 per cent of the less-educated, rate the grades of "full" or "very full" disclosure. At the other extreme, "meager" or "very meager" communication characterizes only 12 per cent of the high school graduates and as many as 41 per cent of the less-educated (Table 11). The difference between the two educational groups persists when the comparison is controlled for the duration of marriage.[5]

Communication between mates tends to decline with the years of marriage. One previous study reports that in families with school-age children the spouses spend less time "talking together" than in families with infants,[6] and mutual confiding has been found by another investigator to decline with time.[7] Similar trends are observed in Glenton. The proportion of "meager" grades are higher for those who have been married seven years or longer than for the young marrieds. But the less-educated husbands present an exception to this generalization; among them the young husbands are more reserved than those who have been married longer. As brought out in Chapter 2, some less-educated men experience special difficulties in transition to marriage and they may require time to learn to share their feelings with their wives.

When men and women are compared educational subgroup for subgroup, the extent of self-disclosure to one's mate appears to be remarkably similar. The only difference between the sexes on this score is the somewhat fuller disclosure of the young, less-educated women in comparison with their husbands. But there is this difference between wives and husbands: if we are to trust the women's testimony, *their* reserve is involuntary, imposed by the indifference or unsatisfactory response of their husbands. The husbands, on the other hand, do not in the same way blame their wives for their own failure to communicate.

That it is the less-educated husband who blocks communication is demonstrated in still another way. Of the 19 couples with unequal levels of education, in 13 cases only the wife is a high school graduate and in the other 6, only the husband. The less-educated wife, married to a high school graduate, reveals herself

---

[5] Murray A. Straus (1964) found class differences in the total amount of communication in an experimental study of 40 families. The working-class families averaged 33.3 interactions per family whereas the figure for the middle-class families was double this, or 65.4.

[6] Harold Feldman, 1961.

[7] Peter C. Pineo, 1961.

as fully as the educated wife. But marriage to a high school graduate does not similarly enhance the self-disclosure of the less-educated husband, whose reticence appears to be self-imposed.[8]

The high school couples disclose themselves more fully than the less-educated. But insofar as they are also reticent, the pattern of reserve is quite similar for the two educational groups. However, the topic of in-laws as an area of reserve is listed more frequently by the less-educated men than by the high school graduates, but the reverse is the case among women. This result is consistent with the high incidence of in-law problems among the less-educated men and the educated women. Another difference lies in the greater frequency with which confidences of girl friends are withheld from husbands among the less-educated women. Since friendships are equally prevalent among the two groups of women, this result may mean that the high school women share these experiences with their husbands more often than do the less-educated women, or that the exchanges of high school friends are less confidential.

The reasons given by the respondents for reserve are again quite similar for the husbands irrespective of their education, but the high school women not only withhold less but do so for different reasons than the less-educated ones. The reserve of the high school women appears to be more voluntary and selective —they mention "husband not interested" less frequently and "to protect husband's self-esteem" and "self-protection" more frequently than the less-educated wives. (See Tables 12a and 12b). In another study, a similar conclusion was reached by two investigators who asked a sample of wives whether or not they ever tell their husbands their troubles on "bad" days and the reasons for their actions; the response of "would not help or reacts negatively" was given by 13 per cent of women with grade school education, but only by 8 per cent of high school graduates and 3 per cent of college graduates.[9]

[8] The few existing studies agree that the total self-disclosure of women (to all of their associates) tends to be higher than that total self-disclosure of men. When it comes to self-disclosure to one's mate, the results vary. One investigation of college-educated respondents reports that wives share their anxieties with their husbands more frequently than the reverse (Irwin Katz *et al.*, 1963, pp. 209-214). Another inquiry confirms the Glenton results that the spouses tend to be alike in degree of marital self-disclosure (Sidney M. Jourard, May 1958).

[9] Robert O. Blood, Jr., and Donald M. Wolfe, 1960, p. 201.

The fuller self-disclosure of better-educated persons is also reported in three other studies. Having compared a group of policemen with ten married college students, one investigator concludes that "the policemen were far less communicative about themselves than were the college boys." The duration of marriage, however, was not held constant in that comparison.[10] In another inquiry women were asked, "When your husband comes home from work, how often does he tell you about things that happened there?" The relative frequency of this particular type of communication went up with the education of the wife. As to occupation, the chief difference in the frequency of conversation about the job was between high white-collar occupations and all others, with the former having the highest frequency. The low blue-collar workers, on the other hand, talked more about their jobs than the high blue-collar men.[11] A third study found that college-educated respondents tended to report more frequently than the less-educated that they "understood everything the spouse was trying to get across" in six specified areas of discussion.[12] Although they differ in their method of inquiry, existing studies, then, agree in attributing higher self-disclosure in marriage to the better-educated respondents.

The fuller self-disclosure of the high school graduates could have been anticipated from what we have learned about their ideals of marriage. But this is only part of the explanation. The following chapter will consider various factors which thwart communication in marriage, including several barriers to interaction which loom higher for the less-educated than for the high school graduates.

[10] Sidney M. Jourard, May 1958, p. 81.
[11] Robert O. Blood, Jr., and Donald M. Wolfe, 1960, pp. 168-170.
[12] Lawrence Eugene Smardan, 1957.

ΛΛΛ

CHAPTER

7

Barriers to Marital Communication

One of every three marriages in this study falls short of the prevailing American ideal of psychological intimacy between married partners. These reserved couples are examined in order to discover the barriers to communication. The emphasis upon barriers unfortunately reinforces the common assumption that high rapport in marriage is natural and requires no explanation. The ability of two individuals to share fully their inner lives is no more natural, however, than their failure to do so. Rapport and the breakdown of interaction are two facets of the same riddle, the solution of which ultimately requires a comparison of both kinds of relationships. But barriers to communication are more visible than conditions which facilitate it.

Socially structured barriers, those rooted in shared values and conditions of life, will be considered first, followed by a discussion of psychological causes of impaired communication.

Sharp Differentiation in the Interests of the Sexes

Husbands and wives need not share identical mental worlds to understand one another, but their two separate worlds must be in contact at some points. This overlapping of interests is so narrow for a number of Glenton couples that neither partner can serve as a satisfactory audience for the other.

Existing emotional differences also block communication. A situation that arouses anxiety, curiosity, pride or guilt in one may have no such effect upon the other. This places excessive demands upon the emphatic ability of married partners.[1]

The upbringing of working-class children undoubtedly contributes to this separation of the sexes. Working-class parents make sharper distinctions than do the middle classes between the social roles of boys and girls. One investigator concludes that "middle-class mothers' conceptions of what is desirable for boys are much the same as their conceptions of what is desirable for girls. But working-class mothers make a clear distinction between the sexes. . . ." [2] In another inquiry, working-class boys and girls were found to be aware of sex roles earlier and more clearly than both boys and girls of the middle-class group, as indicated by the recognition of "appropriate" toys and behavior.[3] Whatever the role of their upbringing, the gulf between the sexes does exist. The following excerpts from the interviews illustrate a variety of reactions to this situation—the boredom of the wives, the contempt and exasperation of the husbands, the resignation of some and the yearnings of others.

A 23-year-old husband, a grammar school graduate, married three years, declared: "What is it about women that they want to talk about things when there is really nothing to talk about? Why do they have to hash it over? They talk about screwy things. Keep quacking, like beating a dead horse." He and his buddies agreed that "it seems to be this way all around."

A 22-year-old man, with ten years of schooling, married three years, confessed that he is often bored with his wife: "What does she have to talk about? Dirty diapers stuff. I don't care about that. She talks about the children, but we both see what is happening. We are both there, it's no use talking about it all the time." This young husband likes to read and when he comes across an interesting situation he tries to "talk her into reading the magazine, but she doesn't like reading, so I stopped bringing

[1] Robert A. Harper, 1958.
[2] Melvin L. Kohn, June 1959, p. 365.
[3] Meyer Rabban, 1950, pp. 140-141.

up these things." His wife was apparently aware of his criticism because she remarked during her interview, "If the wife is home all day, what has she got? Just the children and what the neighbors have said or done."

Another wife, a 28-year-old grammar school graduate, reflected about such sex differences: "Men don't like women so much. They think we are silly and talk too much. They think that women gossip a lot and they are against it." And another husband confirmed this view: "Women talk about the silliest details that don't matter and they don't want to talk about interesting things. This isn't just my wife. It is almost any woman." The same theme was expressed by a 25-year-old woman with ten years of schooling: "Regular guys don't mess around with women except when they want what a woman's got to give them. Men and women are different. The fellows got their interests and the girls got theirs, they each go their separate ways."

A high school graduate of 36 stated: "One thing that gets my wife mad is that I don't talk enough. She wants to sit down and talk. And there is nothing to talk about. I have been married to her for thirteen years and I am talked out. I can't find anything to talk about. The kind of things that she wants to talk about are kidstuff and trivial, like Mrs. X. had her tooth pulled out. I'd rather work around the house or work on the car." When the interviewer reminded this husband that, having been on his job for 13 years, he still enjoyed lively discussions with his fellow workers, he replied, "Sure I can talk to the fellows about the things I like to talk about—cars, sports, work. They are interested in every detail of baseball, but before my wife will pay any attention some pitcher has to hit something extraordinary. That's the difference."

Similar dissatisfactions were expressed by a wife who was trying to explain why talking with girl friends frequently proved more satisfying than conversations with her husband. When she once told her husband about a young woman in the community who had an illegitimate baby, he ended the discussion with: "It happens all the time." But with her girl friends she can talk over such matters in detail. (Does the girl really want to give up her baby? Should she? Would she marry the father of her baby if he asked her to? And so on.)

This pattern was detected in case after case. A 26-year-old

wife of a truck driver, with grammar school education, described their social life, largely confined to friendship with one couple. When they visit, they usually split up: "Jane's husband doesn't know what to talk to women about and Jane doesn't know what to talk to a man about," she explained. Another wife: "I get angry when he doesn't talk to me—he doesn't like silly conversation—it's no fun for me to go fishing with him—when he goes fishing, he doesn't talk—when he works with his tools, he doesn't talk—of course if I have a great problem that has been bothering me for a while, he says, 'Let's sit down and talk it out,' but otherwise he is quiet." A 21-year-old wife: "Men are different; they don't feel the same as us—that's one reason men are friends with men and women have women friends." "Does your husband ever talk about boring things?" the interviewer asked a 23-year-old woman. She answered, "I don't have to listen to him when he does," explaining that he does talk a lot about motorcycles, carpentry, local politics and sports and that she is not interested in such matters.

Generally, having neither competence nor interest in the mate's topic of conversation, each complains that the other "goes on and on about boring things" in unnecessary detail. One of the conditions causing this gulf between the interests of husbands and wives is the exclusion of the wives from their husbands' world of work.

The Wife and Her Husband's Job

There is scarcely a couple among these Glenton families who does not occasionally discuss the husband's job or his occupational plans. But these matters head the list of topics which the husbands admittedly disclose least to their wives. The interviews reveal several grounds for this reserve.

The monotonous nature of the job. This is one reason for limited conversation. "There is nothing to elaborate about my job," said a 36-year-old steeplejack, "I just mix paint all day and put it on. It is monotonous." The men frequently note that if something humorous or unexpected takes place during their work day, they are apt to tell their wives about it. Thus a garbage collector told and retold of the time he had to get a cat out of the sewer, and the story of the escaped pig was a favorite of a meat packer.

A 33-year-old hand truckman's testimony is characteristic: "I'm glad enough to be away from there. When I get away from the plant, I'd rather just let that rest till the next day. After all, it's no great fun; it's just something I got to make a living by. That's all." When asked, "Does your wife take an interest in your job?" another husband replied: "I don't take much interest in it myself so I wouldn't expect her to if I couldn't."

The job is usually felt to be too technical for women. Every husband was asked whether his wife understood the problems he encountered during his working day. Although a few of the husbands claimed that anyone, including their wives, could easily understand their work, the great majority, many of whom held semi-skilled jobs of low technical level, agreed with the man who said, "She'd have to work alongside of me to understand. I don't expect her to." They often felt that only a man in the same line of work could comprehend the technical problems, the irritations, and the satisfactions of the daily routine. The social relationships on the job were seldom discussed at home and social contacts with co-workers were extremely rare (see p. 153).

Talk about the job carries the connotation, for the husband, of "griping," which is thought to be unmanly. Our repeated question, "Can you talk to your wife about your job?" brought forth an unmistakable expression of a value: "I don't believe in bringing my job home." To talk about the job meant to "gripe about it." A 40-year-old sash fitter said apologetically, "Sometimes things go wrong and you come home and you got to get it out of your system and you can't help it if it spills over a little bit." A 23-year-old sanitation worker, in answer to the question about talk (a question which made no reference whatsoever to complaints), said, "Yes, I guess I do blow my stack sometimes: I try not to, but sometimes it sort of busts out of me."

The wives also tend to equate talk about the job with "griping." The item "tells wife about what happens on the job" was included in the schedule of "What makes a good husband?" Only 18 per cent of the women rated it as an important quality. And even this minority endorses conversation about the husband's work because of its presumed mental health function—"Let him talk if he has to get it off his chest." A more prevalent attitude is expressed by another woman who said, "When the hours is done, that is the end." In fact, the only women who complain that their husbands do not tell them enough about the job are a few unhappy wives for whom this silence seems to be another manifestation of the general withdrawal of the husbands.[4]

However self-critical their attitude towards "griping" about the job, we estimate about one-fifth of the husbands wished nevertheless that their wives were more interested in their work problems. On occasions when they wanted to share their work experiences they found their wives preoccupied with the children or uninterested.

Work and home should be kept separate. The great majority of the wives, some 80 per cent, have no social contact with their husbands' work-mates. The friendships husbands may form on the job do not include their wives. Indeed, in more than one-half of the cases the wives either never met their husbands' co-workers or saw them only once or twice when the latter delivered messages to, or called for, the husbands. In about 30 per cent of the cases, the wife did meet one or more fellow workers at some social gathering, a Christmas party or an outing. And in the remaining one-fifth of the cases, wives had more frequent contacts with co-workers. In several instances co-workers were relatives of the couple.

The feeling that work-mates do not belong in one's home was expressed by a 32-year-old painter: "It isn't nice to bring work people home. Homes are not for that. At home you raise children and relax. If you have friends from work, you're going to talk things over with them, and not want to have to hear babies crying or to go out shopping. When you're home you want to ease up and not have to keep on your toes." The idea that the home is too "pure" for masculine comradery was also expressed by several men who noted that the talk among the fellows at work is too rough and vulgar for women. Thus a 38-year-old cable layer said to us, "Nah, they ain't got no call to come on home with me, what would they do there? We might feel like having a drink, or raising a ruckus, and you ought not to do that at home. It is a lot better in the tavern, or the dog-wagon or hanging around the street someplace."

[4] The wives, as well as the husbands, were questioned about the job as a topic of conversation. This served as a safeguard against the possibility that the husbands minimized the extent of their talk because, in their own minds, this was "griping."

Some husbands opt for reciprocal reticence. Instead of mutual sharing of daily experiences, some husbands recommend reserve. Thus a 31-year-old truck driver declared: "It don't do no good to go home and belly-ache to your wife. If you don't want to know about what happens with the washing and with the neighbors' kids, you shouldn't ought to tell her about what goes on at the plant either." And another husband: "The only things we don't tell each other are things the other don't want to hear. She don't want to know what I did in the warehouse and I don't want to know if the baby is sick, so long as it ain't really sick."

The general picture of the exclusion of the wife from the work world of the husband is not altered by an occasional exception, as in the case of a motel worker who married the daughter of the motel manager and stated: "I'm likely to tell her anything that happens out there. She knows what it's all about. It makes it kind of nice. She'll ask me what about it and it makes it interesting. Though some days I wish she'd lay off because I'm sick of the job."

The working-class situation stands in sharp contrast to the frequently reported involvement of the "corporation wife" in her husband's career.[5] The daily assessment of office politics, the prudent entertaining of superiors and associates and the resulting feeling of personal participation in a husband's career are all lacking here. If the workingman, in contrast to the corporation careerist, misses the opportunity to share his world of work, he enjoys a greater immunity from his wife's scrutiny of his daily performance. In any case, for better or worse, the husband's job is not an area of active common interest for the large majority of our couples.

In all social classes, to be sure, the sexes are bound to have some separate interests because their social roles differ. Neither husband nor wife can be expected to be interested in the purely technical aspects of the other's daily tasks. A woman friend, confronted with similar problems, will naturally have a more lively interest than the husband in the baby's diet, a new recipe or a bargain. Similarly, a fellow worker will be more competent than one's wife to discuss the technical problems of the job. Insofar as the husband is drawn into the domestic sphere or

[5] See, e.g., William H. Whyte, Jr., October and November 1951.

the wife gets involved in her husband's career, their interests converge. Neither of these conditions obtained for most of Glenton's families.

Men and women, however, may have their separate tasks and still share common interests in the psychological problems of child rearing, in their personalities, in social life and aspirations for the future. But it is only a slight exaggeration to say that for many of Glenton families life contains little else apart from the immediate daily tasks. The impoverishment of life and of personality curtails the development of shared interests.

The Impoverishment of Life

Writers concerned with the meagerness of marital communication sometimes imply that it would flow abundantly were we only able to open the floodgates. However, the impoverishment of the quality of life not only narrows the overlapping of interests and consequent sharing of experiences, but also stunts personal development. There may be little or nothing to communicate. Speaking of television, for example, typical comments by the respondents were: "We both see it, why talk about it," and "What's there to talk about other than to say it's good or bad." In more general terms, one woman put it this way: "We tell each other things, but I don't know as how we talk about them. He'll tell me or I'll tell him something has happened, but there ain't nothing much to say." In contrast, one father reported that he and his wife "go on and on" discussing the different reactions of their children to discipline. Another man and his wife spoke of their frequent debates about whether good character or success in life is the more important goal of child rearing. Such topics require a psychological sophistication lacking in many of the families. "We don't have any back-and-forth on it," explained one woman when asked whether she and her husband ever talked about their child's reaction to discipline.

If external life is restricted for these families, so is their inner world. For example, the meagerness of joint social life deprives the couples of conversation about mutual friends, gossip, planning of social affairs and "party post-mortems." Over one-third of these couples either never visit with another couple apart from relatives or do so only very infrequently, a few times a year on some special occasion of an anniversary or a

New Year's celebration. Low level of interest in reading, in current events and in cultural subjects has a similar impoverishing effect.

Couples who are exposed to the middle-class values of companionship, but whose mode of life does not stimulate common interests, are sometimes acutely aware of this discrepancy. They know that husbands and wives are supposed to talk with one another, but they do not have anything to say. Characteristically, one young husband, a high school graduate, said: "I wish we had more things to talk about, but when I try to think of something I don't know anything to talk to her about. I wish we could get out and see the shows or something like that." And another man expressed a similar dissatisfaction: "If my wife and I had a little more education maybe we'd have what you call it—more interests? Maybe we could come together better, maybe life would be more interesting for us."

The barriers to communication described so far derive from the meager content of common interests. Deficient skills of communication, especially on the part of the less-educated husbands, also hinder the sharing of experiences.

The Trained Incapacity to Share

The phrase "trained incapacity to share" aims to convey a certain view about the men's inarticulateness. The ideal of masculinity into which they were socialized inhibits expressiveness both directly, with its emphasis on reserve, and indirectly, by identifying personal interchange with the feminine role. Childhood and adolescence, spent in an environment in which feelings were not named, discussed or explained, strengthened these inhibitions. In adulthood they extend beyond culturally demanded reticence—the inhibitions are now experienced not only as "I shouldn't," but as "I cannot." In explaining instances of reserve in marriage many more husbands than wives say: "It is hard to talk about such things." (See p. 141.)

"I used to try to ask him when we were first married," said a 26-year-old woman about her husband, "why he gets into those real flippy moods, but he used to say nothing was wrong, and asking seemed to make him worse. The more I tried, the worse he'd get. So I found out that if you just don't bother him, it wears off." Another young woman described her husband: "Sometimes he could get real black and quiet and you'd just better keep out of his way and not say anything."

The wives endorse the therapeutic value of talk more frequently than the husbands. Thus a 30-year-old woman:

> "Lots of people say it's not good to go around shooting off your lips about what's eating them, but I think the good thing is to talk it out and get it out of your system. But I have to leave him alone because if I try to get him to talk he'll get really sore, or he'll go off the deep end and walk out of here. Or maybe he'd tell me something else, lying like, just so I wouldn't get at the thing that makes him sore. He is strictly hands-off if something hurts him. . . . It makes it rough . . . not knowing what's eating him hurts you worse than it hurts him."

The foregoing remarks were made by less-educated women, but a 39-year-old high school graduate, married to a man with ten years of schooling, told a similar story:

> "He can clam up and not talk for a long time. Sometimes I ask him what are you so clammy for, spit it out and you'll feel much better but he'll answer me coarsely or just say, 'Oh yeah.' Sometimes I can worm it out of him but I believe in leaving him alone. When he begins to work it out then I'll say 'something is the matter with you' and then he'll say, 'Oh —that foreman.' Maybe he'll tell me or maybe he'll just get over it. I watch other people and they have the same thing. Sometimes they ask me what to do and I tell them, 'leave the man alone.' "

These comments are not exceptional. Twenty-six per cent of the wives, but only 9 per cent of the husbands, in answer to questions about dissatisfactions with communication, complain that their mate "does not reveal worries." The responses to the projective story about the husband who doesn't talk enough (see pp. 117-120) convey the same idea. Although the story contained no reference whatsoever to worry, 11 per cent of the respondents agreed: "He might not want to talk because something is wrong." Of 23 qualities of a good husband, the women ranked "speaks his mind when something is worrying him" as the second most important quality. These rankings reflect current deprivations—not merely ideals. The wives value the trait of speaking out precisely because they miss it in their husbands.

The ideal of masculinity accepted by the men is certainly one factor in their meager disclosure of stressful feelings. To gripe about the job carries the connotation of weakness. A strong man bears his troubles in silence and does not "dump his load on the family"; he does not ask for solace and reassurance. Indeed, an adult male does not even experience hurt, much less admit it. "When I don't feel good," said one husband, "I light out and don't dump my load on them." Speaking of his wife, a 40-year-old carpenter (with eight years of school) described the masculine norm quite explicitly: "Sure she gets hurt. Men are supposed to be braver than women, but women is bound to get hurt, it's in their nature, ain't it?"

The strength of such norms is demonstrated in the section of the interview dealing with feelings of hurt and of anger. When asked for sources of hurt feelings, almost twice as many men as women expressed disapproval of the very experience of hurt in an adult: "After a man gets on his feet, he shouldn't be hurt deeply about anything"; "You ought to outgrow it." More men than women say, "Nothing can hurt me anymore," or "Don't know what could reach me anymore." They generally add that at some earlier time—in childhood, "before the army," "before marriage," their feelings were hurt. Among the less-educated, 30 per cent of the men, but only 15 per cent of the women, denied completely that they experienced hurt at present. The sexes, however, report the experience of anger with nearly identical frequency: only 5 per cent of the women and 8 per cent of the men maintain that they are never angry.

It may be argued that the men experience hurt feelings less frequently (thus not merely concealing such feelings) than the allegedly more sensitive females. But the testimony of the high school graduates weakens this argument because the difference by sex in the reporting of hurt feelings narrows: 12 per cent of women and 17 per cent of the men in this educational category deny feelings of hurt. The high school men may have a less rigid norm of masculinity and be more willing to admit being hurt than the less-educated men. Consistent with this idea is the similarity between the two groups of men in their admission of anger: only 8 per cent of the less-educated and only 6 per cent of the high school graduates denied the experience of anger. Unlike the experience of hurt, anger does not carry the connotation of weakness to the less-educated men.

Socialized to identify the expression of certain emotions with a lack of masculinity, the men inhibit self-disclosure. Lack of education plays an independent role in limiting the capacity to identify, interpret and express feelings. The consequences of these factors are amply demonstrated in the next chapter. Of the four subgroups (high school and less-educated husbands and wives) the less-educated husbands are consistently the most withdrawn. They reveal less of themselves to their wives, are less inclined to find relief by openly expressing emotion, and tend to react to marriage conflict by withdrawal. Of all the aids in overcoming emotional stress listed by the uneducated husbands, only 28 per cent involve interaction with others, as against 42 per cent of such aids for the less-educated wives. These men seek relief in action rather than in talk.

The reticence of the less-educated husbands is also apparent in the relative scantiness of their replies to the section of the interview on self, personality and psychological relationships. The questions called for sources of feelings of hurt, happiness, worry, self-satisfaction and guilt, and for assessments of one's strong points and shortcomings. The less-educated husband lists fewer items per person than any of the other respondents. For example, in describing his strong and weak traits, he lists 5.4 fewer traits than does the less-educated woman. But among the high school graduates the sex difference is narrowed to only 2.1 items in favor of women. The inhibitions of the less-educated men are further revealed by the fact that, of all the four subgroups, the less-educated husbands are the only ones who list fewer items about their own personality than about the personality of their mates.

Psychological Barriers to Communication

Husbands and wives will not share their experiences if the sharing is unrewarding, threatening or downright painful. In some cases the chief cause of estrangement lies in the personality of one mate who finds any close relationship threatening for a variety of psychological reasons. These persons would have probably been withdrawn no matter whom they married. Few persons, however, are so rigid in their psychological make-up as to be immune to their environment. Generally speaking it is not the personality of one mate, but the interplay of the two personalities that impairs communication. We shall presently illustrate several of what must be a great variety of such marriages.

In other cases some particular issue creates a tabooed topic and the taboo then spreads a pall of caution and hypocrisy over the whole relationship. Such a problem may have existed from the outset of the marriage, as in some instances of religious intermarriage and in certain marriages marked by in-law conflict. In order to avoid conflict the couple may abstain from discussing topics "too sore to touch." Sometimes alienation can be dated from some external adversity which befell the family, as, for example, an accident suffered by the husband, or his loss of a job. But while some one issue or some external blow may initiate the processes of alienation, in itself this seldom offers sufficient explanation: even in such cases the interplay of the two personalities contributes to the estrangement.

The following cases all illustrate "psychological barriers to communication," but each case brings out the significance of a specific type of factor restricting interchange between husband and wife.

The personality of the husband may impair communication. One man, suffering from ulcers, quoted his doctor: "He says I keep my feelings all bottled up." His warm, sociable but perplexed wife asked the interviewer: "What about him? Did he tell you why he doesn't tell me anything?" The husband admires her sociability. "Oh, she never met a stranger. She's a wonderful woman that way. She has real personality." But that does not make it any easier for him to talk to her about his own feelings. He has recurrent moody periods during which, the wife says, he "picks"on her and on the children. She knows that "something is bothering him but he only gets madder if I ask him what it is." Neither her questions nor "trying to honey him up" does any good.

This man is an extremely ambitious, 30-year-old Southerner, who is striving to become a foreman and who has already raised himself from poverty to comfort. His current income is $6500 a year and he owns his house and has a car. "He is trying too hard," remarked his wife.

He revealed some conflicts in the course of the interview. A deep hostility towards a Catholic man who, he felt, unfairly blocked his promotion, and hostility towards Negroes broke through his reserve. He flushed, started moving about the room and said: "Well, I'm sorry I brought it up. Don't get me wrong, we get along fine. I'm sorry I gave you the wrong impression." This hostility conflicts with his religious ideals because he is an active member of his church and tries to be a good Christian.

Whatever the psychological sources of his violent emotions and his fear of expressing them, it is his own personality that blocks communication in marriage. Only a warm and outgoing wife would not be completely discouraged by his reserve. His wife has learned to leave him alone during his moody periods and to find an outlet for her sociability in daily meetings with women friends.

This man is a strong and striving person who asserts himself at work and at home though at a great psychic cost to himself. His reserve is at least partly due to his fear of giving vent to his hostile feelings. In contrast, other habitually reserved husbands appear more afraid of arousing the hostilities of their associates. Perhaps their own aggression is merely more deeply repressed, but they seem more fearful of "starting a fire" in others than in themselves. They repress irritations in all their social relationships. When such persons encounter marriage conflicts they tend to play safe by withdrawing from the relationship.

The cautious man may withdraw to escape his wife's emotional demands which he cannot satisfy. A 27-year-old truck driver, with ten years of schooling, has been married for four years to a grammar school graduate. This man generally feels that it is safer to "keep some distance" from people, and his marriage has intensified this tendency. He told the interviewer that he liked his work associates well enough, but:

"If you work together and you get too close you have trouble. It's better to keep some distance." Again, speaking of his church activities, he said he is "generally a listener at church." He had been deeply afraid of marriage, but he likes it now. "I am satisfied in the home that I built, I have no real dissatisfactions. I was only hanging around before, and I'm not sorry I lost that. I have a great deal of comfort now." He is a devoted son, but his relations with his parents are somewhat distant. His brother may be his one confidant. His wife is a self-centered woman who has a great need for reassurance. She has difficulty in describing her husband's feelings and turns the conversation to herself. She said, "I'm possessive and very jealous. I was a stinker when we were first married. I wanted everything my own way. Because of his kindness and love, I became a better person. He is a very religious man. That has a lot to do with it."

In explaining why he is not always open with his wife, the husband declared: "I don't like to tell personal things to anyone. Even when you say what you think, you are sorry afterwards. Many men tell their wives what happened before they are married, and later this has been held up against them. A little something may become a long-drawn-out thing. It gets boring. It even grows into an argument. It is so silly. There is no use starting a fire. She feels blue because I don't talk more to her. It is just that I don't talk a great deal. When I relax I like to do it completely, mentally and physically. She feels I don't love her as much as I really do."

He had to drop some of his church activities because his wife resented his absence. She asked, "Don't you want to stay home?" "When she is mad," the husband said, "I try to leave the room till she cools off." The husband mentioned the frequent discussions that he has with his brother about the Bible. The Bible says that looking at a woman is the same thing as committing adultery, and he often discusses with his brother how to stop thinking about it.

When asked about the kinds of things which angered her, the wife answered, "My husband has a great habit of not talking. It happens daily. I yell, 'For God's sake, will you answer?' He answers, 'I don't feel like talking, I'm tired of talking.' " He is not ambitious enough: "You have to push him even if he wants to go." He admitted to her that he needed to be pushed a little. "I would like him to get more drive, get further ahead, do more with his life." Speaking of sexual relations, she said, "I'm not as cold as I was. During pregnancy and after, I began liking it more." Pregnancy "brought her out of her bashfulness."

Whatever makes emotional intimacy generally threatening to this man has been further aggravated by his marriage. His wife is an insecure woman and he is not able to give her the kind of reassurance she wants. He confesses being troubled by his adulterous thoughts. By withdrawing, he seeks to protect himself from her "harping" and her demands.

The tendency to play safe by concealing feelings is also ex-

hibited by some wives. In a strongly patriarchal family such behavior may be a realistic adjustment to life. But some wives are
more cautious than appears to be required, given their position in
marriage and the personalities of their husbands. For example, a
23-year-old high school graduate, married four years, is somewhat dissatisfied with her husband's lack of drive, his nightly
T.V. viewing, his neglect of her, and their lack of social life. Although she has never informed her husband explicitly, she feels
that he ought to treat her parents with more respect. Both are
somewhat reserved, but the wife is more so. She conceals dissatisfactions in order "not to start an argument." When asked
about her moods the husband said, "I don't know. She'd know
better about that." The husband feels that they are still very romantic about each other, saying that he often has slight palpitations
when he meets her suddenly.

These cautious persons occasionally described the process of
alienation. In the beginning of marriage, in moments of rapport,
they would drop their guard and yield to the temptation to discuss some experience, perhaps to atone for some guilt or in a bid
for reassurance. "I used to confide in her but now I know better,"
said one husband. When asked, "Why is that? Can't she keep a
secret?" he replied, "Oh no, that is not it. It's just that I don't
want her bugging me." Generally in such cases, the lower the
tolerance for conflict, and the more full of conflict the relationship, the rarer become such moments of disclosure. To yield to
the impulse to reveal oneself is to supply the adversary with a
weapon which can be turned against one in the next battle.

In contrast to these cautious persons, the reserve of others
seems to stem not from fear but from self-sufficiency. These self-
sufficient persons do not hesitate to express dissatisfactions or to
take a stand on issues of married life, but they can endure a great
deal of solitude and have less need to unburden themselves.
Possibly they are also unable to express their feelings, differing
from the man with the ulcer only in degree. In any event, they do
not appear to suffer such emotional stress, nor do they suppress
dissatisfactions. Their reserve does create a certain distance but,
unless the spouse feels threatened by this reserve, the marriage
relationship can be a satisfying one. (Having cited these examples
of masculine reticence, it should be noted that a woman provided
the clearest instance of self-sufficiency.)

A CASE STUDY OF PROGRESSIVE ESTRANGEMENT

The following analysis of an estranged couple illustrates the deliberate use of withdrawal as punishment. An embittered wife withdraws periodically to punish her husband in a self-defeating strategy to win his response. It also demonstrates the interplay of personalities since both husband and wife contribute to the unhappy end result.

The Jones family consists of the 31-year-old husband, his 30-year-old wife and their 8-year-old daughter. Mrs. J. cannot have any more children as a result of an operation. They have been married for ten years.

The J.'s had been "real friendly" when they were first married. The thin, sallow woman described the circumstances of her marriage.

"He met me and I guess he liked me. Anyway, he got to coming around and hanging around. My family began kidding about him. He got along fine with them and I thought that was good. I liked him pretty good too. So when he asked me to marry him, I did.

"The first year we was married he'd do all kinds of things for me. He couldn't do enough. He'd be sitting around talking, making jokes, sometimes he'd dry the dishes. I'll tell him to get out of the way, he'd kid me and help me anyhow.

"I don't know what happened. We didn't have no real trouble. You couldn't hardly say what went wrong. He just wasn't so interested."

"Oh sure," said the husband in his interview, "everybody likes it [marriage] at first but soon the troubles start."

Mrs. J. is a lonely woman, sensitive to criticism. She still mourns her mother who died five years ago. She is very bitter towards her two sisters and her brother. She was the youngest in her family, and had trouble with her sisters since she was about ten. Her father died at that time and her sisters accused their mother of having spoiled her. "They gave me nothing but gun-fire sarcasm all my life. My other relatives belittled me but I got so I could be sarcastic and give it right back to them."

Her sisters married Catholics and they "turned" [converted to Catholicism]. She hardly ever sees them but she felt hurt that they did not invite her to a recent wedding of her niece and did not send a Christmas present to her little girl.

When Mrs. J. was married, she asked her husband whether she could take in her ailing mother to live with them. Her sisters "crabbed about taking care of Mother." Mr. J. was very good about this, saying that as long as Mrs. J. was prepared to work to cover the expenses he had no objection. "You know I must have liked her a lot if I'd clean offices at night. She lived with us for five years until she died, and he never blamed me for it."

With the death of her mother, Mrs. J. lost her one close friend. Significantly the only person she sees frequently is an older woman who lives on the same block. There are two or three others whom she meets in church and on the street when she is out shopping. Both she and her husband explain her present lack of women friends by the fact that she is a stranger to this community, having moved there from an adjoining town ten years ago when they got married. One old friend from her home town does visit her occasionally.

The J.'s have no regular contact either with her relatives or with his. Mr. J. said that he, too, had been hurt by his family years ago. But it was Mrs. J.'s conflicts with her in-laws that further estranged the couple from his relatives. His parents are now dead and some of his brothers now reside out of town, but one brother lives in the next house. The two families "speak on the street to pass the time of day" but do not exchange home visits.

The marriage conflicts of the J.'s ostensibly center around the discipline of their daughter, but Mrs. J.'s real problem is her husband's withdrawal from her.

"We don't work together as man and woman. We fight a lot. I'd say no to the child and he'd say yes. Like for example about manners. He says I'm too strict, I'll holler at her not to do something and he'll say 'go ahead.' I'll hit the child and she says she'll tell him and I'll say go ahead and I'll hit her again in front of him. That sort of thing works on the nerves and aggravates you till you can't take it. If I had a home to go to I wouldn't be here, though I know it isn't good for a kid to be brought up without a father."

Between our repeated interviews with this family Mrs. J. appealed to the minister of her church to go to the school to find out why her little girl did so poorly. "He comes back," said Mrs. J. "and tells me she is a bright little girl and she is sensitive. 'She is not afraid of her father but she is terrified of you. She is scared of your temper.' " Mrs. J. admitted that she had "a dirty Dutch temper—I don't talk, I hit."

The interviewer witnessed the following scene: the 8-year-old daughter came bursting in with her homework but she had not done well. The mother raised her voice to a scream and scolded her for not paying attention and for being too slow. She berated her for watching the children around her rather than doing her own work. The child was polite to her mother and evidently frightened and most anxious to please her. After trying to justify herself she burst into tears. She came running to her mother and flung her arms around her. The mother continued to shout at her for several moments. When she quieted down the two of them sat there together with their arms around each other, both very obviously fond of each other.

The mother continued to scold a little bit in a quieter voice while the child repeated over and over again, "I'm sorry, Mother." The child then let go of her mother to plead, "Don't tell Daddy." The mother said, "Of course I'll tell your Daddy, and wait till you hear what your father gives you." At this the daughter burst into tears again. The mother told her to be still, but embraced her and the two of them rocked back and forth with a tenderness very obvious between them.

The rages aroused in Mrs. J. by the little girl have, it would appear, another target. This is one way she gets a response from her withdrawn husband. True enough, she wants her daughter to do well in school. She has high standards in general. She is a compulsively meticulous housekeeper, an efficient manager who does not allow the family to incur any debts. She attends church regularly and wants to do the best by her child, but the sources of her temper are suggested in her husband's description of a quarrel.

The quarrel involved the disciplining of the girl: "She trains her good but she is too strict with the kid. I think she ought to leave her alone more." He interceded for the girl and his wife "left home for half a day. I don't know to this day where she went. Me and my daughter rustled for ourselves taking things out of the icebox." When his wife came back she did not talk to them. He wouldn't have minded at all if his daughter had not been so worried.

Referring to his wife's long silences, the husband remarked, "You don't know how to take her then, so now when I get mad I don't show it because when she is quiet like that it's hard on the kid."

When asked whether he got worried when he did not understand his wife's moods, Mr. J. answered, "Only when I think it's bad for the kid." Mrs. J. confirms this in her own interview: "When I get real mad, I won't talk to them for days; they feel it after a while."

"He sees me but he don't say anything, he keeps to himself," said Mrs. J. Answering our questions about sex relations, Mrs. J. replied: "Oh, we had our good time when we started out. It's no fun anymore; it's like I heard the fellows say they use a woman like they go to the toilet." As if confirming this observation Mr. J. said, "She is there when I want her." On a rating scale of the ideal mate he gave "responds to husband's love-making" the rating of moderate importance, and added, "it doesn't make too much difference to her."

There is no doubt that the husband shuts himself off. On rare occasions, when both "make a fuss" over high marks or some other happy event in the life of the little girl, the talk is pleasant. Much more frequently, the child is the subject of a quarrel. The breakdown of communication is conveyed by many facts. For example, Mrs. J. wonders whether he visits his brother next door; she doesn't know. She doesn't know anything about his job or his attitude towards the union and despite the fact that union affairs and Hoffa were in the news at the time of the interview, they never exchanged any words on this subject. She suspects that her husband saw the minister but, again, she is not certain: "He is like that, men never tell you what they do. I don't know who saw who or who said what."

Again, although Mr. J. is generous with the money he never wants to talk to her about budgeting. "Money means nothing to him, I'm the one who saves." It is "when he is nice" that she warms up to him, she explained, "when he isn't sarcastic or mean," not when he gives her money. She wishes she could discuss her budgeting problems with him.

Nor is there, in this case, any sharing of leisure time interests. Mr. J. is a homebody but he hardly talks to her evenings. He watches T.V. and if she interrupts his viewing he might say "shut up" or "get the hell out of here." Mr. J. confirms this picture. There is no occasion, he stated, to talk about what they see on T.V. He doesn't say anything "no more than to say what program I'm going to have on if she's got something else on or I don't even bother to say anything, I just change it." They used to fight about religion because she wanted him to go to church with her. He thinks "religion is a lot of hypocrisy," and they no longer discuss it. As for politics, she remembers voting one year when somebody they knew ran for a minor office. She never votes and "he doesn't always bother," and thus politics is never a topic of family conversation.

The interviewer's direct observations confirm Mrs. J.'s portrait of her husband.

The interviewer first met Mr. J. when he returned from work and found her talking to Mrs. J. When the interviewer explained the study he said "That's very nice" and walked into the living room, turned on the T.V. and opened a newspaper. No, he said, he was too tired to answer any questions; maybe some other time, though he wouldn't like to promise.

"You see, it's like I told you," said Mrs. J. to the interviewer, "he's not very nice, he doesn't like nobody. But you didn't make him mad, I can tell. If you come back and strike him right, he might even talk to you a little bit."

Shortly after their first encounter the interviewer met Mr. J. accidentally near his house one rainy afternoon when another prospect turned out to be unavailable. Mr. J. asked her gruffly whether she would like to step in his house to get out of the rain. Mrs. J. and the little girl were out. At the end of the interview Mr. J. was asked whether he would tell his wife about the interview. "I ain't got no call to tell her nothing," he said. "I'll just go on watching T.V. like always when she comes in. I don't care what you do, you can tell her."

Mr. J.'s self-portrait depicts a man who reacts to any threat to his restricted and routinized existence by further withdrawal.

"I do a lot of thinking before I open my mouth. . . . I leave people alone and they leave me alone and everybody's happier." And again: "As long as I can work a fair day and get fair pay and can take it easy at home—I don't ask no favors. I used to be ambitious but it's a good thing to settle down." Mr. J. likes his job, driving a lift-up truck inside a factory. He eats lunch with his work-mates and may play a hand of pinochle. Once in a while he stops for a beer on the way home. "Once I get home I stay put. I don't understand why some people run around to other people's houses." They never go visiting.

Apart from the union he has no group memberships. His pleasures in life are a good meal and the T.V. He spent his last vacation at home because he thought he could get a better rest than at the beach.

His wife's tendency to quarrel with her own relatives and her in-laws exaggerates Mr. J.'s inclination to withdraw, with the result that the pair is almost completely isolated. Mr. J. avoids his wife to escape a contest of power.

"She is a good hard-working wife but she is nervous and she doesn't mix in," said Mr. J. "My wife's got a lot of trouble with her brothers and sisters. I always tell her to leave them be. But she's got to go monkeying around with them. She gets all cut up when people talk, and she shouldn't." Asked to describe his wife's means of overcoming bad moods, Mr. J. replied that he did not know. As for him, "I just sit and watch T.V. I forget it. I just let things blow over." When his wife answers in ways he does not understand—"I just don't listen."

Mr. J. could not be expected to express fully to the interviewer his dissatisfactions with his wife. He explained at one point why "a man wouldn't complain about his wife," to a co-worker. "A guy likes everybody to think he is boss and that he makes things run smoothly at home." Nevertheless, he did describe their fights over the girl. "She gives in to me about everything but the girl. She leaves me be. I don't like to be crowded."

A man who feels so keenly that the husband should be boss must be exasperated by his helplessness in the face of her temper and her punishment of their daughter. His own withdrawal is, we believe, also punitive. Mrs. J. senses his motive when she refers to his "mean" moods.

Mrs. J. is a lonely woman, easily embittered by any sign of criticism and rejection. In order to avoid being drawn into her quarrels with relatives and in-laws, Mr. J. withdraws. But his withdrawal aggravates his wife's loneliness and hostility. She "hollers" about repairs and about his refusal to discuss their economic problems but she repeatedly admitted that it wasn't the repairs and the money—she just wanted him to be "nice."

Mr. J. has another motive for shutting himself off: he feels that the husband should be boss. A wife who nags and makes a man do what she wants makes a fool of a man, he said. But while she is a conscientious woman who fulfills her wifely duties, her rages are too much for him. In addition to escaping interaction to ward off a power struggle, his avoidances seem to be motivated by a wish to punish his wife.

Mr. J. might have succeeded in "leading his own life" (work

during the day and the T.V. at night) had it not been for his love and concern for his daughter. He remarked on several occasions that it is because of his daughter that he worries about his wife's prolonged and punitive silences. Mrs. J. senses that she reaches him only by attacking the girl. But his defense of the girl in itself infuriates her as a criticism of and a further rejection of herself.

The yearnings back of Mrs. J.'s bitterness became apparent on successive interviews. Having given vent to her bitterness, she was able to express the other side of her ambivalent feelings.

"We don't have such a wonderful marriage but when I see other people's I think ours isn't so bad. He is absolutely regular. He never stays away overnight and he's never looked twice at another woman. He doesn't get drunk. I've been thinking about your questions. They are real interesting. I'm a funny person. I'll cry but I don't want no one around. I want to be alone. Sometimes I think he knows when I've been crying and he doesn't say nothing because he knows I wouldn't like it, I don't know."

The strains put upon this marriage are all the greater because life contains so little else for the pair. They are almost completely isolated from any meaningful social contact and their low income restricts recreational activities. In a more affluent situation, Mrs. J.'s need for reassurance would remain, but a pleasanter life would provide some diversions and would siphon off some discontent—she spoke with warmth about a bus trip to Florida she and her husband once made together to visit relatives.

The Educational Factor in Communication

The foregoing pages have dealt with socially structured and psychological barriers to marital communication. We have seen that communication between husbands and wives is hindered by certain traditional values. Having embraced these values, some men contemptuously relegate conversation about persons to "old women's gossip," and attribute self-disclosure of painful emotions to lack of self-sufficiency. Question: "Do you talk to your wife about this?" Answer: "Yes, once in a while I might *cry on her shoulder*" (emphasis ours), they admit shamefacedly. The separation between the masculine and the feminine spheres of interest also thwarts communication. The humdrum or the technical nature of the man's job makes it of little interest to the wife. The husband wants some "peace and quiet" upon his return home. Moreover, the unhappy marriages illustrate psychological barriers to sharing—for example, withdrawal as escape or punishment.

The above analysis helps to account for the fuller self-disclosure of the high school graduates. Better education and associated social conditions help to lower a number of the barriers. Role differentiation in marriage is not so sharp among the better-educated as among the less-educated families. The high school fathers are somewhat more active in child care. And there is more discussion of the husband's job: of 18 high schol graduates, 39 per cent and, of 40 less-educated men, only 15 per cent discuss their jobs with their wives "quite a lot." [6] In the former group, an overlap in activities promotes communication by supplying a common content of experience. The high school graduates also exceed the less-educated in the extent of shared leisure-time activities. (See Chapter 14.) Furthermore, the better-educated husbands admit feelings of hurt and describe their personalities in fuller detail than the less-educated men. Economic failure of the husband affects adversely the freedom of communication, and there are more such failures among the less-educated men. (See Chapter 13.) The high school wives have more power in marriage in comparison with the less-educated women. (See Chapter 10.) It is our impression that enjoying this power they are able to control the relationship more effectively and to give expression to their interest in sharing experiences. Finally, the high school graduates have relatively fewer very unhappy marriages in which marital conflict leads to a breakdown of communication. All such circumstances combine to raise the level of self-disclosure to mate among the high school graduates.

It should be stressed, however, that higher education by no means guarantees effective marital communication. To be sure, the marital dialogue of the high school graduates is, on the whole, fuller than that of the less-educated couples, but the overlap between the self-disclosure ratings of the two educational groups is substantial. Some better-educated couples are characterized by moderate or meager self-disclosure for a variety of psychological

[6] Robert O. Blood, Jr., and Donald M. Wolfe, however, found that low blue-collar husbands were more likely than high blue-collar husbands to report happenings on the job to their wives (1960, p. 168).

reasons. Conversely, many less-educated couples enjoy deep and close relationships. Some of the latter are the poorly educated, who, apart from their few years of formal schooling, resemble the high school graduates in their values and mode of life. Some less-educated respondents, for example, expressed "middle-class" values on the projective stories.

More interesting, because more revealing of new insights, are the less-educated couples who enjoy satisfying communication and at the same time hold values and display the mode of life typical of the less-educated in general. We shall examine such a case.

EXISTENCE OF CLOSE, HAPPY MARRIAGES AMONG THE LESS-EDUCATED

Mr. and Mrs. King are both 26, married for eight years and expecting their fourth child. Both had ten years of schooling. They share few general interests and spend much of their leisure separately. They express many working-class norms of marriage. Do cases of this kind imply that social factors are, after all, unimportant—that perhaps "love" does conquer all?

The clue to the paternal role played by Mr. K. in this marital relationship was provided by his wife, who, the youngest of six siblings, found her marital role congenial.

> "He is no older than I am but he sure knows how to handle me if I get a head of steam on," said Mrs. K. "He can steady me sometimes by just looking at me in a very nice way with his real blue eyes." She described an argument about making the boy eat his breakfast. Her husband slammed his hand on the table and told her not to discuss it in front of the children. "That made me mad enough to cry." So she got up and started washing up, slamming dishes and pots around. "Well, he came over and put his arm around me and he made me hold still and just looked at me and he said he had to go out and he hoped I'd be over this when he came back. So then I began to cry and he kissed me a little and left. All of a sudden I started to laugh at myself crying into the dishpan."

The K.'s gave typical working-class responses on the test stories. Their interests are sex-linked, and each (especially the wife) is deeply involved in their respective relationships with same-sex groups.

Both Mr. and Mrs. K. felt that the wife who wanted her husband to give up evenings with his male friends was unreasonable and so was the husband who resented his wife's intimacy with her mother. The husband who comes home and does not talk to his wife should be left in peace by his "selfish" wife.

Apart from their answers to the stories, the couple expressed some attitudes closer to the middle-class pole. "We don't yell and holler at each other the way some folks do," said Mr. K. His wife reprimanded him for saying "This damned fool" in front of the children. Their families sometimes discuss with the pastor the meaning of some biblical injunctions concerning family life. Mr. K.'s standards of personal relationships appear higher than those of some other less-educated husbands. "I understand her because I take the trouble to understand her," he said with a touch of pride.

Mrs. K. is the youngest of six children and Mr. K. has five siblings—the parents of each are living in the same community and none of the siblings is far away. The extraordinary closeness of family and in-law relations is a fact of great significance in the life of this couple. Economically, emotionally, recreationally—their daily lives are interwoven with the lives of their parents and siblings.

Mr. and Mrs. K. described a typical working-class division of interests. They talk little of his job. He discusses politics, sports and hobbies with men because she is not interested in these subjects. Mrs. K. on her side described most eloquently how "women should stick together and men should stay by themselves because they don't understand some things." She is in constant and intimate communication with mother, sisters, sisters-in-law and girl friends. Although she is shy and modest about sex, this subject is also discussed among the girls.

Mrs. K. gives the impression that she is more at ease in her female world. Her great respect for her husband and the desire to please him makes her cautious: "If he is feeling dopey I don't want to talk to him because he might get mad at me and I'd feel terrible."

Many an evening a week, Mr. K. goes out for a walk, to see his brother or to the tavern. He often does not tell his wife where he is going or when he expects to return.

Mr. K. does not help with housework or the care of children. Though sometimes he "sticks around" and wipes the dishes and baby-sits if Mrs. K. has something special she wants to do, the task allocation is traditional. Mr. K. is a devoted father. He can "make them mind him better" than their mother, but child care and discipline is Mrs. K.'s responsibility.

Mr. K. describes the typical male difficulty in expressing unhappy emotions and tends to withdraw when he is depressed. Mrs. K. said that she is not quite sure how her husband overcomes his bad moods: "He never bawls me out and he doesn't talk to me." Perhaps, "when he goes out he talks things over with his brother, I used to ask him why he was 'flippy' but it seemed to make him worse. . . . So I found out if you just don't bother him it wears off."

Mr. K. dislikes his job, despite its adequate pay, but does not reveal the full extent of his unhappiness so as not to worry his wife. He feels depressed at times, does not always understand the reason for these moods, and does not discuss them with his wife. She wishes that he did: "It would make it a lot easier for me if he'd explain why he felt the way he did sometimes when he comes home. I'd know if I had to shut up or if I could go on. This way I keep wondering what's the matter with him."

Despite many features which might be expected to estrange the couple, the marriage is close and deeply satisfying to both.

The personality needs of each are fulfilled at the emotional core of the marriage. Sex relations are satisfactory also.

Mrs. K., as the baby of the family, was always teased affectionately and is still easily hurt. "They sometimes called me a dumb Dora—it's on account of I can't talk sometimes. He bawls me out for minding what the others say and he says I'm not so dumb." Her husband gives her a combination of support, protection and appreciation which makes her say fervently, "Oh, he's the most!" He always compliments her when she cooks an especially good meal. His praise matters, she said, because unlike the in-laws who praise out of politeness, he doesn't say things he doesn't mean. He is the stronger of the two, she tries to please him and he rewards her adequately: "Whenever she's done a good job, I tell her so."

In his interview Mr. K. said:

"I don't know if she'd tell you because she's kind of bashful but she's real good in bed. . . . I think you might call it ideal: a woman who is bashful and keeps to herself with everybody else and who's better than anybody with you." Once in a while she seems not to enjoy it and that sometimes bothers him.

Mr. K. is, in turn, fulfilled in marriage. He had a vulnerable spot of his own. He never cared for school and his brothers used to "ride him about being a dummy." His "wonderful mother" would tell them to lay off him. Now he enjoys the deep respect of his wife—"I am the skipper of this marriage." She often tells him how very patient he is. His wife sums up this aspect of their marriage with deep insight: "He ain't stuck on himself at all. Him and me is a little bit alike that way. We have to tell each other not to mind things and that we're better than we think we are. Only he bawls me out more than I do him because he's a man." And Mr. K.: "When I got something to say she listens. She don't sit there and wish I'd stop or be thinking about something else. Sometimes she'll be talking about the babies that aren't my work, but I listen to her."

Both Mr. and Mrs. K. have patience and capacity to get along with people. Mrs. K. said that both have good dispositions. One of his brothers was teasing them and said, "There goes the patient couple." Mr. K. said in discussing her moods, "She is too nice to get furious, but she gets upset."

To return to the question posed at the outset of this analysis: do occasional marriages like this one indicate that the lower-class norms of marriage—segregation of interests along sex lines, reticence, and separate leisure-time pastimes—do not impair communication after all?

For one thing, a marriage which is so deeply satisfying can apparently affect behavior even in the absence of certain norms. The gratification derived from the relationship leads to mutual concern—"It isn't that I'm that much interested in the neighbors, I am interested in her," explains Mr. K. in describing their conversations. It appears also that the content of shared experiences must be distinguished from the scope of sharing. The sense of closeness is apparently compatible with a very specialized pattern of sharing: *what* specifically is shared may be more important for the feeling of intimacy than *how much* of one's life is shared.

But if "love" does offset the potentially estranging social factors, it isn't love alone that does it. These factors do create typical vulnerabilities. To maintain its happy equilibrium this type of marriage requires some special supports.

The equilibrium of this marriage is maintained by the availability of close relatives and friends who fulfill for both, but especially for the wife, functions lacking in marriage. "No, [Mr. K.] don't give a hoot," said Mrs. K. about many things which are very important to her, and about which no man, she added, could be expected to care. If Mrs. K. were isolated or, like some of the other women in Glenton, not on good terms with her relatives and in-laws, and had to depend upon her husband to be her audience, the marriage probably would be strained. As it is Mr. K. is somewhat irritated by his wife's "gossip." Mr. K., in turn, spends much of his leisure in masculine company and his wife suspects that, in his "flippy moods," his brother is more of a help to him than she is.

Mrs. K.'s deep involvement with her mother and sister is tolerated by her husband partly because he likes his in-laws and they like him. Mr. K. was asked, "Do women have more need than men for heart-to-heart talk?" and he replied, "Well my wife sure in hell does and that's for sure. I could go for a month without talking to anybody but she's gotta talk to them just about every day." It is easy to imagine how this mild irritation would be aggravated were his relations with his in-laws less satisfactory or his position in marriage less secure.

Moreover, satisfactory economic conditions and common economic aspirations add to the assets of the marriage. The K.'s have recently purchased a house with some help from their families, but also as a result of joint planning and effort. "I feel real happy and real proud," said Mrs. K., "I had a lot to do with it, working between having babies and living cheaply and saving up." Their satisfaction in this accomplishment was revealed when in answer to a question, "When did Mr. K. last tell you he loved you?" Mrs. K. replied, "He don't do it regular like a school kid but a couple of nights ago we were watching T.V. and the kids had gone to bed. We were feeling kind of good about the house and he just up and said he loved me."

The case of Mr. and Mrs. K. illustrates how close and satisfying marriage can be despite a very specialized pattern of sharing. Even within the strictly personal sphere (her hurts, enthusiasm and problems) Mrs. K. makes a sharp distinction between what is appropriate to share with her husband, on the one hand, and with her girl friends and female relatives, on the other. Deeply satisfied in their emotional needs, Mr. and Mrs. K. live large segments of their lives apart from one another.

This chapter has specified social and psychological factors that tend to limit the sharing of experiences with the spouse. Being more prevalent among the less-educated than among the high school graduates, many of these factors account for the relatively meager self-disclosure of the poorly educated respondents. The final case study advances the analysis further. The close and happy marriage of the poorly educated Kings reveals some conditions offsetting the estranging factors. Deep psychic congeniality, for instance, can create mutual concern even in the absence of the social norm of companionship. This case demonstrates still another fact—that satisfaction with communication and a sense of closeness do not, apparently, require that the totality of one's experiences be shared with the mate. Such emotions may co-exist with a very specialized pattern of sharing. But we have indicated some other factors as, for example, availability of congenial relatives and friends and satisfactory economic conditions, which, apart from emotional complementarity, support this type of marriage.

CHAPTER
8

Interpersonal Competence[1]

Constant association of married partners does not necessarily ensure deep mutual understanding. As one woman wryly remarked, "You get so you know which way they'll jump, but you don't always know why." Understanding of the mate varies widely from one Glenton respondent to another. "When I was first married," said a 23-year-old motel attendant, "half of the time I didn't know what she was driving at." After three years of marriage this husband has learned that teasing upsets his wife, that finding a bargain gives her a thrill, that she worries about his lack of religion, that she feels especially pleased with herself when she has done a good deed, and so on. But the description he gives of their current relations hardly betokens high empathy:

"It is real funny how hard she takes things. She cries if she thinks I'm wrong and she cries if she thinks she's wrong. Sometimes, I'll come home and I won't know what hit her, I find she's all teary and I'll think hard about what it is and I've even forgotten what she's talking about. So I'll tell her I'm sorry if I made her cry (for whatever it was) and everything

[1] The concept of interpersonal competence was developed by Nelson N. Foote and Leonard S. Cottrell, Jr. (1955). Our classification of component skills, however, is not identical with the one proposed by these authors.

will be all right. It's so easy just to say that. She comes out all smiling. Sometimes I just can't believe it's true."

At the other extreme are persons who appear to understand their mates better than the latter understand themselves. A 39-year-old patternmaker, after 12 years of marriage, interprets, apparently correctly, the motives underlying his wife's "gripes" about money and housework: "She needs a lot of sympathy. We both need it, but she gets it from me more often than I get it from her." It is doubtful whether his wife recognizes so clearly that she needs constant reassurance and that his own desire for support is frustrated by her inability to give it. Similarly, a 40-year-old wife of a sash-fitter sees deeply into the troubled personality of her alcoholic husband. Again, a 28-year-old taxi driver, with nine years of schooling, describes his marriage: "We go to pieces differently. She's like a powerful engine that shakes itself to pieces. I'm likely to run down. I make her calm down and she makes me stick together." A 33-year-old woman heard her husband say to the interviewer, "I don't know how she can stand me because I'm such a cantankerous, crabby man." "Yes," she said, "you get cranky and then you holler at me and you don't feel so good about it afterwards. I think you really feel guilty but you don't know what makes you crabby." These excerpts illustrate individual variations in understanding; we now turn to some general patterns underlying them.

Mutual Understanding

The interview was so planned that every respondent had to speak about his spouse almost as much as about himself. Every person, for example, rated his own and his mate's attitudes to some 50 activities and interests on a threefold scale: "enjoy very much"; "average enjoyment"; "enjoy little, if at all." Moreover, identical questions were addressed to both spouses about sources of happy and unhappy feelings and their typical means of overcoming bad moods; each was asked, "What helps you when you feel low?" and "What helps your husband (or wife) when he (or she) feels low?"

Some sections of the interview provided quantitative ratings of understanding, based upon the degree to which the description given by the mate agreed with the self-portrait. Such quantitative ratings raise a number of problems. Can it be assumed that the self-portrait is the real truth and that a divergence indicates a lack of understanding? Clearly, it is the self-portrait that may occasionally conceal the facts. Moreover, a person may give himself a low rating on empathy because he withholds what he knows about the other out of loyalty. Again, the particular items entering into such a rating vary in their significance. Not every "correct" description of the mate is equally indicative of understanding. By giving only superficial answers a couple can spuriously earn a high rating. For example, the wife and the husband may both state that the children are at times a source of irritation to the wife, but such an agreement does not necessarily betoken high empathy on the husband's part. Contrast this with another husband's awareness that his wife worries (though she tries to conceal it from him) about her rejection of one of their children. It would be misleading to use the total proportion of correct answers as an index of understanding without a system of weighing the significance of component items.

To offset these dangers several approaches were used and compared. We put the most trust, however, in a qualitative assessment of each person based upon all the interviews with a given family. These assessments could weigh the probability that loyalty to the mate, rather than ignorance, dictated a particular answer or that the self-portrait concealed an unflattering characteristic. The results of such assessments are presented first.[2]

Using the threefold ratings of "high," "moderate" and "low" understanding, we find that the 116 respondents fall into three nearly equal groups, 32 per cent with "high," 31 per cent with "moderate" and 30 per cent with only "low" understanding of their mates. The evidence was inconclusive in the case of 9 persons, 7 per cent of the total. It will presently become evident that it is the less-educated couples who contribute largely to this picture of little mutual understanding.

Educational Level and Sex in Relation to Understanding

The male high school graduate knows more of what goes on in his wife's world than does the less-educated husband. Only 17 per cent of the educated husbands rate "low" on understanding,

---

[2] We do not have any measure of the reliability of these assessments similar to the test of coding reliability for ratings of self-disclosure.

as compared with 40 per cent of the less-educated (see Table 13). At the other extreme, 50 per cent of the high school graduates and only 20 per cent of the less-educated receive the rating of "high" empathy. Educational level makes less difference in the case of the women. The better-educated wives have fewer "lows," but the two categories of women do not differ in the relative frequency of "high" ratings. Thus, the difference between the sexes proves greater among the less-educated couples, the wives surpassing their husbands. Among the high school graduates, on the other hand, women lose their superiority in understanding.

The quantitative indices of understanding in general confirm the results of the qualitative assessments. The high school men describe more accurately their wives' attitudes toward a variety of leisure time interests than do the less-educated husbands. Of 260 ratings made by the high school men, 60 per cent are identical with the self-ratings supplied independently by their wives. But the less-educated give fewer "correct" answers—only 57 per cent of their 504 ratings are identical with self-descriptions of their wives.

The less-educated wives again score higher than their husbands. They rate "correctly" their husbands' attitudes in 61 per cent of total ratings; but the husbands, rating their wives, do as well in only 57 per cent of the total. Among high school graduates the proportion of "correct" answers is nearly identical for both sexes: 60 per cent of the ratings of their wives' interests given by the men, and 61 per cent of the ratings of their husbands' interests supplied by the women.

Again, the educational level makes less difference in the empathy of women than of men. In fact, in regard to the rating of their husbands' interests, the less-educated wives do quite as well as the high school graduates. Of 785 ratings given by women, 61 per cent are "correct," and the proportions of correct answers are identical for women in both educational categories.

To recapitulate, the qualitative assessments and the quantitative ratings of understanding agree with respect to the influence of education and sex upon the degree of understanding of the mate. In the case of the men, understanding increases with education, but for the women education brings no such improvement. Wives show superior understanding only among the less-educated

—the high school husband is no less understanding than his wife.

The first discrepancy between the qualitative assessments and quantitative ratings occurs with regard to another index of understanding. The latter consisted in describing "correctly" the means employed by the spouse to overcome bad moods. The "correct" answer is again defined as agreement with the mate's self-description.

The wives, as will be shown, quite accurately describe their own role in the mental well-being of their husbands, whereas the latter overestimate their importance in the emotional sustenance of their wives and correspondingly underestimate the importance of other personal and impersonal aids. This occurs on each educational level: the high school men exaggerate their role as much as do the less-educated husbands.

The women quite accurately perceive not only their own role but the nature of all the other means of emotional relief employed by their husbands. Of the aids enumerated by the less-educated husbands in describing themselves, "my wife" constitutes 15 per cent of the total. Their wives, speaking of their husbands, give an identical weight to their role. "I help him" constitutes 15 per cent of all the aids they list for their husbands. The high school women do equally well. Their estimate of their relative role is nearly identical with the self-description of their husbands, 25 per cent and 24 per cent, respectively.

The husbands, however, are far off the mark when they describe how their wives overcome bad moods. "I help her" constitutes 47 per cent of all the aids listed by the less-educated husbands in describing their wives. But the wives, describing themselves, indicate a great variety of aids—and "my husband" amounts to only 24 per cent of their total. The high school men claim that their own aid constitutes 42 per cent of the aids, whereas their wives give their husbands credit for only 23 per cent of the various means they (the women) employ to restore emotional balance.

We considered the possibility that a sense of chivalry caused the husbands to appear ignorant of their wives' mental health. They might have been reluctant to say that "hollering," drinking and breaking things help their wives, whereas women may have felt freer to report such outlets for their husbands. But other activities carrying no such derogatory connotations are equally underrepresented in the descriptions men give of their wives.

Moreover, another measure, free of possible effects of chivalry, yields identical results. This is the frequency with which the members of a given group mention the mate (number of times mate is mentioned per number of persons in the group). Again, women come close to the truth, while the men exaggerate their own helpfulness.

In contrast with the other tests of understanding, this last test does not indicate any superiority of the educated husband over the less-educated man. The former is more likely to feel that emotional therapy is part of the husband's duty. Does this norm color his self-perception and obliterate his superior empathy? But this norm, shared by the high school wife, does not cause her to exaggerate her own service to her husband. Whatever her wish to live up to the ideal, she is quite realistic in assessing her actual role.

The husbands, regardless of their education, exhibit a similar bias in another respect. They underestimate their own contribution to the unhappy moods of their wives. The women, asked to describe the occasions for irritation, depression, anger and other "bad" moods, name their husbands among other causes. The frequency (number of times husbands are mentioned per number of women in the group) is higher than that with which the husbands report themselves as sources of their wives' bad moods (see Tables 14a and 14b). The husbands do not similarly underestimate the extent to which relatives and children contribute to the unhappiness of their wives. They describe their wives' relationships with others more accurately than they do the interaction in marriage.

As for the women, they hold themselves responsible for the "bad" moods of their husbands *more* frequently than the husbands are willing to implicate them. If both sexes err, they err in different directions: the husbands understate their role in causing their mate's unhappiness, and the wives exaggerate it. The explanation may lie in the greater willingness on the part of the women to admit to the interviewers, and possibly even to themselves, the stressful aspects of marriage.

The empathic ability. Are women more "intuitive" than men? Does education enhance empathy? The measures of understanding employed so far do not purport to describe empathic ability as such. In order to arrive at a somewhat more precise test of empathy, we considered the degree of understanding exhibited by the respondents in relation to the difficulty of the task which confronted them, that is, the degree of their mates' self-disclosure. It does not require high empathy to fathom a simple person who freely reveals his feelings. A person's insight is all the keener if he penetrates his mate's reserve, and all the more deficient if his understanding is shallow despite the other's expressiveness.

Having considered understanding in relation to the mate's self-disclosure, it becomes evident that most of the group differences in understanding can be explained by variations in self-disclosure. The educated couples know more about each other because they tell each other more than do the less-educated husbands and wives. Confronted with a reticent mate, the high school graduate does not penetrate reserve any better than does the less-educated person (see Table 15). The one remaining difference is the inferiority of the less-educated husband in comparison with his wife. The latter is more likely to understand her husband if he is reticent than he is to understand her in a similar situation. Moreover, a greater proportion of less-educated husbands than of wives show little understanding even when married to outspoken persons.

The explanation of this sex difference may lie in the relative lack of concern on the part of the less-educated husband. His greater power in marriage means that he need not scrutinize his wife's motives. He can assert his will—while she needs to "handle" him. If he does not like her mood, he's freer to leave the "field," while she has to adjust herself to his behavior. "If something is bothering her," remarked one husband, "I tell her sometimes I have to do something outside and I go out, walk around and maybe drop in at the tavern for a beer and then come back."

Such lack of interest may fully explain the husband's relatively low empathy. But he may also be less attuned to psychological facts. His inarticulateness about his own feelings may blur his understanding of others. It is through personal interchange that feelings are distinguished and related to their manifestations in gestures and behavior. In contrast to their husbands, whose manual jobs provide only limited opportunities for social contacts, the less-educated women are daily exchanging experiences with others.[3]

The high school woman, on the other hand, does not prove

[3] For a report of a positive association between self-insight and empathy, see Rosalind F. Dymond, 1948.

superior in empathy to her husband. He matches her insight. He is more involved in the marriage relationship than the less-educated husband and he wields relatively less power. He consequently has a greater need to understand his wife. Whether or not his higher education further enhances his psychological skills is an open question. Higher education of the female high school graduates does not improve their empathy in comparison with the less-educated women.

Except for the less-educated couples, this study does not support the stereotype of superior feminine insight. This is all the more surprising because women's social roles are said to require a special sensitivity to personal relationships. Had the wives been found to be consistently superior in empathy to their husbands, the explanation would have been ready at hand. Three other investigations failed to reveal sex differences in empathy. One contrary finding is not comparable because it pertains not to the mutual empathy of men and women but to male and female understanding of relatives.[4]

Neither the present, nor one previous, study shows any consistent effect of education upon empathy.[5] This is contrary to expectations because, for one thing, the more highly educated respondents have been shown to be more introspective and self-probing than the less-educated.[6] Such self-awareness should augment the capacity to understand others. Exposure to differences should similarly increase empathy, and the better-educated are more likely to enjoy a greater diversity of experiences through reading and personal encounters.

The largely negative findings concerning educational and sex differences in empathic ability are far from conclusive because too little is known about empathy to permit rigorous comparisons. Is empathy a highly generalized trait or does it vary with the nature of the relationship and spheres of interaction? Some individuals may be perceptive in relation to their superiors but not to their subordinates. Some may be quicker to gauge new acquaintances, but less profound in understanding old friends. Others may possess the opposite trait. The similarity between

---

[4] See Clifford Kirkpatrick and Charles W. Hobart, 1954; Charles W. Hobart, 1956; Sheldon Stryker, 1962. Unlike the above studies of American samples, Reuben Hill *et al.*, 1959, investigated the Puerto Rican family.

[5] No consistent differences in role-taking accuracy by educational levels was found by Sheldon Stryker, 1962, p. 56.

[6] See Gerald Gurin *et al.*, 1960, pp. 80-81.

people probably facilitates understanding, but some persons may be more imaginative than others in dealing with diverse types. Even those high in empathy may have their characteristic blind spots. This complexity makes it difficult at present to isolate the association between empathic ability and some single characteristic of the individual, such as his sex or education.

Emotional Support

The ability to give and to receive emotional support is, like empathy, a component of interpersonal competence. Numerous students have referred to emotional sustenance as one of the primary functions of modern marriage. Glenton data show the extent to which marriage has fulfilled this function for the 116 interviewed individuals.

The main evidence concerning the mate's role in providing emotional support is contained in the responses to the question, "What helps you when you feel bad, unhappy or worried about something, or generally low?" This question was asked after the discussion of sources of happy and unhappy feelings. Unhappy moods are not, of course, all of a kind, but no attempt was made to distinguish worry, depression, irritation or anger.[7]

Members of the whole group list 278 "aids" in overcoming unhappy moods, including such passive reactions as "time," "I try to forget it," "sleep it off." The role of the married partner in providing emotional support is measured by the frequency with which he or she is mentioned among the other aids.

As Table C indicates, for the group as a whole, the married partner emerges as the most important single person who dispels unhappy moods, being mentioned more frequently than parent, sibling, friend, child, minister or others. But as many as 44 per cent of the group do not mention the mate at all—they list either other persons or impersonal aids, such as exercise, drinking, shopping, crying and other activities. The relative importance of the spouse may be gauged in still another way: "my husband" (or "my wife") constitutes only 22 per cent of all the different forms of aids which are mentioned by the group as a whole.[8]

[7] Gerald Gurin *et al.*, 1960, found some differences in the typical modes of coping with "worries" as against "periods of unhappiness." (See pp. 364-381.)

[8] Whenever the mate was not spontaneously mentioned, the interviewer asked: "What about your husband (wife)? Does he (she) ever help, and how?" The affirmative answers to these follow-up questions were included

TABLE C

"WHAT HELPS YOU IN BAD MOODS?"

*(specified aid, as per cent of total aids,
by education and sex of respondent)*

	Wives' Education		Husbands' Education	
Aids	Under 12 Years (n = 94)	High School (n = 63)	Under 12 Years (n = 77)	High School (n = 44)
Husband or wife	23	25	12	30
Child	3	5	1	7
Friend	5	11	13	7
Mother	4	6	—	2
Father	—	—	1	2
Sister	3	8	—	—
Brother	—	—	—	3
Relatives	1	—	—	—
In-laws	—	3	—	2
Other persons	3	—	1	—
Total interpersonal	42	58	28	53
Walk out	4	—	4	5
Drink	3	—	10	2
"Holler," curse	4	—	3	2
Hit	—	—	—	2
Break	3	—	—	5
Cry	4	—	—	—
Shopping	1	2	—	—
Church	1	—	—	—
Activity	29	24	35	18
Time, nothing	8	16	18	14
Don't know	1	—	2	—
Grand total	100	100	100	99

The emotional relief given by the mate took many forms. Some examples are given in the following comments: "He is especially tender and yet he leaves me alone and doesn't bother

in the totals. Some persons explained that they hadn't mentioned their spouses because they took their help for granted.

me when I am blue"; "He boxes with me"; "He brings me a gift"; "Going to bed with my wife"; "Talking it over with my wife (or husband) and getting it off my chest"; "He just holds me in his arms without saying much and that makes me feel a lot better"; "Going out to a movie with my wife (or husband)." Since in some cases the activity may have been as important as the companionship of the spouse, our index may overestimate the role of the latter.

In explaining why the mate offers little help in stressful moods, some blame themselves, recognizing their deep-rooted problems, such as "How can I expect her to understand when even I don't know what's eating me?" But the mate frequently offers no relief in even the more ordinary problems. For example, "When something makes me angry he doesn't help because he doesn't usually think it is important"; "He doesn't help because he thinks there must be a reason for everything"; and "I tell her to simmer down, and it only makes her boil up harder." If there is no emotional identification with the mate, the phrase "Don't worry" or "Simmer down" is merely another way of saying "Stop this nuisance." Contrast this empty gesture with the succor given his wife by one less-educated man: "When my sister was being so snotty to me," reported this woman, "Jim came in and said 'Gee, kid, this really got you deep and for real this time.' I'll never forget the way he walked across the room and put his arms around me and sort of rocked me like a baby."

The wider the gulf—segregation of roles, disparity of interests—between the sexes, the more difficult it is to empathize with the daily frustrations of the other. "It would take someone working alongside of me to understand what I am up against in my job," says the husband, and the wife knows that another *woman* would not consider her daily frustrations trivial.

The wife plays a smaller role in the emotional sustenance of the less-educated man than of the high school graduate. "My wife" constitutes only 12 per cent of the total aids listed by the former, but 30 per cent of the aids reported by the high school men.

The less-educated man does not find emotional relief in marriage for the same reason that he does not find it in social interaction in general. Aids involving social interaction constitute only 28 per cent of his total aids, while for the better-educated husband the figure is 53 per cent of the total. The contrast can be illustrated by citing the following two cases. A 27-year-old truck driver, in answer to the question as to what helps him in a bad mood, said, "To talk about it. When we were first married, we made it a point if anything was wrong, to bring it out into the open and talk it over." Asked, "Do wives have a greater need than husbands for intimate talk?" he replied, "They both need it, this is one of the purposes of marriage. They need each other physically and mentally." On the other hand, a 23-year-old garbage collector overcomes bad moods by "trying to get action of some kind, sweating it out. I don't feel like talking when I am mad. . . . I'll hit the wall real hard and it makes me feel a lot better." Another husband explained that when he "got bottled up," he would go in for "bowling or anything that would get me into a sweat. When I'm just out of sorts and kind of grouchy, the best thing I can do is work with my hands around the house." Going to ball games, watching T.V. and drinking are some of the other aids mentioned by the husbands.

The tendency to find relief in physical activities rather than in social interaction fails to explain, however, another fact about the less-educated husbands. They present the only exception to the earlier generalization about the mate's primacy over other persons in providing relief. For the less-educated husband, friends are as important as his wife; friends constitute 13 per cent and "my wife" 12 per cent of all the aids. The comparable percentages for the high school men are 7 per cent for friends and 30 per cent for wives. The friends assume so important a role partly because the less-educated men spend relatively more of their leisure with friends and partly because the proportion of unhappy marriages is larger among them than among the better-educated husbands. As one wife reported in a matter-of-fact way, "After that quarrel, he was away from home a lot with the fellows to work it out of his system."

Level of education does not affect the therapeutic pattern of the wives as much as it does that of the men. True, the female high school graduates also tend to find more relief in social interaction—impersonal sources of aid comprise only 42 per cent of all their aids as compared with 58 per cent for the less-educated women. But for both groups of women the help rendered by the husband comprises about one-fourth of all the reported sources of aid.

The extent to which the wife receives emotional support from her husband depends more upon his education than upon her own. Perhaps all women are ready to use the support, regardless of their education, but the educated husbands are more likely to offer aid. Seventy-seven per cent of the women married to high school graduates, but only 55 per cent of the wives of the less-educated men, include "my husband" among the aids.[9] The less-educated husbands, who do not find emotional relief in social interaction, are less able to avail themselves of the therapeutic function of marriage and to fulfill it for their wives.

The aid given by the spouse in the handling of stress has been studied in two other investigations, but differences in method restrict possible comparisons. The different phrasing of the questions apparently yields widely differing results as to the *overall* frequencies of resorting to spouses.[10] On the other hand, *differences* by sex and education reported by the three studies lend themselves to more valid comparisons. One investigation, in agreement with our findings, reports that less-educated wives are more likely than the educated to say that it would not help to tell their troubles to their husbands. The same study concludes that wives of white-collar workers, as a whole, have a slightly higher tendency to resort to their husbands in periods of stress than the wives of blue-collar workers (though within these broad occupational categories the relationship is erratic).[11]

The one sharp disagreement in findings pertains to a sex difference in passive or active coping reactions to worries. In one national sample of respondents, women were found to be more passive than men, and the authors explained this by the general passivity of the feminine role.[12] But among less-educated persons in Glenton, it is the husbands more frequently who report "time" and "nothing," while women are more likely to seek help from associates. Glenton's male and female high school graduates are

[9] This result was not controlled for the duration of marriage.

[10] Robert O. Blood, Jr., and Donald M. Wolfe (1960, p. 185) addressed the following question to the wives: "After you've had a bad day, what do you do to get it out of your system?" A longer question was presented to both men and women in a nation-wide sample studied by Gerald Gurin *et al.* (1960, p. 364): "If something is on your mind that's bothering you or worrying you and you don't know what to do about it, what do you usually do? . . . Do you ever talk it over with anyone?" Gurin distinguished between worries and periods of unhappiness.

[11] Robert O. Blood and Donald M. Wolfe, 1960, p. 201.

[12] Gerald Gurin *et al.*, 1960, p. 370.

alike in the relative frequency of passive as against active reactions to stress. Perhaps college graduates, included in the nation-wide study, account for the divergence in the results. Whatever the cause, the less-educated men in Glenton, in contrast to men in the cited study, are more likely than their wives to "do nothing" in periods of stress.

Coping with Conflicts

Willard Waller and Reuben Hill once noted that not all marital quarrels are destructive—that some can actually strengthen the relationship.[13] They referred not merely to their function of "blowing off steam," a function of a quarrel widely recognized by Glenton families. A productive quarrel, they maintained, can do more: it can clarify motivations and help redefine the relationship in a more satisfactory fashion.

Many quarrels described by the respondents do not appear to harm the marriages. Some happily married couples relish a high-spirited contest of wills in frequent arguments. Others engage in provocative teasing which creates pleasurable tension and relieves boredom. Almost no happy couples are free of occasional "hot little flare-ups" in which irritations are expressed. But, to anticipate our conclusions, some typical reactions to conflict could scarcely do anything but aggravate it. What is more, these defective techniques are not merely idiosyncratic but are consequences of patterns of communication previously discussed.

Attitudes expressed by our respondents towards various modes of conflict will be set forth prior to describing their actual behavior. The attitude towards physical aggression ranges from tolerance—"He socked me a couple of times when he was drunk but it's nothing like some around here"—to so severe a sanction against it that respondents do not even mention the possibility of it. Between the two extremes are the husbands who claim credit for "never laying a hand" on their wives. One wife, for example, said that her husband "raised his arm a couple of times" but never struck her. This self-restraint earns no special gratitude from many educated wives who take it for granted. Physical aggression is more frequent among the less-educated (see Table 16).

Although some reiterate that "talking don't do no good" and "if they'd just keep their mouths shut, everybody would be much

---

[13] Willard Waller and Reuben Hill, 1951, pp. 309-312.

better off," the majority uphold the ideal that, in case of conflict, husbands and wives should talk things over. But this norm does not always carry the meaning that it has for the educated middle classes—a fact which illustrates that social classes may attach different meanings to what superficially appears to be a common cultural norm. The value of talking, as these families see it, lies almost exclusively in the catharsis it provides. It helps to "let off steam," to "get things off your chest," as contrasted with keeping feelings bottled up, walking out of the house or sulking. Only rarely do the less-educated point out, as does one husband, that talking can increase understanding, reveal motives and correct misperceptions: "I feel a lot better if I understand [what the trouble is]. When I'm working in the dark, it's likely to make me more jittery."

The reports of marital conversations suggest that there is little mutual probing of motives, labeling of feelings and self-explanation of the kind familiar in highly-educated circles: "Were you disappointed or a little relieved?" or "Did you feel angry or hurt?" or "No, that is not why I did it, the reason was . . ." and the like. We have the impression, supported by reactions to our questions on moods, that not only the male respondents but some women too have a low tolerance for such probing of motives.

The moralistic framework observed in parent-child interaction is also apparent in marriage. One husband, upset by his wife's drinking, expressed his disapproval: "It doesn't look good with the children"; "I can't kiss you when you smell of liquor"; and "If you don't look out, you'll become a drunk like your uncle." But neither he, nor his wife, in reporting their conversations, described any attempt to discover the reasons for her increased drinking. If the "why" of behavior is not explored it is not for lack of concern. Ignorance of psychological dynamics stops such speculation short. Explanations fall back upon moral weakness, inherited traits or individual idiosyncracy. "I shall never understand why she buys things the children don't even need," puzzles the husband of an extravagant woman unable to reach any other conclusion than "I guess that's the way she is." (See similar limitations in the attempts to interpret the behavior of children, pp. 78-79.)

Mutual dissatisfactions are discussed in terms of the "right and the wrong of it" rather than in terms of meanings for the individual. One husband is often late for meals on week ends, infuriating his wife. Since his irregular schedule often makes him late on weekdays, and she accepts it, he cannot understand why she makes "such a fuss" on week ends. The quarrels over this issue, reported separately by the husband and the wife, contain references to their respective rights, not to what the issue might mean to each.

The maxim "Don't go to sleep on a quarrel" was repeated by several young wives who pride themselves upon following this rule even if, as was noted, only ritualistically, "We kiss before we go to sleep even when we are still mad at each other."

The manner of dealing with conflicts was described in answer to the question about "your last spat or quarrel." Each respondent was asked to describe in detail the last quarrel, as well as his or her manner of quarreling in general and this was followed by questions as to who made the first move at reconciliation. The dominant reactions to conflict were then classified. Conflict took a variety of forms: "hot little flare-ups"; explosive and prolonged quarrels with cursing or yelling; violence, including striking or throwing things at each other, or breaking and hitting objects; provoking or baiting each other; crying, not talking, walking out of the house or isolating oneself in a room; talking it out, using arguments to persuade the other; repressing irritations but using children as scapegoats; getting drunk; manipulating by means of deceit or blackmail; and others. (See Table 16 for the results by sex and education of respondent.)

SEX DIFFERENCES IN COPING WITH CONFLICTS

Confronted with a marriage conflict, a greater proportion of the husbands than of the wives withdraw, either physically or psychologically, by such means as walking out of the house ("I say what I have to say and then I go zoom out of the house") or by silence ("I don't pay any attention until she cools off"). Forty-three per cent of the husbands, but only 24 per cent of the wives, exhibit some type of withdrawal in relation to conflict. A reaction was termed a withdrawal only when it was more prolonged than the coolness frequently following any quarrel.

The withdrawal on the part of the husbands is of several kinds. Lack of concern causes some men to shut out the "hollering" of their wives. But other men "clam up" because they are too emotionally involved and unable to express their feelings or otherwise cope with the conflict. "Keeping calm" may also be a deliberate weapon: "I have no one to argue with," wailed a young wife, "it only makes me madder that he doesn't argue back, if he did I could work up a good sweat and feel better." Her husband confirmed her description: "I put on the silent treatment. She does all the yelling." "He doesn't argue like a man," complained another wife, "he goes out of the house."

Most of the withdrawal reactions involve a cessation of interaction during or after quarrels. But also included in this category was suppression of dissatisfactions to avoid quarrels—"I keep my mouth shut so as not to start a fire." In some cases the withdrawal is the sole typical reaction to conflict; in others it coexists with violent outbursts or other behavior. In some cases it is selective, by avoidance of a sore subject, and at other times it spreads over many areas of the relationship.

The wives, fewer in number, who react to conflict by withdrawing also vary in their motivations. Some turn sullen ("I learned to keep my mouth shut") in reaction to their husbands' indifference. Others repress dissatisfactions because they "don't want to start trouble," being married to men with violent tempers, or feeling particularly threatened by conflict. And stronger personalities use withdrawal as punishment. Fewer women than men walk out of the house—instead, they stop talking. A 38-year-old man with six years of schooling who in general admires his wife explained: "We don't exactly quarrel but sometimes, I have to work hard to get her to start talking again. Sometimes it is almost like I have to ask her to marry me all over again, it is as if we was courtin'." Another bitter and unhappy wife said, "I slam around the house. When I get real mad I just won't talk, sometimes I won't talk for days. I won't say a word. They [husband and daughter] feel it after a while. I have one kind of mad and I holler at them; then the other times I keep quiet. I think that that's the worse time."

The greater tendency of the husbands to withdraw in the face of conflict and of the wives to argue, "holler" and cry is consistent with the descriptions of sex differences in communication presented in previous chapters.

EDUCATIONAL DIFFERENCES IN COPING WITH CONFLICTS

The most frequent behavior of the less-educated husband in coping with conflicts is repression and withdrawal, interspersed with violent quarreling. Wife beating is infrequent but it occurs oftener than among the high school graduates. A typical sequence was described: "You don't know quite what you feel, you're just sore and mad so you don't say nothing and it gets worse, after a while you blow up." One woman remarked in the presence of her husband that she sometimes wondered what went on in his mind when he was "real quiet." He said: "Well, I'm just boiling and boiling and I have to work up to a point before I explode and that's it."

The high school husbands quarrel less violently, and fewer get drunk after a fight. "Talking out" of differences is more frequent than among the less-educated—it is reported by 33 per cent of the high school husbands, but by only 12 per cent of the less-educated men. On the other hand, violent quarrels, at times accompanied by beatings, are mentioned by 17 per cent of the high school men and by 27 per cent of the less-educated.

Withdrawal, however, is just as frequent on the part of the male high school graduates as among the less-educated men; the former also tend to avoid sore subjects and withdraw in the face of demands they cannot meet. Occasionally they also walk out after a quarrel. But the case analyses disclosed only one high school marriage in which the breakdown of communication was as extreme as in the worst 10 per cent of the less-educated couples. Moreover, contemptuous dismissal of the wife, noted on the part of some less-educated husbands, was less frequent among the high school graduates.

Level of education affects women's reactions to conflicts as it affects those of the men. Violence decreases and "talking out" increases in frequency as the level of education goes up. The high school wives tend to withdraw somewhat less frequently, but the difference between them and the less-educated women in this respect is very slight.

The function of a quarrel cannot be judged by its overt form. Cruel words can be spoken softly and a slap on the face in at least one quarrel led to sexual satisfaction: "He took me kind of rough that time, I liked it," remarked one wife. The same act may carry different meanings. The wife, for example, may be the one who generally makes the first conciliatory move after a quarrel because she is the weaker of the two or because she is less involved. Loud voices are not to be equated with destructive quarrels. But it is difficult to escape the conclusion that the techniques employed by the less-educated husbands (withdrawal, getting drunk and explosive quarrels) are unproductive. At best these techniques allow a periodic release of irritations and at worst they lead to progressive alienation of the kind illustrated on pages 138-140. The greater frequency of talking over disagreements on the part of the high school graduates provides at least an opportunity (ruled out by withdrawal) to clarify motivations and to redefine the relationship. It is no accident that the most completely estranged are the less-educated couples. Whatever else brought about the atrophy of their marriages, their defective techniques of coping with conflicts must have contributed to the outcome.

The defective techniques of the less-educated husband might have been predicted from the earlier discoveries about him. His difficulty in expressing his feelings, his relatively low empathy, the relative absence of the norm of sharing, the identification of emotional self-expression with weakness and femininity—all these play a part in his approach to marriage problems.

Dissatisfactions with Communication

The dissatisfactions about to be described are those voiced by the couples. These expressions of discontent were not always given in response to direct questions. The interview included a series of direct questions, such as "Is your husband (wife) an easy or a hard person to talk to? Why?"; "How often do you find his (her) behavior puzzling?"; "Do you think it is generally hard for a woman to understand a man? for a man to understand a woman?"; "Would you wish that you could talk more about some things to your husband (wife)? Why don't you?"; and "Do you think that women in general have more need for heart-to-heart talk than do men?" [14]

These direct questions tended to evoke clichés about differences between the sexes. Moreover, they called for an evaluation of a relationship, which is no easy task for anyone. The tend-

[14] The author is indebted to Mark Flapan for permission to use these questions from his unpublished manuscript.

ency of the less-educated persons to miss the more subtle grada-
tions led many, no doubt, to interpret the questions too simply. "Is
your husband (wife) a hard or an easy person to talk to?" appeared to be interpreted as a choice between two extreme alternatives: a husband with whom it is quite impossible to talk and one
with whom some communication is possible. Unless a respondent
was deeply dissatisfied he tended to choose the second alternative
without registering qualifications. These direct questions turned
out to be occasionally misleading because the frame of reference
of the respondent could not always be made explicit. "Sure, I can
talk to my husband about anything," one wife stated, who had
previously told the interviewer how uninterested her husband was
in shopping and interior decoration. When confronted with this
discrepancy, she exclaimed, "But I don't even try to bring up these
subjects."

Our respondents expressed their dissatisfactions more fully in
other sections of the interview when they explained, for example,
why some experiences were not shared with the mate. The two
test stories dealing with communication also elicited personal
grievances. Finally, the ratings of qualities deemed important in
a mate, when compared with the ratings given to their own
spouses, supplied another clue to dissatisfactions.

Answers to direct questions on dissatisfactions, as well as all
other available data, were assessed to decide what, if any, dissatisfaction existed in a given case. When the whole interview is thus
used as a basis for judgment, very few of the marriages turn out
to be completely free of grievances—90 per cent of the wives and
80 per cent of the husbands reported some dissatisfaction with
communication. Table D presents the major themes of dissatisfaction: boredom, overall meagerness of communication, mutual
misunderstandings and the mate's indiscretions.

The expressed dissatisfactions probably understate the extent
of experienced deprivations, and not solely because of possible
concealment. The expression of a complaint requires some degree of introspection, a conception of a possible alternative and,
perhaps, a disappointment of expectations. And, as we shall see,
a person may experience a vague sense of unhappiness without
being able to give it explicit expression.

The wives express greater discontent than the husbands. The
findings on dissatisfactions with communication add up to one

TABLE D
DISSATISFACTIONS WITH COMMUNICATION

(Per Cent of Husbands and Wives
with Specified Complaints)

Complaints	Husbands (*n*=58)	Wives (*n*=58)
BOREDOM—Mate often talks about boring things	21	34
INDISCRETION—Mate often talks about personal matters to others	21	7
MISUNDERSTANDING*—Mate's behavior often puzzling	34	33
Mate "doesn't understand me"	17	24
MEAGERNESS OF COMMUNICATION		
Mate doesn't listen	15	40
Mate doesn't reveal worries	9	26
"We have nothing to talk about"	7	10
Mate doesn't talk enough in general	7	20
Mate "criticizes me about not talking enough"	14	—

* Two dissatisfactions, that the mate's behavior is often puzzling, and that the mate "doesn't understand me" turn out, strictly speaking, to apply not to communication but to disagreements in general. When these statements were pursued further, the illustrations were "I can't understand why she buys things the kids don't even need" and "Yes, he puzzles me because he is late to dinner on Saturdays."

major result: the women are by far the more dissatisfied sex and what they want is more interaction. They certainly want their husbands to be better listeners, 40 per cent of the wives but only 15 per cent of the husbands registering the complaint that the mate does not listen and does not say the helpful thing when concerns are shared. These complaints varied in intensity from moderate to bitter and appeared to express many different yearnings, such as just for sharing for its own sake, or for reassurance, counsel, appreciation and encouragement.

The wives are also prepared to listen, 26 per cent of the wives and only 9 per cent of the husbands complaining that their mates do not reveal worries. To be sure, the motivation back of this complaint may not always be altruistic. "Is anything wrong?" or "What is eating you?" is asked when the other is "glum," withdrawn or unusually irritable, and it is asked not only to proffer sympathy but with the hope of improving his disposition. The wish for more interchange is seen in still another grievance. Only 7 per cent of the husbands, but 20 per cent of the wives, complain that their mates do not talk enough. Indeed for 14 per cent of the husbands the problem lies precisely in their wives' "nagging because I don't talk to her enough." Women, however, want not only more conversation but more satisfying conversation, 34 per cent of them complaining that their husbands talk too much about boring things.

These findings are consistent with data cited in Chapter 6 about incomplete self-disclosure. Women attribute their reserve to their husbands' indifference or unsatisfactory reaction, but men do not equally blame their wives for their own failure to disclose feelings.[15]

Women are said to be the "passive" sex. In this area, however, it is the women who nag, demand and complain, and the husbands' action is largely a *reaction* to women's demands, and one which often takes the form of leaving the field of battle.

The tendency of women to express more dissatisfaction with marriage has been noted in a number of studies. The tendency apparently runs through various social classes. In a recent survey women were found to be not only more dissatisfied, but to blame their husbands for marital unhappiness more often than the husbands blamed their wives. The authors suggest that the failures in the more active male role may be "more easily pinpointed than failures in the female's more passive and supportive role." [16] As the following pages will demonstrate, no single explanation does justice to this problem.

The attempt to account for the greater discontent of the Glenton wives in comparison with their husbands began with a plausible hypothesis which was, however, eventually discarded. The alleged isolation of the wives during the day was thought to be the cause of their greater yearning for interaction with their husbands. But this assumption of isolation must be challenged. Truck drivers, steeplejacks and some factory operatives have little social life on the job. A few of the housewives are indeed

---

[15] Indifference or unsatisfactory reaction of the mate constituted 43 per cent of 256 reasons for instances of reserve cited by the wives, but only 29 per cent of the 168 reasons listed by the husbands.

[16] Gerald Gurin *et al.*, 1960, pp. 115-116.

very lonely during the day and all are isolated on rainy days (with an occasional telephone conversation as their only contact with an adult), but many women do enjoy daily meetings with friends, neighbors, and relatives. More women than men have confidants. (See Chapter 9.) It is far from certain, then, that women as a rule are more deprived of social life and therefore more in need of evening companionship.

A second possibility is that the men were simply more reticent with women interviewers and did not admit their dissatisfactions. The extent of error caused by such possible reserve is not known but, in any event, there exist, we believe, other reasons for the greater discontent among the wives.

Men express fewer complaints because, in the first place, the *accepted beliefs about feminine personality lead men to take certain deprivations for granted.* The wives are occasionally protected from criticism by virtue of the very contempt which men feel for certain characteristics of the feminine mind. The husbands who wish they could share their interests in sports, cars, their jobs or politics with someone do not expect that someone to be a woman. The inability of women to share these interests is so fully accepted that it does not disappoint expectations and does not arouse indignation. If men experience such deprivations they are more likely to say, "I don't have any buddies in the neighborhood" than "My wife doesn't listen to my interests." Forty-three percent of the husbands declared that the job was one area of incomplete communication with the wife, but only 14 per cent complained that she "doesn't listen enough" to daily concerns. The wife, on the other hand, feels that there is nothing technical about *her* concerns "if he'd only pay attention, he'd understand."

Secondly, *the husband's admitted difficulty in expressing emotions deflects the blame from his wife to himself.* Among the reasons given by the husbands for incomplete self-disclosure, "hard to talk about such things" was the second most frequently mentioned, but for the wives it was only the sixth in the order of frequency. Recognition by the men that their own reserve curtails communication serves to curb criticism of their wives.

Thirdly, *the ideal of masculinity tends to inhibit the direct expression of certain grievances.* The norm "Don't dump your load on the family" and the belief that the experience of hurt is unmanly restrain the less-educated men from a direct plea for solace. Women feel freer to complain and become aggrieved if husbands refuse to listen.

Finally, in comparison with women, *the men tend to seek relief from their frustrations less through talk than through action.* This tendency, described earlier in the present chapter, would again curb, if not the need of the husbands to unburden themselves, then their ability to do so. In an unhappy mood the wife would be more likely than the husband to want to talk and to feel resentful if he refused a sympathetic ear.

Our interpretation of these differences between the sexes gains additional support from the internal consistency of the findings. The male high school graduates differ in two respects from the less-educated men: they more readily admit feelings of hurt, and a higher proportion of them find relief from emotional stress through some form of interaction rather than through drink or physical activity. It was argued that this behavior affects the verbal expression of discontent with communication. And indeed the male high school graduates express greater dissatisfaction than the less-educated husbands.

In explaining the lesser dissatisfaction expressed by the husbands it was assumed that they may have suffered similar deprivations but were either unable to express them or failed to perceive their wives as the cause of their deprivations. There exists, however, the possibility that the husbands express fewer dissatisfactions because *they experience fewer deprivations in this particular sphere of marriage.* In the first place, the fuller self-disclosure of women means that the husbands have less cause to complain that their mates are withdrawn. We found an inverse relationship between the self-disclosure grades of married persons and the frequency with which their partners complained about the excessive reserve of the other. By and large women do reveal their worries, and their husbands have fewer complaints on this score.

Another feminine characteristic may explain why their partners are spared another frustration. It is possible that women, because of their greater interest in personal relationships, are more creative listeners on occasions when their husbands are willing to unburden themselves. For example, one woman has always worshiped her father but a recent episode suddenly revealed to her that her father "wasn't God." She wanted to discuss this with her husband but the latter merely shrugged his shoulders— "he figured it was my business." On the other hand, when it comes to her husband's "dark secret" (some uncertainty about the circumstances of his birth), a source of great anxiety to him, she is only too ready to discuss fully any shred of disclosure he is willing to make.

Finally, there exists the possibility that men basically need less intimate interaction than women. But even if this be the case, social factors can apparently either mute or exaggerate this sex difference. When ideals of masculinity permit men to express their emotional needs, the sexes become more alike in the demands they place upon communication. Excess of feminine discontent characterizes the less-educated couples; among the high school graduates, the differential between the sexes is narrower. Moreover, in another study, college-educated men complained about the lack of closeness in marriage more frequently than did college-educated women, 13 per cent of the husbands as compared with only 4 per cent of the wives. Among non-college respondents in that study 8 per cent of the wives and 5 per cent of the husbands cited lack of closeness as a problem.[17] The more frequent expressions of this discontent with the rise in the husband's educational level are consistent with the analysis presented in the preceding paragraphs.

Aspirations and Contentment

The degree of satisfaction with marriage is widely used as a yardstick of marital success. But if marital satisfaction is to be assessed in any meaningful way, we must know both the objective level of experience and the subjective reactions to it. Otherwise no distinction can be made between satisfaction with modest goals, on the one hand, and fulfillment of high aspiration, on the other. In the words of Samuel Johnson, "a small drinking glass and a large one may be equally full, but the large one contains more than the small" [18] and cognizance must be taken of the size of the glass. As far as marital communication is concerned, this study contains three sets of data which illuminate the comparison between the high school graduates and the less-educated: their

[17] Orville G. Brim, Jr., et al., 1961, p. 224.
[18] Cited in Joseph Wood Krutch, 1963, p. 13.

absolute level of communication as measured by the ratings of understanding and self-disclosure, their ideal expectations and the extent of their discontent.

The high school graduates were repeatedly shown to have higher expectations with regard to marital communication. Do their high ideals "pay off"? As we shall presently see, the answer is affirmative with regard to the actual fullness of communication but not always with regard to contentment. The high school women are more content with communication than the less-educated women, but only during the early years of marriage; this advantage disappears in older marriages. Among the young marrieds the only complaint made more frequently by the more-educated was that the husband does not talk enough. The less-educated women, on the other hand, report an excess of several grievances: that the husband does not listen, that he does not reveal worries and that he "often talks about boring things." Among the less-educated there was a group of young women who experienced little of the alleged euphoria of the early years of marriage. The sharply different interests of the sexes, economic deprivations, the low empathy and self-disclosure of their husbands—all produced discontent. These young women did not expect as much companionship as the high school graduates but reality thwarted even their modest aspirations.

The passage of the years affects the two educational groups differently. The women high school graduates experience the disenchantment which other investigators have found in the older marriages.[19] Those married seven years and over are more dissatisfied with communication than the young high school graduates. We know that the older educated husbands disclose themselves less fully and have a slightly lower degree of empathy than the young men. But the greatest increase is in the frequency of the complaint that the husband does not listen enough. Among the less-educated, however, the older women are, if anything, somewhat more content with communication than the younger ones. True, the grievance that husband does not listen increases in frequency, but fewer complain that the husband does not talk enough or does not reveal his worries. This is no mere resignation on the part of the women: the older less-educated husbands have higher empathy and disclosure ratings than the younger

[19] See, for example, Peter C. Pineo, 1961.

men. Possibly, the less-educated man experiences such difficulty in intimate communication with a woman that he requires a longer period of socialization in marriage.

With the years of marriage, women of the two educational levels become more alike in extent of satisfaction. In fact, the older high school graduates complain more frequently than the less-educated that their husbands do not talk enough and that they "have nothing interesting to talk about." Since the high school graduates enjoy fuller communication, their discontent may be attributed to their higher expectations.

The small number of high school husbands renders a similar comparison by duration of marriage inconclusive, but the pattern is repeated. The dissatisfactions with communication increase with the duration of marriage for the high school graduates and decrease for the less-educated. What is more, the older high school graduates list more grievances than the older less-educated men. A greater proportion of them criticize their wives for not listening and for talking about boring things. Since they actually enjoy fuller communication than the older less-educated husbands, here again their problem may be explained by their higher expectations.

We conclude that in this instance, as elsewhere, high aspirations carry with them the risk of more discontent but also a chance of far greater fulfillment. In the early years of marriage, the better-educated score well on both counts. They enjoy fuller communication and reality comes relatively closer to their expectations than is true among the less-educated couples. But with the duration of marriage the gap between expectations and reality widens for the educated. Thus, among the older couples "we have nothing interesting to talk about" is a complaint voiced by 16 per cent of the high school women and only 6 per cent of the less-educated; by 17 per cent of the high school but only 3 per cent of the less-educated husbands. But it must be remembered that the educated couples who are dissatisfied with the quality of their conversation in fact enjoy more companionable talk than the less-educated.

CHAPTER
9

"Significant Others": Confidants Outside of Marriage

Marriage is generally thought to be more important to a woman than to a man. This may be the case and yet we found in Glenton that women continue to maintain close and confidential ties with others more frequently than men. Conversely, for more men than women marriage is the sole deeply personal relationship in life.

The friendships to be examined in this chapter all fall into the sociological category of the "primary" relationships as generally contrasted with the impersonal, "secondary" ties—the kind, for example, that exist between teacher and pupil or employer and employee. Whereas the former relationships are said to involve total personalities, secondary ties are segmented and specialized. The latter vary in the functions they serve, but the primary ones, allegedly, tend to vary only in degree of intimacy.[1] But we found that age, sex, kinship and other social factors fashioned intimate friendships in patterned ways. Primary, personal relationships here turn out to be also, in some ways, specialized and segmented. What is shared with a sister, for example, may be withheld from

[1] Talcott Parsons, 1939, p. 462.

one's mother, and understandably so. The very devotion and partisanship of a particular confidant is a disadvantage if one feels penitent and wants to be reprimanded, not exonerated. A person may wish to share some experiences with others who suffered an identical fate. In other areas the difference between oneself and the confidant promises greater objectivity. Absolute discretion is more important in some confidences than in others. This specialization of relationships is confirmed indirectly by women who have serious conflicts with their mothers. Five such women in their twenties, who have an older woman as a confidant in addition to friends of their own age, quite explicitly say: "She is more of a mother to me than my own mother." Because the mother is not available, a substitute is chosen to perform the function of an older, maternal woman.

The stranger as a recipient of an occasional confidence also plays a distinctive role. As often noted, the lack of emotional involvement is one of the stranger's advantages. For example, Mr. Daniels, whose marriage was described in Chapter 4, took a mistress during his wife's pregnancy and spoke to her more freely than he did to his wife about his passion for "juicing up" old cars, thus enjoying the luxury of self-expression without the risk of arousing criticism or concern. The same man revealed another, and a less well recognized, advantage enjoyed by a stranger: "I knew I wasn't going to see her regular. My wife would want to know when I didn't feel like talking about it. I guess your wife's kinda got a right to ask questions. But if you got a woman on the side she ain't got a right to ask you nothing." The fact that his mistress, unlike his wife, had no rights to his "mental private property" [2] enabled him to control the flow of confidences and this in turn prompted self-disclosure. Still a third feature of the stranger's role was observed in the case of a husband who talked of his occupational ambitions in the bar but never at home. His wife would have instantly pricked the bubble of his illusions, but with strangers he could temporarily enjoy a flattering image of himself.

Discovering Confidants

The method of discovering the existence of confidants was presented on pages 134–135. The respondents were asked to describe emotionally significant experiences in various spheres of

[2] The phrase used by Georg Simmel, in Kurt H. Wolff, ed., 1950.

life and to indicate in whom, if anyone, they confided specific feelings and thoughts.

Not every close relationship with a sister, brother or friend was classified by us as "confidential." (We termed "doubtful," for example, one case in which the wife's mother lived in the same house with the couple and the relationship between mother and daughter was harmonious. "It isn't that I'd rather talk to her and tell her what's on my mind," said the wife, "but she's right here. I don't have many worries, but if you have something on your mind you are likely to tell your mother or your friend." The reason for our classification: we lacked any proof that the kind of experiences shared with the mother were anything deeper than the "women's talk" of babies, household worries, and minor marital irritations. The term "confidant" is here reserved for a particularly close relationship involving areas defined as sensitive either by the investigator or by the respondent himself. Confidences given in professional contacts with ministers or doctors are excluded as are occasional intimate conversations with persons who are relative strangers. "Certain external situations," Georg Simmel wrote, "may move us to make very personal statements . . . usually reserved for our closest friends only, to relatively strange people. But in such cases we nevertheless feel that this indiscreet conduct does not quite make the relation an intimate one." [3]

A person is said to have a confidant if he shares with the other such matters as suspicion of his spouse's infidelity; his own unfaithfulness; pleasant or unpleasant facts about his sexual life; regrets about marriage; details of serious quarrels; some of his deeper disappointments in himself; disappointments about the spouse's ambition, intelligence or other traits; and confidences about the spouse's relationships with relatives and in-laws.

In addition to such topics, defined by us as sensitive, we included others that the respondents themselves gave evidence of considering confidences, such as the amount of one's savings or earnings, some deep personal anxiety, and the like. A few examples of the "secrets" actually shared by men and women with their confidants are:

> A wife told her friend that she only pretended to enjoy sexual intercourse during the first two years of marriage and that she felt she succeeded in deceiving her husband.

[3] See Georg Simmel, in Kurt H. Wolff, ed., 1950, p. 127.

A wife told her friend that she pretended to be tired at night when she did not want her husband to make love to her. This woman worries about her lack of sexual response, but does not discuss this with her husband.

The full extent of one woman's irritation with her husband's lack of initiative was not revealed to her husband for fear of hurting him but was shared with a sister.

A husband talked to a "couple of fellows" with whom he works about his marital problems. This began when he discovered that they had difficulties in their marriages too.

A husband discussed his marital dissatisfactions with a divorced friend because he knew that his friend "was even worse off than I am."

The interviewer made the original judgment as to the existence of confidants in each case. The reliability of these decisions was tested by having an independent judge assess 58 case records. Disagreements were limited to 7 per cent of the judgments.

The Wives' Confidants

Two-thirds of the wives have at least one person apart from their husbands in whom they confide deeply personal experiences. In 35 per cent of the cases the wife not only enjoys such intimate friendships but shares some significant segment of her life *more fully* with her confidants than with her husband (see Table 17). These confidants, however, need not give husbands any ground for jealousy. All but two (and these two are fathers) are women, and 63 per cent of all are mothers and sisters of the wives. Of all intimate associates, only 27 per cent are not related to the wives by blood or marriage. This is eloquent testimony to the persistent importance of kinship ties. Among the confidants are two adolescent daughters. In one case the marriage is strained and the 15-year-old daughter is her mother's ally in marital conflicts, but the second wife is a happily married woman. The middle-class interviewer found such mother-daughter intimacy surprising. It seemed to her unlikely that under normal circumstances a middle-class mother would confide marital intimacies to a 15-year-old daughter. Since most of the couples are too young to have adolescent children, we could not ascertain the general prevalence of such mother-daughter ties.

Confidential relations with others decline in frequency as the wives grow older: eight of every ten women under 30 years of age, but only four of ten women in their thirties, enjoy them. The main reason for the lack of confidants at any age is not far to seek. The women who do not have confidants are those whose mothers and sisters are not available. Some of the older women have lost their mothers, or live at a distance from them. In four cases, relations with the mother are strained, and in two others, the mother-husband conflict restrains the wife: "My mother is so set against him anyhow." Of 16 wives lacking confidants, 8 either have no sisters living in the community or have quarreled with them—and 2 women are strangers in the community.

A variety of explanations accounts for the few remaining women who lack intimate associations despite the availability of female relatives. One was a sullen, employed mother of seven children, too weary and broken by life to have any friends. An interesting woman, whom the interviewer nicknamed the "silent one," reiterated throughout the interview the view that "talking does no good" and "people talk too much." Still another woman is described by her neighbors as "a deep one, you never quite know what's on her mind." Unhappily married, guarded and reserved about her life, she apparently receives some satisfaction from playing the role of a confidante to her two neighbors.

Level of education does not affect the proportion of women who have confidants, nor the proportion of the latter who are relatives. The high school graduates do not, in other words, reach out for confidants beyond the kinship group any more frequently than the less-educated. Among the wives there are only two true "isolates," women whose marital communication is seriously impaired and who have no confidants. Both are grade school graduates. One is the grim working mother of seven earlier referred to; the other is an unhappily married woman in her thirties whose mother is dead, and who has quarreled with her two sisters over their conversion to Catholicism. She says of herself: "I don't mingle, I keep to myself."

Although the high school graduates and the less-educated enjoy close friendships outside of marriage with equal frequency, the groups do differ in one important respect, discovered in our attempt to compare the confidant's role with the mate's. In only 35 per cent of the cases does the wife share some significant confidences more fully with someone else than with her spouse. And even in such cases it of course does not follow that the confidant is in general more important to the wife than her husband is; it is only that some sensitive sectors of life are shared more fully with the confidant. In comparing the two educational groups we find that of 31 uneducated women, 14 have confidants with whom they are more open in some significant respects than with their husbands. But of 21 high school graduates, only 4 have such confidants. The better-educated wives consequently more closely approximate the ideal, dominant in our society, that one's husband should be also one's most intimate friend. As one high school graduate expressed it: "You can't just live the two of you all alone, you have to be talking to other people or you'd get bored with each other. The thing about marriage though is that it has to be number one all the time." Such attitudes, as well as the fuller communication that the better-educated wife does in fact enjoy in marriage, undoubtedly explain the unrivaled position of her husband as a sharer of confidences.

A few of the poor and less-educated families live in a low-cost tenement. It appeared to the interviewer that these women discussed intimate family matters with their neighbors more openly than was true of residents of private houses. Furthermore, they tended to vent their pent-up irritations; homeowners were more deliberate and selective in their disclosures to trusted friends. The thin walls of the tenement make concealment difficult. "Did you hear us fight last night?" asked a women of her neighbor in our presence. Punishment of children, marital quarrels and drunkenness all were audible or visible to the neighbors. But if loss of privacy made reserve futile, and the temptation to "let off steam" was ever-present—so also was the fear of gossip: women mentioned unfair gossip as a frequent source of worry and irritation.

PATTERNS OF SHARING

The sharing of experiences with mothers, sisters, in-laws and friends is not random. Each relationship tends to have its peculiar content. Two women respondents agreed to prepare for us a joint statement as to preferred confidants in various spheres of life.

One of the women is a 28-year-old mother of four, with eight years of schooling; her friends is 26, a mother of three, with ten years of schooling. The marriage of the first is strained by poverty, but the second woman is very happily married. Their reports follow:

> Mother as confidante: "You tell her kinds of secrets that you don't tell other people. You tell her secrets that are sort of sad, and that she won't tell other people because she'd be ashamed for your sake. Sad things like a sickness, cancer or T.B. or it could be if your husband had been bad, maybe he'd gone with another woman, and nobody else knew it and somehow you found out all by yourself. Then there would be another kind of secret that you wouldn't know whether it was a secret or not, but you asked her advice about it and she'd decide.
>
> You can tell a lot of that kind of secret to your sisters too, and they can give you advice. And then when you got things that are puzzling, close stuff. Like maybe you think your husband's bad, but you don't know, or maybe you wonder if you're pregnant, or maybe you got trouble in the neighborhood and you don't know how to handle it, that kind of thing you can tell your sister when you don't want to bother your mother, it isn't sure, it isn't sad, it isn't bad."

> Sisters and mothers as confidantes: "One reason you can tell your sister something you can't tell your mom is on account that your mom worries too much. Besides the stuff that you might tell either one of them, of the sad and bad things, there's fun stuff too, and there's lots of news about people and what you call gossip. If it's about a friend of yours and you aren't sure about it, you ask them first. If it's about somebody you don't like, you tell anybody, 'cause it doesn't matter if it gets around."

Despite the frequency with which mothers serve as confidantes they are not the preferred confidantes in certain areas. For example, mothers are thought to be too "old-fashioned" about sex. Of nine wives who withheld from their husbands some sexual reaction, attitude or experience, only one confided it in her mother, while eight discussed it with their sisters or girl friends. The mother's partisanship is sometimes felt to be another disadvantage. A 19-year-old wife, who telephones her mother daily and sees her several times a week, prefers to discuss her in-law problems with an older woman friend. Her mother, the young wife explained, always takes her side, whereas her friend listens to her complaints and sometimes suggests, "Why don't you try this or that." The mother's partisanship is a threat in another way. Some women explained that they restrained themselves with their mothers so as not to arouse antagonism and conflict between their mothers and their husbands. The wives needed a sympathetic but relatively uninvolved listener who allowed them to "let off steam" with impunity. The communication between wives and their mothers is reciprocal in the sense that the latter in turn confide to their daughters worries about sickness, financial matters and various family secrets. Occasionally a woman reported that her mother was more open with another daughter, from whom the woman eventually learned her mother's news.

To continue with the report of the two informants:

Sister and husband as confidants: "You can tell husbands some kind of jokes that are sort of smutty. But then some husbands can't stand that kind. They can hear them from everybody but their wives. But it's a lot of fun stuff that both your husband and your sisters would be interested in. But you don't tell your husband's friends, you tell him, and if he wants to tell them, he can. Or if you tell his sisters, then they can tell his brothers or anybody they want to. But if you told your brother-in-law, he might think you were smutty or not very nice. You have to be careful about these things, they're sort of tricky."

Friends as confidants: "You tell friends anything that you don't care if it gets around. You tell them all kinds of little trouble, things that you can't puzzle out by yourself and gossip and lots of regular funny stuff. Sometimes you can tell your women friends worse jokes that you can tell your husband."

Women-neighbors as confidants: "You gotta watch out for them unless the neighbor was also a friend. If you got a real close neighbor, it's the next best thing to a sister."

Father as confidant: "We couldn't quite make up our minds about whether you should tell fathers anything or not. When your fathers ask you questions after you're married, you should try not to tell them lies. Some fathers are closer to their daughters on account of maybe the wives and mothers are dead. And then we both know women who like their fathers more than their mothers. They say they can tell their fathers anything, but not their mom."

The two women believed that most of the women in the neighborhood feel as they do, although there are a few "odd ducks" who have different ideas about talking to their fathers. Asked why women have to be so careful about what they tell their fathers, one of the two women said, "Some girls hate their fathers because their fathers have been unfair to them or had beaten them when drunk."

"I guess we get used to it when we're kids. If your father socks you, it'll knock you off your feet. And sometimes your mom's scared of your father, especially if he's been drinking. Then it's like I told you about my brother. He couldn't sock me and make me get in line. He was going to tell my old man, and then it was like my old man was going to kill me." Asked if boys felt the same fear of their fathers, she answered, "Some do and some don't. It all depends on what kind of dad you got. Some of them are real soft, do anything for you. Some of them spoil the kids, but I wasn't spoiled by nobody, not my mother, or my dad, and all my older brothers and sisters jumped on me and made me get in line."

Husband and brother as confidants: The women could not think of any matter which is generally shared only with one's brother—perhaps "one kind of joke you could tell a brother and maybe not a sister." One of the women knew two wives who asked their brothers' advice about how to tell their husbands bad news, but these were girls whose fathers had died and "who were used to looking at their brothers like the head of the family. You have to talk to your husband about things that you don't want to bother your brother with, things like bills; and there's the junk that happens every day. You gotta tell your husband, it's part of his business and his job, and your job. And you don't have to bother your brother none.

"We decided that some brothers and some husbands is different from others and it's the kind of person. When people flip when you tell them something, after they've flipped a couple of times you keep off. If they don't seem to mind or if they seem to like it you tell them some more."

The wife's world of intimate communication is an almost exclusively feminine world. The foregoing personal document and the overall summary on confidants convey the prevailing reserve towards fathers and brothers. One's husband is the one close link with the inner world of the other sex. Occasionally, among the more puritanical couples, even he cannot bridge the gulf between the sexes.

The reserve between the sexes creates a roundabout network of communication. If a wife wants her father-in-law or even her own father to know some personal matters, she is likely to tell her mother-in-law or her mother and depend upon the older women to transmit the information to their respective husbands.

Intermediaries are used not only to communicate across sex lines. A woman might find it too painful or embarrassing to tell her contemporaries of her husband's serious sickness. She tells her mother who tells her friends, and they in turn transmit the news to their daughters who give the wife of the sick man their discreet understanding.

The relationship with a confidant is affected, as the women themselves perceive, not only by age and kinship but by psychological factors. Through trial and error some wives worked out for themselves an intricate pattern of sharing. In one case, a 26-year-old mother of five, with six years of schooling, the wife of a freight handler with an annual income of $3400, worries mainly, she says, about possible sickness and, secondly, about lack of money. She knows that the Lord will provide, but sometimes she lacks faith. She shares her worries with her husband who often has words of wisdom that comfort her. When she is worried or depressed, "he is a staff to lean upon." But he does not help when she is angry, and he does not always find matters which hurt her feelings to be serious enough. Her sister, on the other hand, fully understands her hurts. Although her mother might criticize her about being irritable with her children, her sister would not.

The psychological availability of husband or mother at a given moment determines the choice of a confidant in another case. "It's hard to say what you've got to talk over with somebody," reflected a 28-year-old wife, a grammar school graduate. "Once I got worried because I was getting headaches and I told Mom instead of him because I didn't want to worry him. But you see Mom goes off beat too, and then you can't tell her anything. You just have to hope that one or the other of them is in the right mood to hear you when you gotta talk to somebody. . . .

I wouldn't talk to my girl friends. They might gossip. I talk to them about all kinds of things that don't matter too much, but not about the things that are really eating me."

The Husbands' Confidants

We turn now to the husbands, who present a very different picture of psychological relationships. Whereas the majority of the women—six out of every ten—enjoy close friendships outside the family, for the husband this proportion is only two out of ten—a finding consistent with the greater reserve of the husbands reported in Chapter 7. Moreover, the proportion of isolates is 12 per cent for men, against only 3 per cent for women. Isolates are persons who, severely withdrawn in marriage, also lack any outside confidants. Several men mentioned that their confidants had marital problems of their own. In fact, it is only when tentative soundings brought out shared difficulties that these husbands felt free to unburden themselves, for the role of a martyr is no doubt less culturally sanctioned for a man than for a woman. The man cited earlier who thought that a complaining husband betrays his inability to control his wife expressed another attitude blocking male self-disclosure.

The husbands' confidants are brothers, friends and, only in one case each, mother and father. It is a very rare father who is included in the network of intimate communications of his married children. (The isolation of these older men is discussed further in Chapter 11.)

With age, the husbands' close relationships with others practically disappear. Whether it is that the need for sharing diminishes with the decline of emotional vitality, or that the opportunities for contacts with male friends shrink, the picture is one of progressive withdrawal from close interaction with others. Between the ages of 30 and 40, only one out of ten husbands has a confidant.

Age for age, the two educational groups do not differ in the frequency of confidants. But the less-educated men tend to belong to a clique of friends meeting regularly in a tavern or a club, while the confidants of the high school graduates consist of individual friends or relatives.

In general even the younger and more gregarious men censure disclosure of marriage problems in bars: "You don't want to drag that kind of thing in the bar—not about all this family stuff; this is bilge. But sometimes you get drunk and I suppose you say things like this." Apart from such catharsis under the influence of drink, the tavern culture permits jocular references to marital difficulties ("I am in the dog-house today") when the transgressions are of a kind that carry prestige in the male group as a sign of successful self-assertion against women.

Fifteen per cent of the less-educated and 6 per cent of the high school graduates are members of cliques. One clique of five friends, who have known each other for over ten years, still meets regularly on Fridays to play pool in a "club" connected with a tavern. This clique was described by one of its members, a 28-year-old man with nine years of schooling. We asked him to refer to the various members of the clique by number, to protect their privacy, and to answer questions as to the kind of personal information each has about the others. The report follows:

This man knows the amount of rent two of his friends pay and the size of the mortgage on the house purchased by a third. Only one member of the bunch is "touchy on the subject of money." (The group does not know what he paid for the house which he bought from his father.) They "know pretty much what each earns a week." If he had debts, he thinks he could count on a loan, though he never had to resort to it.

Asked whether in-law problems are ever discussed, this man replied that he heard his buddies say occasionally "My father-[or mother-]in-law is a pain in the neck." None had the problems, suggested by the interviewer, of having to help one's parents without letting one's wife know about it. He thought if he had such problem he would not hesitate to discuss it with the fellows. As to relations with one's own parents, one of the fellows did complain that his brother "clipped his old man for a lot of money," whereas when he himself once asked for some little favor, his old man refused.

The fellows do complain about the extravagance of wives: "She thinks money grows on trees." He "never heard anyone cry that his wife was stingy with money for his own expenses." (In the beginning he himself turned over his pay envelope to his wife, but it didn't work out. Whenever he needed money for gas, cigarettes or lunches, he'd have to ask her and she'd say, "Gee, why do you need this?" Now he takes out his expense money and as she "never has the money she doesn't miss it." He makes sure, of course, that she has enough for the household.)

Do the fellows complain, he was asked, about excessive demands on the part of their wives to help with the kids? "They are the kind of guys who just wouldn't do it if they didn't want to do it. They wouldn't be crying about it," he replied.

As to extra-marital affairs, "They'd tell you if they had a girl the night before, they'd trust you because they know it would not go any further," but "if a fellow suspected that his own wife was running around he wouldn't say anything unless they were ready to split up." He himself "wouldn't tell anyone if I was just suspecting my wife, if I wasn't sure." If he saw a wife of one of the fellows with another guy he wouldn't say anything to his friend, he wouldn't think it was his business to interfere.

"Yes, that is the kind of things we do say," he answered when asked whether a fellow might complain that he doesn't get enough sex. "Suppose it was the other way around and the wife wanted more sex?" He laughed: "No, that's not the kind of thing anyone would want to get around. Why, the house would be full of fellows the next day!" None of the friends ever said as far as he could remember that they wished they had married a different woman. They did say, "Gee, I wish I never married."

He never heard anyone make any reference to an especially good time he had in bed with his wife. "No, they never give details like this. It isn't when they are happy, it's when they don't get enough, that they talk."

The minority of husbands belonging to such cliques obviously enjoy friendships of considerable intimacy. Understandably reticent about weaknesses which would lower their status in the group, they are less likely to "cry" about their own inadequacies as lovers than about the shortcomings of their wives. But they share with each other secrets from which wives are excluded and support each other in the face of what they deem excessive feminine demands. They protect a friend who violates the ideal norm of marriage in a way that is still within the permissible limits of the "working moralities" of the clique.

Confidants and Marital Adjustment

"The secrets of marriage," wrote Willard Waller and Reuben Hill, "are among its most important assets . . . upholding the fiction of solidarity tends to strengthen the marriage." [4] Conversely, revealing marriage dissatisfactions to outsiders they hold to be detrimental to marriage. This generalization, plausible as it may appear, applies, we find, only to marriages of a certain kind. The stability of other marriages is not damaged but actually enhanced by close interaction with others. This finding again illustrates the relativity of socio-psychological generalizations—a seemingly "universal" process turns out to be limited to a particular set of norms and conditions.

To begin with some facts supporting Waller and Hill's thesis, we note that the unhappily married women are more likely to have confidants than the happy ones. Of the 39 women whose marriages were only moderately happy or unhappy, as many as 30 had confidants. There were only 8 with confidants among the 14 very happy wives.[5] The unhappy wife has a greater need to seek out a confidant. Her disclosure may in turn cause further estrangement between the spouses. In some cases the very existence of a confidant was in itself so resented by the husband that it caused conflict.

Despite this association of confidants with marital problems, confidential relations with outsiders can prove compatible with a happy marriage. Marriages which are not harmed but helped by confidants are primarily those in which a close friendship between the mates is not expected. Otherwise the husband might feel the jealousy expressed by a 28-year-old high school graduate: "I know that my wife talks to her step-mother more than to just about anybody else and I don't like it. I think I'd like her to be that way about me."

The husbands who do not expect a close friendship in marriage tend to be more tolerant towards feminine ties, although they, too, are occasionally uneasy about the disclosure of personal matters to outsiders. Their uneasiness stems from fear of gossip or of interference on the part of the confidants: "I know the two gals talk to each other all the time but I blew my stack because she [his wife's friend] was butting in when it was none of

---

[4] Willard Waller and Reuben Hill, 1951, p. 326.

[5] A possible source of error lies in the fact that the existence of a confidant may have been easier to discover in an unhappy marriage. Try as we did to avoid such distortions, it may have been easier to pinpoint the disclosure of a marital problem than the more diffuse but equally personal communication of a happily married woman.

her business." If these men also experienced the jealousy of the high school graduate quoted above, they did not express it. They did not want their wives to talk more to them—only to talk less to outsiders. The relatively meager communication between the spouses which characterizes these marriages serves to obscure the extent of disclosure to others. "I had no business talking about sex to my girl friend. John would be mad if he knew," said one wife. But John and the other men often did not know, and their ignorance played its part in their tolerance of confidants.

As for the wives, it is difficult to see how some of the women could maintain emotional balance if they had no outside friendships. The confidants enabled some women whose communication with their husbands was meager to be nevertheless quite content with their marriages.

ΛΛΛ
CHAPTER
10

Marriage and Power

The power structure of marriage is, generally, classified into husband-dominated, wife-dominated and equalitarian types, and a similar approach will be followed in this chapter.[1] This classification shows which spouse, if either, has more power in a given marriage, but this is all it shows. It does not capture the manifold facets of power, as a few examples drawn from Glenton will demonstrate. Thus, one maternal and anxious wife carries the responsibility for the family while her charming braggart husband holds the center of the stage. In another marriage, a benevolent patriarch is adored by his dependent wife. Again, a pair of enemies, using their wretched child as a weapon, engage in constant warfare in which they are stalemated. Another wife is a complex, fiery person, emotionally dependent upon her steady, simple husband, who is exhilarated, but also occasionally overwhelmed, by her drive.

In order to do justice to such complexity a typology of power should include the sphere of the marital relationship in which power is exercised, the source from which it is derived and the techniques used to maintain it; but the inclusive typology re-

---

[1] Syncratic and autonomic (or colleague) categories are recent refinements of the equalitarian types. See P. G. Herbst, 1954, and D. R. Miller and G. E. Swanson, 1958.

mains to be formulated.[2] In the following pages we shall attempt to assess the relative power enjoyed by Glenton's husbands and wives and to distinguish five sources of conjugal power.

The term "power" is here defined as the ability to control the mate whatever the sources from which such power is derived. In the past, in theoretical discussions, both "influence" and "power" have been proposed as the generic term; the latter was chosen in the interest of maintaining continuity with previous studies of marriage.

Assessments of Power

Three kinds of evidence were used to assess which partner, if either, enjoyed superior power in a given marriage. The reliability of these assessments was tested by having two judges independently rate 13 consecutive cases. In 10 of the 13 the judges agreed, in 2 they disagreed, and in 1 other case both judges declared the power balance to be inconclusive.

The ratings of power were based, first, upon the outcome of marital disagreements. Six hours of interviewing yielded many instances of past and current conflicts and we studied their outcome. Power is most visible in contested decisions ending in the victory of one partner. But it exists irrespective of conflict because the powerful partner may so influence the wishes and preferences of his mate that a contest of wills does not even arise. Therefore, secondly we also considered the total feeling-tone of the marriage—who deferred to whom, who "tiptoed" around whom, who conciliated or influenced whom.

The third basis for assessments is the most widely used index in studies of power, the role of each spouse in decision-making. Our experience argues for caution in the use of decision-making as an index of power. Obviously, were *all* decision-making vested in one partner there would be no doubt of his superior power. But it does not follow that decision-making in one or several areas is necessarily a reliable index of general power. It depends upon the saliency of such areas for each partner. The useful distinction between "who makes the decisions" and "who

[2] The concept of power as "based on differential control of resources of value to others for need-satisfaction," proposed by Donald M. Wolfe, 1962, pp. 582-600, may provide a general orientation, but elements of this definition still remain to be classified in fruitful ways to yield a typology of power.

carries them out" [3] must be pushed further—"who decides who is to make the given decisions?" Not merely an activity, but a whole field of decision-making may be relegated to a weaker partner by his dominant mate. Some husbands thrust the responsibility for managing the budget upon their reluctant wives and others turn over the task of child rearing entirely to their wives. The latter may appear to the grocer, the advertiser or the children to wield superior power and still be, in the marital relationship, the weaker of the two. Even so sensitive a matter as receiving the husband's paycheck turns out not to be a wholly valid index of power. The dominant wives, it is true, are most likely to get the paycheck.[4] But the dominant husbands also give the paycheck to their wives in one-half the cases. The wife is least likely to get it in the "balance-of-power" marriages. We noted that in a few patriarchal families the husband had nothing to lose by giving the paycheck to his wife because his wishes were decisive in any case. On the other hand, a weaker husband has more to gain in keeping control of the paycheck and he may put up more of a struggle to secure this control. Nevertheless, even the wife who is forced by her stronger husband to assume the job of budgeting, may acquire in the course of day-to-day decisions some power to realize her own preferences. Whatever the circumstances which initiated her activities, the latter have latent functions for the structure of power which must be taken into account.

The Power Structure of Marriage

Two diametrically opposed images coexist in the references to working-class marriages. On the one hand, the working classes are allegedly more patriarchal than the middle classes, being the

---

[3] P. G. Herbst, 1954, pp. 118-130.

[4] Eight out of 10 dominant wives got the paycheck. The comparable figures are 11 out of 21 husband-dominated and 3 out of 9 equalitarian marriages. We excluded the working wives.

Robert O. Blood, Jr., and Donald M. Wolfe, 1960, pp. 33, 52, found the power score of the husbands to be higher when they were the ones who always handled the money than when their wives performed this task. Their sample included a wider range of economic classes than ours and higher classes have a "larger increment of money beyond the level of daily necessities." The higher-class husband is more likely than his wife to handle investments, insurance and similar financial matters. But he is also more likely to have the superior power on other grounds.

If we are to isolate the association between handling money and conjugal power, we must control for the socio-economic status.

last remaining stronghold of the tradition of male dominance. On the other hand, another stereotype portrays the low-status family as a matriarchy, nonetheless so because it may be one by default, due to the husband's poor economic performance and irresponsibility.

Neither portrayal describes reality as we found it. In the total group, the husbands are dominant in 45 per cent of the marriages; the wives in 21 per cent; and in the remaining 27 per cent the balance-of-power couples, neither enjoys superior power.[5] The last is a mixed category consisting of three subgroups: the "equalitarian" couples who make decisions jointly; the "stalemate" relationships in which each spouse is strong enough to frustrate the wishes of the other, but is unable to realize his own; and the cases in which each partner enjoys supremacy over different but equally important spheres of marriage.[6]

Glenton society is clearly no matriarchy: husband-dominated marriages are twice as frequent as those dominated by women. But neither is this a patriarchal group. In about one-half of the marriages the wives enjoy as powerful a position as their husbands.

In comparison with the findings of most American studies of conjugal power, male dominance is more pronounced in Glenton. This is all the more surprising because many of the other investigations included white-collar providers who have been found to wield more power than blue-collar workers.[7] This disagreement in findings may be due to differences in methods.

---

[5] The relative frequency of various types of marriages among Glenton's families:

	No.	Per Cent
Husband dominates	26	45
Wife dominates	12	21
Balance-of-power	16	27
Uncertain	4	7
	58	100

[6] The equalitarian couples have been termed "syncratic" and the third kind "autonomic" by P. G. Herbst, 1954. The "veto power" or stalemate category appears to be similar to the "conflict" one used by Murray A. Straus, 1962.

[7] The equalitarian type has been found to be the most prevalent by the following studies: Robert O. Blood, Jr., and Donald M. Wolfe, 1960; Martin Gold and Carol Slater, 1958; Russell Middleton and Snell Putney, 1960. William F. Kenkel's 1957 study of 25 college couples did find that, though most men and women had only a medium degree of influence, husbands were more likely than wives to have a high degree of influence.

With the exception of three experimental investigations, existing studies are based upon reports of decision-making supplied by wives, children and, only rarely, by both partners. Possibly respondents tend to exaggerate the degree of equalitarianism in answer to direct questions.[8] And conceivably the decisions which have been previously studied did not tap all the dimensions of power included in the present investigation.

Who Are the Dominant Men?

There were good reasons to expect that the better providers, the more skilled, and the better-educated men would enjoy more power in marriage than the men of lower socio-economic status. The good providers can use money as a means of control. Higher occupational and economic status entails a higher social rank which in turn tends to evoke deference. Better economic performance betokens a more effective personality, capable of exercising leadership. Past studies show that the husband's power rises with higher economic and occupational status.[9]

Contrary to the above expectations, however, the better providers in Glenton turn out to be the less powerful husbands. Of the men earning under $4000 a year, 64 per cent are dominant in marriage, but only 41 per cent of men with incomes of $4000 or over enjoy the superior power. Chances of dominance decline with better education: 47 per cent of husbands with less than high school education, but only 35 per cent of the high school graduates, have the greater power in marriage. Eighteen skilled workers included only 4 dominant husbands, but there were 16 such husbands among the 34 semi-skilled and unskilled men. Moreover, the superior power of the less-educated husband persists when duration of marriage is taken into account.

These surprising results have been foreshadowed in one study which shows a curvilinear relationship between occupation and social status, on the one hand, and the husband's power, on the other. The low blue-collar men exercised *more* power than the high blue-collar men and in white-collar occupations the power of the husband rose again. Similarly, white-collar men in the two lowest social status groups enjoyed *more* power than in the next higher

8 Suggested by P. G. Herbst and by Fred L. Strodtbeck.

9 Robert O. Blood, Jr., and Donald M. Wolfe, 1960, Fred L. Strodtbeck, 1951, and David M. Heer, 1962.

status category, though less than in the highest status group. The authors of this study suggest that these low-status men may be older, but otherwise do not explain the relatively high power of the men at the bottom of the occupational and social hierarchy.[10]

It is surely not their low achievement that gives Glenton's less-educated and unskilled husbands their relative power advantage. They must derive some compensating power from other sources. The explanation is suggested by the following comparison of two groups, the first consisting of the less-educated couples with both husband and wife with less than high school attainment and the second comprised of couples in which both spouses are high school graduates. Among the less-educated, patriarchal couples outnumber the matriarchal two to one; among high-school graduates the percentages of husband-dominated and of wife-dominated couples are identical.[11]

Ideologies: Patriarchal or Equalitarian

The traditional acceptance of masculine dominance has not disappeared in Glenton. The authority attached to the husband's status is certainly one source of his power in some of the families. This becomes especially visible when the husband takes selfish advantages of his position and the wife accepts frustrations as the normal lot of married women. The joyless mother of seven described on pages 89-93, is a case in point; she submits to her husband at least in part because she feels it to be her moral duty. She is an unhappy woman, but one of the happiest women in our sample is also the wife of a patriarchal husband. The traditional source of the latter's power is inferred from the manner in which this couple discussed marriage roles; the very question as to who should have the greater authority in marriage evoked surprise. Both husband and wife gave traditional answers on the male dominance schedule.

Patriarchal attitudes are more prevalent among the less-educated. Men and women were asked to check one of four possible responses to the following statements: "Equality in marriage is a good thing, but by and large the husband ought to

[10] Robert O. Blood, Jr., and Donald M. Wolfe, 1960, pp. 31, 33.
[11] The less-educated couples consist of 14 patriarchal, 6 matriarchal and 6 balance-of-power marriages, whereas the corresponding figures for high school graduates are 4, 4 and 5.

have the main say-so in family matters," and "Men should make the really important decisions in the family." The responses ranged from "I agree a lot," "I agree," to "I disagree," "I disagree a lot." [12] Eighty per cent of the uneducated men and women agreed with these statements, and some 30 per cent checked "I agree a lot." On the other hand, only 57 per cent of the high school graduates endorsed these propositions and only 17 per cent checked, "I agree a lot." The comments of the high school graduates in answer to the schedule further supported equalitarian values: "The really important decisions should be discussed and a decision reached by both"; "Marriage is a fifty-fifty proposition"; "Both husband and wife should have equal say in important matters"; and the like.

Some weak husbands, we noted, vociferously proclaimed patriarchal views and others made use of equalitarian ideology to rationalize their own defeat. Similarly, some strong husbands accepted equalitarian ideals all the more readily because they were secure in their supremacy. If expressed values and actual behavior do not always coincide, in the group as a whole they do tend to be consistent. Moreover, in at least some cases, the internal evidence indicates that it is the ideals that influence behavior rather than the converse.

Related to their equalitarian attitudes is the further fact that the high school graduates do not grant males the privileges they enjoy as a matter of right among the less-educated couples. Masculine privilege is not identical with patriarchal authority. The latter refers to the sanctioned dominance of the husband, whereas privilege is a sanctioned advantage. The possession of a privilege removes an issue from the arena of possible contest by ensuring victory prior to any struggle. The high school wife expects and demands much of marriage. "This is not the kind of marriage I want," remonstrated one wife whose husband spent many nights in church work away from home. The husband told the interviewer that he felt that her complaint was justified and that he had reluctantly acceded to her demands. Standing on her rights, she was supported by her husband's sense of guilt. Another high school graduate is not always as helpful to his wife in the evenings as she would like him to be. "The worst of it," he confessed,

---

[12] These questions were adapted from the Male Dominance Ideology scale of Lois Wladis Hoffman, 1960, p. 31.

"is that I don't feel right watching T.V. when she has all this **work** to finish." Thus, with respect to both patriarchal authority **and** masculine privilege, the less-educated men enjoy an advantage in comparison with the high school graduates.

Physical Coercion as a Source of Power

The threat of violence is another ground of masculine power. "Women got to figure men out," remarked a 23-year-old wife, "on account of men are stronger and when they sock you, they could hurt you." Another woman said of her husband: "He is a big man and terribly strong. One time when he got sore at me, he pulled off the banister and he ripped up three steps." With the evidence of this damage in view, this woman realized, as she put it, what her husband could do to her if he should decide to strike her.

Superior physical strength is of little avail to the male when social norms prohibit the use of force. The outrage of the wife, if not the husband's own guilt, makes physical aggression too costly for the husband. This illustrates how the same attribute may either enhance or weaken an individual's power, depending upon his social environment. By the same token, a woman can grant or withhold sexual favors but this "resource" cannot be "actualized" if the wife considers it her duty to submit sexually.

Some high school graduates in Glenton have been known to slap their wives, but wife-beating is less frequent than among the less-educated. One educated woman married to a man with nine years of schooling took him to court because he beat her. Superior masculine strength gives the less-educated man an advantage which the high school graduate cannot generally enjoy.

Personal Leadership or Competence

The superior power of one spouse may derive from his personal resources, such as intelligence, self-confidence, willingness to assume responsibility, or possession of specific knowledge required for certain decisions. Persons so endowed tend to exercise influence because they are persuasive. Their claim to lead may be recognized even if their mates should feel reluctant to honor it. "My taste is hopeless," said one wife. "He does most of the planning for the home. He even picks my clothes." "He is deeper," she maintained in another connection. "I don't always know what goes on in his head; he reads me, I can't read him." His more complex personality gives this husband the advantage of quicker responses and superior insight.

The description of another man given by his wife serves to illustrate personal leadership:

> "He is very sure in the way he moves and does things and says things. Many of the boys I went to school with act as though they don't know what they want. He's very easy about what he does and it is because he's so sure. You want to please him. He says things definitely and everybody likes it—the children, his friends. I like it very much myself."

The case records suggest that among the less-educated the husband is more likely to excel in personal resources for the exercise of influence, and that this margin of male superiority narrows among the high school graduates. This tends to be the case because the more equalitarian attitudes of the high school graduates have cumulative consequences for power relationships. These attitudes provide opportunities for the wife to exercise her judgment and to reach out beyond the walls of the home and this, in turn, trains her abilities and helps release whatever potential resources she possesses. For example, the high school woman enjoys the privilege of a "night off" more frequently than the less-educated wife. She may spend such an evening gossiping with her relatives, but she may also join the P.T.A. and be elected to office. The self-assurance and competence provided by experiences such as these affect her position in marriage. "He asked me how to vote on the school question because we discussed it at the P.T.A.," reported one wife. Increased respect for the wife leads to a greater tendency on the part of the husband to share matters of importance with her and to consult her.

Among the less-educated, the husband has wider contacts in the community than his wife. He represents the world to his family, and he is the family's "secretary of state." In contrast, a few of the more educated wives enjoy wider contacts and a higher status outside the home than their husbands. Thus two wives are P.T.A. presidents while neither of their husbands occupies a position of such eminence. The husbands go to the meetings at which their wives preside. The telephone messages and the correspondence received by these families are largely for the wives. We found no similar cases among the less-educated women, either because their families are larger or because they lack resources for positions of leadership. The less-educated husband may not belong to more organizations than does his wife (the rate of participation is identical for the two), but he is more mobile, and his experiences on the job, in the labor union, and in the tavern lead his wife to feel, as one woman said, that "he is in the middle of it." Her somewhat more frequent attendance at church does not appear to carry much weight with her husband. If he himself is unaffiliated, this is often because of hostility or indifference to the church.[13]

The relative educational attainment of the spouses was found to affect their degrees of power.[14] Of 36 husbands whose education is at least equal (or superior) to that of their wives, 21 enjoy superior power. But there are only 5 dominant men among the 18 husbands with less formal schooling than their wives.

The effect of educational inequality appears to explain the lower power of the skilled workers in comparison with the semi-skilled.[15] The skilled worker is more likely than the semi-skilled to marry a high school graduate. In one or two cases the better-educated wife urged her husband to learn a skilled trade. In other cases, the husband held his skilled job at the time of marriage. By virtue of their relatively high earnings skilled workers may be able to marry better-educated women, but by marrying "upward" they lose the degree of power enjoyed by the semi-skilled over their less-educated wives.

There are personal determinants of power other than individual competence. The readiness of one partner to take advantage of the vulnerabilities of the other may give him an advantage. Other manipulative skills have a similar effect. Again, a neurotic person may indirectly control his more insightful partner because the latter makes the major adjustments. It has even been suggested that a stupid, irresponsible and thick-skinned person is

[13] Studying the husband's power by comparative church attendance of the spouses, two authors found that he had less power when his attendance was less frequent than his wife's. See Robert O. Blood, Jr., and Donald M. Wolfe, 1960, p. 39. That study included a wider range of socio-economic classes than the present investigation. Comparative church attendance of the spouses may have a different significance for power in various classes.

[14] Robert O. Blood, Jr., and Donald M. Wolfe, 1960, pp. 37-38, found a similar relationship.

[15] Out of 18 skilled workers only 4 (or 22 per cent) are dominant as compared to 9 (or 35 per cent) out of 26 semi-skilled.

"superbly equipped as a fighting machine for the matrimonial battles" when pitted against an intelligent and sensitive mate aware of the consequences of his actions.[16] These sources of power are distinct from "personal competence" because the manipulative person does not usually make his purpose explicit and, in any case, his claim to power is not recognized as legitimate by the spouse even if she is forced to submit.

Social Rank and Deference

Persons of high social rank enjoy a margin of power because of the deference that high rank commands. Prestige gives power apart from the presumption that the high-ranking person has competence. In this way, a position of importance in the community lends a halo effect to the husband's status within the family. Perhaps implicit in this type of situation is a norm of equivalence in social relationships. The inferior in rank exchanges, as it were, his subordination for the privilege of association with his superior.

Within the family, men and women are ranked informally on the basis of both similar and dissimilar criteria—beauty, for example, usually being more important for women than for men. Each spouse is tacitly rated on a scale of matrimonial desirability. "I don't know how I was so lucky," exclaimed one husband of a younger and good-looking wife; he dances attendance upon her in part because he feels that her superior position on the scale of desirability somehow entitles her to this consideration.

Although personal leadership, of course, is not identical with social rank, it is often difficult to distinguish these in practice. It is, however, our impression that with regard to social rank, as in regard to personal leadership, the less-educated husbands tend to be superior to their wives, whereas the high school graduates do not enjoy this advantage to the same extent.

The Relative Stake in the Relationship

The bargaining position of each spouse depends in part upon the degree of emotional involvement in the marriage.[17] The high school husbands are more emotionally involved in their marriages. This gives their wives a leverage of power. "My wife" as

[16] See Clifford Kirkpatrick, 1963, p. 342.
[17] See, for example, Willard Waller and Reuben Hill, 1951, pp. 190-192.

a source of comfort in periods of stress was mentioned twice as frequently by the high school graduates as by the less-educated men. Both the less-educated and the educated wives, on the other hand, resorted to their husbands with equal frequency. The high school husband tends to confide in his wife, talk about his job, and enjoy joint leisure-time activities more frequently than the less-educated husband. Greater social interaction between the spouses tends to deepen emotional involvement,[18] and this in turn makes the educated husband more vulnerable. His wife can control him by granting or withholding emotional rewards. In sum, in comparison with the less-educated men, the high school graduates exchange superior power for a deeper companionship in marriage.

Insofar as their bargaining position is affected by economic dependence, the high school wives may be less vulnerable than the less-educated women. The parental family constitutes a second line of defense for the wife if her husband fails her. One wife reported that had she had a home to which to return, she would have left her husband during her first year of marriage. In similar circumstances another wife did return to her parental home, and this forced her husband to come back on her terms. We found that a higher proportion of the high school women than of the less-educated enjoyed favorable relationships with their mothers. This may to some extent have mitigated their economic dependence upon their husbands.

Wife-Dominated Marriages: A Study of Deviance

Though some couples believe that women should have a relatively high position, no one in our sample thinks it proper for a wife to dominate the relationship. Social norms do not sanction a superior position for the wife in the sense in which patriarchal attitudes of some families uphold the husband's supremacy. Women do not draw strength from economic support—in none of our families is the husband completely dependent upon the wife. Without such bolstering, dominant women attain their superior powers by virtue of their personal resources. Some are obviously strong personalities; others are merely wives of exceptionally weak husbands.

Marriages dominated by wives violate the norms of the cou

[18] See George C. Homans, 1950.

ple, but this discrepancy between the ideal and the real does not always cause problems. A few very happy marriages are of this kind. Various factors affect the degree of adjustment to this deviant pattern. In the first place, the visibility of the wife's supremacy varies with circumstances. It is not easy to conceal the husband's inferior education or his economic failure, whereas his emotional dependence upon his wife may be hidden from public scrutiny. While some common adaptations cushion the potential strains of wife-dominated marriages, these adaptations are not equally available to all.

A recognized adaptive technique of the dominant wives is to maintain in public the fiction of masculine dominance. Speaking of voting preferences, one woman said: "A wife shouldn't go against her husband in public. She should agree with him or else keep her disagreement to herself until they are alone and then voice her views." Another wife, who bragged that her earnings enabled the couple to pay cash for the living room set, was severely criticized, even though "the public" in this case was her sister's family. Not every strong wife, however, could play this game of public deference. Some, indeed, found it easier to spare their husband's self-esteem in private than in the presence of others. They became more intensely irritated by some defect in the husband when viewing it through the imagined reactions of others. The need to excel, dormant when they were alone with the husband, was stimulated by an audience.

Another explicit technique is the familiar "building up the male ego" by "letting on he is the boss." This tactic is a ritualistic adherence to the norms coupled with their violation. But not every husband lends himself to such manipulation, and not every wife can or will resort to it. For example, a young high school graduate who calls himself an "oddball" is happily married, but confesses that his wife "hurts him deeply when she tries to build up my ego, especially in company." Possibly, his wife does not do this skillfully enough, with the result that she appears to be merely apologizing for him. On the other hand, this sensitive young man would probably see through even subtler strategy. Again, the technique of "building up the male ego" is not available to a wife who takes pleasure in humiliating her husband, as does Mrs. Miller (described in Chapter 12). And even apart from such sadistic needs, "letting on he is the boss" is too costly a stratagem for some wives. "I ask him to explain things to me that he knows and I don't, but he don't ask me to tell things to him," complained one wife who prided herself upon her competence. The self-respect of some women is tied precisely to the successful manipulation of their husbands. Several young women envy their mothers' skill in getting their own way without challenging the men's illusion of supremacy. Some husbands even admire such skills: "I wouldn't mind if my wife played it that way," one husband remarked.

Manipulation by the wife is occasionally successful in the sense that the relationship proves stable and rewarding to both. At least one husband, married to an independent and self-sufficient woman, adapts to the situation by maintaining the illusion that he is the "strong wall" on which she leans. Admittedly, this husband may have concealed from us the truth which he knew only too well. But the evidence of his total interview belies such an interpretation—he appears secure and content. The marriage has many other assets, and the husband is able to cherish some fictions that his wife leaves undisturbed.

Some husbands react to dominant wives by making much of their superiorities in relatively trivial matters, at times with the connivance of their wives. For example, their wives' poor sense of direction or some habitual awkwardnesses are reiterated with glee and built into the family's folklore.

The self-esteem of a man married to a dominant wife sometimes remains intact because in some deeply important area of the relationship he remains the stronger of the two. For example, a taxi-driver described his marriage: "Even if she is a lot smarter than I am, there's some things that I can do a lot better than she can. We hit it off real good together. We suit each other. . . . I make her calm down and she makes me stick together."

Among the matriarchal couples, some illustrate the familiar type of dependent husband and maternal wife. In one such marriage the complementary emotional needs are fully satisfied and the relationship is mutually rewarding. But the deviation from the norm exacts its price: the emotionally dependent husband is not aggressive enough on the job, with painful consequences for the family's economic status.

Another mode of adaptation on the part of weak husbands is to redefine the relationship. A weak man who persists in making demands that he cannot enforce tends to irritate his wife and lower his status still further. Several husbands are able to modify their claims and to offer compensatory services to their wives, thereby renouncing their claims to high marital status but achieving a rewarding relationship nonetheless. One poor provider who helps his wife with housework did say, "Beggars can't be choosers," but he was certainly not "henpecked."

Rage, violence, drink, frequent absence from home and perhaps infidelity are still other reactions of weak husbands who could neither accept defeat nor settle for half a loaf. (A detailed illustration of such a case is given on pp. 262-267.)

Summary

The expectation that the better providers and the better-educated husbands would wield superior power in marriage is belied by the facts. This does not signify, however, that economic and educational achievement in general play no part in the husband's power. Glenton's families represent, after all, a relatively narrow segment of the socio-economic hierarchy. The difference of $2000 in annual earnings, or the difference between a semi-skilled and a skilled occupation, may not be crucial enough to offset the contrary influence of patriarchal attitudes or other sources of power. In the population at large, the relationship between the socio-economic status of the husband and his conjugal power appears to be curvilinear—at the very bottom of the pyramid there exists, perhaps because of the relatively larger proportion of Negroes, a matriarchy by default.[19] The power of the husband rises in the low blue-collar and declines in the high blue-collar classes. With ascending class status, the husband's power rises again because once more he appears to outstrip his wife in resources for the exercise of power. For example, in higher socio-economic classes, the husband is more likely to excel his wife in formal education than he is among blue-collar workers. The United States Census of 1960 shows that men predominate among college graduates, but that adult women have a higher median education (10.9 years of schooling for women to 10.3 years for men).[20] More intensive comparative studies, we believe, will confirm the lesson of Glenton that the power structure of marriage in a given class is the net result of a great variety of social factors, reinforcing and occasionally offsetting one another. Patriarchal or equalitarian mores; patterns of mate selection; the relative bargaining position of each sex in a given social milieu; the relative personal, educational and economic attainments of men and women; and the roles men and women play in the community—all together give the conjugal power structure of a socio-economic class its peculiar character.

∧∧∧
CHAPTER

II

Kinship Relations

We could imagine Glenton's families carrying on their lives even if they were suddenly separated from uncles, aunts and cousins, but life without parents, brothers and sisters would leave a great void. Every aspect of life from the most fundamental to the most frivolous would be drastically altered. Daily existence centers about relatives all the more because there are so few competing social ties or interests. Anxiety over the father's ill health; delight with an unexpected little gift from an in-law; pique caused by favoritism shown by the mother to a brother's child; shame over some misbehavior of a "wild" young relative; plans for a family reunion at Sunday church services; the temptation to reveal, in talking to one relative, the secret which was entrusted by another; the rivalry of two brothers for parental approval—these and similar family experiences constitute a large part of the substance of daily life. "Your relatives can hurt you more than anybody because you love them the most," remarked a 38-year-old cable-layer.

Our findings, therefore, add another chapter to the recent rediscovery of the importance of kinship in modern industrial society. To be sure, industrialism, mobility and other social changes over the past century have no doubt weakened the extended family and have correspondingly increased the independence of the nuclear unit of parents and children. But while sociologists have assessed correctly the direction of the change, they may have exaggerated its extent. Turning from speculation to empirical studies of contemporary kinship, they are finding kinship ties to be still surprisingly strong.[1]

The relatives considered in this chapter and the following ones are primarily parents and siblings. Contacts with aunts, uncles and cousins were not studied systematically, but it is our impression that these more distant relatives play a much smaller role in the lives of the families than do parents and siblings.

There is hardly any function of family life to which relatives make no contribution. Other chapters of this book consider the part played by relatives in the socialization of the married couple, in providing emotional support, as confidants, and as companions in recreation.

With respect to financial aid, the parents of these couples are usually in no position to help their children to buy a home or establish a business: in only two or three cases were homes purchased with a loan from parents. But some financial aid is frequently provided in emergencies. Many persons agreed with the remark: "It is a comfort to have your people near. We both feel if it's really bad, our families will step in." The families do step in with the payment of a doctor's bill or overdue rent or with a gift of clothing. The bulk of financial aid is from the parents to their married children because many of these couples are young; perhaps one-half of the couples received such help in the recent past. In about one-fifth of the cases, financial help is given by children to their parents. But a frequent economic arrangement is one of reciprocal aid. Thus, a widowed father shares his home with a married son who pays no rent but is responsible for household expenses; a widowed mother residing with her daughter works as a waitress, paying rent and her share of the grocery bill; a widow and her bachelor brother inherited the parental home and rented rooms to a married daughter who is the homemaker for the whole group and expenses are shared.

Apart from such more or less permanent arrangements, relatives frequently exchange services which among wealthier fam-

---

[1] For guides to the extensive literature on kinship relations, see bibliographies in Marvin B. Sussman and Lee Burchinal, August 1962, pp. 231-241, and William J. Goode, 1963, pp. 381-388.

ilies are purchased from specialists—such as house painting, carpentry, repair, laying linoleum, building partitions, and help in moving.[2]

The main principle governing aid is that of reciprocity. The severity of the need and the ability to help generally determine the direction of aid, but aid is expected to be given without favoritism to either older or younger generations. The principle of reciprocity appears to explain why grandmothers are frequently paid for baby-sitting with grandchildren. This "contractual" transaction was reported to us in a matter-of-fact way with no mention of such extenuating circumstances as financial need or sacrifice on the part of the grandmother. In one case, the mother refused payment but accepted a gift. Another grandmother asserted that it would not be right to accept money because she loved her grandchildren. The mothers who accept payment are not necessarily in dire need. Occasionally, this situation is undefined and troublesome. For example, a widowed mother baby-sits for her daughter and gets paid for it. But this mother lives with another married daughter who occasionally also asks her to baby-sit. Since the older woman would be likely to spend the evening at home in any case, no payment would seem to be called for, yet the daughter is not sure whether her mother expects to be paid.

More impressive than economic aid given by relatives is the social role they play. For some families, relatives provide their sole experience of group membership. One-third of the couples either never spend any leisure-time with another couple (apart from relatives) or do so only a few times a year; were it not for the circle of relatives, they would be completely isolated. A few of the couples belong to closely knit cliques of friends and a few others are members of church-based social circles. But for the great majority, neither the labor union nor the church, nor any other cultural, fraternal or purely social group provides the experience of social participation.

When the circle of relatives is congenial and large, it can provide not only a satisfying but a rich social life, as the following cases illustrate. One man who has five siblings is married to a woman who is one of seven children, and the two families happen to be congenial—they enjoy picnicking together: "Some

[2] See Marvin B. Sussman and Lee Burchinal, November 1962.

times we'll have thirty or forty people out there, all coming from the same families, all whooping it up and having a wonderful time." Again, a woman takes her children to her mother's home for Saturday lunch where she regularly meets all her sisters and sisters-in-law and their children while the husbands come and go. "Our families," testifies another man, "are like a large council. If this one knows more about legal problems, we talk to him, if another knows more about cars, we talk to him." Family relationships, of course, are not always this harmonious. Close interaction (amicable or strained) with relatives is facilitated by residential proximity.

Residential Proximity to Relatives

Among these working-class families, the ideal norms with regard to residence are clear: a married couple and their children should live in a home of their own apart from relatives. Sharing a household with parents or relatives is thought to be undesirable, especially during the early years of marrige when the newlyweds are still "strange to one another." The final decision as to residence should be made by the husband as the head of the family and the family provider. Lastly, while it is considered to be desirable to live close to one's parents, the opportunity to improve one's economic position should take precedence over sentimental ties to kin.

These norms emphasizing the primacy of the nuclear over the extended family are not matched by actual behavior. Relatives play, as will be shown, a more important role in reality than is granted them in principle. Economic obstacles hinder the realization of some ideals, and improvement in material living conditions would no doubt accelerate the trend towards the nuclear type of family. However, the discrepancy between ideals and practice will be shown to stem from circumstances other than economic conditions. Professed ideals of the supremacy of the conjugal relationship come into conflict with sentiments generated by other elements of the kinship structure. These sentiments give rise to patterns of behavior that are recognized and sanctioned even though they run counter to the "official" norms.

Responses to the following two test stories revealed attitudes towards competing claims of spouse and relatives:

1. A woman, 25 years old, is engaged to a man who is 28. She is an only child and lives with her father in an apartment and keeps house for him. She would like to continue living in the apartment after marriage so that she could continue to take care of her father. But her fiancé says that her father could go to live with his sister who has a big house. He wants them to have an apartment of their own and not to have his father-in-law around. What do you think of such a problem?

2. The husband was offered a better job out of town, and he wants to take it. The wife says she doesn't want to move and leave her mother and her sisters. She doesn't care about the extra money and thinks he ought to try to be happy where he is. What do you think about such a problem?

All but 1 of the 97 persons who commented upon the first story clearly endorsed the ideal of starting married life alone without the father-in-law. This does not mean that they feel no scruples about the old man: about one-half voiced some qualms, such as: "Is he willing to live with his sister, maybe they have a real hate on?" and "You can't shove an old person around like this—does he want to go?" A few (15 per cent of the group) noted the economic advantages of doubling up: "If it's cheaper with the father, they could save up for a place of their own." But whatever the concessions to expediency or filial duty, the *ideal* of separate residence is universally upheld.

The comments upon the second story again reflect an agreement on principles. Only 3 of 97 persons take the part of the wife who refuses to leave her relatives; all three are women and, significantly, they did not attempt to invoke any ethical justification for their position. The others, in stating that the wife must follow her husband, referred to three principles—the importance of upward mobility, the husband's right to dictate the place of residence, and the primacy of the spouse over consanguineal relatives. Both men and women often responded to the second story with considerable feeling, as illustrated by the following comments: "The wife should get the lead out of her pants and go"; "If she doesn't want to move—husband should send her packing off"; "She's looking for a divorce—if a man can better himself, she shouldn't hold him back"; "Man should be the head of the family and have the final say"; "Husband comes before family"; "Parents ain't going to live forever—everybody gotta look out for their own kids coming up"; and "Mother and sisters don't pay the bills."

Thirty-seven per cent of the women but only 12 per cent of the men qualified their answers: "If it is a fly-by-night job you couldn't blame her"; "How far out-of-town? If it is Alaska, maybe they ought to think twice"; "He might make a deal to see her family whenever they could"; and "If it is just a passing job, she shouldn't have to give up her family." One or two men expressed helplessness: "Whatever you do, you're going to be in hot water. If the husband takes the job, the wife is going to be dissatisfied." Most of the qualifications were made by the less-educated wives. Women with high school education tend to give priority to economic advancement and loyalty to the husband. Education makes no difference in the husbands' responses.

What these men and women say does not always agree with what they do. Many couples were unable to realize the ideal of a separate household for economic need and obligation to kin forced them to reside with parents or other relatives. Over one-half of the couples lived with relatives at some time during their marriage. Forty per cent started married life in the same household with relatives. Normally, after a year or less, the couple did move into an apartment of their own. Thus circumstances forced the young couples to "double up" with relatives at a stage of marriage which they felt to be crucial for adjustment and one which required privacy. At the time of the study, 16 per cent of the households included a parent or parents, and an additional 7 per cent occupied a separate apartment in the same building with their parents or relatives.

"Doubling up" with relatives tends to cause stress. The majority of the couples, though not all, were disturbed about such living arrangements (as brought out in some detail in Chapter 12). A separate apartment in the same house with relatives tends to be less stressful than a joint household as judged by the relative proportions of families dissatisfied with their living arrangements.

While the great majority of the couples live apart from their parents, they do live close by. Sixty-eight per cent of all husbands and wives reside in the same community as their parents. The parents of others reside in nearby communities, easily reached by car or bus. In only 7 per cent of the cases do parents live farther than "two hours away by car."

The brothers and sisters of our couples are somewhat more scattered. Nevertheless, of the 331 siblings only 11 per cent live farther than "two hours away by car." Information was lacking for 7 per cent of the siblings, but even if the latter are assumed to reside in other cities the proportion of out-of-towners would amount to only 18 per cent.

Do these couples, in common with the English working-class families, tend to settle closer to the wife's than to the husband's parents?[3] In Glenton, the matrilocal tendency is slight and is similar to that reported for the country as a whole.[4] Sixteen per cent of the couples live in the same house with the wife's parents, while only 11 per cent reside with the husband's. Only 5 per cent of the wives have parents living farther than "two hours away by car," while the comparable figure for the husbands is 9 per cent.

About two-thirds of the husbands and the wives have originally come from Glenton or neighboring communities. This may account for the almost equal distance of residence from both sets of parents. In 18 per cent of the cases, however, a move out of the community had been desired by the husband at some time after marriage, and was successfully resisted by the wife who did not want to leave her relatives. In one of these cases, a temporarily unemployed husband was promised a job by his father in another city, but his wife did not want, as he put it, to "give up her family"; he added that the job would have been something of a gamble and that he "wouldn't take his wife away from her family for a gamble." Three or four husbands, commenting upon the projective story, said that they would be most reluctant to leave their own relatives. In another case, the wife of an ambitious high school graduate who is determined "to get out of the laboring class," described the couple's problem in looking for a house. They want to move to a better neighborhood because of the children, but at the same time they wish to remain near the rest of the family; the wife's parents reside in the South, and the

<hr>

[3] See Michael Young and Peter Willmott, 1957, p. 16.

[4] Of married females living with their spouses in households of parents, about 60 per cent were daughters and 40 per cent daughters-in-law. U.S. Bureau of Census, *U.S. Census of Population: 1950*, Vol. IV, Special Reports, Part 2, Chapter D, Marital Status, Table 1.

"family" for this couple refers to the husband's parents and his married brother.[5] We conclude that in about one-fifth of the cases, kinship ties (usually those of the wife) tended to impede residential mobility.

Frequency of Contacts with Relatives

The frequency with which Glenton couples see their relatives is one index of the importance of kin in the scheme of life. Table 18 presents the frequencies of contacts between various relatives irrespective of residence, as well as frequencies of contacts with relatives who reside in Glenton. As would be expected, the families see the latter more frequently than they do relatives who live farther away, but the ranking of particular relationships in terms of frequency of contacts remains the same. The following discussion will be limited to relatives residing in Glenton, but whether we count all relatives or only residents of Glenton, the wife and her mother see each other more frequently than any other pair of relatives. Sixty-six per cent of those wives whose mothers live in Glenton see their mothers several times a week or daily. For wives married under seven years, the proportion is 92 per cent (Table 19). After seven years of marriage, the frequency of daughter-mother contacts declines to 59 per cent. Decreasing dependence upon the mother is one reason for fewer contacts, and another is the growing burden of domestic responsibilities. Moreover, some of the mothers are working and this limits the time available for visits with daughters.

The wives see their fathers less frequently than they do their mothers. Only one-half of them see their fathers several times a week or daily. With longer duration of marriage, contacts with fathers also decline in frequency. Mothers are seen more frequently because they visit their daughters during the day or baby-sit at night. Indeed, knowing the relatively distant attitudes towards the father, we suspect that, while he is frequently seen in the parental home, the real purpose of the visit is to see the mother.

The husbands also see their mothers somewhat more frequently than they do their fathers, but the difference is slight, existing only among the older couples. Forty-eight per cent of

[5] For a study of family cohesion and mobility, see Eugene Litwak, February and June 1960.

the older husbands, married seven years and over, see their mothers as often as "several times a week or daily," but only one-third see their fathers that frequently. Upon scrutiny, the explanation of fewer contacts with fathers lies partly in the fact that the older husbands are more likely to have widowed mothers than widowed fathers living with them, since there are more widows than widowers in the population at large. A husband might also see his mother at his own home as she frequently drops in without his father.

The wives' contacts with other relatives, ranked in the order of frequency, are: sister, sister-in-law, brother, brother-in-law and aunt. The five relatives most frequently seen by the husbands are: brother, sister, sister-in-law, brother-in-law and wife's aunt. The frequency of contacts reflects not only the person's own tie to a particular relative, but the tie of his spouse. If the husband is close to his brother, the wife is bound to see more of her brother-in-law. Similarly, if the husband frequently sees his sister-in-law it is because she tends to be close to his wife. Any association which may exist between frequency of interaction and sentiment is therefore obscured by the joint social life of married couples.

The tendency to associate more frequently with the wife's family is contrary to the ideal norms. The couples often express the view that both sets of parents should be treated equally with respect to gifts and visiting. These ideals were elicited by a test story:

> The wife is close to her parents and they like to have her come over with the family every Sunday for the midday dinner. The husband says that he has nothing against her family, but he doesn't like to be tied up every Sunday and he doesn't want to go so regularly. What do you think about this problem? If it were the husband's parents who wanted to see the couple, would this make a difference?

One-half of the husbands and the same proportion of the wives thought that such weekly visits were "too set" and "monotonous." A few smilingly noted the advantage of a free meal. But with only two exceptions, they held that the side of the family issuing the invitation should make no difference in the frequency of visits. Contrary to these attitudes, in fact only 46 per cent of the wives see their in-laws as often as several times a week or daily whereas the comparable figure for the husbands is 63 per cent.[6] Christmas, Thanksgiving, birthdays, anniversaries, and joint vacations are much more likely to be spent with the parents of the wife. We estimate that couples with both sets of parents residing in Glenton are three times more likely to celebrate these occasions with the wife's than with the husband's parents.

Two factors explain the more frequent association of the couple with the wife's relatives—the woman's greater attachment to her parents and her dominant role in planning social activities. But this discrepancy between the ideal of symmetrical obligations to both sets of parents and the matricentric bias causes no problems. This deviance is widespread, and it acquires a kind of legitimacy. "It is natural," remarked one man, "to go with the wife's family," and another said: "I think men generally go with the wife's family, don't they?"

It requires some exceptional circumstances for the husband to rebel against frequent contacts with his in-laws and to invoke the "official" norm. As long as his personal interests are not frustrated, the departure from the ideal is tolerated; but a husband who dislikes his in-laws or has especially warm relations with his own relatives begins to question the accepted practices.

"Every time I turn around, it looks like I am having dinner at Mary's parents," complained one husband. "Even on holidays, Thanksgiving and Christmas, she wants to go to her mother's because she says that her mother is lonesome" [the wife's brother is in the service]. "I feel a stranger with her parents," he went on to say. "Her father is funny. I don't see eye to eye with him and I just keep quiet. It's the funniest thing. I feel more at home visiting her aunt and uncle than her parents."

Another husband would like to see his aunt and uncle more frequently, but he says: "If there is any question as to whom to visit, it is two-to-one in favor of her family." This is all the more unfair, he feels, because his in-laws live a distance away, whereas his aunt lives nearby. He volunteered the observation that they often meet, at the home of a couple they visit, the

[6] A slight matrilineal tendency was found also in an upper middle-class sample. Males maintained interaction with a slightly higher proportion of their in-laws than did females. Paul J. Reiss, 1962, p. 334.

wife's sister and her father, but that he "doesn't even know whether my friend [the husband] has a brother!" His personal frustration heightened his perception of these patterns.

A personality plagued by the fear that "people will step all over you if you let them" made another husband sensitive to the discrepancy between belief and practice. He resented the fact that his wife invited her own family and not his to the first meal at their home after their marriage.

Such resentful husbands form a small minority. The husbands as a rule are free to see their relatives as often as they wish. Indeed, the surprising finding is the frequency with which the husbands interact with their own parents and the frequency with which even their wives see their in-laws.

The Wife and Her Parents

The wife's emotional involvement with her mother remains strong. All three interviewers noted the hold that mothers frequently had over their married daughters. We have no comparable data for middle- or upper-class Protestant families, but merely record the impression that many a wife in her late twenties and thirties exhibited a vulnerability to her mother's criticism and a desire to win her approval which we had associated with a much earlier stage of life.

A 38-year-old woman, whose widowed mother lives with the couple, reported that her mother can hurt her:

"It's the way she will look about something and you know she doesn't like it, especially after you have tried so hard to please her. And then, sometimes she will say something real cutting, but you have to hear it at the time to know it's cutting."

A 28-year-old woman in answer to the question, "Does your mother ever hurt your feelings?" replied:

"I don't know how to explain it. It used to be awful when I was a kid, but she can still get under my skin and it makes me jump." She went on to tell a story of decorating a room. Her mother "made some dirty cracks about my bad taste. It made me feel so lousy I had to cry about it." This woman is one of the few of these dependent daughters who feels that such reactions are a sign of immaturity, as is evident in her remark, "I'm a big girl and shouldn't cry if mother says something like that . . . I was so ashamed."

A 26-year-old woman responding to the same question, said:

"Mother thought I was lazy and that bothered me very much. I try to do the best I can, but Mother is a strong woman and doesn't understand." When asked if her husband knows of her feeling, she answered, "He found me crying once or twice and so I told him about feeling hurt by Mother's criticism."

Respectful restraint in relation to the mother is illustrated by a 40-year-old woman, herself a mother of ten:

"My mother has an awful sharp tongue. She doesn't hold anything back. She just lets fly at you and sometimes it can be pretty bad." As an example she told of an incident in the hospital after the death of a premature baby when her mother happened to be with her. She quoted her mother as saying, " 'I don't know what you're cryin' for. You got enough home waiting for you.' " She said that even though her mother makes her mad and hurts her feelings she "hardly ever had a spat with her."

Similar control of irritation is seen on the part of a 31-year-old woman, the mother of a 2-year-old boy. The woman's mother expects too much of the child and though this disturbs the daughter, she does not reveal her resentment: "I keep it bottled up." She explained that if she ever had a fight with her mother, the latter would "never forget or forgive."

In assessing current relations between the wives and their mothers, we found that six wives out of every ten enjoy "close" or "very close" relationships. This category includes some very warm and harmonious relations, but also others with minor conflicts. In all cases the wives share their experiences with their mothers, see them as frequently as circumstances permit, and express positive feelings towards them. They frequently say about their mothers: "We are close."

At the other extreme, two out of every ten are bitter towards their mothers. The hostility may be so strong that contacts are infrequent and conflict is avoided by relative estrangement.

This leaves two out of ten who fall into an intermediate category of "fair" relationships. These wives are more distant towards their mothers than the first group but not as estranged as the second. Others in this category have more serious conflicts than the first, but, again, not so serious as the second group of wives (see Table 20).

The hostile daughters disclosed three main themes of strain in relation to their mothers. Some women claimed that their mothers had rejected them in favor of another child, generally a son. The following excerpts illustrate this first theme:

"I got a big brother . . . he and my ma worship each other. My dad liked me better, he was a real sweet guy. He was quiet but I know he loved me. He made me feel all warm and good."

"My brother John is my mother's absolute favorite. When he is in trouble she mopes around all the time worrying about his problem. That makes her crabby at me. She gets disgusted that my kids are healthy and his is sickly."

The second—and a frequent problem of the hostile daughters —is conflict with their mothers over sexual behavior. A 31-year-old woman reported that her mother hurt her feelings by saying that she was a "bad girl."

"Ma thought," she explained, "that I was flirting when I wasn't doing anything of the kind. My brother and sister joined up with Ma and sat in judgment on me. I lied about my age and joined up as a kitchen helper with the U.S.O. I was glad to be transferred South to get away from home for a while."

"There's nothing that I just can't stand as much as somebody being unfair," said another woman. "It was bad enough when other people were unjust, but when your own mother thought you were bad—you were licked."

It was not always possible to judge the justice of the daughters' accusations that their mothers were prudish, suspicious and restrictive. In some cases, however, the process of alienation from the mother can be traced. A 26-year-old woman with ten years of schooling described her troubled life. An unsatisfactory relationship with her mother led to precocious sexual behavior which, in turn, increased mother-daughter conflict.

"I eloped when I was sixteen. I think I did it just to get away from Ma more than anything else. But this guy and I, we was crazy in love. He was a lot older than I. He made good money but he got to playing pool all the time and drinking beer. He drank so much beer he didn't eat and then he got the D.T.'s and it was awful. After my baby was born he would be so drunk sometimes that he would bump into the crib and once he picked it up and dropped it and that was what finished me. I took the baby and went home to Ma, to dear old home where I came from. We had a stinking lousy divorce trial. I wasn't doing anything but looking after the baby and acting like a paid servant without any pay from my ma. But they accused me of running around with fellows and being immoral. His mother swore herself black and blue in the face that he never touched a drink. I sat there in court while they lied in their teeth. I was beat. They got my kid. After they took my baby, I didn't care what happened. Mother wanted me to go on making like her servant. She'd have bridge parties and she'd get all dressed up and I had to serve the ladies and not play bridge.

"I don't know if I'll ever be able to forgive her. I really think it's as much her fault as anybody else's that I lost my child. She hurt me plenty—more than anybody else in the whole world. She's cold and selfish and I can't stand her. As long as they thought such lousy things about me in that way, what difference does it make. So one day, I just lit out with this guy and we hitchhiked just to get away from my ma. We went down South and he sort of conned some people into giving us a good time. I got a job as a waitress in a dog wagon but I had plenty of time to lie around the beach too. It was real nice. One day a fellow came in and began asking questions about this guy I'd run off with. When I got to the room I asked him if he was in debt or something or if the cops were after him and he slapped me so hard I fell down. After that, I knew it was all over."

She met her present husband when he came into the diner: "He had class about him, he got all the way through high school." At the time of our interview, they had been happily married for seven years. The sexual tie in the present marriage is very strong. The husband enjoys her emotional dependence upon him, and says that he has "tried to make it up to her for all the trouble she has had" before she met him.

An alignment with the father against the mother in the marital conflict of parents constitutes the third variety of problems disclosed by hostile daughters. The daughter's resentment of her mother is illustrated in the following case:

"What makes me maddest about Mother is the way she treats my father," confessed a 26-year-old woman, "Ma puts on airs. She wanted to be somebody and my father is only a guard in a bank. It's a wonder he doesn't have ulcers. There is no pleasing my mother. She is always criticizing and complaining. She was a good mother as far as feeding and dressing and trying to bring us up, and she worked hard, but she made you feel awful and you could never do anything to please her. So finally everybody just shut up, including my dad. We'd try to leave her alone and go talk with Dad but my brother ain't got no use for my dad. Dad caught him stealing some stuff and licked the tar out of him and my brother was sore as hell about it. He didn't appreciate that Dad was trying to make him do right. He just thought if he was slick and got away with it, that was the thing to do. Ma was all worked up about it and she didn't say so in so many words but the general idea was don't get caught and everything will be all right.

A few years ago this woman told her mother that if she "couldn't stop riding my father she should at least keep quiet. After that my ma let out after me like a wildcat. The day I tell my ma anything I care about, I should have my head examined."

This account of parental relations was confirmed in the interview with this woman's husband: "There's one thing you can count on for sure—her old lady really does get her down. She rides her old man—he's a queer duck—my wife loves him a lot and it's a shame that it goes on like this."

These hostile daughters are more numerous among the less-educated women, constituting 23 per cent of the total, as compared with only 5 per cent among the high school graduates. There are several possible explanations of this difference. The fathers of the less-educated wives were unskilled and semi-skilled workers, whereas the fathers of the high school graduates had more skilled occupations. Possibly disappointment with the husband's economic performance led some women to channel affection towards their sons with the result that their daughters felt rejected. The less-educated women come from somewhat larger families than the high school graduates and this raised the possibility of maternal rejection on the part of an overworked mother. But upon examination the hostile daughters turned out to come from average, not the largest, families; in fact, several had only one sibling, a brother.

The hypothesis that the greater frequency of hostile daughters among the less-educated may have been the result of selection was not confirmed by the records: in only one case was the conflict with the mother the major cause of leaving school. Possibly the mothers of the less-educated wives were more restrictive and less understanding, or the daughters more sexually precocious, but these hypotheses could not be tested. The age composition of less-educated and educated wives is nearly identical, but the average duration of marriage is greater for the less-educated. Duration of marriage could hardly affect the frequency of severe conflict with the mother. But the greater dependence of the young wife upon her mother may have contributed to the higher proportion of "close" ties among the high school graduates.

The relationships of the wives with their fathers are more distant than those with their mothers. This is true regardless of educational level. Only 34 per cent of the wives enjoy "close or very close" ties with their fathers, whereas the comparable figure for the mothers is 62 per cent. The most prevalent relationship to the father is the more distant one, designated as "fair," with 40 per cent of the cases falling into this category. The proportion of "hostile" relationships is identical for both parents, but the hostile daughters tend to be more estranged from their fathers and more bitter towards their mothers. In general, then, the feelings towards the mothers are more highly polarized. The intensity of feeling is greater and, in case of friction, the resentment is stronger.

The complaints against the father expressed by the hostile daughters sometimes refer to his excessive strictness and lack of affection, and in other cases, concern his alleged failure as provider and head of the family.

"I don't respect my father," declared a 23-year-old woman. "He and my mother separated two years ago. Although they slept in the same bed, I don't think they were husband and wife for years. I'll tell you about my father. They would fight and maybe he would or wouldn't be in the wrong—and the only thing he would do is to have an attack of asthma. He's a cheap one, very tight. He once asked me to use my charge account to get some drapes. He wouldn't pay and I had to pay up. It would be no use to go to him. He'd say, take your drapes back. I never see him, I never even think of him." This woman also complained of economic hardships she suffered in childhood.

Although all wives are closer to their mothers than to their fathers the high school graduates have warmer attitudes towards their fathers—"close" and "very close" ties are twice as frequent among them as among the less-educated women; the proportion of "hostile" daughters, however, does not differ in the two educational groups.

The fathers of the high school graduates represent a higher occupational level and, it may be surmised, a higher income and educational level in comparison with the fathers of the less-educated women. Does the gulf which exists between the sexes among the less-educated create a distance between daughters and fathers? The less-educated husbands in this study do not participate in child care to the extent true of the high school graduates, and this may have been the case in the parental generation as well. Is the coolness of the adult daughter the fruit of paternal aloofness? These questions will be examined in the light of the husband's attitudes towards his father.

The Husband and His Parents

The husbands are not as close to their parents as the wives are to theirs.[7] This sex difference is especially great in regard to attitudes toward the mother since only 43 per cent of the husbands, but 62 per cent of the wives, enjoy "close" relations with their mothers. The proportion of "close" relations with the father is 34 per cent for the wives, and only 27 per cent for the husbands.

This does not mean that most of the men are uninvolved with their relatives or unconcerned about their welfare. The frequency of contacts with parents is one sign of such attachment. But to be classified as "close," the son has to share his experiences with the parent, express some warmth and appreciation or explicitly describe the relationship as a close one. The husbands, especially the less-educated men, tend to be generally reserved about their emotions. This general reticence may, therefore, be reflected in the relatively low proportion of "close" relations with parents.

Considering the segregation of the sexes, it is noteworthy that not only the wives but the husbands are closer to their

---

[7] Several studies reporting a similar finding for a college-educated sample, are summarized in Mirra Komarovsky, 1950.

mothers than to their fathers.[8] Forty-three per cent of the husbands enjoy "close" relations with their mothers, but this proportion drops to 27 per cent with the fathers; the proportion of hostile (or estranged) sons is only 9 per cent in relation to mothers, but rises to 25 per cent in relation to fathers (Table 21).

Only a few husbands see in their fathers' occupational careers a model worth emulating. A stationary engineer sponsored his son at the union and the son has followed in his father's occupation. One young husband hopes to inherit his father's luncheonette business in partnership with his brother. A high school graduate works in his father's garage. A 25-year-old high school graduate strives to measure up to his father's achievements; the latter is a section manager in a mail-order business who helped his son get a job in the stockroom of the same company. According to his wife, this young man "hero-worships his father, though he gets sore because his father still treats him like a boy." This man reported an incident in which his father lost his temper and the son said to him: "Dad, you have managed men all your life, why can't you manage your own family?"

But the men who respect their fathers' success are the exceptions. Generally, when a son does express admiration for his father, the reference is to his father's character rather than to his attainments. "He is a prince of a fellow," said one man about his father. "He has tremendous patience—he has more patience than I have with my own kids. When I lived at home, he'd always listen to me and give me good advice." Another man commented: "Dad's a prince of a guy—he'll do anything for you, give you the shirt off his back."

Turning to the hostile sons, we distinguished three types of problems. Some sons complain of paternal indifference combined with strictness and beatings:

> "My father-in-law has been more of a dad to me than my own dad ever was," stated a 23-year-old man with eight years of schooling. His own father had a hot temper and had taken his belt to him many times when it wasn't necessary. He had been too strict with all the children. "I hope," added this man, "I will be a lot easier on my own kids."

[8] Similar findings are cited for college-educated men. See Mirra Komarovsky, 1950 and 1956.

A mixture of contempt, pity and resentment towards a weak father characterizes another group of hostile sons:

A 32-year-old man with eight years of schooling, an only son, is bitter towards both parents. He speaks with anger about his domineering mother. The one relative he admires is his deceased grandfather: "He was a real man. He carried a knife around with him as does any good Scot. He was not afraid of anyone." His father allowed himself to be completely dominated by his wife. This was confirmed by the wife of the respondent: "You should see his old man. He just sits around and never says a word. His wife hollers at him in front of people, but he doesn't say a thing."

One woman described a similar resentment on the part of her husband towards his weak father.

The 23-year-old husband is a high school graduate and the only son in a family of five children. His parents' marriage is unhappy. His father is not a good provider and his domineering mother makes life miserable for the family. "She fascinated my husband but he was scared to death of her as a boy. He tried to be domineering like his mother but he resented the way she tried to make a man of him."

This young husband said of his mother: "She was disappointed in my father and tried to mold something out of me, but that didn't work either."

A combination of a weak father and a strong mother does not always result in resentment towards the father. In one such family the son clearly reserves his admiration for his mother, but relations with his father are affectionate.

This man's father was a truck driver who lost his arm in an accident. Another accident affected his eyesight. When our respondent was nine years old, his mother had to go to work, with his grandmother taking care of the large family of eight children. "Father used to drink quite a lot," said the interviewee. "He wasn't violent or anything, he would just come home drunk and go to sleep. Then we moved to a new house and mother said to him, 'Well, we have new neighbors and you wouldn't want to make a fool of yourself and come home drunk.' Father stopped drinking and doesn't take a drop now. He cannot work because of his accident, and gets compensation. He just works in the cellar and keeps the house in repair." Asked who was boss in his parental family, the respondent said that his father "made a lot of noise," but his mother "got her way most of the time." His mother is "a wonderful woman, nothing fazes her." She brought up her own eight children and is always ready to take care of her grandchildren. An employed daughter-in-law leaves her child with his mother during the day. Our respondent visits his parental home three or four times a week. He occasionally slips a few dollars to his mother. The latter visits her married children occasionally, but she goes alone; his father generally does not go out. Nevertheless, he sees his children and grandchildren frequently when they come to the parental home, and the whole family comes to see the father on Father's Day.

We interviewed the parental couple in this case. The father appeared to be a good-natured, talkative man with a sense of humor, and the mother—despite her deeply lined and tired face—a strong woman who held her large family together and continues to be the head of the family. Nevertheless, the father also enjoys a degree of affection. His good nature, the more-or-less satisfactory marriage, the fact that his poverty was caused by his accidents and not by personal failure—all of these circumstances protected him from the resentment directed against weak fathers by other sons.[9]

Hostility to a father occasionally stems from paternal rejection. Failure to win love and recognition from his father continues to oppress a 36-year-old man, a high school graduate, in the following case:

When asked for examples of hurt feelings, his response at first was negative—neither his wife, nor his boss or workmates, nor yet his in-laws or friends ever hurt his feelings. "What about your father?" asked the interviewer, and he replied: "You've got something there. I don't know how to express it—he doesn't give me credit. He always sided with my sister, ever since I can remember. I built this porch. I enclosed it all by myself. Father came over and I showed it to him. He acted as though it was nothing. He started bragging about what his son-in-law did, and I went over to look at it and

[9] In this case, the son, our respondent, is Catholic. The few Catholic husbands among our respondents appear to have particularly warm ties with their mothers. One husband stops over at his mother's home, if only for a few minutes, every afternoon on the way home from work. The wife of another complains that her husband goes to buy a loaf of bread and spends a couple of hours at his mother's.

I could do it with my eyes closed. A child could do it. But my father is always the same. We bought a new gas range and I called to tell him. We wanted to get a new car and I tried him out. When I tell him, he doesn't act the right way, he never gives me any credit." This man remarked that he had a very bad memory and that he hardly remembered his childhood.

In addition to the patterns of strain described above, a few hostile sons reported that their fathers were alcoholics who failed to provide for the family. In one or two cases, the fathers had left their families.

Parental relations of the less-educated men are less satisfactory than those of the high school graduates. This proves especially true of relations with the father. The small number of high school graduates leaves these findings inconclusive, but the differences are striking and consistent. Over one-half of the high school graduates, as compared with only 14 per cent of the less-educated, are "close" to their fathers. The proportion of bitter or estranged sons is almost twice as high among the less-educated. The better-educated husband enjoys a higher proportion of "close" ties with his mother, also, but the proportion of sons hostile to the mother is the same for the two educational groups.[10]

The fathers of the male high school graduates are superior in occupational level to the fathers of the less-educated. Over one-half of the former are skilled men, and there are no unskilled workers among them. By contrast, almost one-half of the fathers of the less-educated men are unskilled. One may assume that the fathers of the high school graduates are also better providers. Certain problems reported by the hostile sons, such as alcoholism and economic failure, can be expected to be associated with low socio-economic status—as its cause or consequence. The smaller involvement of the less-educated fathers in child rearing may also contribute to estrangement from children. Moreover, the lower the occupational status of the fathers, the less likely is the son to turn to him for occupational guidance.

It has been shown that both wives and husbands remain

[10] The high school graduates are on the average younger than the less-educated. But youth does not account for their superior relations with parents, because, holding the age constant, the result still gives less-educated men an excess of hostile sons.

closer to their mothers than to their fathers. The earlier discussion of confidants bears witness to the same fact. The older men in Glenton appear isolated—much more so than their wives. The latter continue to perform instrumental and emotional functions for their married children. They act as guides in homemaking and child care, all the more so because their daughters and daughters-in-law have not, in middle-class fashion, discovered the professional expert on child rearing. The older woman is called upon to baby-sit and to help in sickness or in other emergencies. The older men, who have no property to bequeath and no background of business experience, have fewer family functions. The younger relatives, brothers and brothers-in-law, are more likely to be called upon for help in moving, building or other physical tasks. If his married children are drawn to the father it is primarily by the strength of personal ties. But the non-involvement of the fathers in child rearing and the difficulties experienced by the less-educated men in communication hinder the development of close personal relationships.

The isolation of the fathers may be conveyed by an incident witnessed at the home of an older couple, parents of a respondent. Two boys, grandchildren of the couple, came in and monopolized the conversation, telling their grandmother the news of the day. The grandfather teased them a little and called them to look at his tropical fish. The boys walked over to the fish and returned to their grandmother, competing for her attention. The woman smiled and, referring to the fish, said: "I call that his family now." Her husband agreed that the fish were "just like children to me." When everybody goes away over the weekend, he often stays at home to feed and to take care of them.

Relatively few older men appear to be intimately involved in the lives of their married children. One such exceptional parent, a timekeeper, is devoted to his 4-year-old grandson, and frequently baby-sits at his son's home. His daughter-in-law reported that he loved children and that he came to the hospital when his grandson was born and seemed more excited about the event than her husband. The husband is devoted to his father. "He'd do anything for you, but he had always had an irregular shift and couldn't spend much time with us children. He's got a regular shift now, and my kid sees a lot more of him than I did." The warmth of the older man ties him to his son's family. The interviewer observed the 4-year-old child running into the arms of his grandfather, who apparently gives him the fathering he was unable to give to his son.

To sum up, the great majority of husbands and wives enjoy moderately satisfactory or even close relationships with their parents. But the study discloses a relatively high frequency of hostile sons and daughters among the less-educated adults, involving one-fifth to one-fourth of the respondents. Characteristically, the unsatisfactory relationships are those of the husband to his father and of the wife to both parents. The high school graduates have warmer relations with parents although both the wives and the husbands are closer to their mothers, with the result that the older men are relatively isolated in the kinship structure.

CHAPTER
12

A Marriage Triangle: The Husband, His Wife, and His Mother-in-Law

Mother-in-law jokes may be popular among men, but according to all existing studies American wives, not their husbands, report greater difficulties with in-laws. More wives than husbands, for example, testify that they dislike their mothers-in-law.[1] Although these facts were derived from studies of predominantly middle-class families, it was anticipated that the in-law problem in Glenton would also be more frequently a problem of women. And indeed the high school graduates conform to this middle-class pattern. One-third of the wives reveal serious dissatisfaction with their in-laws, whereas the husbands enjoy relatively satisfactory in-law relationships. The surprising finding, however, is the prevalence of in-law problems among the less-educated husbands. One-third of these men experience strain in relation to their in-laws, the same proportion as that of women with in-law grievances, irrespective of the women's education (see Table 22).

[1] Evelyn Millis Duvall, 1954, Paul Wallin, 1954, Peggy S. Marcus, 1950, Judson T. Landis and Mary G. Landis, 1953.

These results are derived from direct questions about in-laws, but supporting evidence is found in responses to questions about sources of unhappy moods. The more-educated women mentioned "my in-laws" as a source of negative moods much more frequently than the male high school graduates. But among the less-educated, the husbands and the wives attributed unhappy moods to their in-laws with equal frequency.[2] The in-laws included in these unhappy relationships are predominantly the mothers-in-law; in only one-fifth of the cases does the major conflict involve another in-law. In this respect the less-educated and the educated men and women are alike.

The in-law problems of the less-educated husbands were all the more unexpected because their responses to the test stories revealed considerable tolerance towards close ties between the wife and her mother. In contrast, the educated men stressed the primacy of the marriage relationship. It could have been assumed, therefore, that the wife's continuing dependence upon her mother might pose a greater threat to the educated husband, arousing his moral indignation and jealousy. It is now clear, however, that even if these factors do give the less-educated husbands some immunity to in-law conflict, they are more than offset by forces operating in the opposite direction.

The strain between the men and their mothers-in-law seldom breaks out into an open and violent conflict. The control the men exercise over the expression of hostility is impressive. "To be polite to your in-laws and to try to get along and not make any trouble" are important requirements of conjugal roles. If relations are cool and frequent contacts are unavoidable, the thing to do is to "keep to yourself." Respect is only one reason for this restraint. Several persons spoke of the risk of spontaneous expressions of feelings; as one of them put it, "You can fight with your wife one hour and forget all about it the next, but if you let off steam with your in-laws, it may be for keeps."

In-law relationships are of course not always strained. Three categories of mother-in-law relationships were distinguished. The first is a "good" relationship, when affection and positive satisfac-

2 In-laws constituted 5 per cent of the total of 242 negative feelings reported by educated women, but only 1 per cent of the 114 listed by educated men. Among the less-educated, the figures are 2 per cent of 356 negative feelings on the part of women, and an identical 2 per cent of 249 listed by men.

tion are coupled with only minor conflicts, if any. An "average" relationship is one in which favorable comments are interspersed with some dissatisfactions, though not serious ones. The third category of "strained" relations is characterized by serious problems and absence of positive remarks.[3] The mother-in-law relationships of the respondents are good in 27 per cent, average in 41 per cent and strained in 31 per cent of the cases. In one case, relations are severed. (See Table 22 for sex and educational differences in mother-in-law relationships.)

The purpose of this chapter is to attempt to account for the absence or presence of in-law conflict and, more specifically, for the unexpected prevalence of in-law problems among the less-educated husbands. To anticipate our major findings, the following conditions tend to be associated with an unsatisfactory relationship between the husband and his mother-in-law: marriage to a better-educated wife; wife's hostility towards her mother; wife's emotional dependence upon her mother; and economic and social interdependence, including a joint household with in-laws. Since none of these conditions invariably causes in-law conflict, the task of the following pages is two-fold—to trace the ways in which each tends to disturb relationships and to discern conditions that occasionally offset or neutralize these disturbing influences.

Marriage to a Better-educated Wife

Marriage to a better-educated wife is found to be associated with in-law conflict.[4] (Another study also reports that the adjustment to his in-laws is particularly difficult if the husband is less well-educated than his wife.[5]) Since persons with over 12 years of schooling were excluded from our sample, none of the male high school graduates is married to a better-educated wife. But in the population at large, men who have not completed high school are more likely than college graduates to marry "up" educationally.[6] The following case studies will illuminate the various ways

---

[3] These assessments were reached independently by two judges evaluating 73 less-educated men and women. The judges agreed in 67 and disagreed in 6 cases.

[4] Of the 11 less-educated husbands with in-law problems, 5 were married to high school graduates; of the 8 husbands who enjoyed "good" in-law relations, only 1 was married to a high school graduate.

[5] Peggy S. Marcus, 1950.

[6] Paul C. Glick and Hugh Carter, 1958, p. 297.

in which educational inferiority tends to produce disturbing effects in relationships with in-laws.

Mr. and Mrs. Miller, aged 21 and 22 respectively, have four children. Mr. M. is a warehouseman in a meat processing plant, earning $98 a week. The couple had saved $1200 towards buying a house. Mrs. M. took a college preparatory course in high school and her mother had hoped that she would go on to a school of nursing and eventually marry a doctor. Instead, at the age of 17 she married Mr. M., then only 16, who had dropped out of school when in the tenth grade.

The mother-in-law's feeling that her daughter has married "beneath" herself leads to frequent criticisms of Mr. M:

> "My mother complains that her children failed her by marrying so lousy. My mother and my husband are friendly on the surface; they even joke with one another, but they hate each other. We don't visit my relatives too often, my mother is ashamed of him. She says, 'He is so ignorant, he can't even carry on a decent conversation.' "

The mother-in-law's criticism extends not only to Mr. M.'s poor education but to the low prestige of his occupation: "I wish Mother wouldn't needle me about John's job. He likes his work, the pay is adequate and I am satisfied with it. If I am mad I bring up the job just to make him mad."

Similar criticisms are reported by another woman whose marriage to a mechanic had been a disappointment to her mother: "My husband says Ma wished I had married somebody with money or some upper-crust person she could brag about. Maybe he is right."

Another feature of such marriages is the demoralizing effect that the wife's superior education may have upon the self-esteem of the husband. Thus, Mr. M. commented:

> "My wife thinks that I ought to go back to night school and finish school, but if she'd think into it, she'd know it just couldn't be done." He did go back once or twice, but he was too far behind to make it up. Anyway, he said, if he had more schooling he might get a different job, but he wouldn't be making any more money.

The couple has recently joined a church and they read Psalms and a devotional book at night. The wife enjoys "very much" reading aloud to her husband: "Usually he can't understand and I explain every line. I don't know if I do it to show him I am smarter. I don't think so. I think I enjoy explaining it to him so he'll be proud of me, though a lot of times he won't listen . . . he says he makes up for it because I am not as smart as a six-year-old. For example, I might set the dishes close to the edge of the table so they will fall off. He'll say, 'For being as smart as you are, you are the stupidest jerk going. Any three-year-old could figure that one out.' "

Talking about this evening reading, the husband remarked: "She calls me a dummy. I admit I quit school early, and I am sorry for it. Still, if I don't understand, I ask her, it is faster than looking the word up." His self-appraisal may be inferred from the fact that he would like his sons to have white-collar jobs rather than follow in his occupation.

His educational inferiority played a part in his losing control of money: "When we were first married, the first three months, I took care of money. She was critical and told me to mark everything down. I told her, 'If you could do it better, you do it.' "

Inferior education often results in a self-defeating strategy of marital and in-law conflict. The weapons taught him by his milieu accentuate conflicts and lead to his defeat. Mr. M. recognizes that he is no match for his wife:

"I don't think I could win an argument with her. If she is wrong, she should say so, but she doesn't."

The very level of his wife's attacks is too much for him. Mrs. M. reports: "I told him, 'You run away from home, you run away from school, and you are running out here, you cannot face it.' " Because he cannot defend himself with words, he turns in helpless fury to physical aggression. He beats his wife, his children, he breaks and throws things around the house, he hides the box with the household money, he drinks, and he leaves home for a night.

"After one fight, I left home and thought I would stay out all night with the fellows but I came back at four A.M. I apologized, but in my heart I knew I was right. If she'd only admit she is wrong. If I am wrong, I am wrong. If she knows she is wrong, she should say so. Later she says she did it to tease me. Maybe I take too seriously the things she says."

Mrs. M. described her husband's violent temper: "It's just a little thing I say to him, and he snaps and goes crazy. I've had two black eyes in three months. I would forgive him after it was all over if he didn't make fun of me." After pulling her hair and knocking her about, he told the kids, "Look at the beauty there." She took him to court a few months ago when she was eight months pregnant and the judge gave him a good tongue-lashing. He told the judge that he knew he was wrong and had to learn to control his temper. He did for about four months, but then it started all over again. The last time, he threw a hot pan at her. She didn't remember what brought it on, but added, "It all boils down to the fact that I stayed at my mother's too late the day before and that he was jealous, he resents her so."

She talked to the minister, who said that her husband was not mature and that she should help by turning the other cheek. When she first threatened him with court action, he said, "I'll tell the judge that the kids aren't mine." She laughed at him because the children look like him. When he becomes enraged, he beats her and the children, and knocks her head against the wall. Sometimes he has his friends come in and laugh at her because she is black-and-blue.

Mr. M.'s violence, however, not only fails to bring him victory, but creates a vicious cycle of marital conflict in which he is ultimately the loser. The beatings get him into court. The judge and the minister are his wife's and his mother-in-law's allies. The attitude towards physical aggression in his social group may be more permissive than in "upper" blue-collar families, but they are not so permissive as to free Mr. M. completely of some sense of guilt. He admitted that he had a violent temper and wished he could control it better. His violent outbursts are used by his mother-in-law as an argument to remove him from control of money and to keep the savings in Mrs. M.'s name. Many of the marriage quarrels are about money:

> Asked to describe the handling of money, Mr. M. said that his mother-in-law thought he should sign his check and put it on the table. But he cashes the check at the bank and gives his wife the cash and the stub. "She always tells me what her mother said, instead of keeping her mouth shut." He wishes his wife would be more interested in "figuring things out with me instead of letting her mother set her mind."

Compensatory sources of power available in other classes to a husband of inferior education are denied to Mr. M. Inferiority in education need not similarly weaken the husband's power in all classes. A successful businessman may compensate for his educational deficiency by his success as a provider and by his position in the community. Although Mr. M.'s wages are satisfactory by the standards of his group, he can derive little strategic advantage from his position as a provider. The wife receives his paycheck and has complete control of the finances in keeping with a common practice in many blue-collar families. Both of his closest pals have similar arrangements with their wives, and he accepts this practice. But he resents the fact that their savings are kept in his wife's name.

Mr. M. has no group affiliations which could lend him prestige, or from which he could draw support for his stand on various issues. He occasionally does cite opinons of his two friends in defending his own stand on marital problems—"The fellows agree with me." Ironically, in making use of this weapon, he incurs his wife's resentment for the alleged violation of privacy. He told the interviewer that he does not in fact discuss his marriage with his friends but merely pretends that he does in order to buttress his case.

Differences in conjugal norms sometimes associated with educational inferiority work to the husband's disadvantage. The "low" blue-collar norms grant the husband somewhat more freedom to behave in ways which the "upper" blue-collar wife tends to consider selfish—to spend some of his leisure away from home, to leave the housework to his wife and to come and go as he chooses. When a man marries "up," these differences work to his disadvantage, he is criticized and, in his opinion, unjustly so.

Mr. M.'s mother-in-law and his wife criticize him for staying away from home for long stretches of time over week ends, for not telling his wife at what time to expect his return, for swearing at the child, for spending money on drinks, and for not paying enough attention to his wife in public on the few occasions when they do go out together. "He goes off with the guys and ignores me. I am sure he loves me, I don't know why he does it. I guess he doesn't want anyone else to know." The only time he tells her that he loves her is when they are having intercourse, and that, she says, "doesn't count."

But Mr. M. considers these criticisms unfair: "Her mother puts her up to nag me. I get criticized for going out to buy a package of cigarettes." (The interviewer was present on one occasion when he stepped out to get some cigarettes and was absent for an hour and a half.) As to spending too much money on beer, how can he spend much, Mr. M. explained, when he never has more than a dollar or two in his pocket.

A contrasting picture is presented by one husband who married "down" educationally and socially. This man tends to judge his own behavior more severely than his wife and his mother-in-law do, and is grateful to them for "putting up with me." In terms of their norms, his behavior is quite acceptable. The sense of injustice experienced by Mr. M. is here replaced by a feeling of gratitude, with differing consequences for in-law relations.

Educational inferiority may lead to in-law conflict in still another way. When coupled with superior education of the wife's parents, it may make for invidious comparisons.

A 37-year-old tool maker, a grammar school graduate, is married to a high school graduate. His reading is restricted to tool catalogues and *Popular Mechanics*. She reads novels and she "can have a more intelligent conversation" with her cousins and her father than with her husband. Her husband resents her attitude toward her father: "Who do you think your father is, God Almighty?" She can never make a decision without consulting her father. For example, "My husband and I went together to look at a house we thought of buying. I wouldn't put down a deposit before talking to Daddy. My husband asked me 'why do you always have to call your father?' "

This was one of two cases in which the in-law strain involved the father-in-law more than the mother-in-law. "She needs an O.K. from her father on anything she does," remarked the husband. "Don't get me wrong, I don't fight with my in-laws. I just like to be far away from them. We get along fine now because they have moved."

These cases illustrate the process of in-law conflict resulting from the inferior education of the husband. But lower education does not inevitably bring about conflict. First of all, the extent of difference in years of schooling may vary from one to several years. Moreover, formal schooling is not a precise index of the critical element affecting the power position of the husband—his verbal skills, interests and intelligence.

A 31-year-old mechanic left school in his second year of high school because his father had deserted the family and he had to go to work. His wife completed high school. His earnings are the same as those of Mr. M., and he had also attempted to return to school. But here the similarity between the two men ends. Mr. M. had given up because he felt he was too far behind, but this mechanic found that the youngsters were "fooling around and that he was wasting his time." He is a deacon in the church and has played an important part in the selection of a new preacher. Despite fewer years of formal schooling, this man is not intellectually inferior to his wife, as indicated by his vocabulary and his interests.

Furthermore, lower education may or may not be associated with the kind of occupation and social status that disappoint the aspirations of the mother-in-law. At least one mother-in-law, critical of her son-in-law's education and "background," remarked: "But he is a hustler. You have to hand it to him; if work is slow in his company, he tries to pick up a job here and there."

But it appears that though the disappointment may be muted, the skilled occupation fails to comfort a woman who is sensitive to the lower occupational prestige of her son-in-law. The big divide is between manual and white-collar jobs. Of the 14 couples with educational differences, some husbands had skilled, while others held only semi-skilled or unskilled jobs. The skilled job did not protect the husband from in-law conflict. Of seven skilled workers (all with lower education), three had in-law conflict, and the proportion was identical for the semi-skilled and unskilled. If there exists any difference in prestige between the skilled and the semi-skilled jobs, it is apparently too slight to satisfy the status aspirations of the mother-in-law.

Even when the factor of lower schooling has its full force in the sense that it does represent an actual educational difference and is coupled with some disappointment on the part of the mother-in-law, in-law conflict is not inevitable. The safeguards against, and the precipitants of such conflict will become apparent as we consider some other factors predisposing the less-educated husbands to in-law conflict.

The Wife's Antagonism to Her Mother as a Source of In-Law Conflict

In a number of families, the husband's conflict with his mother-in-law reflects his identification with his wife—he is her

ally against her mother, occasionally acting as the buffer between the two women. This type of in-law conflict runs counter
to the familiar stereotype which pictures the wife and her mother
in coalition against the husband or the wife acting as an unhappy
buffer between the other two. The preceding chapter reported
that the proportion of hostile daughters was more frequent among
the less-educated than among the high school graduates and may,
thus, contribute to the proneness of the less-educated men to in-
law conflict.

Mr. and Mrs. N. illustrate this pattern of in-law strain.

"The things that bother us isn't marriage," said Mr. N.,
the 38-year-old taxi driver and father of three, "it is things like
our family. There is one thing you can count on for sure and
that is that her old lady really does get her down. It is a shame
that it goes on like this. I try to keep her away from her family
as much as I can on account of they do hurt her a lot."

They go to visit his in-laws and the in-laws sit around as if
they were mad at each other, not saying much of anything.
"It's a real nasty way that they've got about them and it gives
you the creeps. She hates to go to see them even more than I
do."

Mr. N. explained that his mother-in-law often needles him
too and gets under his skin. He controls his irritation because
his wife "cusses them out so much, that I find I'm sticking up
for them, sometimes."

Mr. N.'s emotional role in marriage is to furnish balance
and support to his high-strung wife. He admires her: "I was
lucky to get her. She takes things much harder than most
people, but then she's smarter than most people."

Mr. N. is hurt by his mother-in-law's needling of him, but
his major resentment against the older woman is caused by his
identification with his wife.

The Wife's Emotional Dependence upon Her Mother

Of ten less-educated husbands who have dependent wives,
six have in-law conflict, which is twice the proportion existing
in the whole group. Moreover, the proportion of dependent wives
is greater among the less-educated: 10 of 33 had dependent wives
as compared to only 1 of the 12 high school graduates.

The assumption that the wife's emotional dependence upon
her mother, in and of itself, may not be as threatening to a less-

educated husband as it is to a high school graduate may be valid. But, as we shall see, emotional dependence increases the potency of other disturbing conditions. A dependent wife tends to create situations in which the husband's will is pitted against the will of his mother-in-law. When the wife is under the influence of her mother, a disagreement between her mother and her husband leads to in-law conflict in areas in which a couple must make joint decisions. With a dependent wife, consequently, it becomes more important for the husband and his mother-in-law to be congenial. Conflict is minimized to the extent that the couple makes few joint decisions, either because roles are segregated or because life is routinized.

A 37-year-old foreman of a construction crew of four men, who has been married for six years, speaks of his 31-year-old wife:

"I would like to get her broke away from her parents. Their influence on her sometimes seeps through."

He comes from Texas and is "lonesome for my folks." He wanted to take his wife and their child to visit his family for Christmas. His wife said that her parents disapproved of their spending the money for such a trip and, anyway, she didn't want to leave her parents for Christmas. She thought the trip South should be postponed till Easter. Asked whether he tried to persuade his wife to change her mind, the husband said, "It wouldn't help."

A 23-year-old Catholic woman with three children is a daughter of a Catholic father and a Protestant mother. Her mother thought that the young couple should have waited before having children. "My mother's idea," the wife said, "is that you ought to have a house and a place to bring up children. She doesn't think that you *make* a place for them whenever they come." Her husband, also a Catholic, felt that they ought to let children come when they come, not to wait to have them at their own convenience.

"I used to go along with everything my mother said," remarked the wife, "and I used to ask her for advice all the time, and my mother is the kind who would run your life if you gave her the chance."

If the children got sick, she would call her mother at once. If she didn't follow her mother's advice, she used to feel very badly about it. Eventually she claimed, she learned to make her own decisions, but this was not her husband's opinion. He said: "The further you live away from your relatives, the better. I tell her something and still she has to go and ask her mother and even if it is the same thing, she feels better if her mother says it." Asked whether there has been any improvement since the first year of marriage, he said: "No change. She still gets too much advice from her mother."

This husband participates in child care, shopping and housework, partly because his wife needs his help and partly as a matter of interest. Because of this participation, they must make many joint decisions. This increases the possibilities of conflict with his mother-in-law.

A dependent wife provides her mother with weapons through her pliability. Confidences shared with the mother supply the mother with ammunition, and if she is a managing and critical person she can frustrate the interests of the husband in various ways. Consequently, with a dependent daughter the mother must be especially discreet and self-restrained if in-law conflict is to be avoided. A husband who keeps from his wife the exact amount of their savings indirectly illustrates this generalization: "Her mother will worm it out of her and will broadcast it all over."

Finally, the dependency of the wife upon her mother increases the frequency of interaction and makes it more difficult to alleviate in-law conflict by at least partial separation.

But the wife's dependency does not invariably create tension; in fact it occasionally coexists with very warm in-law relationships. In one such case, the young couple lives at some distance from the wife's parents. But physical separation is not the only safeguard. In-law relations are exceptionally harmonious in another case despite the fact that the widowed mother-in-law shares the household with the couple. This exceptionally understanding and discreet mother-in-law shares the nurturing role towards her daughter with the latter's kindly, somewhat stolid, gentle and well-adjusted husband. Exceptional personalities, compatibility of emotional needs and a good marriage combine in this happy outcome.

Another case is instructive precisely because everything in this marriage would seem to point to inevitability of conflict—the marital relations are strained; the wife is deeply dependent upon her mother; the husband is a troubled and inconsiderate person who surely provides both women with grounds for criticism. Each of these potentially threatening factors is neutralized by some countervailing condition. The complex dynamics of these relationships is revealed in the following description of the case:

Mrs. Clark, whose sexual life was described in Chapter 4, is a 30-year-old, immature and unhappy woman, deeply dependent upon her mother. She gave numerous illustrations of this dependency. Whenever she is unhappy or worried about something, talking to her mother "helps very much." As to her husband, "I don't want to bother him too much. He's got a lot on his mind already." Speaking about some difficulties she had in sex relations she said: "I asked Mother about it. I was afraid that there was something wrong with me." Her mother assures her that she will learn in time to handle her domestic duties more efficiently.

The husband, a troubled man, is the only son of a dominant mother, towards whom he is very hostile, and a "henpecked" father. His father is an electrician. The parents own their home, and a plot of land on a lake. They are greatly disappointed in their son because he did not want to become an electrician and did not continue his education. "My husband got away from them," said Mrs. C. about her in-laws, "and now he is boss in his own home and that is the way it should be." Mr. C. used words which the interviewer thought would be above the head of his wife and mother-in-law ("personality," "paranoid," "skillful"). He said that he reads "good magazines such as *Harper's* and the *Atlantic Monthly*." His ambition is to develop his hobby and make a fortune in his own business. He had one or two schemes that did not work out. He started a correspondence course, but he is still in his first year of high school.

His wife said of the husband: "He worries because he don't make something better of himself when he wants to so bad." His frustrations manifest themselves in periods of deep moodiness and withdrawal. What helps him at such times is to go out for a drink. He spends a good deal of time away from home alone or with male friends.

His mother-in-law, who was also interviewed, fears that he may want to try his luck in a new community. She would not like them to move, but she said nothing about it, either to him or to her daughter.

His wife's dependence upon her mother does not trouble Mr. C. in the least. There is nothing in the coalition of mother and wife to frustrate his interests because he is master of the situation. Both women are trying to please him. The mother's advice to her daughter is usually "to bear and forbear" in marriage. His influence over his mother-in-law was revealed when his mother-in-law first refused to be interviewed; Mr. C., in learning about it, said: "Why don't you tell me what it is about, I'll talk to the old girl, and I think she'll probably do it for me."

There is another reason why his wife's ties to her mother do not arouse anxiety in Mr. C.—he is neither concerned nor particularly interested in his wife; in fact he is relieved that her mother takes the burden of emotional reassurance off his shoulders. Moreover, the full extent of his wife's dependence upon her mother may not be known to Mr. C. They do not tell him, for example, that the mother-in-law frequently comes over to clean the apartment. Finally, the respect accorded him by his mother-in-law offers Mr. C. some surcease from the criticism and humiliation he feels he received from his own mother.

The circumstances cited above account for the friendly feelings of the son-in-law, but the mother-in-law's tolerance of this selfish man remains to be explained. Why do not the two women combine to attempt to defeat him over various issues of married life? Both women look up to him. He is difficult, but he is "smart" and somewhat superior to them in class background. The older woman said that his parents were well off and "kind of uppity."

Because of class differences in conjugal norms, the two women do not judge his behavior as severely as he judges it himself. He expressed some gratitude to them for "putting up with me."

In answer to the interviewer's question: "Don't you think Mr. C. should stay home and keep your daughter company more often?" the mother-in-law remarked: "A man has a right to go out if he wants to." She went on: "He can't be as big as he tries to be, but I think he is going to be somebody. People say that he is stuck on himself and impolite a lot of the time and I guess maybe he is but he is smart and I stick up for him when people say things about him." Mrs. C. expressed similar views. A husband who gives his wife his weekly check is entitled, she thinks, to spend his overtime as he chooses. As to her husband's evenings away from home: "He has to work very hard while he is working, he ought to have some fun after work."

Even when Mrs. C. admits her husband's faults, she deflects some of the blame towards herself. She feels that in marriage it is up to the wife to secure her interests by faithful manipulation. "A man should be master in his own house, but men like their psychologies too. You should see the way my ma handles my dad, smooth as silk. I would like to be able to do that with John."

Mrs. C. is resigned about her marital problems. Her immaturity, passivity and bewilderment play a part in this resignation, but it is partly caused also by her conception of marriage and the absence of any realistic alternatives to her plight.

When Mrs. C. defended her husband's right to have his fun, she was asked whether she had any fun. "No, that's part of the women's life now, ain't it?" The interviewer pressed her: "So you think it's all right for a man to have fun, but a woman shouldn't expect it." She thought that over a while and then said, "Well, that seems to be what everybody thinks." She continued, "It seems kinda funny, don't it? Women are supposed to enjoy their children, but they are the biggest heartache of all. They say a woman is supposed to enjoy her home, but it's a big job. I don't know how they figure." The interviewer asked whether she was going to talk this over with her mother or anybody; she smiled and said, "I might say something about it to Mary" [a girl friend].

The mother-in-law's tolerance of her turbulent and restless son-in-law derives in part from her recognition of her daughter's failings.

Her daughter is not a good homemaker and that provides Mr. C. with a margin of immunity from her criticism. Her daughter cries often and "when she feels blue she just lets everything go. Sometimes I go over and give her a hand myself; he told me once that it was the worst thing about my daughter. He told me that sometimes she gets him down so much that he wants to walk out of the house."

Mrs. C. pays for her docile adjustment to the needs of her difficult husband by periods of depression during which she can hardly carry on her household duties without physical and emotional support from her mother. The older woman helps to sustain this marriage. Mr. C. consults his mother-in-law about his marital dissatisfactions, and talks freely to her in general.

"Do you think," asked the interviewer, "you can talk more easily to your son-in-law than your daughter can?" "Yes, in some ways I'd say I could. I can laugh about some things more than she can. She takes things awful serious. Sometimes, I'll say things to her like 'Have yourself a good time,' but she don't know what I mean. He knows all right, he never misses a thing."

The harmonious relationship between Mr. C. and his mother-in-law prevails in the face of his wife's dependence upon her mother, a far from satisfactory marriage, and the husband's troubled personality. The interpretation of this case has centered upon the circumstances which appeared to offset these potentially disruptive influences.

Economic and Social Interdependence and Joint Households

The interdependence of in-laws makes it difficult for uncongenial persons to go their separate ways. These coercive bonds, therefore, tend to exacerbate the conflict, which might have been muted by infrequent contacts. Economic interdependence is greater among the less-educated families than among the high school graduates. The average income of the former is lower and the frequency of joint households with the wife's relatives is higher.[7]

The feeling of economic dependence upon relatives is frequently expressed. One man, urging his wife to curb her irritations with her mother, said: "We have to keep in good with her [his mother-in-law]. We might need her real bad." A mother of three children, whose husband earns $3600 a year remarked: "His folks will back us up if we get into real trouble."

That the mode of life and the social norms create close bonds with in-laws is clear from the fact that a complete break with them is very rare. It occurs only when the marriage itself has seriously deteriorated, or when the wife is so bitter towards her own mother that contacts between them are infrequent. The association between the husband's sentiments towards his in-laws

[7] Of 33 less-educated men, 6 reside in the same house with relatives of the wife; the corresponding figure for the high school graduates is 1 of 12. See also Alvin L. Schorr, 1960, for data on joint households by income.

and frequency of contacts with them is suggestive. Husbands with "good" in-law relationships see their in-laws more frequently than those with "average" relationships. However, husbands with "strained" relations do not stay away from their in-laws, as might have been expected, but see them as frequently as do those with "good" relations. Case studies show that at least some "average" cases are protected from deterioration by avoidance, a solution unavailable for various reasons to the other men.[8]

Economic and social interdependence reaches its maximum in joint residence, with a variety of consequences for in-law relationships. Joint residence tends to perpetuate the wife's dependency upon her mother by exposing her behavior to daily surveillance by the mother and, if she returns to her parental home, by perpetuating the environment of her life before marriage.

"My wife is close to her mother and this is as it should be, but she should behave as a married woman," said one husband who has lived since his marriage four years ago in the home owned by his widowed mother-in-law. When they were first married, the husband reported, his mother-in-law would get angry with his wife if she didn't do something the way her mother wanted it and would scarcely talk to her daughter for four or five days. Sometimes he himself might do something which the mother-in-law disapproved and she would tell it to her daughter, who would be caught in the middle trying to please both. He knew that "such things would pile up and he took a stand on it," telling his wife: "You are a married woman and you have just got to learn to stand on your own two feet. If you talk it out, it would blow over." He did not think it was right for a mother not to speak to her daughter for days and to make her unhappy. The wife remarked during her interview that her mother still treated her as though she were a child.

This shy woman, eager to placate everybody, is moving from her dependence on her mother to dependence upon her husband, but the transition is not without strain because of the joint household.

In another case, a 27-year-old woman returned with her husband and their three children to her parental home, now owned jointly by her widowed mother and the mother's unmarried sister and brother. Throughout the interview the wife referred to

[8] The association between sentiments and interaction posited by Homans is here modified by forced interaction. See George C. Homans, 1950.

her relatives as the "grown-ups" and this term symbolized the whole of her "little girl" behavior towards them.

Joint residence is an exceptional, and not an institutionalized, pattern. Consequently it presents many situations undefined by custom. In such undefined situations, participants are freer to act in terms of their own selfish interests, to invoke different principles of action or to be ambivalent. Allocation of tasks is one such undefined situation, and allocation of financial responsibility is another.

A mother of two young children keeps house for the household, which includes also her mother. Since her mother works near the shopping center, the wife usually delegates to her the shopping for the children. She has to conceal this fact from her husband, who feels strongly that it is a mother's, not a grandmother's, responsibility to select and purchase clothes for the children.

In one joint household both the husband and the wife felt hurt because the wife's mother never offered to pay for the storm windows and the curtains in her own room in addition to her normal, monthly contributions towards the expense of the house.

How fully the parent is to be included in the life of the family is perhaps the most troublesome question. The right of the married pair to some privacy is generally acknowledged, but there is also a large undefined area. What rights, for example, does a parent living with the married couple have in the living room when the family is home alone or when friends are visiting?

A woman, whose father-in-law lives with them, complains that at first the latter used to stay in his room when the couple had company but now he comes down and "cramps our fun." Ambivalence and guilt create strain even when the parent makes an effort not to be in the way. One man is irritated by the way his mother-in-law jumps up from the comfortable living room chair whenever he enters the living room. He is apparently upset by her martyrdom, all the more so because, while recognizing her right to share the living room, he does not like her. Asked for sources of "guilty feelings," he spontaneously mentioned his mother-in-law.

Another man spoke with pride of his father because the latter never criticizes his grandchildren if their parents are present. "They can break the T.V. set and he won't say a word if one of us is in the room." But this self-restraint did not protect his father from his wife's request that he eat his meals in his own room instead of the dining room because of the "noise and confusion in feeding three boisterous boys." It was not easy for the husband, he admitted, to put this request to his father, but the latter graciously replied that he was about to make a similar suggestion himself.

Sharing a household increases opportunities to clash over differences in conceptions of conjugal and parental roles. Moreover, interdependence of daily life calls for adjustments that may frustrate individual interests.

One toolmaker believes that it is a wife's duty to prepare her husband's breakfast. His mother-in-law, however, maintains that, because all he ever has for breakfast is coffee, her daughter should not have to get up so early to make her husband a cup of coffee.

Another mother-in-law is irritated by her son-in-law's inefficiency and lack of helpfulness about the house. Whenever her daughter's family has to go out, her son-in-law instead of helping his wife comes downstairs to her living room to smoke a cigarette and to complain that his wife is late.

A man disapproves of his mother-in-law's old-fashioned remedies and insists on calling the doctor when the children are sick. In minor sicknesses, however, the wife, to avoid conflict with her mother, uses those remedies, to the great annoyance of her husband.

One educated wife, sharing an apartment with her parents, longs for a home for her and her husband. With her parents in the same apartment, she and her husband cannot begin to make love in a spontaneous way—they have to get into bed, and this "takes the surprise out of it" for her.

Further Factors in Adjustment to In-Laws

The comparison of "good," "average" and "strained" in-law relationships reveals some additional circumstances which account for these different types. One of them is the ability of some in-laws to play the role of parent-substitutes to a man who has been deprived of parental affection. Of eight less-educated husbands with good in-law relations, five are either orphans or are in conflict with their own parents. "My mother has always made me feel like two cents," remarked one man, contrasting his mother with his "very nice" mother-in-law.

"He [the husband] never got along with his own parents," explained one woman. "When he married, it was like suddenly finding a mother for the first time." Another husband exceptionally friendly with his mother-in-law had lost both his parents in childhood.

The strategy of a wife who finds herself "in the middle" between her mother and her husband is another factor in the outcome. Some wives succeed in muting in-law conflict by suppressing facts that might tend to aggravate it. But other wives tend to accentuate the in-law conflict. This tends to be the case when the wife has not resolved her own conflicts with her mother. Mrs. Miller, described earlier in this chapter, is such an ambivalent daughter, who uses her husband as a weapon in punishing her mother and, conversely, her mother as a means of tormenting her husband.

The ambivalence of Mrs. M.'s feelings towards her mother is apparent from her dependence upon her mother and her feeling of having been rejected by the latter. Mrs. M. has no friends and sees her mother daily. Mr. M. said: "If she has a choice of visiting, she'll always visit her mother." Mrs. M. gave many examples of her mother's unfairness to her. Her mother refuses to baby-sit for her but she does sit for her sister. When their T.V. was out of order, she asked her mother to lend them her set "to keep my husband at home nights, but she refused." Her brother had only to ask and he got her mother's set. Mrs. M. fully reveals all of her husband's misdeeds to her mother, which deepens her mother's feeling that her children humiliated her by having married "so lousy." Mrs. M. is equally "frank" in reporting her mother's criticisms to her husband. "I wish," said Mr. M., "she wouldn't repeat what her mother said to her."

Mrs. M. may bemoan the unhappy relationship between her mother and her husband but she herself plays an active, though unconscious, role in promoting it. Asked what might improve her marriage, Mrs. M. replied: "To move out of here. We'd get along better if Mother weren't around." But she added that she liked Glenton and wouldn't want to move away.

Another condition related to the presence or absence of in-law conflict is marital estrangement. We had anticipated a strong positive association between marital happiness and in-law adjustment, if for no other reason than the presumed fact that in-law strain in itself causes marriage conflict. But, surprisingly, there are more unhappy marriages among men with "average" than among those with "strained" in-law relations.[9] This paradox is explained by the fact that "average" in-law relations are of two kinds—one in which husbands are quite involved with their in-laws and experience a normal combination of satisfactions and irritations, and another in which husbands succeed in remaining on "average" terms only because they "keep to themselves," because contacts are more formal or less frequent. This may be brought about by marital strain. A husband may be less involved with his in-laws because he is less involved with his wife. In some strained marriages husbands and wives escape into their own families; each visits his own family separately and sees his in-laws only on special occasions. Similarly, it is only a devoted husband who will identify himself with his wife to the extent that her antagonism towards her mother will become his problem as well as hers. This explains why the association between happiness in marriage and in-law harmony is not as high as was anticipated.

To recapitulate, the prevalence of in-law problems among the less-educated workers is caused not only by an excess of conflict-producing situations but also by the inability to escape them once they arise. The mode of life and the social norms of these workers create close dependence upon relatives. Because previous studies have shown repeatedly that in-law conflicts involve women predominantly, it was tempting and plausible to attribute this fact to the psychological sex differences—woman's lesser objectivity, greater sensitivity and perhaps greater pettiness and jealousy. It now seems likely that when the mode of life forces husbands to associate closely with their in-laws regardless of personal congeniality, the chances of strain can be as great as for their wives.

[9] Of 11 cases with in-law problems, only 3 marriages were unhappy, but among 14 "average" cases there were 8 unhappy marriages.

AAA

CHAPTER

13

The Long Arm of the Job[1]

The men in this study are white, native-born Americans whose parents are also native-born. This background exposes them to the American tradition of upward mobility. As one man put it: "A man should strive to better himself." However, although a third of the men had moved up the occupational ladder in comparison with their fathers, all but six still hold blue-collar jobs. How do they feel about their jobs, and more generally, about their place in society?

An Overview

Only a few of these men feel a strong pride in occupational achievement. Some 10 per cent of the men say that they have "made good." These are skilled and semi-skilled workers in their thirties who are proud of the gain in their earnings over the years, of their occupational skills, and their paid-up homes, cars, modern dinette sets and washing machines. Another 14 per cent, not quite so self-satisfied, are content enough to want to remain in their present jobs for life, despite no prospect of advancement other than some slow improvement in pay or in working conditions.[2]

[1] This phrase was first used by Robert S. and Helen Merrell Lynd in *Middletown*, 1929, p. 53.
[2] The proportion of "very satisfied" workers is similar to that found by

The largest single group of Glenton men, 45 per cent of the total, is not wholly satisfied, but has no plans for upward occupational mobility. These men express some dissatisfaction with their jobs: low pay, unpleasant working conditions, night or shift work, or low status of the job. A 26-year-old man with ten years of schooling unloads and washes hogs in a meat packing business. The job is steady, but he is very dissatisfied about the smells of the place and "the whole set-up"—the smell nauseates him so that he often is unable to eat his lunch. But he has just bought a ramshackle bungalow and cannot afford the risk of changing to another, possibly less secure, job. A 33-year-old man, a bottler in a beer company, struggles to support his wife and three children on $3000 a year pay. He does not like his job, but he also feels that he cannot risk giving up a secure job.

Of the dissatisfied men, over one-half are trapped in their present jobs: "That's as good as I could get." The rest are eager for a change: "I think I'll soon make a break for it." The projected change, however, does not involve a move out of blue-collar status. Even the men who feel trapped in their present jobs are not apathetic, as their moonlighting indicates: many search for occasional repair or carpentry evening and week-end jobs and are, in the words of their wives, "hustlers."

The upwardly mobile constitute a minority of 22 per cent. These men hope and plan not only to change jobs, but to move out of their blue-collar status. Excluded from this category of the upwardly mobile are men with only dreams of escape, as reflected in the casual comment, "I'd like to have a little business of my own someday, maybe a tavern." Only serious plans for change were included, as testified by frequent discussion of the plan with wives and relatives, efforts to save, correspondence courses, interviews with management and systematic search for opportunities. Not all of these men will succeed. The prospects

---

some other investigators, although the differing indices of satisfaction hamper comparisons. Studies generally agree in reporting a higher degree of job satisfaction as one ascends the occupational ladder. In one inquiry, 27 per cent of blue-collar but 42 per cent of white-collar workers were rated "very satisfied" with their jobs (Nancy C. Morse and Robert S. Weiss, 1955). In another, the proportions of satisfied were 23 per cent for the former and 41 per cent for the latter (Elizabeth L. Lyman, 1955). A more detailed classification of occupations reveals one departure from the general rule: the skilled manual workers are slightly more satisfied than the lower ranks of white-collar personnel (Alex Inkeles, 1960, p. 5).

of achievement appear tenuous, for example, in the case of a 27-year-old fish market employee who supports his family, with three children, on $50 a week. But he is determined to learn the business and save up enough over a period of ten years to buy a fish-store business of his own and this is a repeated topic of conversation with his wife and his brother. Prospects of success appear more promising, however, in some other cases of these aspiring men.

The particular channels of upward mobility vary with the education of the mobile minority. Those with less than high school education hope to establish a small business of their own: a garage, a store, a trucking business, a motel business (with parents-in-law). But one plans to rise through the union bureaucracy, and another to become a policeman.

Among the high school graduates, one husband also wants to join the police force and another to own a grocery. The rest hope to rise through the administrative channels of the firms in which they are presently employed. One attends the training school of the firm, has joined the Masons and has started to read newspapers regularly "to be well informed about business conditions." Another is taking a correspondence course, and a third intends to enroll in a college evening course.

Nine per cent of the men seem to be completely defeated. One has gone downhill after an accident, while others cannot find full time jobs for a variety of reasons. Large families add to the difficulties of some. A description of two such families will be found on pp. 294-299 and 303-309.

Some Sources of Occupational Strain

The low status of the job, in addition to low pay and unfavorable working conditions, is a frequent source of dissatisfaction. Eliminating the upwardly mobile, it is estimated that some 30 per cent of the remainder feel some uneasiness about their rank on the occupational totem pole. Not many experience the constant irritation of the sanitation worker whose friends are "always ribbing" him about his being a "dirty old . . . garbage man." But their lack of self-satisfaction is reflected in such remarks as "If I had the opportunity I might have made something of myself"; "With my lack of education that's about the only kind of work I could do"; "I guess I have no ambition." It is difficult to take at face value the satisfaction expressed by one truck driver: "I know I'll never be an executive, I'll always be a worker and I'm happy about it. I think I am average. When you think that you're better than others, you're in for a downfall." Yet, speaking of his son, this man said with some feeling: "I want something better for my son. I want him to have a college education."

With all the lack of pride in their status, the men appear to place themselves somewhat higher in the socio-economic hierarchy than the middle-class interviewer would have placed them. While no systematic study of self-placement was made, the frequent statement "I guess I am average" conveyed the impression that their picture of the classes above them was foreshortened into a narrow "upper class" of the executives and bosses. One semi-skilled factory worker in answer to our question called himself "middle-class." "You wouldn't then call yourself a working-class person?" pursued the interviewer. "I figure that is the same thing," he countered; "the working class *is* the middle class."

This telescoped view of the class structure is not shared by a high school graduate who has increased her social contacts through her presidency of the P.T.A.: "We are definitely working-class. If my husband went to an office in a collar and tie, even if he didn't earn more, we would be middle-class." Describing a social visit, she commented: "They are a rung above us. They are the kind who give cocktail parties."

Although in terms of education and style of life, this woman ranks above the factory worker just quoted, unlike him she places herself in the "working class." Apart from the lack of standardization in the criteria of class membership, this contrast points to another conclusion.[3] The factory worker is isolated from contacts with the middle classes. On the other hand, the P.T.A. president's exposure to the higher ranks has led to finer discriminations and a different view of the shape of the hierarchy.

The dissatisfied men generally blame themselves for their low achievement, usually attributing it to their lack of education. Their individualistic ideology deflects blame from society to the individual. There is little projection of blame upon the govern-

[3] On perception of rank, see Joseph A. Kahl, 1957, pp. 82-84, Bernard Barber, 1957, pp. 186-231, and James West, 1945, pp. 128-133.

ment, political parties, the "bosses," or any ethnic or religious group. Occasionally they refer to their "bad luck" as some impersonal, amorphous force of circumstances. Even the men who were forced by poverty to leave school express little bitterness but tend to reproach themselves for not having gone back to complete their schooling in later years. Our interviews do not, then, substantiate the current jeremiads about the growth of dependent ("society-owes-me-a-good-living") attitudes. Whether or not the Glenton respondents are representative of other blue-collar families, they tend to accept personal responsibility for their condition.

It seems to the author that society played a greater part in their unsatisfactory occupational status than the workers themselves were able to perceive. Their work histories tell the story of frequent shifts from one unskilled or semi-skilled job to another. They ran elevators, drove taxis, handled freight and worked in a variety of factory jobs. Sometimes they were laid off, but more often they changed jobs to improve working conditions or pay. Granted that those who had dropped out of school contain a certain proportion of incompetent or unmotivated persons, but whatever their personal limitations, their schools and communities did not provide adequate guidance, training and information.[4] The men attempted to improve their position but lacked the resources for doing so. They relied upon chance remarks and help of associates: "I heard good jobs are opening up in the West"; "I told everybody to be on the lookout for a good job for me." Their chief sources were the union, for those who were members, and relatives. Only two men capitalized upon the occupational training they received in military service.

Lack of education and isolation from many institutions of the larger society limit utilization even of such assistance as the community provides through the printed word and existing social agencies. In the case of an economic or moral breakdown, existing institutional help does reach working-class families, but the more stable families appear to be at a disadvantage in this respect.

Certain dilemmas of occupational choice are peculiar to some

[4] See Bernard Barber, 1961, pp. 110-112, for proposed social measures to improve educational life chances for children of lower socio-economic classes.

positions in the occupational structure. Conflict between the desire for status and for money is such a dilemma. When the monetary and the prestige rewards attached to jobs are not closely associated, the worker is confronted with a difficult choice between them. For example, a 27-year-old high school graduate, a truck driver's helper earning $5900 a year who had a chance to become a driver with an income of $7500, described his conflict:

> "I don't know what I want to be. I am trying to get something that will raise me and my family in society. I don't want my child to grow up hearing 'Your father is a truck driver.' I know that the average person thinks truck drivers and teamsters are hard-driving, lower-class in society. I am thinking of becoming a policeman. But when you're used to living at a certain pay level, think of dropping to one-half of it. I have come to believe that money means a lot in this world."

A semi-skilled factory worker reports that his wife wants him to take a desk job: "Something that is important and that she can talk about." As for him, "I don't care what they call me as long as I make a lot of money." Another man made a similar choice. He was a stock boy in Woolworth's, but found that he could make more money as a laborer. The opposite decision was made by a high school graduate who earned over $100 a week but did not like working with colored people. He changed to a job with lower pay because "I wanted to raise my social status." But he is very anxious to make more money again and is still looking for a job which will combine status with adequate pay.

The men caught in this conflict between status and economic drives are, with one exception, high school graduates, who understandably tend to have higher status aspirations than the less-educated husbands.

The Shape of the Future

As we have seen, only one-fifth of these workers hope to get out of their blue-collar jobs, but this does not mean that the rest have no hope for improvement. Quite the contrary, the vast majority appear to feel that the future will be brighter than the present. This optimism may in part be explained by the fact that about one-half of the men are still in their twenties. The hopes for the future include higher wages, steadier jobs without the threat of seasonal layoffs, pleasanter conditions of work and more convenient work shifts.

A universal ambition is to own a home, a goal which one-fifth of the families have already achieved. An additional fifth live in parental homes, which in some cases the couple expect to inherit. Something akin to moral disapproval was occasionally expressed towards a man who still "rents" despite good earnings. Other economic aspirations include a car, modern appliances, better furniture and, very infrequently, the luxury of a summer cottage. Only one person referred to "travel," though several mentioned vacations in Florida. "My sister has it good," said one woman with ten years of schooling, "a great big refrigerator, nice house, two irons, a regular and a steam iron, three radios, a beautiful T.V. set. She's got everything you could want."

Few would be so naive in a post-Veblenian era as to assume that these economic strivings are free from status overtones. But more explicit forms of status-seeking are also expressed. The most frequent of these is the desire to move to a "better-class" neighborhood, usually for the children's sake. And there is the wish of the men to join a lodge and other organizations. Club membership for women is not regarded as a channel of upward mobility, even though it actually had such effects in two cases. The high school women belong to the P.T.A. and church groups and are Girl Scout leaders more frequently than is the case for less-educated women, but there is nothing resembling the middle-class housewife who joins the prestigeful clubs in the community to gain entry into the next higher social stratum. In general, social life, in the sense of cultivation of the "right" people, plays a very minor role in the efforts to improve status. Nor do the upwardly mobile men expect any help from their wives through social contacts.

"Keeping up with the Joneses" is disapproved of by these families and in fact there appears to be little competitive consumption among them. In the restricted social life of Glenton's families, apart from relatives, few couples ever visit each others' homes. There is, consequently, less incentive for competitive consumption and there are fewer models to inspire emulation. As one woman put it: "You wouldn't want the things that your aunts and uncles have because they are probably old-fashioned, and there aren't that many people your own age among the relatives." Mass media provide models and stimulate desires for possessions, but the limited social contacts reduce competitive display in comparison with the middle classes.[5]

The few who express the wish for cultural self-improvement through correspondence courses or hobbies consider this either as a means of upward mobility or a compensation for lack of economic success. A 28-year-old grammar school graduate said: "If I can't make my success in the world of material things perhaps I could become something like a poet."

Aspirations for the future find their fullest expression in parental hopes for children. Among themes mentioned repeatedly in reference to children are good character ("We hope they'll turn out all right and be nice people") and improvement in the life situation ("We'd like to give them the chances we didn't get"). When asked, "Would you like your son to follow in your line of work?" the great majority of fathers replied, "Oh no, I'd like him to go much farther." These fathers certainly do not see themselves as occupational models for their sons. Nearly all fathers want their sons to go to college, although some doubt their ability to help them: "Perhaps if he has the ability he can get some scholarship." A number of young couples have taken out insurance policies to send their sons through college.

If college education is valued in Glenton for other than vocational purposes, there is no inkling of it. Only one person, a woman high school graduate, suggested another value: "College offers an experience which one should have if one can afford it." The others agreed with the view that "by the time he is ready to go to work a good job will require a college degree." Partly because college is regarded as an avenue towards occupational mobility, college education for the daughters of the families is considered to be a dispensable luxury—"She'll get married"; "Let her husband support her"; "We can't afford giving a college education to both the boys and the girls and it is more important for the boys." The few exceptions are not the mothers, but several fathers who want their favorite daughter to attend college. One such couple quarreled because the husband wished to take out an insurance policy for the education of their little girl and the wife thought it an unnecessary expense.

With a regularity that suggests a strongly held value, mothers

[5] In a study of grades of residences in an urban area, clerical workers were found to have higher mean dwelling ratings than blue-collar workers at the same income level. Charles Tilly, 1961.

and fathers disclaim any preferences for a particular occupation for their children: "It is up to the children to pick their own occupations." At times the futility of planning is also stressed: "It don't do any good—children have ideas of their own and the times change." Only rarely do parents express the hope that a daughter might become a nurse or a musician; business, engineering, and other professions are mentioned for the sons. Incidentally, not a single parent expressed regret that he could not afford to send his children to a summer camp. Only one family each wished they could afford dancing and music lessons for their children.

Men and women in general share similar aspirations. Among the young couples in their twenties, one wife of every four wishes that her husband were more ambitious, and only one of ten thinks that her husband drives himself too hard. Thus one-fourth of the young husbands have to contend with an unfavorable evaluation of their performance on the part of their wives. It was noted that, among the less-educated, the wives tended to explain poor earnings of their husbands by his "bad luck" or lack of education, whereas the high school graduate married to a poor provider spoke more frequently about her husband's lack of drive or lack of ambition.[6]

The Effects of Poverty upon Marriage

Poverty may be a relative matter, but one-fourth of these families are poor by any American standard. The annual income of the poorest one-fourth of these families varies from the low of $2000 to the high (in only two cases) of $3500. Some of these poor couples are young and hopeful; others, in their thirties, are deeply discouraged. Daily life is a constant struggle to meet the bills for rent, groceries, a pair of shoes, a winter coat, and the T.V. set and the washing machine. The oppressive, almost palpable burden of bills seldom lifts. "What sort of things make you happy?" asked the interviewer and a 25-year-old woman answered: "I had myself a ball once when I came out two dollars over the budget that we didn't have to pay out all at once. I know it sounds goofy that a couple of lousy bucks make you feel good, but it sure does." A 31-year-old woman, the

[6] For guides to the extensive literature on mobility aspirations, see textbooks such as Bernard Barber, 1957, and Joseph A. Kahl, 1957.

mother of three children, remarked: "There ain't much call to get set up about much when you're so broke."

Dread of illness is ever-present because serious sickness means getting into debt or losing furniture or the house. "We had no money, the children were sick and he was half out of his mind," said a mother of five children, whose 28-year-old husband earned $3400 a year as a freight handler. Speaking of her husband's desire to find a better job, this woman explained that if he lost a week or two of pay, they would "really starve"—he cannot take any chances.

Possessions are few and the hold on them is precarious.

A 23-year-old wife of a street cleaner was describing the helpfulness of her older sister. "She even got socks for my husband once when he was out of them. He was wearing a pair with the front half of one of them missing. I had it fixed up with a piece of yarn to hold it over the toes. We were having it rocky and I don't know how she saw it, but she got him some army surplus socks so I didn't have to wash those out every night and iron them dry."

Another incident was described by a 26-year-old woman, mother of two children.

"We'd made a down payment on this bedroom set. It was second-hand anyhow. Something happened, we couldn't keep up the payments and the guy said he was going to take it away. We slept on the floor before, but I got used to the bed now. I was so down about this I couldn't see straight. The men came to take the bed away. When I heard them coming, I took the kids out and locked the door and hid in my neighbor's place. She came out to talk to them and said that I was out and wouldn't be back till the next day. When my husband got home and saw how I felt about it, he went out and borrowed the money. I don't know where he got it, but he got it somehow. He went around to that bastard's shop in the morning and gave him a piece of his mind. We weren't troubled no more after that even though we were slow on some payments. I sometimes wonder if he [the husband] said he'd smash his windows if he didn't lay off."

The same woman describes the pleasures of her life: "I got a deal with a hock shop downstairs. He is a real sweet guy. I got a little player in hock down there. Sometimes I scrape together enough money to get it out of hock for a couple of hours and maybe over a week end we all listen to records and then I take it back to him the next day. He don't charge me much more than a quarter for taking it out over the week end."

A father with eight years of schooling talked of his difficulties in supporting a family of five children. At one time he had to let most of his furniture go, but kept the bed, chairs and T.V. set. He had to sell some books which, he felt, he should have kept for his children, but he decided that it was more important for them to have the T.V.

This is one of many illustrations of the view that a T.V. set is a necessity. As another man put it, "I guess everybody knows you gotta have a place to live, something to eat, clothes. Just about everybody gotta have a T.V. now, too." One woman said: "I had to make up my mind if I wanted the T.V. or the phone the most. You can count on T.V. any old time but if you want to talk to somebody on the phone he's got to be there."

Unhappy marriages are somewhat more frequent among the poorest families than in the rest of the group. Of 15 couples with incomes of $3500 or less, 7 are unhappily married, whereas among the remaining 44 there are 15 unhappy couples. But these facts understate the effects of poverty. The good marriages among the poor also manifest the corrosion of poverty even when the destructive effects are not so marked as to place a marriage in the "unhappy" category.

Economic deprivations, anxiety about the future, the sense of defeat, concern about the failure to give one's children a good start in life, the bleak existence—these and other features of poverty are found to affect marriage in a variety of ways. These features tend to produce tensions in the personalities of family members, with inimical consequences for the marital relationship. They also create dislocations in institutional roles. For example, the relative failure of the husband as a provider disturbs the reciprocities inherent in conjugal roles. Poverty is found at times to hamper marital communication. All of these effects tend to be interdependent, and the task of unraveling them may begin at any point.

The adverse effects of poverty include the loss of self-esteem on the part of the poor providers. The men in their early twenties are still hopeful, but those over 30, with one or two exceptions, reveal a deep loss of self-esteem. A Southern couple who had migrated North some ten years prior to our interview had failed to "make good":

> "The reason he drinks so much here," remarked his wife, "is that he cannot stand to think he'd been a flop. He thought he was going to get himself a fine job. He said we'd shake the dust out of our shoes and we'd show them all. Well, we haven't showed them much. His wages sound good down South and I wrote my folks that we're doing just fine, but they live better down home than we do."

These disappointed men tend to blame themselves even more than their wives blame them. Many wives restrain their criticism out of pity, or expediency, or because they do not hold their husbands completely responsible for the plight of the family. After all, slack seasons, low pay, even being on relief had been familiar experiences for a few of these women in their parental families. But even the wives who do not voice any criticism could not conceal their disappointment—a worried face can be enough of a reproach. Eventually, however, all but the most compassionate and restrained wives are provoked into some criticism.

The women's deprivations and anxieties lead to a more critical scrutiny of their husbands' personalities. A barely perceptible weakness, one which might be tolerated in a good provider, tends to be seized upon as a possible cause of the husband's failure. This excessive sensitivity to the husband's faults unhappily feeds into another typical tendency: fault-finding is easy because economic failure is likely to magnify shortcomings. The poor providers are, themselves, frustrated and anxious. Not many men can handle these destructive emotions without further painful consequences, such as drinking, violence, irritability, increased sensitivity to criticism, and withdrawal. Whatever temporary relief some of these reactions may provide for the men, their long-range effects are to deepen the husband's sense of guilt and to antagonize his wife.

There is another reason why even the more considerate wives are drawn occasionally into disparagement of their husbands. The poor providers offer their wives too obvious a weapon not to be used in a fit of anger. Thus, a wife insisted that her child finish the food on her plate and her husband took the daughter's part, saying that he sympathizes with his daughter's dislike of this particular dish. The wife "hollered at me at the table and said if I'd make enough money she could get the food they liked."

The extreme shortage of money might be thought to rule out quarrels over expenditures because every dollar must be spent on necessities. But this is not the case. The couples quarrel over the order in which bills are to be paid—the milk bills first, so that the children can be fed properly—or the electric bill, so that the light is not turned off. They quarrel over the few discretionary expenditures that do remain—beer, cigarettes or clothes. Every minor difference in economic preferences may cause a conflict because the shortage of money necessitates choices.

Conflict is intensified also because lack of money deprives some husbands of the use of certain rapport devices to decrease marital tensions. When money is available, an apology often takes the form of a gift to break the ice after a quarrel, even if it is only a coffee ring and "Let's have some java to go with it." Thus husbands lack the resources to alleviate marital strain at a time when the strain is exacerbated by poverty.

Some common means of coping with the problems of poverty often provide temporary relief only at the cost of long-range losses. A certain remoteness in marriage and a loss of spontaneity are a case in point. To talk about what matters most—the bills, the fear of sickness and of the uncertain future—is only to intensify the anxiety, and by suppressing these topics one hopes to find some relief. But avoidance of one's uppermost concern blocks other sharing as well. A slightly dishonest tinge to the whole relationship is given by still other suppressions. For example, the wife curbs her irritation out of pity and, more frequently, out of fear of driving her husband to drink or intensifying some other defensive reaction. Again, among the economically more secure and aspiring couples, common aspirations for the children, the purchase of a house and other plans constitute one of the strong ties of marriage. But for these poor couples the future is not an enticing prospect to be relished in repeated discussions; it is uncertain and threatening. Asked whether she and her husband ever discussed their dreams for the children, a 29-year-old woman said: "Nah, that's too sore." The avoidance of painful subjects in turn increases the loneliness of each partner, at the time when each is most in need of emotional support.

Some poor couples continue to have a very full sex life, but even these reported some adverse effects of poverty. Worry about having more children is one problem. The effect of anxiety and of drink upon the husband's potency is another.

Speaking of her husband, a 29-year-old woman remarked: "Things have been going hard for him and the soul takes it out on the body. Sometimes he's so down in the mouth he just hasn't got his heart in it." She confessed another difficulty. When her husband is very drunk he wets his bed, so that when he comes in drunk, he sleeps on the iron cot in the front room and she lies in bed "just like a wild cat raging in the woods." She might not have wanted him in the first place when he returns in this state, but somehow she "gets raging inside" anyhow and feeling disappointed.

The strain of doubling up with relatives for the sake of economy (discussed in Chapter 12) is another problem of the poor.

Not every poor couple experiences each or all of these problems with equal intensity. For one thing, the poverty of a young couple hopeful of a better future is not the same experience as poverty ten years later. Of six poor husbands who are 25 years old or younger, only one is unhappily married; out of nine older poor men, six have unhappy marriages. There are many other factors affecting the reaction of the family to poverty even within the same age category. To explore these differences we shall compare three marriages in some detail. None of the three is immune from the adverse effects of poverty, but each exemplifies a variety of sustaining forces which keep the marriage from complete breakdown. It was to be expected that psychological resiliency of individuals and their stability in the face of adversity would safeguard a marriage. So would, clearly, the presence of assets in the relationship itself which might offset external deprivations. But the following cases were selected to illustrate the more unusual situations. We shall see, for example, that psychological resiliency may actually weaken the marital bond and, conversely, that the bond may remain strong despite considerable deterioration in the husband's behavior.

The Relative Vulnerability of Marriages to the Stresses of Poverty

Of the two couples to be described first, the Parkers and the Roberts, the latter are happier. The major difference between the two couples lies in the quality of the marital relationship. For the Roberts their marriage is in itself so supportive and rewarding that in the face of adversity the couple turn to each other for emotional aid. The Parkers, apart from their strong sexual tie, are unable to help one another. They seek escape in drink and in other relationships. But the Roberts also show the disturbing effects of poverty. As deprivations continue and anxieties mount, the demands for emotional support become excessive and neither can dispel the worries of the other.

The Parkers have four children, aged 7, 6, 4, and 2. Mr. P. is 33 years old and his wife is 28. Both are grammar school graduates. Mrs. P. said that she did not like school and was "put back a couple of times." This was also true of her husband, she reported. The fathers of both parental families had been on relief in the 1930's.

> "I don't remember it so good," said Mrs. P., "but he does. He was only a little boy but he said it was awful. He said they could never have any fun, they just sat around and nobody played or did anything. His folks were real mad about everything and they'd yell at him and he said it was hell."

Mr. P.'s morale is low. He cannot get full-time work and his earnings for the past year were about $3500. He said:

> "I was born five or ten years too late. I'd have done all right during the last war, but now I am in a jam. I have learned all I can about metal work without working. Now I have to have experience in work and seniority and that's something I never get. I go from one place to another, and I don't get union rights because of it. Oh, sure, they'll help me look for another job, but when there ain't no jobs, what are you going to do? Who could have been more sure about being right than I was in metal work? And look at me now.
>
> "We have gone down-hill ever since we've been married eight and one half years ago. We had one good year and we thought we had the world by the tail. But then with the lay-offs and the babies coming we was wised up."

Asked about his wife's attitude towards their economic plight, Mr. P. expressed some appreciation of her:

> "I can't say my wife stands by me or don't complain, but she don't make you feel bad like my mom. Mom's a good

woman, a wonderful woman, but even if she don't say nothing or don't ride me, she makes me feel I don't do good enough. But my wife was the one to tell me it was just bad luck when I got mad at myself and thought I was no good. She don't ask me for nothing she shouldn't." He did complain that she was lazy about housework and that she drank too much beer. "I wouldn't drink at home so much, but I hate to see her starting down to the tavern. I wouldn't even mind it so much if she would just quietly have a drink and go out, but I hate to have her talking down there and have people tell me what she had said. I told the bartender to throw her out and not to serve her," and the bartender had chided him for this. "Beer's good stuff to help you get along in life but it can ruin you. I wouldn't want the kids to be ashamed if I got in trouble with the cops if I got drunk. That's one reason we lay off."

Speaking of his children, Mr. P. said: "Maybe one reason that I like them so much is that I can't do enough for them, and I cannot do what I want to. I would like to see them go to college." He then said very sadly that he didn't think he'd be able to help them, but he had "heard that some boys were smart enough to work their way through." When asked if his wife knew about his wanting the children to go to college, he said rather bitterly, "She'd think I'd gone nuts if I told her."

Mrs. P. was resting on the davenport in a dirty pink quilted wrapper when the interviewer first visited her, unexpectedly. The two older children were in school, the two younger ones were napping and her girl friend was visiting her. This friend and Mrs. P. exchange baby-sitting services to enable each to pick up an odd job now and then. Mrs. P. works at the diner and baby-sits. Asked whether her husband helped her with the shopping, Mrs. P. gave a picture of their life:

"He gets paid Friday and shops is open Thursday nights. By Thursday night we ain't got no money left. If he does a full day's work on Friday, he don't get home in time. Friday night he goes to the tavern and he usually can't get up in time to help me Saturday morning. Friday and Saturday nights is a big deal with him." Saturday night is also spent at the tavern "having a hand of cards over beer. . . . So it winds up with me doing most of the shopping in the afternoon and about a dollar's worth just about every day. The milk and the bakery come here, but I usually spend four or five dollars on Saturday while he is sleeping it off."

Mrs. P., at the end of the interview, summed up her husband in these words: "Like I told you, he is kind of good-looking and he can still have awful good manners. He is poor, he ain't got much ambition and sex is a big deal with him." "Isn't he smart enough to get a better job?" she was asked. "He is much smarter than he needs to be for the job he is in now. A lot of men that knows less than he and isn't as good workers have better jobs. He's just unlucky. I know he's tried; sometimes when he ain't got a full day's work he goes and tries other places around." "Well then, he really is ambitious," said the interviewer. Mrs. P. explained: "What I mean, he ain't set on buying any Cadillacs and we ain't figuring on buying a house. We'd just like to get all our bills paid off and we'd like to know for sure we weren't going on relief."

As to marriage, here again is Mrs. P.'s summary: "You have fun and then you have babies and then you get scared of having more babies. He worries about the same kind of things I worry about, mostly about bills and how everything is going to turn out, what will happen if we have more kids. No, we don't talk about that. We worry too much about it if we talk about it—it's bad enough as it is." Their sexual relations are very satisfactory, but are beginning to be disturbed by Mr. P.'s anxiety. "Do you think," she was asked, "that this [sex] is one of the most important things in marriage?" She replied: "For us it is. We were lucky that way. It turned out right. But he can't do much when he is lit. When he's a sourpuss he'd practically knock you down if you touched him."

Despite all the sympathy they have for one another, the Parkers turn outward for emotional support, Mr. P. to drink and male companionship at the tavern; Mrs. P. to drink and to her family and girl friends. She derives much pleasure out of earning an occasional $5 to $10 baby-sitting or waiting on tables. The communication between the pair is inadequate and the signs of this inadequacy are numerous:

Asked what usually arouses his wife's anger, Mr. P. said: "God knows what's going to set her off next—when the children are disobedient or when she thinks I am holding out too much money on her. She talks too much, but I guess she has to let off steam somehow." When the interviewer asked him whether he did not think it would help if he stayed home and let her talk to him to let off steam, he said, "That would be all very nice, if I could take it, but I can't take it." He, in turn, is unfulfilled in marriage, because it is difficult to talk to her: "It ain't that she couldn't understand, but she's busy with the babies or something else most of the time. I go my way and she has a right to go hers." Can he discuss his job with his wife? "About the best news that I could tell her was that I landed a good job." When the interviewer tried to pin him down about his wife's interest in his daily work, asking whether she was perhaps "too interested" or not interested enough, he replied, "She's not interested enough."

Mrs. P. presented her side of the story in her interview, explaining why she tends to "go my way and let him go his":

"I don't like him to talk about the bills, nothing you can do but pay them and I wish he'd shut his trap. No good talking about it." "If you both gave up drinking," tried the interviewer, "and both worked, couldn't you get a house one day?" The wife answered, "About the time we was sixty when we'd already killed ourselves with work, maybe we could get a place." She was questioned further, "And you think it's all right that he goes to the tavern with the fellows?" She said hopelessly, "What can you do? You'd go nutty if you couldn't do something. Anything that's fun costs money. You can't take a drive, you can't go to a movie, you can't go anywhere without spending two or three bucks."

Asked about her husband's moods, Mrs. P. said: "Sometimes everything is going all right and suddenly he's a sourpuss. He'll just sit there with his sourpuss sticking out a mile. He's more likely to go sourpuss than to blow his top. He gets the slow burn on about things and I don't know exactly what it is that sets him off. He stalks around and he mumbles along and sometimes he'll go out and get a drink, that is, if it isn't the wrong time of the day like early in the morning when he is real sourpuss sometimes." "Can you help him when he is like that?" asked the interviewer. "Not me," she answered. "I'm too busy over the babies the time that he is going off, they're yelling around making an awful racket. Sometimes I wish I could stomp out to work myself. . . . When he feels good, there's no need for him to go out to the tavern. He goes out to see the fellows on the week end and in the evening sometimes. He'll go out earlier, but that's only when he is a sourpuss. When he feels good, he'll play with the girls and even with the boys. He'll do something like wind up their toys, or sometimes he'll feel so good he'll come home and bring a present of some kind, maybe a little bit of candy or a ballpoint pen for the girls."

"Sure—we fight sometimes. I ride him and he rides me too; I don't know what gets into us but those things just happen. One word leads to another and sometimes he will hold out his hand like he is going to hit me but he don't. Then he'll go out and get a drink."

Illustrating the things that hurt her husband's feelings, Mrs. P. described the time when their oldest girl wanted to go on a picnic and her husband "had to help out somehow but didn't want to be bothered. The big girl just said, 'You're not like the other dads with their kids, what kind of dad are you?' Honestly you would've thought she had hit him in the mouth with a truck. He looked like he was going to cry. He went out and got a couple under his belt and then he came and he fixed the kids up like they wanted." Does he cheer her up when she feels blue? "No, I'm the one who has to cheer him up. He comes home and tells me about what's going on and I tell you, he is lower than I am and I have to tell him, 'Have a drink and get over it.'"

Mrs. P. enumerated some of the things that made her feel happy: "Well, they say I am the cheerful sort. I'm happy if I get a big tip down in the diner or if I pick up a nice piece of change from work or can get a new dress cheap. I guess everybody knows it if I have enough beer to feel happy." She does not usually tell her husband when she makes this extra money: "It isn't always a good idea to tell him." She feels that when she earns the money, she has a right to spend it the way she wants to "because as long as I keep the house clean it is up to him to support us. He likes to drink beer a lot more than I do and it is only fair that I can keep what I can pick up." She thinks her husband doesn't approve of that. She gets "awful mad with him because he won't tell me things he should. People will tell him to tell me about a job and he'll forget—at least he says he forgets. The other day a neighbor of ours had a job for me and I lost maybe five or ten bucks. Wouldn't it make you mad? I suppose he thinks because I don't toss it in the kitty and let him drink it all up, he is not going to let me make anything. He hurt his foot once and I got a case of beer for him from money out of my table-waiting and he sure appreciated that. Golly, he laughed and carried on. I told him he wasn't to give none of it to the fellows. This was just for him and me, and that time, he made a grab for me and he squeezed me and he really got all sloppy about that."

Although her secrecy about her own earnings is acknowledged to be a source of friction, Mr. and Mrs. P. have never talked about this directly. This lack of communication tends to spiral marital tension. Mr. P. (at least in part because he cannot talk out his problems with his wife) seeks escape in drink. His wife sympathizes with this reaction because she also drinks, but at the same time she resents his expenditures at the tavern, especially when she suspects that he "holds out" on her on payday. She makes a little money on her own, but does not "put it into the kitty." With her, it is partly a matter of principle—a wife who meets her role obligations is entitled to her husband's support, while her own earnings are none of his affair. Moreover, his "holding out" on her gives her a further excuse to keep her earnings. But her secrecy leads Mr. P. to exaggerate the amount of her earnings and he uses this to justify his own behavior. Mrs. P.'s pattern of avoiding talk about the painful subject of bills leads to lack of communication about money in general. This, in turn, deprives the couple of a chance to iron out their different principles: she *thinks* he doesn't approve of her withholding her earnings, but they have not discussed these differences.

The marriage of the Parkers has some strong assets. One is their sexual tie and the other is the wife's attitude towards her husband, which is relatively free of nagging or belittling. Nevertheless, this marriage is vulnerable because, sex and mutual sympathy notwithstanding, neither can offer the other enough understanding and support in the face of economic hardships. "I go my way and he goes his," said Mrs. P., and Mr. P. described their relationship in almost identical words.

Whatever the psychological forces at work here, some social conditions contribute to this centrifugal tendency. The Parkers view the sharp separation of masculine and feminine interests as the natural pattern. "But they are girls," Mrs. P. exclaimed when the interviewer noted that she apparently talked more freely to her girl friends than to her husband. Admittedly, the couple does share many instrumental domestic concerns. But these sooner or later lead to the painful subject of money. The kinds of interests they do share, then, are tinged with the gloom of their poverty and hopelessness.

This case also illuminates the role of the wife's personal adjustment in the marriages of the economically deprived families.

Understandably, the wife's discouragement and too-close identification with her husband may intensify his stress, but so occasionally does her relatively good adjustment. Mrs. P.'s personal adjustment, which is superior to that of her husband, is based upon a variety of supports which do not involve her husband. These are the job at the diner, kidding with the customers, beer, her girl friends, her family, and her relationship with her oldest daughter. But her good cheer makes Mr. P. feel all the more lonely.

The Roberts present a contrasting case. Mr. R. is 27 years old, had seven years of schooling, and is now a fish cleaner in a fish market, earning about $50 a week. His family consists of his 25-year-old wife (who had ten years of schooling) and their three children, aged 4, 3 and 1. They share an apartment with Mr. R.'s brother and his family. The R.'s have little privacy: in their bedroom two screens and some cardboard partitions separate the half of the room in which they sleep from the other half, which is actually a hall opening into the common bathroom and the kitchen.

The relative resiliency of this marriage in the face of economic hardships derives in part from certain features of the marital relationship. Mrs. R. is deeply dependent upon her husband's emotional support and homage to her. Moreover, the exceptional personality of the husband, unimpaired by his economic difficulties, plays a role in the stability of the relationship.

"My mother," Mrs. R. told us, "didn't want me to marry John because he had trouble with his eyes and was poor. 'You had to go and fall for a big hunk like that,' she said. But I'm not sorry I married him. He don't make much dough and I sure hope things will get better, but he is an easy guy to have around and he is a good husband and a good father." The children like him better than they like her, but she thinks this is natural because when he comes home at night, he plays with them. She has to work at home, and is always having to "shoo the children out of the way." He can make a formula and feed the baby its bottle, and he has helped out a lot in giving them baths. She said, "He gets a kick out of it." He also almost always helps her with the dishes. And sometimes when she has heavy marketing to do, he helps to carry things up the stairs to their third-floor flat.

Her husband appears to be helpful to Mrs. R. in other ways.

She is an insecure woman and he reassures her. For example, she often wishes she weren't so tall, and he says, "I like big women." At other times, when she is depressed, he advises her to stop housework and watch T.V. for a while or to go out with the children and see her girl friends or her mother.

Perhaps the best clue to the relationship is given by her remark that she feels better when her husband is around. "He enjoys life, likes food, T.V., bright colors, and he is real popular with the crowd."

The emotional dependence of the wife upon her husband characterizes not only the Roberts but three other "poor but happy" couples. The emotional security of these women is so bound up with their husbands that they are ambivalent about week-end and evening jobs which take husbands out of the home, despite the chance of some needed additional earnings.

In three cases, including the Roberts, membership in a clique serves to offset to some extent the adverse effects of poverty. Clique membership has this salutary influence because in these cases the husband is the acknowledged social leader of the pairs. "They ask us because of him," admitted one wife, "mind you, it's not just that he's my husband. Women I meet in the afternoon often tell me how nicely he sang or tell me they liked some story or joke he told." The popularity of the husbands raised their own self-esteem and their status in the eyes of their wives. Mr. R. remarked: "I tell my wife those stories but she ain't interested but when we are in a crowd and everybody laughs, she laughs too."

The clique, also, provides some shared pleasures when pleasures are scarce. "Life is no good," said Mrs. R. "if you can't have a good time sometimes. All the good time we got is watching T.V. and going around with the crowd."

The clique serves as a form of group therapy. The interviews of the two men were punctuated with such comments as: "We talked about it with the crowd" or "The crowd kidded us that time." Relatives, also, offer such support, but an advantage of the clique lies in the similar ages and stages of the family cycle, not always present in the kinship group. Moreover, clique relationships lack the intense and sometimes ambivalent character of kinship ties.

But the ability to use the support of such a clique is not a matter of accident. It presupposes the existence of a pattern of joint social life which is not universal even among the gregarious families. It may also require an exceptional social talent for the husband to obtain a reward from "the crowd" great enough to off-set the humiliation of economic failure.

Despite the sustaining forces, the economic deprivations of the Roberts have begun to affect their marital relationship.

"We ain't fixed so good," said Mrs. R. "He got no education and he has trouble with his eyes. When we got married it looked like things were going to be good, but things ain't so good now . . . gee, I'd like to have a different house, this place is a pig-pen." The fish market offers no chance for pro-motion. Their only hope is that he and his brother can one day open a fish market of their own; Mr. R. told us it would take, at best, many years to accumulate the needed capital, and neither side of the family can help them.

Apart from worry about subsistence, Mrs. R. is very unhappy about living together with her sister and brother-in-law. Her nerves are frequently on edge.

"It's all right for a little while to be doubled up like this, but when it goes on and on, you can't stand each other," Mr. R. told us. "Much as my brother and I like living together, we got our family to think of. Our wives would like to live apart. It would be nice if we could live beside each other, but in dif-ferent apartments." They heard of a place in a neighboring town, where there were two flats, "sort of run-down," but convenient. "The girls," he said, "will have to make up their minds whether they want to move so far away from their mothers and their folks." (It would be about a fifteen-minute bus ride.)

Another source of anxiety is the fear of pregnancy. The couple would have liked to have six children but "We ain't got enough dough. We want to give the children good food. Food is real important to him, too. Vitamins cost an awful lot of money." The R.'s have been married for six years. Much as she appreciates her exceptionally kind and supportive husband, Mrs. R. has expressed some disappointment with his economic performance, and there are no prospects for improvement. Furthermore, her depressions are already beginning to strain the marriage.

Mrs. R. expressed the regret that neither of them had much education. "But I guess he couldn't help it with his eyes. He gets tired if he tries to read. Funny thing," she added, musingly, "it don't seem to bother him when he cleans fish or watches T.V." She described her husband as "more ambitious than able." Speaking about herself, she said she wished she could be a more cheerful person. "Yes I get moody, any little old thing can set me off, maybe coming out behind with the budget, maybe the kids not feeling well and squabbling. The baby got sick a couple of months ago and we were scared for a while. The doctor thought maybe we should send her to the hospital and we didn't have no plans for it [insurance]. The downer you get, the downer you go; you have to get some breaks or you might wind up jumping in the river."

And now from Mr. R.'s interview:

"When she feels good, she kind of skips. She kind of jumps and dances around. I like to see that. It makes me feel good too. I tell her I like her to be cheerful. But she gets cranky, she says she's nervous, I don't know what it is. I sent her to the doctor, and he said it wasn't nothing but her imagination. I asked him and he told me, and I told her as long as she is moody, she had better have good moods."

Unlike Mr. P., whose personality remains intact and who compensates his wife for economic privations by the good-natured homage he pays her, Mr. Smith, the husband in our third case, is far from being a model husband. He drinks and squanders money required for the daily necessities of life. He spends three to five evenings away from home, usually in the tavern, leaving his wife alone and completely isolated, since she has no relatives or friends in the community. If he has not actually been unfaithful there is enough gossip to give his wife uneasy suspicions, but with all that, the marriage is an exceptionally stable one. What enables this marriage to withstand such adversities?

The S.'s, born in South Carolina, left the South soon after their marriage because Mrs. S.'s family was "uppity" towards Mr. S. and his own people, according to his wife, "weren't very nice and certainly weren't good to him." Mr. S. is 33, had nine years of schooling, and earns $3000 to $3500 a year operating a hand-truck for an express company.

"I haven't got any skills. Just push a truck around. This damn thing called automation is not something I can do much about. Sure, I'd like to have more education. I'd like to have it shoved at me. I'm not energetic enough to go out and get it. . . . Well, I work all day. I'm tired when I get home."

His job is steady, but he cannot always count on a full week's work. He picks up odd jobs and he once got into trouble with the union because he was doing unlicensed porter's work.

Mrs. S. is 29 years old, and had nine years of schooling. The couple lost two children in infancy and they still mourn their loss. Their love for their only child, a 9-year-old girl, is intense.

The S.'s have moved around a great deal during their stay in Glenton. Their furniture was made by the husband, who salvaged some second-hand chairs, a table and an iron cot and remodeled these pieces. Mrs. S. made attractive pillows for the chairs and the sofa. Complimented on their handmade furniture, Mrs. S. drew herself up with a certain pride and said that her husband was very good with his hands. With all the pride in their handiwork, she looked around at the two-room apartment and said rather bitterly: "If you can call this a home." Mrs. S. would have liked to have returned to her home in the South. She longs to be back with her large family, but Mr. S. is still bitter about her folks so that she tries to "keep her mouth shut" about her homesickness. Mr. S. does want news from home when she gets letters, but she has to be careful as to what she can tell him. During the fourth visit to the family, the interviewer saw Mr. and Mrs. S. together. Mr. S. has admitted his defeat in the East and has begun talking about trying his luck in some other part of the country. This is the conversation that took place in the presence of the interviewer:

Mrs. S. said: "I had a hankerin' to get back home ever since we got here. I didn't say nothing because he thought he was making better wages. But if he can get as good wages down there I think we'd better get up and git." Did they ever talk this over, asked the interviewer. "No! I didn't say nothing because I didn't want to make him uneasy." Mr. S. broke in and said: "I knew it anyhow." In his own interview Mr. S. said: "It would be a lot easier back home because she would have somebody to talk to. She ain't got any friends up here and it gets real lonesome."

The direct and indirect effects of poverty strain this marriage and we shall trace the vicious circle of influences. Mr. S.'s disappointment in himself leads to his drinking. His excessive drinking, as well as his discouragement, is destroying their sex life.

Mrs. S. said with some pity: "He drinks because he can't stand to think he'd been a flop." He leaves after dinner, usually for the bar, but he doesn't always tell his wife where he is bound for or when he will be home. In the joint interview Mr. S. was talking about his drinking and he turned to his wife to ask belligerently whether she thought he was a drunk. No, she said, but he did drink too much for his health. Mr. S. suddenly became all smiles and said he knew he drank too much for the health of his budget, but what does a working man have outside of his wife and the bar. "Yup, I can get a lot out of my system talking to people at work and in the tavern. If she'd come to the bar she'd feel a lot better. I try to get her to come out to have a beer but she thinks it's wrong."

"A bar is no place for a woman to be," commented his wife. "Drinking is bad enough but drinking in a bar is terrible." When the interviewer turned to Mrs. S. and asked whether it might not be harmless to keep her husband company in the bar, Mr. S. at once came to his wife's defense, smiling benignly, "She's kinda religious." Mrs. S., like her folks in the South, thinks that drinking and even smoking is wrong.

The sex life of the S.'s is now rarely satisfactory. The remark, cited earlier in this chapter, that "the soul takes it out of the body" was made by Mrs. S. in describing how his discouragement affected her husband's sex life. She described a spat they had had the night before the interview:

"He came home drunk and was mushing it around kissing me. . . . I would not have minded it if he could stand straight and if he didn't stink so much. After he has some coffee and a bath I don't mind him by me in bed and I'd be awfully disappointed if he didn't kiss me goodnight."

Whether because his wife is a witness to his economic defeat or for other reasons Mr. S. is, in all probability, occasionally unfaithful to his wife. The suspicion of unfaithfulness was aroused by Mrs. S.'s staunch defense of her husband against the gossip of their neighbors.

"I get furious," said Mrs. S., "because the neighbors' children tell my daughter nasty things about her father's drinking and maybe flirting with somebody. One time a man came in boiling mad, because one of the neighbors had said that my husband was going with this man's wife. He came to the house a little tipsy to look for his wife. I almost took a stick to him and pushed him out of the door and told him if he ever came to our house and said anything like that in front of our daughter I'd take a knife to him. He wanted to search the house and I told him he would do it over my dead body. He came around and apologized the next day, quiet, when the girl was in school. He stayed off from work to do it." She said she would not dream of discussing anything like this with the neighbors as she would not want her daughter to find out. When her daughter grew older she said she would have to explain some things to her and try to keep her loving both of them.

When Mr. S. was asked about sources of happy moods, he included "seeing pretty women walking along the street with nice airy dresses, nice limbs and all that sort of thing."

The husband's status in the marriage is still high, but it has been adversely affected by his failure. Lack of money has created for Mrs. S. a conflict between her conjugal and parental roles.

"Down home." said Mrs. S., "they say your first duty is to your husband. They say a child can die and your husband has the power for a new one, and he is your lord. When you marry him you say you are going to obey him." The question of the conflicting demands of her husband and her daughter admittedly troubles Mrs. S. a great deal. She apparently feels guilty because she occasionally makes a decision in favor of her daughter's interests, concerning food preferences, for example.

Speaking about conjugal roles, Mr. S. said in the presence of his wife, "A poor man ain't a king nowhere, not even in his own family." His wife looked hurt and said that she knew it was a woman's duty to look after her husband but that they just hadn't enough money for him to get the kind of food and service that he expected. She had after all to look out for the health of their daughter and to make their own clothes.

Marital communication between the Smiths has deteriorated in the sense that an increasing number of topics are "too sore to discuss. He is touchy," said Mrs. S., "because he can't do things better for me so he grouches and sulks and I had to learn to keep my mouth shut." Throughout the interview Mrs. S. repeatedly explained that she was unable to share this or that worry with her husband because she feared that he would become moody and leave for the bar.

This reserve in marriage draws the wife closer to her nine-year-old daughter who is becoming her confidante. This is not to suggest that there is a coalition of mother and daughter against the father. The daughter adores her father and is in turn deeply loved by him. Mrs. S. cautions her daughter against re-peating the gossip of the church women for fear of disturbing her husband.

Mrs. S. has no friends in the community. She feels herself superior in morals and manners to her neighbors, but her com-plete isolation is also an indirect result of their situation. She cuts herself off from the women in her church as well as in the housing development in order to guard her daughter from what she describes as the mean gossip about her husband. She gives a picture of a sad and very lonely work-driven woman, anxious about the future of the family. Asked about sources of happy moods, she said that making a pretty dress for her daughter, so that she would not ask for one in the store, made her feel light-hearted. She feels pleased with herself when she can get all her work done. Once in a while when her husband is in a good mood then everybody is happy. He'd shuffle around, half-dancing, singing and "talking sweet" to her. And once she had a wonderful day when a family from her home town came to Glen-ton and visited them.

When, at the conclusion of the interview, Mrs. S. was asked what, if anything, she would like to change about her marriage, she laughed loudly for the first time in the interview: "If I wasn't so crazy about him I'd change the whole thing from A to Z." She'd start off all over again by falling in love with another man, a rich man who would buy them a big house and a car and she'd have a lot of kids. Then in a more serious and sad voice she added that the only thing she'd change about her husband would be to make him luckier.

Among the sustaining forces of this marriage are the firm patriarchal convictions of the wife. Mr. S. may say that a poor man is not the king of his family, but he enjoys high status in his own marriage. Mrs. S.'s patriarchal attitudes blunt her resentment against her husband. She takes upon herself the burden of adjustment to her bleak and lonely life. She explained her loneliness not by his neglect of her but by her separation from her family. To the extent that these attitudes help maintain Mr. S.'s status in the family, they also bolster his self-esteem and safeguard his personality from more serious disintegration.

Mr. S. explained that his wife does not expect him to help with housework: "She is old-fashioned that way." However, he does help on his own initiative and is always rewarded by her gratitude. Where another wife may demand help with housework precisely because the poor provider does not fulfill his own role obligations, Mrs. S. is grateful for his aid. Such aid, offered as a voluntary gift, does not lower his status. Mrs. S.'s patriarchal attitudes are revealed in other ways. Asked whether he is an easy man to talk to, she said: "Yes, when he is not troubled but he usually wants to talk about himself more than about her, and men are supposed to talk more."

The common values shared by this couple are all the more binding because they still feel themselves alien in the East; even Mr. S. with his wider contacts and his gregarious personality finds the Eastern attitudes on race and other issues different from his own. This isolation in an alien environment makes Mrs. S. all the more dependent upon whatever attention and support her husband is willing to give her. In the discussion of T.V. preferences, she said that she feels so much better when her husband is home that she is only too glad to let him watch whatever he likes on T.V. irrespective of her own preferences.

Another sustaining force is the deep mutual empathy and affection characterizing their marriage.

Mrs. S. describes their mourning after the death of the two infants. "We was grieving together without saying a word." She felt they were very close to each other then. Sometimes, she said, he can be very comforting, he can understand her "real spooky, but, of course, if he has other things on his mind you might as well talk to yourself." Her pity for him is shown in her attitude towards his drinking: "He takes an awful lot of money for his beer, but he has had it awfully hard and it is one of his few pleasures." Asked whether he ever shows any appreciation of her, she answered: "He acts as though I was the most marvelous movie star in the world and he is a great kisser." When he is happy he waltzes around with her and just before they go to sleep he often tells her how much he loves her. Once in a while he even brings her a little present, such as a handkerchief. "Once or twice he got some flowers for me free from a florist. He brought the flowers home, cute and bashful like a high school kid . . . kind of like he is trying to say he is sorry for what he is, but I don't mind what he is, although I get awfully griped with things the way they are." Mr. S. in turn expressed great satisfaction with his wife as a mate, as a mother and as a housekeeper.

Mrs. S. is not as subservient to her husband as it might appear. She gave several illustrations of their arguments—once they had planned to do some errands together and instead he got cross and went to the bar. "I was fit to be tied. I went and did some of the errands myself, not the ones he wanted done, and then he came in and hollered at me about it and I bawled him out real good, and told him to go and do the errands himself, that it serves him right if he was going to run off to the bar in the morning. We had a real bust-up but it was all right in a little because I was so tired and he too."

The Smiths illustrate that the wife's tenderness and pity for the husband can survive not only economic privation, but excessive drinking, marital neglect and, perhaps, unfaithfulness. As we have seen, her patriarchal attitudes, the common values she shares with her husband in an alien environment, his empathy and romanticism are among the other sustaining forces.

Too sum up, none of Glenton's poor families is immune from the destructive effects of poverty and economic failure, but the effects vary in degree and in kind. The cases illustrated the variety of factors that made some families more vulnerable to these stresses than others. A cluster of such factors centers around the marital relationship itself—for example, the interpersonal relations, as seen in the compatibility of emotional and sexual roles. The Parkers turn outward for emotional support with progressive estrangement in marriage, whereas for the Roberts and the Smiths the spouse is often a shield against external hardships. The norms of marriage also play a role in the outcome. Mrs. Smith's patriarchal norms, for example, provide some immunity to the effects of poverty. Interpersonal competence is still another feature of a marriage which was traced in the foregoing case studies. The lack of communication between the Parkers tends to increase mutual suspicion and Mr. P.'s loneliness.

In addition to the marital relationship, the interplay between the pair and their social environment comprises another category of relevant forces. The isolation of the Smiths among neighbors of whom they are critical deepens their sense of mutual respect and dependence. Mr. Roberts' high position in his "crowd" buttresses his self-esteem and in part compensates his wife for his lack of achievement.

It is to be expected that psychological resiliency of the husband and of the wife in the face of economic hardships will benefit marriage, and indeed this is amply borne out. The more surprising finding, however, is that under certain conditions personal integration actually undermines the solidarity of the couple. Mrs. Parker's cheerfulness makes her husband feel all the gloomier. The cohesion of the pair requires something more than the stability of the two personalities.

The cases also document the circular processes of marital interaction—the vicious circles which undermine the solidarity of the couple and the "virtuous" circles sustaining the marriage despite external stresses. An act having an unfavorable effect all too often starts a chain reaction. But so also does a salutary act, and seemingly small initial differences therefore may lead to increasingly divergent marital patterns.[7]

[7] For a discussion of and bibliography on family adjustment to crises see Reuben Hill, 1963, and Howard J. Parad and Gerald Caplan, 1963.

ΛΛΛ

CHAPTER
14

Social Life and Leisure

Our guiding concern in this book is with marriage. The uses of leisure will be considered in this chapter only insofar as they constitute one aspect of marital interaction or have consequences for it.[1]

Joint Social Life and the Marital Relationship

In Glenton, joint social life with friends is far from being the important leisure-time pursuit that it is in higher socio-economic classes. This applies to exchanges of home visits as well as to joint visits to public recreational places. About one-fifth of the couples never visit with another couple apart from relatives. An additional 16 per cent do so only very infrequently, a few times a year. And these social occasions may include so impersonal an event as a Sunday school picnic or a company Christmas party (see Table 23).

Even those who maintain social relations with other couples have a very small circle of friends. For one-half of them this circle consists of only one or two couples. Only 17 per cent see as

[1] For references on the extensive literature on class and leisure see the following sources and the included bibliographies: Floyd Dotson, 1951; Reuel Denney and David Riesman, 1951, Leonard Reisman, 1954, Clyde R. White, 1955, Alfred Clarke, 1956, Morris Axelrod, 1956, Robert J. Havighurst and Kenneth Feigenbaum, 1959.

many as four or more different couples in the course of a year (included in this count are couples seen at least a few times a year).

When asked, the respondents attribute their meager social life to lack of money and other external obstacles. At first glance this explanation appears sufficient. In comparison with the middle classes, the poorer couples can hardly afford the cost of coffee and cake for their guests, much less a theater or a restaurant. Moreover, the working wives and their husbands often dovetail their work-shifts in such a way that they have little free time together. The cost of baby-sitters is prohibitive and, apart from the cost, strangers are not trusted in this role and relatives are not always available. Some families are newcomers to the community and attribute their lack of friends to that fact.

But there are other impediments to social life in Glenton. Opportunities of enlarging the circle of friends are limited when social life is confined to two or three couples and when the husband's job neither requires social entertaining nor serves as a source of new contacts. The friendships that these families enjoy have often been acquired in school. Because the choice of friends is made within so small a group, the chances of finding congenial persons are relatively small. A couple may lack social life simply because a husband does not like his wife's girl friend or her husband. Occasionally the husband gives a similar explanation—his wife does not like the woman his buddy married and hence they do not meet as a foursome.

But while external obstacles may limit social life, a favorable external situation does not necessarily ensure it. A pattern of joint social participation must exist before a family avails itself of propitious circumstances. The weaker the interest in social life, the more easily will it be dissipated by even a slight hindrance. A few of our respondents appear hardly aware of the pattern of entertaining non-relatives at home. Thus, an older woman said that such a custom may have existed in the past but must have gone out of fashion because no one she knew followed it.

Lack of common interests between men and women is another deterrent to joint social life. In the words of one woman, "Jane [her girl friend] doesn't know what to talk to men about and Jane's husband doesn't know what to talk to women about."

Where the pattern of joint social life is firmly established, marital strain does not preclude an active social life. The fiction of marital solidarity is maintained in public, and social life may even provide a welcome escape from the emptiness of marriage. But in these working-class families a reasonably satisfactory marriage appears to be a necessary condition of joint social life. Because separate social life is accepted, it takes very little to tip the scale in its favor.

A feeling of awkwardness at social occasions was expressed by some husbands.

"You work all day," said a 31-year-old truck driver (with six years of schooling), "and you're on your feet a lot and when you come home, you like to get comfortable. You don't want to get all dressed up, to be bothered. You see enough of the fellows at work and you'd think the women see enough of each other all day long. It don't make any sense, this rushing around to everybody's house." This man spends evenings in front of the T.V. set. Another young man feels awkward eating in public, unless he is alone with his wife.

The case of Mr. and Mrs. Taylor illustrates the leisure hours of a couple in their twenties who never visit with mutual friends. Since the external circumstances create no obstacles to joint social life, the case highlights the less obvious deterrents.

Mr. and Mrs. T., aged 28 and 25 respectively, have been married for eight years and have two children. Mr. T. is a truck driver and neither has completed high school. They are a good-looking pair. Mrs. T.'s hair, always in curlers during the morning interviews, was combed stylishly on a Saturday afternoon when she was leaving to meet "the girls" in the park. The afternoon visits in the park with other mothers and their children are a daily occurrence, but the women obviously dress up on Saturdays.

The T.'s occupy the second floor of a wooden-frame house owned by Mrs. T.'s parents. The house was recently bought for $18,000. The parents-in-law live on the ground floor and tenants occupy the top floor. The T.'s apartment is conventionally furnished with an upholstered living-room set, a modern coffee table with a big glass ashtray and a new dinette set in the kitchen. They have a T.V., a radio, a washing machine and a car. There are two bedrooms; the bathroom has a box of tissues matching the color of the walls.

As soon as she gets up in the morning, Mrs. T. turns on the radio: "I know by the program whether I am getting my housework done on time." The best part of her day, she said, was the afternoon visit with her girl friends in the park, with all the children playing nearby. If they have shopping to do, the mothers may wheel the carriages to the main street only a block away from the park. Her mother helps with the main shopping twice a week by taking care of baby or by coming along. Mr. T. dislikes shopping and, although he may occasionally drive his wife to the store on a Saturday, he helps less than most husbands in the neighborhood. Mrs. T.'s maternal grandparents live across the street and she may drop in for a visit with the children any time during the day. On Sundays they have the midday meal downstairs with her parents. They do not attend church. In the afternoon they usually drive over to see Mr. T.'s parents. In the summer they often spend Sundays at Mrs. T.'s maternal aunt's place in the country where a number of her relatives gather for a picnic lunch. They often drive to the shore for a swim.

Mrs. T. would have liked to go driving on week ends, but Mr. T. explained to the interviewer: "I drive all week and on week ends she says, 'Let's go for a ride.' It is like a ditch-digger. He digs all week and when he gets home his wife says, 'Go dig a ditch in the yard.'"

Mr. T. has a night off every Friday and he spends it at his club. He explained that a man owns a poolroom with card tables and a Coca-Cola machine. His four buddies come to play some pool or pinochle and ten to fifteen other fellows gather there of an evening. Then they usually go over to the tavern to have some beer. Saturday afternoons are also usually spent at the club with the fellows. They kid around, they talk about cars or sports—and try to stay away from religion and politics. "It's no use talking about this, you just get into an argument." He doesn't discuss his job because it would take another truck driver to understand what he is up against, and there doesn't happen to be anyone in his line of work at the club. While Mr. T. is at his club on Friday evenings, Mrs. T. entertains two or three girl friends at home. She is usually asleep by the time he returns.

Asked what he would do with two more hours a day, Mr. T. was stymied: "I wouldn't know what to do with the time." Mrs. T.'s answer to the same question was a quick "Two more hours in the afternoon with my girl friends."

If Mr. T. returns from work early, he usually goes out to see whomever he can meet in the neighborhood or goes downstairs to have a cup of coffee with his in-laws. Otherwise he and his wife watch T.V. Once in a while he puts on his paja-mas, lies on the floor and lets the kids climb all over him and play with him. Every two or three weeks he and his wife go to a movie together, leaving the children in the grandmother's care. If he doesn't care to see the movie, he baby-sits and his wife goes with a girl friend. In answer to our question as to what he would do with $100 to spend on fun, Mr. T. made no mention of his family and said he would go riding at a ranch for a week.

Mrs. T. also discussed her leisure-time preferences. She would have liked to go dancing but her husband doesn't enjoy it. Going to restaurants is no fun with small children. One of her main pleasures is shopping for new clothes for herself and the children. She gets something new for them every month or so, shopping alone or with her mother. Mrs. T. corresponds with a girl friend who moved out of town. She gave the inter-viewer a year's set of letters received from her friend. These letters contained detailed descriptions of clothes bought or made for the children with many references to Mrs. T.'s pur-chases, which were apparently reported in her own letters in similar detail.

Neither Mr. nor Mrs. T. reads books—the only book she read in the past year or two was *Peyton Place*, at the sugges-tion of a girl friend and her husband didn't read it. At one time Mrs. T. had a subscription to the *Ladies' Home Jour-nal* and the *Saturday Evening Post*, but these ran out and now her reading is confined to movie magazines. Occasionally she does report what she reads to her husband. The one remem-bered example was an article about an epidemic of boils in a children's hospital and, because their own infant had boils, Mr. T. read the article at her suggestion.

Mr. T. reads two daily newspapers (he does not bring them home), and sometimes sees *Look* magazine. His wife doesn't read any newspapers and once in a while, if there is something interesting in the papers, he tells her about it. He told her, for example, of a bombing of a synagogue. He was indignant because he knew how he'd feel if it were his house of worship. He also told his wife about a picture he saw of a little boy in Quemoy with his hand blown off. They don't discuss politics: "What is the use, all the politicians talk sweet and promise you anything until they are elected." Mrs. T. sometimes talks about the atom bomb blowing them all up, which makes Mr. T. very angry.

The T.'s have a car and live within 15 miles of a metropolis.

Yet they have never been in a museum of any kind, in a theater other than a movie, and have never taken their child (now 5 years old) to the city zoo.

One explanation of the T.'s segregated social life lies in their lack of mutual interests. Each prefers the companionship of his own friends because the interests and the talk of the opposite sex appears trivial or boring. Mrs. T. still feels the scars of her husband's neglect of her in favor of his buddies in the early years of their marriage. Nevertheless, she would be willing to entertain and to go out with other couples, but Mr. T. had never observed such a pattern in his own family and discouraged her attempts to organize such social affairs.

Unlike the T.'s, the majority of the young married people do have some joint social life. Mr. and Mrs. V., one of the most active couples, belong to a "bunch," consisting of three other married pairs, all old school friends. The V.'s, married for three years, are grammar school graduates in their early twenties. The wife reported that when all of their friends began to think about getting married they took an oath that they "wouldn't get like their parents, who stay home and never do anything." They were "going to keep on having fun as long as they could and were going to do things together." They make it a point to play cards together at least once a month. They also bowl, hike and go swimming with the other couples. Mr. and Mrs. Taylor also met each other in school. During their long period of going "steady" (Mrs. T. was 15 when they started), Mr. T. was "terribly jealous," and he punched a couple of fellows because he thought they paid her too much attention. Whether due to his jealousy or to other causes, the T.'s never belonged to a mixed clique in school. This may have contributed to their lack of joint social contacts.

Most of the couples fall between the two extremes of the T.'s and the V.'s, with the majority seeing another couple about once a month. Couples drop in or arrange in advance to spend an evening together. We have not heard of a single dinner party; the men may go out to bring a pizza for late evening refreshments, but only relatives have meals together.

Unless the couples play cards or watch T.V., men and women form separate groups. Although questions were asked about this in every interview, only one woman expressed a concern about this segregation. One of her peeves, she said, is that people leave their T.V. on when they have company. Neither does she like to see all of the men bunched in one place and all women in another; she tries hard to have the conversation general. (This unusual, upwardly mobile woman was described on p. 76.)

The differences in the extent of joint social life appear to be explained less by external obstacles than by attitudes towards it. Neither presence nor absence of young children, length of residence in the community, or level of income affects the relative frequency of joint social contacts. The surprising irrelevance of income is explained by the fact that under certain conditions poverty is no barrier to an informal social life. Indeed, in the case of three families who are neighbors on the same floor of a tenement, proximity, poverty and the need for mutual aid weld them together: "We see each other all the time, even too much." But in other areas of the city, lack of money probably hinders social life. The majority of the respondents resided in two- or three-family houses, with five or six houses on their block. Usually the curtains were drawn shut and there were few persons seen on the porches or in front of the house during the period of the study, between September and June. The contacts between neighbors are infrequent—even families who lived at their present address for several years had difficulty recognizing the names (obtained by us from the Directory) of other persons on the block. The identification might eventually be made with a remark such as: "Oh, they must be the people in their fifties across the street who have a married daughter." "I still don't know the names of my neighbors," said a woman who had lived in a three-story corner apartment house for the past six years. "We say 'Good morning' and 'How are you,' but I don't get into their homes and they don't come into mine."

Given this lack of neighborliness, a poor family residing in such areas cannot enjoy the informal sociability possible in housing development or tenement. Unless friends are also neighbors, social life entails the expense of telephone calls, transportation, more elaborate refreshments for visitors coming from a distance and, if children are left at home, the provision of babysitters.

The factor which is most highly associated with the frequency of joint social life is the age of the couple, especially the age of the husband. Such activity is the pastime of couples in their twenties; it declines sharply with age. Forty per cent of the men in their thirties visit with other couples only twice a year, if that often. On the other hand, among men under 30 years of age only 7 per cent are that inactive socially. That the age of the husband is more decisive for the extent of social life than the age of the wife reflects, we believe, his greater power in this respect (see Tables 24a and 24b). More wives than husbands attribute their limited social activities to the disinterest of their partners: "There is no point in having friends over when he sits and watches T.V. instead of joining in the conversation."

The more active social life of the younger couples may represent a new trend that will continue into their later years. But we suspect that for them also social life will decline with age. Old friends move away; interest in sports, dancing and other physical activities which brings the younger people together declines; some marriages will deteriorate; and prudential considerations dictate less spending on "fun" and more on necessities.

The decline in joint social life with age is especially great among the less-educated. At the start of married life, education does not affect the frequency of social contacts, but, among couples in their thirties, the high school graduates tend to surpass the less-educated. The small number of cases studied makes their comparison by age and education inconclusive, but the result proves consistent with the findings of another study showing that the leisure patterns of middle and lower classes grow more divergent with the age of the respondents.[2]

We turn now to the implications of these facts for the marital relationship. One consequence of social gatherings is that they may expose facets of personality which are subdued in marriage: joint social life may enable a person to see his mate in new roles. For example, Mr. Roberts, described in the preceding chapter, prides himself upon his wit, but has no adequate outlet for his humor at home. His wife, he remarked, does not laugh at his jokes when they are alone but "when the others laugh she laughs too." He is very popular with the "crowd," and his wife admires his social talent.

If social life can reveal assets otherwise hidden, it can also re-

[2] See Clyde R. White, 1955.

veal defects. Both attractive and unattractive aspects of personality come into play with the increase in social life. The spouse will be observed when he wins an argument or loses it; when his story falls flat and when he is the life of the party; in his attitude towards those who are more successful and to his inferiors, towards male and towards female friends. Conversely, the couples whose social life is limited to relatives lack opportunities to observe their mate with friends and to react to newly revealed facets of his personality. This reaction may, in turn, evoke a response from the mate and a chain of further consequences.

Joint social life has another important consequence: a comparison with others increases self-awareness. In order to know oneself, one must know others. The greater the diversity of persons with whom one interacts, the greater the chance that some characteristic previously taken for granted will become the object of reflection. A woman remarked, for instance, that her friend is more demonstrative towards her husband in public than she herself would dare to be. It is highly probable that the difficulty respondents manifested in perceiving and reflecting upon relationships stems in part from their limited range of social contacts.

Comparison with others, then, may allay or arouse dissatisfactions with oneself or with marriage. A woman, an officer of the P.T.A., said of her husband: "I wish he went out among different people the way I do. He would see that his children are not so different as he thinks they are." The greater the diversity of contacts, the greater the range of such possible comparisons.

The processes cited do not exhaust the functions of social life. The couple with a joint social life has the experience of being treated as a unit, and this tends to heighten their sense of interdependence. Being identified with the mate, one winces at his blunders and feels pride in his triumphs. The reserve imposed by the presence of others upon the couple may sharpen the sense of the intimacy they share. Post-mortems after social gatherings may bring mutual recriminations, but they may also provide the couple with common interests in personalities or ideas to which they were jointly exposed.

By providing contacts between men and women social life may occasionally create attractions that threaten marriage, but it may also stabilize it. Playful flirtations are generally controlled, serving as an outlet for desires that might otherwise seek more radical satisfactions. Moreover, the attention paid one's mate by others may refresh one's perceptions of him.

In sum, social life does not have uniform consequences for marital adjustment; it may strengthen or weaken a marriage. But one generalization may be safely made. The one-third of these couples who lack joint social contacts are cut off from an important means of development, self-knowledge and recreation.[3]

Separate Social Life

The case of Mr. and Mrs. Taylor demonstrates that lack of joint social life does not necessarily imply withdrawal from social contacts. Couples can enjoy an active separate social life with friends of the same sex. Among the Glenton husbands, the less-educated have more frequent contact with male friends than the high school graduates. Sixty-nine per cent of the former, and only 41 per cent of the high school graduates, see male friends once a week or more frequently.[4]

These educational differences are related to differences in normative expectations, as attested by responses to a test story. Both husbands and wives were asked to comment upon the following story:

> The Williamses have been married for five years. They have two small children. Every Monday the husband goes bowling with his buddies and every Thursday he plays gin rummy with some friends. His wife says that twice a week is too often to leave her alone with the kids. It isn't the money—it is just that she doesn't like to be alone. She is after him to give up one night. What do you think about this couple?

[3] Perhaps even this generalization requires a qualification. Joint interaction with friends may occasionally develop one mate at the expense of the other. In segregated social life each mate may be forced to play out a wider range of roles. This occurs because a married couple, interacting as a unit in social gatherings, develops a tendency towards some specialization. A mate superior in some respects usurps, or is forced into, a particular role allowing his mate to remain more passive.

[4] See Tables 25a and 25b for frequency of contacts by sex and education. We did not count as a social contact a chance meeting with a friend on the street. Many, in fact most of these contacts, take place outside the home but if four men play cards in one another's homes without their wives (often giving the host's wife a "night off" since the husband can baby-sit) the contact is judged to be "separate" and not joint. See Table 26 for wives' separate social contacts.

The wife in this story aroused the indignation of some husbands:

A 31-year-old laborer with seven years of schooling: "She's a stinker. What could be more natural than that guy, and she wants to cramp his style."

A 40-year-old carpenter with eight years of schooling: "The husband earns the money, don't he? He has the right to get away as often as he wants. If my wife tried to butt in like that I'd really let her have it."

A 29-year-old semi-skilled worker, a high school graduate: "Mr. Williams probably has to get out to let off steam. My wife doesn't seem to mind being left alone a couple of times a week. That's the way it should be."

A 25-year-old sanitation worker with eight years of school: "She should mind her business. He should spank her."

Similarly, some of the wives defended Mr. Williams:

A 37-year-old woman, a grade school graduate: "He's got the right to spend his own money any way he wants to. He should go out."

A 30-year-old wife with seven years of schooling: "She shouldn't be after him—it is his affair if he wants to go."

Those who take the side of the husband in the story occasionally agree with the view expressed by one of them that "she should have two nights off also. What is right for one is right for the other." More frequently, Mr. Williams is urged to give his wife some time off, but not necessarily equal time.

But the wife in the story also has her supporters. A novel element is introduced by her defenders—the idea that something is wrong with the marriage if the husband wants to spend that much of his leisure away from his wife:

A 27-year-old taxi driver, a high school graduate: "It's rough on a dame, if she loves a guy and he don't love her and wants to get away."

A 26 year-old wife, a high school graduate: "She's right even if they do have the money. If she likes him around, he ought to try to stay with her more. I'd want to be with my husband on my night off."

A 32-year-old pipelayer with ten years of schooling: "If they don't like each other's company then they should at least take turns. He should let the wife go out too."

When the defenders of the wife were asked whether the appropriate solution may not be to give Mrs. Williams equal time off, they declared that four nights were too many to be apart. Instead, they endorsed Mrs. Williams's request: "Let him give up one night and take her out once in a while."

The first type of comment, favoring the husband, is more frequently voiced by the less-educated men and women. The high school graduates tend to take the part of the wife: Mr. Williams was defended by 57 per cent of the less-educated but by only 35 per cent of the high school graduates. Conversely, the wife's view that one night away from home is enough, was supported by only 26 per cent of the less-educated but by 41 per cent of the high school graduates.

As one would expect, women at each educational level tend to side with the wife more frequently than do their husbands. But among the less-educated, even the wives find Mrs. Williams unreasonable, 50 per cent of the less-educated women defending the husband (Table 27).

The less-educated men and women are not far apart in their disapproval of Mrs. Williams, while disagreement between the sexes is wider among the high school graduates. Were we to prophesy the frequency of marital conflicts over the husband's absences from home on the basis of professed attitudes, that of the high school couples would be expected to exceed that of the less-educated. But the actual behavior of the men, although it tends to be consistent with the attitudes, is influenced by other factors as well. The less-educated husbands tend in practice to exceed the accepted limits, while the high school graduates do not exhaust their rights. And one reason for the latter fact is the competing right, claimed by the better-educated wives, to have an evening away from home at a club or with girl friends. They enjoy this privilege more frequently than the less-educated women: 42 per cent of the high school graduates, but only 28 per cent of the less-educated, have a "night off" weekly—usually with the husband serving as the baby-sitter. The wife's night off is sometimes spent with her social club, a group of six to ten women meeting in the members' homes, usually not for such activities as card playing and sewing, but just for sociability. Weekly club dues are saved for splurges in the neighboring city —a dinner and a movie; the men, acting as baby-sitters, are generally not included in these outings. In contrast, the less-educated women see their own friends during the day or informally in the evenings without having a regular night off.

Membership in Organizations

The number of organizational ties for our respondents is higher than it would be in a random sample of Glenton blue-collar workers since we reached 18 of the families through their churches. Nevertheless, as many as 28 per cent of the respondents belong to no organized group whatsoever, neither to a church nor a union, nor even an informal sewing circle. For an additional 31 per cent of men and women, the church is the sole organizational affiliation, although the latter itself often includes a variety of subsidiary affiliations, such as Bible classes, missionary societies, choirs and the "Mr. and Mrs." clubs.[5]

The union is the second most frequent affiliation of the men. Only one-fourth of the latter belong to associations other than the church and the union. One-third of the women are members of groups unaffiliated with the church. The other organizations include the P.T.A., Masonic lodges, singing societies, women's clubs, bowling groups and social clubs. A minority of some 10 per cent who belong to three or more clubs seem to follow the busy schedules of the middle-class suburbanites. For example, Mr. Y., aged 36 and a high school graduate, and Mrs. Y., a 31-year-old woman with similar education, are the parents of two children. Mr. Y. bowls every Tuesday as a member of the church bowling league. Every second Friday the couple attends the Mr. and Mrs. club of the church. He is a member of the union and he regularly plays chess. Mrs. Y. is a member of the Executive committee of the P.T.A. and chairman of the Parents'

[5] Morris Axelrod, 1956, p. 16, states that 40 per cent of his operators and craftsmen belonged to some organization other than a church. In our sample, 41 per cent of all the respondents had at least one affiliation other than the church.

Education Study Group (each of these groups meets monthly). Mrs. Y. also belongs to a women's social club which meets weekly in the homes of the members.

Almost non-existent among the organized activities of these couples is volunteer social service, apart from what may be carried on under church auspices: only two women are scout leaders and only one does volunteer hospital work.

The less-educated men, largely because they are affiliated with unions, have a higher rate of organizational membership than the less-educated women—70 per cent of the men, but only 54 per cent of the women, belong to one or more associations (including the church). But among the high school graduates, the women are more active than the men. Of the small number of male high school graduates, three are white-collar workers who do not belong to unions or any other local groups. The organizations of the women high school graduates include churches, social clubs, the P.T.A., the high school sorority and a few others.

Leisure-Time Preferences

A list of 50 leisure-time activities and interests was presented to each respondent for rating on a three-fold scale: "enjoy very much"; "average enjoyment"; "enjoy little if at all." These activities were to be rated independently of the frequency with which an activity was performed. Each person was given an opportunity to add interests omitted from the schedule.[6]

The ten most enjoyable activities of the women (only those rated "enjoy very much") follow in order of frequency for the group as a whole: (1) T.V., (2) playing with children, (3) having friends over, (4) gardening, (5) having family over and planning home improvements, (6) planning Christmas gifts, (7) swimming, (8) attending church, (9) visiting relatives and friends, (10) shopping for clothes. The husbands' preferences, in order, include: (1) T.V., (2) playing with children, (3) swimming, (4) smoking, (5) visiting relatives and having friends over, (6) having family over, (7) visiting friends, (8) going to a restaurant, (9) planning home improvements, (10) having a drink in the tavern.

---

[6] The list of activities was adapted with some modifications from an article by Clifford Kirkpatrick, 1937. The theory underlying this and the next section is based also upon a work of Jessie Bernard, 1933.

Some interests and activities included in the schedule received few, if any, votes. Missing in the listing of the ten most enjoyable interests are "reading a magazine or a book," "talking about myself," "attending a sports event," "going to movies," "card playing," "talking about what I read in a newspaper," and "talking about what makes people tick."

With age and duration of marriage, the number of interests enjoyed "very much" declines in frequency. For example, husbands under the age of 30 listed 15 enjoyable interests per person, but this average declines to 11 for men 30 years and over. The comparable figures for women are 15 and 13. The reduction of the number of interests is all the more significant because the interviewees were not asked to indicate the frequency of performance of these activities. Moreover, many of the listed interests do not call for any outlay of money. And yet men and women in their thirties could not think of as many interests they enjoyed "very much" as did the younger respondents. This is a numerical index of the shrinking of interests and partial withdrawal from social life which we noted among the older couples.

The husbands with high school education included among their ten favorite interests some that do not appear on the listing of less-educated, (who are on the average older). These are photography, dancing, card playing and dreaming of the children's future. The tavern is listed by the less-educated among the top ten enjoyable activities but not by the high school graduates. The high school wives gave first place to "going to a restaurant," while for the less-educated television took the top position. "Planning home decorations" is rated higher by high school graduates than by less-educated women.

Each respondent was asked to indicate his preferred companion in each of the 50 activities and interests presented for rating. The replies enable us to compare the role of the spouse as the preferred associate in various kinds of activities, particularly those enjoyed "very much" as against those enjoyed only moderately.

The spouse emerges as the single most important companion for both men and women, but he or she is one of many others. Of all the preferred companions in "most enjoyable" pursuits listed by the husbands, "my wife" constituted 25 per cent and "my friend" a close second, with 21 per cent of the total (Table 28). For the wives, the husband is more frequently the preferred companion, constituting 30 per cent of all the associates, with friends amounting to only 17 per cent of the total.

A comparison of companions in the two categories of activities, those "most enjoyable" and those "enjoyed only moderately," is instructive. Wives are relatively less prominent as companions in their husbands' favored leisure-time pursuits than in those they enjoy only moderately. And this is the case in both educational categories. Wives constitute only 25 per cent of the preferred associates in their husbands' most enjoyable activities, but 32 per cent of the associates in the moderately enjoyable ones. The wives name husbands as favored companions with almost equal frequency in both categories of activities and this is the case irrespective of the wives' education.

Duration of marriage affects the choice of leisure-time companions (see Table 29). Among those married seven years or less, the wives named their husbands as preferred companions more frequently than husbands named wives. But in marriages of longer duration the pattern of preferences changes: The older husband curtails associations with friends and relatives: he prefers to be "alone" or with "children" relatively more frequently. The relative role of the wife does not change. But the older wife, in listing her preferences, named friends and relatives with increasing frequency and her husband less often. The husband is still the single most important associate in the wife's most enjoyable pursuits, but after years of marriage he has a relatively smaller role than he had during the first seven years of marriage.

Men and women with high school education named their spouses as preferred associates in their most enjoyable activities more frequently than the less-educated men and women. This result was not controlled for duration of marriage, but this factor had no influence upon the choices of the less-educated men in any case. We are unable to separate the influence of the duration of marriage, on the one hand, and education, on the other, for the women (see Table 30).

Reading

The men read the daily newspapers more regularly than do their wives, at each educational level. High school education increases the newspaper reading of the husbands, but seems not to influence the reading habits of the wives. Thus only 6 per cent of the male high school graduates, but 26 per cent of the less-educated men, "seldom or never" see the daily paper, whereas almost one-half of the wives, irrespective of their education, are non-readers. The wives explained that when anything of importance happens somebody is bound to tell them about it anyway or they hear the news on the radio and T.V. Almost one-third of the less-educated husbands said that they never discuss items read in the newspapers with their wives, but only one-fifth of the more educated husbands could not remember any occasions when such topics were discussed. Such newspaper-oriented conversations as do occur are initiated, according to their recollection, by the husband in one-half of the couples and by the wife in only one-fifth. In the remaining cases the spouses initiate discussions of news with equal frequency.

Education does not appear to increase the reading of magazines on the part of the men, but this may merely reflect our less detailed inquiry into the extent of magazine reading. About one-third of the husbands, irrespective of their education, "seldom or never" read a magazine but, at the other extreme, almost one-half at least "see" two or more magazines. We did not ascertain the regularity or thoroughness with which these are read.[7]

The magazines mentioned include *Popular Mechanics*, *TV Guide*, trade magazines, *Mechanics Illustrated*, "How to . . ." pamphlets, *American Home*, *Saturday Evening Post*, *Coronet*, *Adventure*, *Reader's Digest*, *Life*, *Look* and others. Only one man each listed *Variety*, *Argosy* and *Popular Science*. *Harper's*, *Atlantic Monthly* and *Scientific American* were mentioned by one respondent. This husband is one of only two of the 58 men who visit a library:

> A 32-year-old grade school graduate, he is the son of a prosperous electrician who wanted him to finish high school and to follow in his own occupation; but the youth felt hostile towards both of his parents and hoped to be independent of them. At 32, he has a semi-skilled job and a wife and three children to support on $70 a week. He has grandiose ambitions of

[7] The question posed was: "Do you ever read any magazines? Which?" The non-readers are those who answered "Seldom," "Hardly ever" or "Never."

taking correspondence courses and becoming a professional man, but his deep moodiness may indicate that he himself realizes how forlorn his hopes are. This reader of *Harper's* is a downwardly mobile and unhappy man.

Women read magazines as often as do men and, once again, education does not affect the frequency of non-readers or the proportion who read two or more magazines. Among the women's magazines are *TV Guide*, *True Story*, movie magazines, *True Confessions*, *Woman's Day*, *The P.T.A. Magazine*, *Ladies' Home Journal*, *Coronet*, *Reader's Digest*, *Saturday Evening Post*, *Good Housekeeping*, *American Home*, *Redbook*, *Look*, *McCall's* and *Cue*.

Three-fifths of the interviewees said that they never read books. Book reading among men increases with amount of schooling, but not among women. The two-fifths of the group who are classified as "readers" may have mentioned only one book read during the past two years. Reading of the Bible is included in the count. The books read by these families during the past two years include the following: paperback mysteries, paperback Westerns, *Reader's Digest* book condensations, *White Tower*, *Rebecca*, *Peyton Place*, novels by Zane Grey, *How Green Was My Valley*, *Home Before Dark*, *The Child's Book of Knowledge*, *The Nun's Story*, *Parliamentary Procedure*, the Bible and a few others.

Since the habit of reading is not widespread and only one of the couple may be a reader, the sharing of interests here tends to be reduced. One-third of the respondents expressed some dissatisfaction with their mates because they could not discuss their reading with them in a stimulating way. Twice as many wives as husbands voiced such complaints.

Summary

Several findings concerning the uses of leisure in Glenton are pertinent to the analysis of marriage. The ideal of marital companionship during leisure hours tends to be more fully endorsed by the high school graduates than by the less-educated, as seen in their respective evaluations of Mr. and Mrs. Williams in the test story. Another test of preferences produced a consistent result. Having first checked their most enjoyable recreational interests and activities, the respondents were asked to name the preferred associates in each. The high school graduates, male and female, chose their mates somewhat more frequently than the less-educated respondents. But men of both educational categories agreed in one respect—their most enjoyable activities involved the companionship of their wives relatively less frequently than recreational activities they enjoyed only moderately. Wives, on the other hand, named their husbands as the preferred companions in both these categories of activities with equal frequency.

Turning from attitudes and preferences to actual practices, we have no measure of the amount of leisure time husbands and wives spent together or separately and are unable to compare the two educational categories in this respect. The less-educated husbands spend more of their leisure in separate social life with male friends than is true of the educated men. But offsetting the influence of the husbands' absence among the less-educated is the greater tendency of the high school wife to have a "night off." Joint social life plays a smaller part in the leisure patterns of all Glenton families than has been reported for middle-class persons, and it tends to decline with age more sharply among Glenton's less-educated respondents. In the examination of effects of a meager social life on the marital relationship, we have indicated some of the former's dysfunctional and also some possibly functional consequences.

ΛΛΛ
CHAPTER
15

Theoretical and Methodological Conclusions

This chapter will view marriage problems discussed in the preceding pages from a wider theoretical perspective and present some methodological and substantive conclusions of the study.

Marital Disorganization

The theory that illuminates Glenton's problems bears little resemblance to some dominant interpretations of social ills. In contemporary sociology, social problems are generally associated with anomie or the breakdown of social norms, cultural ambiguities and institutional conflicts.[1] Relevant as these concepts are in a period of vast world changes, they may lead to an overemphasis upon consensus. Glenton's families are generally stable, respectable, and law-abiding, sharing deeply internalized and common values. Stable though they are, one-third of these marriages fail to rate our assessment of "moderately happy." In 14 per cent of the cases the marriages are "very unhappy." There is no doubt about this latter diagnosis; in these very unhappy cases all but one of the wives (and she was also wretched) voiced strong regrets about their marriages. Slightly over one-third of the marriages are rated

[1] See, for example, Robert K. Merton and Robert A. Nisbet, 1961, p. 13.

as moderately happy. At the other extreme, slightly less than one-third are happily or very happily married. Their numerous problems will serve as a reminder that, if social ills are frequently the product of moral confusion, it does not necessarily follow that clear moral directives and consensus are synonymous with social health.

Some violation of social norms were no doubt concealed from us. Allowing for such under-reporting, the evidence nevertheless strongly suggests that deviant behavior plays only a minor role in the marriage problems of our respondents. Illegitimacy, adultery, juvenile delinquency, alcoholism, refusal on the part of the housewife and the provider to fulfill their obligations appear to be rare exceptions. The husbands are not all adequate providers but it is not for want of effort and devotion. There are many other examples, as we shall show, of failure to attain desired and culturally sanctioned goals but this failure does not generally lead to violations of legal or moral codes.

Social disorganization, however, may exist in the absence of deviant behavior.[2] The distinction between the two concepts proved its usefulness in the case of Glenton. Deviant behavior refers to violations of normative codes. Social disorganization, on the other hand, has been defined by Robert K. Merton as "inadequacies or failures in a social system of interrelated statuses and roles such that collective purposes and individual objectives of its members are less fully realized than they could be in an alternative workable system."[3] Social deviation may be one cause of disorganization but it is not the only one, and it must not be permitted to obscure the other causes. Moreover, the distinction between the concepts of deviation and disorganization enables us to raise significant problems as to their interrelationship. For example, what are the consequences of particular kinds and degrees of deviance for the ability of specified social systems to fulfill their goals? How do other deficiencies of social systems affect the patterning of deviance?

Social disorganization in Glenton is not the result of deviant behavior, nor yet of the other conditions strongly emphasized in current theory, i.e., institutional conflict and moral dissensus. Our respondents are relatively alienated from many institutions of the

[2] See Robert K. Merton and Robert A. Nisbet, 1961, pp. 697-737.
[3] *Ibid.*, p. 720.

community. Having few institutional ties they are consequently spared the conflicts caused by competing demands of various statuses. For example, the familiar conflict between career and family life does not plague the workingman. His emotional investment in the job is relatively slight. Irregular work shifts occasionally create problems for the family but no workingman's wife need feel jealous of her husband's job and he himself does not feel guilty because his career leaves too little time for his family. The workingman's wife does not resent her husband's career but neither does she feel that she contributes to it by social entertaining or advice. The husband cannot count on her assistance but he is protected from critical scrutiny of his performance on the job.

Though rare, competing loyalties do exist. The union, the church, and a youth group each absorbed the interests of three men to the extent that their wives felt neglected. In two of these cases the marriage is problem-ridden and the wife sensed that her husband's preoccupation is motivated by the wish to escape the unhappy home.

Conflicts in marriage are sometimes created by the outside affiliations of the wives, several of whom are more active in churches and in clubs than their husbands. One man with ten years of schooling, married to an intelligent high school graduate, active in the affairs of her church, confessed to the interviewer:

> "I might not have told you but she said she already told you, that nothing in the world gets me more than coming home and finding she's not here and not knowing where she is. I get to thinking, maybe she's out gabbing with the women in the church and that gets me mad and blue. She usually comes home in the middle of church suppers and things like that to fix my meal for me. I like that a lot. I think I'm an average man. I enjoy my family. A little untidiness is O.K., but if it's there all the time, you can't take it, *especially if it's because she has outside interests*" [italics ours].

Another woman, also a high school graduate, is active in the P.T.A. and in the church. The church has created the one serious problem in an otherwise happy marriage:

> "He didn't want me to teach Sunday School. I cried plenty and it was a real problem in our marriage. It wasn't only the Sunday School. It grew into the teachers' meetings and afternoon services. He now feels a little more a part of it. They

asked for volunteers to serve coffee during the coffee break at the church and he volunteered and had a good time talking to people. But he still doesn't like to go to church and still doesn't let me do everything I'd like to do."

Both of these men find their main gratification within the home whereas their wives are enjoying the heady wine of leadership in outside organizations. The first husband is patently dependent upon his wife. The irony of the second case is that the husband has succeeded in transforming his shy and insecure wife into a more outgoing person. She gives him full credit for this metamorphosis. But having become self-confident, she is reaching out into community activities. "He doesn't like to share me with anyone or anything"—all the more so, we might add, because he himself has no strong interest either in his work or in civic participation.

It is no accident that in both cases the wives are high school graduates. The latter exceed the less-educated women in church and club memberships. In our sample, the educated women also exceed their husbands in group memberships. The less-educated couples conform more closely than the high school graduates to the specialization of the roles posited by Talcott Parsons.[4] Among the former the husband is not merely the provider but the "secretary of state" concerned with the family's relations to the external world. But the high school wives tend to be more involved in community affairs than their husbands.

One problem caused by multiple affiliations is, however, quite prevalent. We refer to the in-law problems (discussed in Chapter 12) that are created by continued interdependence of the married couple and their parental families.

Another allegedly prevalent contemporary problem is also rare among these families. Ambiguous definitions of conjugal roles or conflicts over different conceptions of marriage cause few marital difficulties because spouses have similar cultural backgrounds. The exceptions to this consist of a few cases of religious and class intermarriages.

The intermarriage that creates the more serious strain is one in which the wife (and not the husband) has the superior class background.[5] The marriage norms of the high blue-collar worker are

[4] Talcott Parsons, 1955, p. 47.
[5] See Julius Roth and Robert F. Peck, 1951.

more egalitarian than in the lower strata and the wife who marries "up" has no difficulty in accepting this improvement in her position (illustrated on pp. 272-273).

But when the high blue-collar woman marries "down," the consequences may be more stressful. A characteristic conflict of such a marriage concerns social life—especially as regards recreational activities without the children. "He likes us all to be together all the time and I'd like to leave the children home and have us do things by ourselves sometimes," said a mother of four children, a high school graduate who married "down." "Sometimes I think it's because he didn't have any education and he has nothing else to do or to think about than just relaxing at home with the T.V." The couple disagree about baby-sitters. The husband shares the frequently held attitude of low blue-collar families: "I wouldn't leave my children with a stranger." The wife, on the other hand, would prefer to pay a stranger instead of depending upon services given by relatives that she would have to repay. Social life is a bone of contention in still another way. The husband expects relatives to join in all the social entertaining but the wife considers personal congeniality on social occasions to take precedence over ties to kin. Education is another subject of disagreements in this family. The husband resents the money spent by his wife on the *Reader's Digest* and its series of abridged books. He does help the young children with their homework but frequently feels that chores around the house are more important than school work, while his wife emphasizes the latter.

The yearning for a more romantic approach to love-making was expressed by one 34-year-old high school graduate who married a rough, less-educated but benevolent patriarch. "I'd be happy if we'd just go along the road and park somewhere sometimes," she said. "What do you think you're doing?" he is likely to say, "we are too old for that kind of stuff." This is a restless, energetic woman with an inquiring mind, married to a good provider who likes his home and wants to be left alone to enjoy his comfort. She tries to stimulate and to rouse him but succeeds only in evoking a stubborn defensiveness. Their previously satisfactory sex life has been harmed by this psychological interplay. She is puzzled by his neglect of her. "It isn't that he doesn't respond, you touch him and he gets excited but he doesn't like to do that any more."

Other differences in class backgrounds of the spouses and the problems discussed so far are, to repeat, exceptional in Glenton. But these families pay a high price for their immunity to some typical ills of our time. This immunity is produced by their isolation from social mainstreams. But the shield that protects them from the disorganizing influences of social change is also a barrier against its benefits. Similarly, if they are spared the conflicting demands of various organizations they are also deprived of the advantages of social participation.

In turning now to Glenton's major problems we shall at the same time qualify the current emphasis upon institutional conflicts and the breakdown of moral consensus as the main source of social disorganization.

It is not the failure to maintain traditional social patterns but the failure to modify them that accounts for some marital problems in Glenton. In a period of rapid social change, effective socialization into traditional patterns may contribute to social disorganization.

The sharp differentiation of masculine and feminine roles and the absence of the expectation of friendship in marriage are cases in point. Even when fully accepted by both partners these cultural patterns create difficulties for each. The husband pays a price for his relative exemption from domestic duties. Irritability, the apathy, the desire for a job outside the home—these are the reactions of some women to the domestic routine unrelieved by companionship with their husbands. Mr. Daniels was not the only husband baffled by his wife's frequent depressions. He consulted a relative who told him that women are subject to fits of "neurasthenia." He could not perceive any connection between his neglect of his wife and her condition because he behaved in what was, for his group, the accepted way. Some situations create frustrations even when they do not violate any norms. The young wife who has no expectation of friendship in marriage can still feel lonely. The young husband who never expected a wife to share his interests can still experience boredom with her conversation.

The reader may cite the case of the Greens to show that marriages can be satisfying even when they are not based upon friendship. This is a fact worth noting. But such marriages require the availability of relatives and close friends. Geographical mobility tends to separate the married couples from kin and trusted friends. The Smiths are only one of several families that demonstrate the burden such separation places upon the marriage to provide the emotional support previously given by other primary groups.[6] The same lesson is implicit in the cases of the Greens and the Kings, whose satisfactory marriages depend upon functions performed for each spouse by outsiders. These older norms of marriage will become increasingly unsuitable if the following prediction by a government agency proves accurate: "Many more of our workers than in the past must have, or develop, the mobility to shift jobs. . . . Many may have to change their residence as well as their occupation." [7]

Traditional patterns have today other unfavorable consequences. Because the need for psychological intimacy could not be satisfied in marriage, some men and many more women exchange confidences with outsiders. But friendship has a dynamic of its own and cannot always be contained within the prescribed limits. Even in a marriage which is "not for friendship," the disclosure of certain matters to outsiders is taboo. Twenty-one per cent of the husbands voiced a complaint that their wives talked too much about personal matters to outsiders. The husbands were distressed to realize that their finances or marital conflicts were exposed to public view. Fewer men than women have confidants; only 7 per cent of the women have a similar grievance. The absence of the norm of friendship created certain psychological pressures to seek confidants outside of marriage. But this, in turn, resulted in violation of marital privacy.

Again, the Glenton ideal of masculinity with its emphasis upon emotional reserve and its identification of personal interchange with the feminine role resulted in what we have termed a "trained incapacity to share." Chapter 8 demonstrates the deleterious effects of these characteristics upon the ability to cope with marital conflicts and to provide emotional support for the mate. Thus, even when a couple was exposed to the ideal of the companionate marriage, this lack of interpersonal competence occasionally hindered its realization. Indeed, the intellectual acceptance of such an ideal aroused in some couples feelings of inadequacy. They knew that

[6] For the effect of mobility upon marriage see Elizabeth Bott, 1957; John M. Mogey, 1956; and Michael Young and Peter Willmott, 1957.

[7] Department of Labor release published in *The New York Times*, September 20, 1963.

husbands and wives should talk to one another, but they found nothing to say. One measure of this problem is conveyed by two sets of figures. In response to one test story, 56 per cent of the wives held that something was lacking in the marriage of the couple in the story who had so little to talk about in the evenings. But as many as 44 per cent of the women, in another connection, complained that they frequently had nothing interesting to talk about with their husbands. For the husbands, the corresponding figures were 45 per cent, referring to the story, and 28 per cent, expressing a personal complaint.

The difficulties that hinder fuller realization of the ideal of companionship illustrate a familiar mode of social disorganization. Socially structured obstacles stand in the way of attaining the newly emerging cultural goal.[8] With respect to marital communication, our data enabled us to compare the magnitude of this discrepancy between aspirations and attainment for men and women at each educational level. The older high school women experience the widest gap between their expectations, on the one hand, and the actual quality of the marriage dialogue, on the other. They are consequently more dissatisfied with marriage communication than the less-educated wives at the same stage of life, despite the fact that they actually enjoy a higher level of sharing and companionate interchange.

The reader may argue that the personal dissatisfactions described above do not constitute social disorganization. Granted that the families continue to function without the social supports or restraints required by more seriously disorganized groups. Nevertheless, since the function of companionship is an increasingly important raison d'etre of marriage, marital unhappiness by definition implies the failure of this social system to attain one of its goals, with unfavorable consequences for the fulfillment of other goals, including that of child-rearing.

The function of companionship has been frequently cited by sociologists as the distinctive feature of modern marriage. Many writers have described the evolution of the modern family with specialization in its functions.[9] The remaining functions have been variously described as affectional or expressive and child-

---

[8] See Robert K. Merton, 1957, pp. 162-164.
[9] William F. Ogburn, Robert M. MacIver, Ernest W. Burgess, Harvey J. Locke, and Talcott Parsons, among others.

BLUE-COLLAR MARRIAGE / 338

rearing or socialization. "We have argued above," concludes one recent discussion, "that the nuclear family is specialized far over in the expressive tension-management and socialization directions." [10]

If Glenton families are at all typical of comparable classes in other communities, then for considerable segments of our population these writings are more prescriptive than descriptive. They define the appropriate functions of marriage in modern society. But the logic of the analysis does not unfortunately bring the required patterns into existence automatically. Possibly even for the unhappy third of the Glenton couples, marriage entails some satisfactions. But these men and women do not turn to one another for emotional support, and it is uncertain whether the net effect of the marriage relationship is to relieve or to increase personal tension.

Let us recapitulate our analysis. Modern marriage is called upon to fulfill new functions of friendship and emotional support, partly as a result of mobility and isolation of the couple and partly in response to new cultural expectations stimulated by the changing status of women and other trends. The fulfillment of these functions is impaired in Glenton by the persistence of some traditional values and definitions of sex roles. These operate directly in sanctioning certain behavior and indirectly, through their detrimental effects upon interpersonal competence. The relatively low educational level of Glenton respondents plays, no doubt, an independent role in retarding the development of skills and attitudes required for psychological intimacy between the sexes.

The survival of dysfunctional values and attitudes is not the only source of social disorganization in Glenton. Were the residents themselves asked to rank their difficulties, the economic situation would head the list. Their relatively low occupational and educational resources create a wide gulf between desired goals and attainments. Chapter 13 describes their economic and status frustrations and the types of resulting adaptations. Not only the poorest fourth of the families, but others also live from one pay envelope to the next, with no savings or insurance to cushion a possible crisis. This explains the undercurrent of anxiety which repeatedly comes to the surface in such remarks as, "He worked

[10] Talcott Parsons and Robert Bales, 1955, pp. 162-163.

good last year. I hope he will this year," or "I hope we'll stay healthy." Public relief is too humiliating to contemplate for these people, and in moments of panic they are much more likely to think of their relatives as a possible source of assistance.

For the man, the economic difficulties have a special emotional significance—they undermine his self-esteem. For example, he is concerned about his parental responsibilities. Our question, "Would you like your son to follow in your line of work?" was generally answered negatively, "No, I would like him to do a lot better." But at the same time the fathers doubted their ability to provide for their children the necessary means of advancement.

The husbands experience some other characteristic strains. Their actual power in the family frequently falls short of their patriarchal aspirations. In contrast, successful professional husbands may occasionally enjoy more power in marriage than is sanctioned by their egalitarian ideals.[11] The twinges of guilt which this latter discrepancy produces are less painful than the working-man's problem. Our respondents thought that "men should have the final say-so in family decisions." However, they found themselves pitted against resourceful wives who held paid jobs prior to marriage and could hold their own in marriage. This is especially true of the women high school graduates. One young wife told the interviewer that her husband's current weekly wages were only $10.00 higher than her own pay before marriage. Even the good providers lack the halo of prestige which high achievement and high community status bestow on a successful business or professional man. The ambivalence towards working wives was described in Chapter 3.

The lack of occupational and educational skills hinders the attainment of desired goals but this does not drive Glenton residents to resort to illegitimate means. Several possible explanations suggest themselves for the low rate of deviancy. In comparison with lower socio-economic groups, especially those with racial and ethnic disadvantages, these native born Protestants may feel less alienated from society and more strongly committed to its moral codes and legitimations. We have already noted, for example, that their individualistic ideology made the Glenton's poor pro-

---

[11] See Peter Pineo, 1961, for a discussion of a middle-class sample. As this book goes to press I note that a similar observation about class differences in patterns of strain has been made by William J. Goode, 1963, p. 21.

viders deflect the blame for their low achievement from social conditions to personal failings (see p. 283). Moreover, the majority of Glenton's families have not given up the hope of improving their own economic position within the blue-collar class. By projecting their ambition to move out of the working class unto their children they feel that they remain true to the American norm of striving.

The relatively poor adaptation to the economic environment is, of course, a familiar theme in the literature on the working classes. Less familiar is the effect upon marriage of the poor utilization of the cultural, recreational and social resources of the community, also associated with this class position. The drabness of life puts a heavy burden upon the marriage relationship. Shortening of the work day, smaller families, and the withdrawal of many economic functions from the home have given these couples long evenings and weekends together. But life in general is impoverished, and marriage assumes a saliency by default. It is questionable whether any relationship can fill so great a void. Even the middle-class suburbanite, who has reputedly forsaken the world for the family nest, bristles with outside interests in comparison with our respondents. Status seeking, the elaboration of living standards, the social life, to say nothing of civic and cultural interests, fill life with tension and struggle but also with emotional involvement and rewards. The romantic ideal which decrees that each find in his mate the fulfillment of all his needs is, after all, only rarely attainable. Many marriages remain satisfying precisely because each partner can draw upon other sources of stimulation, amusement, response and accomplishment. These rewarding experiences may be shared in marriage thus nourishing the relationship. They may also compensate for whatever frustrations may be entailed in marriage. Of course, outside interests occasionally become so all-absorbing as to divest marriage of any emotional significance or they may violate the limits of cultural permissiveness as in the case of extra-marital sex. But given some psychic congeniality, the richness of life enjoyed apart from the marital relationship per se may sustain the latter and make it not merely tolerable but rewarding.

As for Glenton couples, those in their twenties still enjoy social life and other forms of recreation. The birth of children and the striving to purchase a home and to furnish it still give life a sense of movement. But many couples in their late thirties, especially among the less-educated, seem almost to have withdrawn from life. There they sit in front of the television set: "What's there to say? We both see it." "If you had two extra hours every day, how would you like to spend them?" asked the interviewer, and a man mused: "This would make the evening awfully long and tiring if you're watching T.V."

The social isolation, especially of the older men, has been repeatedly noted. We have described the relatively low involvement of the men, as compared with their wives, in the lives of their married children. Social life with friends also declines with age. Only infrequently do the men appear to enjoy emotionally significant ties with work-mates. They lack even the kind of segmented, though intense, relationships that business and professional men frequently have with co-workers.[12] If this social isolation is characteristic of working-class men of other ethnic, religious, and regional groups, it may play a role in explaining the relatively lower level of mental health in blue-collar strata as compared with the middle and upper classes.[13] In any event, this social isolation, we believe, tends to strain the marriage relationship. It robs life and therefore marriage, of stimulation and novelty and it closes outlets that might siphon off marital irritations.

We were slow to perceive the problem brought about by a drab existence and constant "togetherness," for a reason that illustrates anew how tacitly held values can distort perception. We approached the study with the image of the East London working-class marriage in mind. Will the American working-class marriage, we asked, show the same estrangement between the sexes? Do husbands and wives in Glenton, as in London, lead their separate lives in work and in leisure? The English pattern fell short of our own ideal of friendship in marriage.

Glenton families were found to differ significantly from the East London ones. Most wives know to the penny what their husbands earn, and economic decisions are made jointly. There is no lack of togetherness in the sense of time spent in each other's physical presence. Indeed, these couples probably spend more time

[12] See Robert Dubin, 1956, for a research finding to the effect that "only ten per cent of the . . . (surveyed) workers perceived their important primary social relationships as taking place at work." For a comparative study of a professional group, see Louis H. Orzack, 1959.

[13] Thomas S. Langner and S. T. Michael, 1963.

together as a family (and probably more time together as a pair, without children, relatives, or friends) than middle-class couples with their more active social and club life. Our own moral set led us to approve these deviations from the East London patterns, and we were temporarily blinded to the problem that togetherness entailed for our respondents. We mistakenly assumed that the greater association between the spouses automatically brought about a deeper relationship than in East London.

Not all of Glenton families experience the difficulties just enumerated with equal intensity. The high school graduates on the whole, are happier in marriage than the less-educated (Tables 31a and 31b). This is especially true in the first years of marriage. The better-educated marry later and delay child-bearing in comparison with the less-educated couples. Consequently, fewer of the former suffer from the syndrome of problems of some young couples: too many infants, parenthood too soon after marriage under difficult economic conditions and in the absence of companionship between the mates. Moreover, the high school men (perhaps because they are younger), do not include the completely defeated men whose sense of failure has such unhappy consequences for marriage.

While high school graduates also believe in the traditional division of labor between the sexes, in practice the husbands help more frequently with the care of infants and with shopping than in less-educated families. Equally significant is their fuller marital communication. They have more faith in the possibility of friendship between men and women. One young high school graduate explained why women have more need of heart-to-heart talk than men: "The husband's job is an outlet for him and her days are more routine and so she needs to sit down and feel the closeness with her husband." When depressed, this wife finds that "a good heart-to-heart talk can do a lot for her morale." A value endorsed so explicitly must surely affect behavior. In contrast, the less-educated tend to feel, as was indicated in an earlier chapter, that friendship is more likely to exist between persons of the same sex and that the principal marital ties are sexual union, mutual devotion and complementary tasks.

But the better-educated have some typical problems of their own. Status frustration is one of them. Generally, status-seeking is not a prominent drive among these families. There is an order of priorities in goals and many are preoccupied with sheer survival. Even the more prosperous families do not live with gazes fixed on their reflected image, and with the constant comparative self-appraisal allegedly so characteristic of our society. This is no "other-directed" group. Many a middle-class couple who have to cultivate the "right" people for the sake of the husband's career would envy the freedom these families enjoy to entertain only the people they like. Their social life, such as it is, is pure sociability. Nevertheless, some pressures for upward mobility do exist and some high school couples exhibit strain because their aspirations for higher status are frustrated. (See Chapter 13.)

We found no difference between the two educational groups in the prevalence of sexual problems or in psychological sources of marital strains. No personality tests were employed in this study, and observations about psychological factors in marital maladjustment here appear inconclusive. But some speculation is aroused by the higher proportion of hostile sons and daughters among the less-educated couples, caused apparently by a number of social factors in their early lives. An unhappy childhood and hostile parent-child relationships tend to affect adversely the marital adjustment of the individual.[14] If this excess of parent-child conflict among the less-educated is confirmed by future studies it will offer another possible explanation of their lower marital happiness.

We limited our summary to problems in marriage, brought about, directly or indirectly, by socio-economic and cultural conditions. But there is hardly a case history cited in this book which does not suggest psychological factors involved in marital strain. Sharing a home with in-laws need not necessarily create an in-law problem, but it requires, as we have seen, a closer emotional dovetailing of personalities if trouble is to be avoided. Given the same degree of congeniality, those residing in separate households will experience less strain. Given a common residence, variations in psychological factors will also produce variations in the outcome. Similar interplay of psychological and social factors is illustrated in every chapter of this book. Maintaining the fiction of her husband's supremacy in public is, for example, an accepted stratagem of a dominant wife. But this adaptation to a deviant situation is not available to some person-

[14] Clifford Kirkpatrick, 1963, pp. 385-386.

alities. We encountered a wife whose competitiveness with her husband, more or less dormant in the privacy of the home, is aroused by the presence of an audience.

The summary of Glenton's problems was further limited to those most likely to be class-linked. The book itself illustrated many other sources of social disorganization: discontinuities in sex roles throughout the life cycle; ethical inconsistencies consequent upon social mobility and social change, yielding unearned advantages to either husbands or wives; situational pressures giving rise to operative norms which occasionally violate the ideal code and others. Among social sources of psychological stress, our case studies revealed an interesting variety. It is well known that culture may cause stress by censuring some desired gratification or by mandating a goal difficult to attain. But social factors may affect the degree of stress also by making it more or less difficult for individuals to mask socially condemned motives. For example, the new social acceptance of working wives has not modified the husband's jealousy, his anxiety over the possible loss of power and other personal objections to his wife's employment. Lacking the support of public condemnation, he is robbed of acceptable rationalizations in arguing his case and must expose, to himself and to others, his "irrational" objections. Again, the well-to-do wife, whose real motive for working is the wish for power, can hardly claim that she needs to contribute to family support. The Glenton working wives, on the other hand, could plausibly rationalize less acceptable incentives in economic terms.[15]

This study did not include any middle- or upper-class respondents, and it contains no data on broad class differences in marital adjustment. Recent evidence shows that divorce rates tend to decrease with higher socio-economic and educational status. The data on marital satisfaction are consistent; satisfaction appears to go up with the rise in the class hierarchy.[16] We have no information about the rates of divorce or desertion

[15] These observations suggest a new dimension to the factor of visibility in social relations. In the past it was the visibility of norms and of role-performance that was the object of discussion. Added to this now is the probability that social factors may determine the degree to which an occupant of some status can succeed in masking his motivations, or conversely, be forced to expose them.

[16] See bibliographies in William M. Kephart, 1961, and in William J. Goode, 1956 and 1963.

among the general population of Glenton's Protestant blue-collar families from which we drew our respondents. Nevertheless, our comparison of the two educational categories of blue-collar families has some pertinence to the question of broad class differences in marital happiness.

Current analyses of this problem seek to ascertain the peculiarly stressful experiences of the working classes in comparison with the upper strata.[17] But it is not certain whether the extent of stress does in fact decline as one ascends the occupational or the educational ladder. The economic and occupational frustrations were indeed more prevalent among our less-educated respondents as they are, no doubt, in a comparable stratum in the society at large. But offsetting these and other difficulties of these workers is their freedom from a number of allegedly typical problems of the higher and better-educated classes. Ambiguous definitions of mutual rights and duties and the resulting ethical inconsistencies, mental conflict produced by an abundance of choices, conflicting loyalties and standards, strain produced by the sheer volume of stimuli—all these are relatively rare in Glenton. Glenton couples are also free from the self-conscious scrutiny of relationships that, some writers claim, robs marriage of its spontaneity among many highly educated persons.

Are we to assume then, ex post facto, that these problems, more prevalent among the higher classes, are somehow less disturbing than those typical of the workingman? [18]

The interpretation of this problem may require a shift in emphasis. It is an open question whether life is less stressful for the higher classes. But it must surely contain richer rewards.[19] The sense of satisfaction with marriage, as with life in general, may depend not so much upon an absence of stress as upon the presence of rewards—a momentary feeling of closeness with one's mate, the occasional excitement of hope, even a fleeting triumph of achievement. True, a low level of expectations inflates the rewards of minor attainments ("I had myself a ball once

[17] See, for example, William J. Goode, 1956, p. 67.
[18] It is possible that the Glenton sample is too stable to be typical of working-class strata that are generally included in the class comparisons of marital adjustment. But the insulation from intellectual currents of the larger society and absence of group affiliations have been demonstrated in numerous working-class studies in other communities.
[19] See Alex Inkeles, 1960.

when I came out two dollars over the budget that we didn't have to pay out all at once"). But even with their modest aspirations, too many Glenton couples find life drab and unrewarding.

The paradox that higher socio-economic classes may experience both more happiness and more tension in marriage is no mere conjecture. The more highly-educated respondents in one study rated their marital happiness higher than people of less education; at the same time they expressed more self-doubt and a greater sense of inadequacy.[20] Further confirmation is supplied by a recent investigation which reveals that "high marital tension or job dissatisfaction may not necessarily produce unhappiness if they are offset by a sufficient number of positive feelings." [21] The better educated, higher income groups in the same study were found to exhibit a higher level of both positive and negative feelings. The authors conclude that "men of higher socio-economic status have a higher degree of marital tension, but at the same time happier marriages . . . [than men of the lower status]." [22]

Not only is the marriage relationship of the educated middle classes—in comparison with blue-collar workers—likely to contain more positive experiences, but so does their life in general. The more abundant life provides, as noted earlier, safety valves to siphon off marital frustrations and compensations to offset them.

Life at its best is economically comfortable and rewarding, but for the great majority life is narrowly circumscribed. A spotlight outlines a small circle of ground around each family, with the relatives, a few friends, the boss and some work-mates, the tavern keeper, the church and the union. Visible also are the top movie stars, baseball players and other athletes, T.V. performers and top national office holders. But beyond that circle extends a vast darkness. These English-speaking, well-dressed, well-mannered, responsible persons do not enjoy full membership in their society. They lack even such bridges to the larger society as may be provided by membership in a women's club or a Chamber of Commerce. The union occasionally (but from what could be ascertained, only infrequently) provides such a channel of information and sense of participation.[23] Verbal and intellectual

20 Gerald Gurin, et al., 1960, p. 116.
21 Norman M. Bradburn and David Caplovitz, 1965, p. 39.
22 Ibid., p. 41.
23 For a similar view see Joel Seidman, "The Labor Union as an Organization" in Arthur Kornhauser, et al., 1954.

limitations curtail reflection even about the immediate environment. In the words of Beatie, the working-class rebel of *Roots:* "Ever since it began the world's bin growin' hasn't it? Things have happened, things have bin discovered, people have bin thinking and improving and inventing but what do we know about it all?" [24] Economically poorer racial and ethnic minorities are no doubt still more deprived, but this does not make the exclusion of Glenton families any less wasteful and disturbing.

This is not merely the judgment of the author. In considerable measure, this is also the respondents' self-appraisal. Why, otherwise, would a father exclaim with such feeling: "No, I want my children to go a lot farther." But for all their fervent hopes and the struggle, these parents cannot provide for their children the environment enjoyed by the average middle-class child. Unless school and society find ways to improve the life chances for all citizens, a proportion of Glenton's children will grow up to live as do their parents, on the fringes of their society.

The Case Study Method

The case study method has its unique functions.[25] The test of causal relationships between known and measurable variables is not one of them. Neither is the study of relative frequencies of some readily ascertainable facts. We have occasionally investigated problems, such as allocation of tasks or contacts with relatives, which have been previously studied with larger and more representative samples. Such value as this book may have does not lie here.

But this statement requires two qualifications. Most previous studies of working-class marriage depended upon wives as informants. The scarcity of interviews with blue-collar husbands lends value to additional data. Moreover, the instruments used in the quantitative surveys to measure such elusive dimensions as authority, empathy and emotional support are still in an early stage of development—on this score the present study may provide a useful check.

In comparing our findings with those of other investigations, two broad conclusions emerge. The agreement between our as-

[24] Arnold Wesker, 1959, pp. 74-75.
[25] A useful classification of functions of qualitative methods is found in Allen H. Barton and Paul F. Lazarsfeld, n.d.

sessments and quantitative studies is high when it comes to group differences. The direction of sex, education and income differences is generally similar. The divergencies are greater with regard to the frequencies of certain patterns *in each group*. For example, our sample is more patriarchal and less equalitarian than are several working-class samples studied by survey methods. We found much more dissatisfaction with communication and more unhappiness in marriage than had been generally reported previously. To cite but one nationwide survey of 2460 persons, 38 per cent of the grade school graduates are classified as "very happy" and an additional 16 per cent are "happier than average." At the other extreme, only 5 per cent are "not too happy." The high school graduates are happier, with 46 per cent in the "very happy" group and 25 per cent "happier than average." [26] We also found that the high school graduates are happier than the less-educated, but both groups have a much higher proportion of unhappy marriages. Fourteen per cent of our total sample were judged to be very unhappy and to have serious regrets about their marriages.

The explanation of these divergencies may lie in the actual differences in the samples or in the cutting-off points of the different classifications. We suspect, however, that they reflect differences in methods. Our detailed and indirect probing may have brought to light unfavorable facts which are not readily admitted in answer to direct questions used in the surveys: for example, "When there's a really important decision in which you two are likely to disagree, who really wins out?" or "Taking things all together, how would you describe your marriage—would you say your marriage was very happy, a little happier than average, just about average, or not too happy?" In our own interview, answers to the direct questions on dissatisfactions with communication were at variance with the admissions made elsewhere by the same people. (See pp. 196-197.) With respect to marital happiness, it must be added that even the well-known measures that include a great number of criteria in addition to self-ratings of happiness have generally yielded higher proportions of happy marriages than in Glenton.[27]

26 Gerald Gurin *et al.*, 1960, p. 105.
27 See Judson T. Landis and Mary G. Landis, 1953, p. 279, for a summary of happiness ratings as revealed by several studies.

The moral of this is not to use expensive case studies on a large scale but to develop measures of authority, empathy and "psychological intimacy" that will minimize such distortions. Of the dimensions of marriage studied here, "psychological intimacy" is the most elusive. Currently used measures are still inadequate. How frequently the spouses discuss a particular topic and with what degree of satisfaction (provided this can be reliably ascertained) can tell us something about communication. But the range and the frequency may not be highly associated with completeness of self-disclosure. And some disclosures are not as indicative of intimacy as others. We show that the feeling of closeness can exist when communication is very selective and specialized. Chapter 6 presents an ambitious attempt to rate the psychological intimacy of 58 marriages on the basis of the total evidence of each case. Here, again, we found a high incidence of withdrawal from interaction. But (despite the encouraging degree of agreement of two coders) our assessments are no substitute for a measure that could be used on a large scale.

One of the functions of case studies is to suggest explanatory clues for empirical generalizations previously derived by quantitative techniques. We encountered in recent researches correlations that have mystified their discoverers because no rationale could be found for them or because they were contrary to expectations. Similarly puzzling have been some negative results, that is, absence of expected associations.

Our cases amplified and illuminated the findings of previous studies on such topics as: the irregular relationship between class, on the one hand, and the husband's power on the other, at the bottom of the socio-economic hierarchy (Blood and Wolfe); the irregular relationship between income and the extent of social life (Axelrod); the positive relationship between education and satisfaction with communication (Smardan); the greater in-law problems of husbands married to better-educated wives (Marcus); and the relatively better marital adjustment of hypergamous over hypogamous marriages—that is, better adjustment in marriages in which the husband rather than the wife has the superior socio-economic background (Roth and Peck).[28] Occasionally case studies add support to a purely speculative interpretation offered by the original investigator.

[28] See Bibliography (pp. 380 ff.) for full references to these studies.

The case study method is not limited, of course, to such refinements of earlier generalizations. Our cases provided full descriptions of attitudes, yielded some new observations, and uncovered new variables:

1. Quantitative studies of attitudes all too often compress answers into the simple alternatives of yes and no. The use of "projective" stories gave us a fuller description of attitudes, including qualifications, links with other attitudes, and depth of conviction.

2. Among the unanticipated observations made in the study are, to cite a few examples, the control that the older women still exercised over their married daughters; the isolation of the older men in the community and in the family; the sense of liberation that marriage brought to men as well as to women; the jealousy experienced by the husbands of the working wives; the contractual relationship that occasionally existed among relatives, such as payment for baby-sitting; the moral homogeneity and relative absence of role conflicts.

3. The search for new variables proceeded through a systematic study of such deviant cases as economically desperate and yet stable marriages; sexually satisfied but unhappily married couples; households shared with relatives that are, nevertheless, harmonious; happy in-law relationships in the face of a whole cluster of potentially disturbing factors, and the like.

The analysis did not stop with the listing of new variables or of isolated observations. The unique function of the case study method is to capture new *patterns* of relationships. We attempted, for example, to reconstruct in some depth a number of processes. It requires a flexible interview (or participant observation) to bring to light the various ways in which a social clique can cushion disillusionment with marriage. Similar methods are needed to show the manner in which a person attempts to socialize his mate, the reactions to such attempts and, in turn, his ways of coping with this backwash of his original efforts.

There are several typologies delineated in various chapters, for example, the classification of relationships between married persons and their parents, and of sexual problems. It remains to be seen whether future research will find these classifications fruitful.

Finally, we presented several detailed case studies. Though they were generally focused upon particular themes, they came closer than the study of isolated processes to the complex reality of marital interaction. The analysis of an estranged couple; the three poverty-stricken couples; the marriage which is "not for friendship"; the happy and close relationship of a less-educated couple—these and other cases sought to reveal something of the complexity of the interplay of social and psychological variables. Since the conceptualization of marital interaction is still inadequate, such descriptions may stimulate its development.

Some Generalizations Reconsidered

A large proportion of current generalizations about marriage owe their derivation to studies of college graduates. Are such generalizations "universals" for our society? It will be particularly instructive to review some negative instances. The comparative perspective of this study brought to light the hidden assumptions and, therefore, the limited scope of some familiar generalizations.

Studies of in-law problems made in this country show these to be predominantly "women's problems." (See Chapter 12, pp. 259-261, for references.) This can be plausibly explained by the greater social involvement of women with relatives, by their greater sensitivity and jealousy and other psychological sex differences. But we found that the less-educated husbands experience in-law problems as frequently as do their wives. Chapter 12 analyzes this anomalous finding. Should future studies confirm this fact, the original generalization about the excessive feminine proclivity to in-law conflict in our society will have to be restricted to a particular social context.

Waller and Hill's idea that "the secrets of marriage are among its most important assets" appears plausible enough.[29] The secrets of marriage both express the solidarity of the pair and, in turn, weld it more strongly. Conversely, revealing marital dissatisfactions to outsiders would naturally appear to weaken the marriage. But in Chapter 10 we argue that a number of the "low" blue-collar marriages are not harmed but actually made more viable because the partners—especially the wife—find emotional support in intimate relationships with friends and relatives. Not only was this support lacking in marriage; more significantly, neither mate expected to find it in marriage. The original gener-

[29] Willard Waller and Reuben Hill, 1951, p. 326.

alization then holds only for marriage characterized by certain norms.

The recognition that marital interaction changes with the stages of the family cycle has led to the interest in the patterning of these changes. Many writers stress the disenchantment that sets in with the years of marriage. We cited, however, several indications that the curves of satisfaction differed for the two educational groups. Dissatisfaction with marital communication, for example, was actually higher on the part of the younger less-educated men than among those married seven years and over. The unfavorable circumstances plaguing some less-educated couples dispelled very soon the euphoria of early marriage. This raises the possibility that the typical curve of marital happiness throughout the family cycle may not be identical in various socio-economic classes. Moreover, the curves of satisfaction may vary from one aspect of marriage to another.

Several studies have reported a correlation between the sexual adjustment of a couple and their happiness in marriage. Our interviews suggest that the size of this correlation may vary with class. Because some of our less-educated women expect little psychological intimacy in marriage, and their standards of personal relationships are not demanding, they were able to dissociate the sexual response from the total relationship. The sole high school graduate who was sexually fulfilled despite marital unhappiness appeared to have a masochistic personality.

The perennial debate about the causes of sex differences lends interest to comparative studies. That the social environment can affect emotional sex differences was demonstrated anew by our findings on empathy, the sources of emotional relief, on admission of "being hurt," and other traits. Women were found to excel men in empathy only among the less-educated couples; with high school education differences between the sexes became smaller. But a constant residue of difference remains: women of both levels of education express a greater yearning for interaction with their husbands than vice versa. Is this a true "universal" for our society? In one study, college-educated men cited "lack of closeness between husband and wife" as a marital problem more frequently than did college-educated women.[30]

Different class backgrounds of the spouses have been found

[30] Orville G. Brim, Jr., *et al.*, 1961, p. 224.

to be unfavorable to marital adjustment.[31] However, we encountered cases in which intermarriage promoted adjustment. For example, one husband who married "down" found that his wife, brought up in a patriarchal milieu, granted him more privileges than he had been conditioned to expect. He was appreciative of her generosity. His wife's lower social background did not interfere with his semi-skilled job as it might have had he been a junior executive in a corporation. Although no doubt they are more often unfavorable, the effects of intermarriage vary with the significance of the particular differences between the spouses in the social context of a given marriage.[32]

One of the more interesting recent developments is the application to the family of theories derived from the study of small groups. The positive relationship between the extent of talking and dominance in decision-making, noted in small groups, has been confirmed by Fred L. Strodtbeck in experimental sessions with married couples.[33] We did not study this problem systematically, but in several of our cases the dominant partner was the less talkative of the two; these may of course have been exceptions to the general pattern. But one can readily see that in a group of strangers a silent person can hardly make his influence count. In marriage, however, we deal not only with a smaller group but an enduring one. Over the years of marriage a person can exert his influence in other ways than through sheer volume of words. "He doesn't say much but he means what he says and the children mind him," a mother says about the father. The same may apply to the couple's marital relationship.

Sidney M. Jourard and Murray J. Landsman found a high degree of reciprocity in self-disclosure in a study of friendship.[34] Our married couples present a similar picture but in a number of marriages one partner is considerably more reserved than the other. Here again the differences between the family and other small groups may account for the divergence. Lack of reciprocity may tend to make friendship less rewarding to the participants and therefore unstable. Marriage, on the other hand, is held by many ties. The more independent, or the more withdrawn,

[31] Ernest W. Burgess and Leonard S. Cottrell, Jr., 1939.

[32] See Anselm L. Strauss, 1954, for a study of American-Japanese intermarriages.

[33] Fred L. Strodtbeck, 1951.

[34] Sidney M. Jourard and Murray J. Landsman, 1959-1960.

partner may reveal less of himself than his mate without thereby endangering the stability of marriage.[35]

Other generalizations have been modified by the findings of this study. Among the questions raised at the outset of this inquiry were some involving dilemmas of choice. Will work or the family claim the major emotional commitment on the part of the workingman? Does he find his greatest rewards in personal relationship or in achievement? Will our respondents spend relatively more of their leisure together or with individual hobbies? Will the conjugal or the parental family claim the primary loyalty? Will domesticity or the job bring the greater gratification to the working wife? We assumed the existence of these dilemmas because time and energy are limited. Moreover, some of these goals are not only competing but conflicting since the means which further one, hinder the other.

But we soon realized that this formula, "The more of one, the less of the other," often does not fit the facts. The workingman neither brings home a briefcase nor spends the evening in social life with friends. He is absorbed neither in his career nor in hobbies. Our high school graduates tend to be both more intent on achievement than the less-educated and more emotionally involved in marriage. The better-educated women enjoy more joint leisure-time activities with their husbands, but also spend more evenings in club work and with girl friends away from home.

Is the day, we began to wonder equally long for all social classes? The answer is that it is not, that the less-educated have a less abundant life all around because neither time nor energy is fully used.

The assumption that all have an identical volume of energy and time was not our sole fallacy. Certain attitudes tend to be considered antithetical because of fortuitous historical circumstances. There may have been a time when only women who rejected domesticity would crave an outside job. But we encountered women who had an exceptionally favorable attitude to both domesticity and work, and others who found few satisfactions in either.

[35] For some differences between the family and other small groups see Fred L. Strodtbeck, 1954, and Talcott Parsons and Robert Bales, 1955, pp. 303-306.

Some sets of values have the sound of a logical antithesis but in fact tend to be associated. The high school women reveal more of themselves to their husbands than the less-educated wives. But they also appear to have a greater respect for privacy. When we asked one high school graduate not to discuss the study with her husband prior to our meeting with him, she voiced a value in her reply: "This was *my* interview and I don't have to share it with him." She was happily married and her communication was rated "very full." Her high standard of personal relationships included both the value of sharing and respect for privacy. A person embracing both values may sometimes experience a conflict between them. But in comparing two groups, we find that one of the same group tends to endorse both. Similarly it is probable that a complex person has an acute need both for occasional privacy and for self-revelation.[36]

To sum up, most generalizations concerning American marriages have been based predominantly upon studies of middle-class and educated respondents. As was indicated throughout the books, many of these propositions withstood the test of this investigation. Others proved to be class-linked. This study of blue-collar marriages brought to light the hidden premises of several familiar generalizations and has thereby enabled us to reformulate them with greater precision.

[36] See an interesting discussion of dilemmas of family living in Clifford Kirkpatrick, 1963, pp. 90-95.

APPENDIX

Description of the Families

Of the 116 interviewed persons, 101 are Protestants and the rest are Catholics. There are 5 religious intermarriages among the 58 couples. All the respondents but one are native-born.

The modal occupation of the husbands is semi-skilled. Using A. B. Hollingshead's occupational classification, the jobs held by the 58 men were grouped as follows: 18 skilled, 22 semi-skilled and 10 unskilled.[1] We termed 6 jobs "white collar" (clerks) and 2 jobs were borderline semi-skilled or unskilled. The average annual earnings were $3,370 for the unskilled, $4,315 for the semi-skilled, $4,739 for the skilled and $3,800 for the white collar workers. The highest income in the group was $7,600. The high school husbands, though younger than the less educated, earned on the average as much as the latter. In fact, among the poorest fourth, there were only two high school graduates. Moreover, having smaller families, the high school couples enjoyed a higher standard of living than the less-educated.

Of the women, 25 completed high school and 33 did not. Only 18 of the 58 husbands were high school graduates. Sixteen wives and 17 husbands did not go beyond the eighth grade.

As to age, 38 of the wives were under 30 years at the time of the interview and the remaining 20 were 30 or older. Of the 58 men, 28 were under 30 years. Twenty-three couples have been

[1] See August B. Hollingshead and Frederick C. Redlich, 1958, Appendix 2.

married less than seven years and 35, seven years or longer. The average number of children was 1.9 for the better-educated women. Women who have not completed high school, although on the average not any older than the high school graduates, have been married longer. They had on the average 2.8 children per family. Thirty per cent of the less educated women and only 20 per cent of the high school graduates married at the age of 18 or younger. The corresponding figures for the husbands are 8 per cent for the less educated and 5 per cent for the high school graduates.

TABLE 1

SEX ADJUSTMENT OF WOMEN, BY EDUCATIONAL LEVEL

	All Women		Under 12 Years		12 Years	
	No.	Per Cent	No.	Per Cent	No.	Per Cent
Good adjustment	16	27	11	33	5	20
Fair adjustment	19	33	8	25	11	44
Poor adjustment	23	40	14	42	9	36
TOTAL	58	100	33	100	25	100

TABLE 2

SEX ADJUSTMENT AND MARRIAGE HAPPINESS OF THE WIVES, BY THEIR EDUCATION

Types of Marriage	Under 12 Years		12 Years	
	No.	Per Cent	No.	Per Cent
Sexually and generally highly satisfactory	6	18	4	16
Sexually and generally fairly satisfactory	6	18	9	36
Sexually and generally unhappy	9	27	5	20
Marriage satisfaction higher than sexual satisfaction	7	21	6	24
Sexual satisfaction higher than marriage satisfaction	5	15	1	4
TOTAL	33	99	25	100

TABLE 3

"THE HUSBAND WHO DOESN'T TALK," BY EDUCATION OF RESPONDENT

	Under 12 Years		12 Years		Total	
	No.	*Per Cent*	*No.*	*Per Cent*	*No.*	*Per Cent*
Lack of conversation is a genuine problem	17	26	20	59	37	37
"Wife is spoiled"	32	49	5	15	37	37
"Let him alone when he is like that"	7	11	4	12	11	11
Others*	9	14	5	15	14	14
TOTAL	65	100	34	101	99	99

* This category consists largely of responses which describe personal experiences without expressing a judgment.

TABLE 4

THE FOX STORY, BY EDUCATION OF RESPONDENT

	Under 12 Years		12 Years		Total	
	No.	*Per Cent*	*No.*	*Per Cent*	*No.*	*Per Cent*
Disapprove of wife because she violates the norm of privacy	11	16	19	50	30	29
No mention of the norm of privacy	51	76	15	40	66	63
Others*	5	8	4	11	9	9
TOTAL	67	100	38	101	105	101

* This category consists largely of responses which describe some personal experience without expressing a judgment.

TABLE 5

THE FOX STORY,
BY SEX AND EDUCATION OF RESPONDENT

| | HUSBANDS | | | | WIVES | | | |
| | Under 12 Years | | 12 Years | | Under 12 Years | | 12 Years | |
	No.	Per Cent	No.	Per Cent	No.	Per Cent	No.	Per Cent
Disapprove of wife because she violates the norm of privacy	7	19	8	53	4	13	11	48
No mention of the norm of privacy	28	78	6	40	23	74	9	39
Others*	1	3	1	7	4	13	3	13
TOTAL	36	100	15	100	31	100	23	100

* This category consists largely of responses which describe some personal experience without expressing a judgment.

TABLE 6

"THE HUSBAND WHO DOESN'T TALK," BY SEX AND EDUCATION OF RESPONDENT

	Husbands				Wives			
	Under 12 Years		12 Years		Under 12 Years		12 Years	
	No.	Per Cent	No.	Per Cent	No.	Per Cent	No.	Per Cent
Lack of conversation is a genuine problem	9	25	7	50	8	28	13	65
"Wife is spoiled"	23	64	4	29	9	31	1	5
"Let him alone when he is like that"	2	6	1	7	5	17	3	15
Others*	2	6	2	14	7	24	3	15
TOTAL	36	101	14	100	29	100	20	100

* This category consists largely of responses which describe personal experiences without expressing a judgment.

TABLE 7a

"THE HUSBAND WHO DOESN'T TALK,"
BY CHURCH MEMBERSHIP, EDUCATION AND SEX
Percent of "middle class" answers

| | Under 12 Years | | | | 12 Years | | | |
| | Church | | No Church | | Church | | No Church | |
	No.	Per Cent	No.	Per Cent	No.	Per Cent	No.	Per Cent
Husbands	15	46	21	10	9	56	5	40
Wives	15	13	14	43	14	76	7	43

TABLE 7b

THE FOX STORY,
BY CHURCH MEMBERSHIP, EDUCATION AND SEX
Percent of "middle class" answers

| | Under 12 Years | | | | 12 Years | | | |
| | Church | | No Church | | Church | | No Church | |
	No.	Per Cent	No.	Per Cent	No.	Per Cent	No.	Per Cent
Husbands	15	33	21	14	10	60	5	20
Wives	15	13	14	36	16	62	7	29

TABLE 8

SELF-DISCLOSURE IN MARRIAGE,
BY SEX OF RESPONDENT

| Disclosure to Mate | WIVES | | HUSBANDS | | TOTAL | |
	No.	Per Cent	No.	Per Cent	No.	Per Cent
Very full	10	17	13	22	23	20
Full	19	33	12	21	31	27
Moderate	14	24	13	22	27	23
Meager	11	20	13	22	24	21
Very meager	4	6	7	12	11	10
TOTAL	58	100	58	99	116	101

TABLE 9

MUTUAL SELF-DISCLOSURE OF COUPLES

Self-Disclosure	No.	Per Cent
Both full or very full*	20	35
Both moderate	6	10
Both meager or very meager*	14	24
Wife higher in self-disclosure	12	21
Husband higher in self-disclosure	6	10
TOTAL	58	100

* Ratings of husband and wife are either identical or differing only by one step, from "full" to "very full," or "meager" to "very meager."

TABLE 10a

MARITAL HAPPINESS AND
SELF-DISCLOSURE OF WOMEN

Self-Disclosure	MARITAL HAPPINESS		
	Happy	Moderately Happy	Unhappy
Full or very full	13	11	4
Moderate	3	8	1
Meager or very meager	—	4	9

TABLE 10b

MARITAL HAPPINESS AND
SELF-DISCLOSURE OF MEN

Self-disclosure	MARITAL HAPPINESS		
	Happy	Moderately Happy	Unhappy
Full or very full	13	9	1
Moderate	1	6	2
Meager or very meager	—	8	11

TABLE 11

SELF-DISCLOSURE, BY SEX AND EDUCATION OF RESPONDENT

(Per cent of respondents with specified ratings)

Self-Disclosure	WIVES		HUSBANDS		TOTAL	
	Under 12 Years ($n = 33$)	12 Years ($n = 25$)	Under 12 Years ($n = 40$)	12 Years ($n = 18$)	Under 12 Years ($n = 73$)	12 Years ($n = 43$)
Full (or very full)	37	68	35	61	36	65
Moderate	26	20	20	28	23	23
Meager (or very meager)	37	12	45	11	41	12
TOTAL	100	100	100	100	100	100

TABLE 12a

EDUCATIONAL LEVEL OF RESPONDENT
AND AREAS OF RESERVE *

Area	WIVES		HUSBANDS	
	Under 12 Years ($n = 146$)	12 Years ($n = 99$)	Under 12 Years ($n = 141$)	12 Years ($n = 48$)
In-laws	2	6	6	2
Confidences of friends	9	5	2	—

* Area as per cent of total areas.

TABLE 12b

EDUCATIONAL LEVEL OF RESPONDENT
AND MOTIVES OF RESERVE *

Motive	WIVES	
	Under 12 Years ($n=155$)	12 Years ($n=109$)
Husband not interested	22	13
To protect husband's self-esteem	9	19
Self-protection	7	10
To protect confidence of others	12	7

* Motive as per cent of total motives.

TABLE 13

ASSESSMENTS OF UNDERSTANDING,
BY SEX AND EDUCATION OF RESPONDENT
(Per cent of cases having a specified rating of empathy)

Rating of empathy	WIVES		HUSBANDS	
	Under 12 Years ($n = 38$)	12 Years ($n = 25$)	Under 12 Years ($n = 40$)	12 Years ($n = 18$)
High	36	32	20	50
Average	24	44	33	28
Low	30	16	40	17
Unknown	9	8	7	5
TOTAL	99	100	100	100

TABLE 14a

THE HUSBAND'S ROLE IN WIFE'S BAD MOODS

*(Frequency of mention of husband per
number of persons in specified group)*

Husband Source of Bad Mood

33 uneducated husbands,	
describing their wives	1.2
Their wives describing themselves	2.1
15 educated husbands,	
describing their wives	1.8
Their wives describing themselves	2.6

TABLE 14b

THE WIFE'S ROLE IN HUSBAND'S BAD MOODS

*(Frequency of mention of wife per
number of persons in specified group)*

Wife Source of Bad Mood

29 uneducated wives,	
describing their husbands	1.2
Their husbands describing themselves	0.7
21 educated wives,	
describing their husbands	1.4
Their husbands describing themselves	0.9

TABLE 15

EMPATHY AND SELF-DISCLOSURE OF MATE

Less Educated Husbands Husband's Empathy*	Their Wives' Self-Disclosure		
	High	Average	Low
High	5	3	—
Average	4	7	2
Low	4	2	10
TOTAL	13	12	12

* Unknowns omitted.

TABLE IS *Continued*

Less Educated Wives Wife's Empathy*	Their Husbands' Self-Disclosure		
	High	Average	Low
High	7	3	2
Average	3	2	3
Low	1	—	10
TOTAL	11	5	15

Educated Husbands Husband's Empathy	Their Wives' Self-Disclosure		
	High	Average	Low
High	9	—	—
Average	2	2	1
Low	1	1	1
TOTAL	12	3	2

Educated Wives Wife's Empathy*	Their Husbands' Self-Disclosure		
	High	Average	Low
High	5	3	—
Average	7	3	—
Low	1	—	4
TOTAL	13	6	4

* Unknowns omitted.

TABLE 16

MODES OF CONFLICT, BY SEX AND EDUCATION OF RESPONDENT
(*Per cent of persons who mentioned selected modes of conflict*)

	HUSBANDS		WIVES	
Mode of Conflict	Under 12 Years (*n* = 40)	12 Years (*n* = 18)	Under 12 Years (*n* = 33)	12 Years (*n* = 25)
Withdrawal and repression	41	44	27	20
Talking out	12	33	12	32
Moderate "flare-ups"	12	28	6	32
Violent quarrels, occasionally beating, breaking	27	17	33	4
Drinking	15	—	3	—

TABLE 17

CONFIDANTS, BY SEX AND EDUCATION OF RESPONDENT

| | HUSBANDS | | | | | | WIVES | | | | | |
| | Under 12 Years | | 12 Years | | Total | | Under 12 Years | | 12 Years | | Total | |
	No.	Per Cent	No.	Per Cent	No.	Per Cent	No.	Per Cent	No.	Per Cent	No.	Per Cent
Isolates*	6	15	1	6	7	12	2	6	—	—	2	3
No confidants	26	65	11	61	37	64	8	24	6	24	14	24
Confidants	2	5	5	27	7	12	21	64	17	68	38	66
Tavern or clique	6	15	1	6	7	12	—	—	—	—	—	—
Unknown	—	—	—	—	—	—	2	6	2	8	4	7
TOTAL	40	100	18	100	58	100	33	100	25	100	58	100

* Persons whose marriage communication is "very meager" and who have no outside confidants either.

TABLE 18

CONTACTS WITH RELATIVES

(Per Cent of Wives and Husbands Who See a Specified Relative as Frequently as Several Times a Week or Daily)

| | Relatives Reside in Same Community | | | | | | All Living Relatives Irrespective of Their Place of Residence | | | | | |
| | Mother | | Father | | In-Laws | | Mother | | Father | | In-Laws | |
	No.*	Per Cent	No.*	Per Cent	No.*	Per Cent	No.*	Per Cent	No.*	Per Cent	No.*	Per Cent
Wives	34	66	25	50	34	46	50	54	40	37	50	32
Husbands	31	52	26	50	35	63	45	38	38	34	50	40

* Number of cases for whom we have visiting information.

TABLE 19

Per Cent of Wives and Husbands Who See a Specified Relative (Residing in the Same Community) as Frequently as Several Times a Week or Daily, by Duration of Marriage

| | Wives | | Husbands | |
	Married Under 7 Years	Married 7 Years or Over	Married Under 7 Years	Married 7 Years or Over
Mother	92	59	60	48
Father	54	43	60	33
In-Laws	50	45	61	63

TABLE 20

THE WIFE'S RELATIONS TO HER PARENTS, BY HER EDUCATION
(*per cent*)

| | Wives to Mothers | | | Wives to Fathers | | |
	Under 12 Years ($n = 30$)	12 Years ($n = 20$)	All ($n = 50$)	Under 12 Years ($n = 21$)	12 Years ($n = 14$)	All ($n = 35$)
Close or very close	50	80	62	24	50	34
Fair	27	15	22	56	36	48
Hostile or estranged	23	5	16	20	14	18
TOTAL	100	100	100	100	100	100

TABLE 21

THE HUSBAND'S RELATIONS TO HIS PARENTS, BY HIS EDUCATION (*per cent*)

| | Husbands to Mothers | | | Husbands to Fathers | | |
	Under 12 Years ($n=31$)	12 Years ($n=13$)	All ($n=44$)	Under 12 Years ($n=28$)	12 Years ($n=13$)	All ($n=41$)
Close or very close	32	68	43	14	54	27
Fair	58	24	48	56	31	48
Hostile or estranged	10	8	9	29	15	25
TOTAL	100	100	100	99	100	100

TABLE 22

MOTHER-IN-LAW RELATIONS, BY EDUCATION AND SEX OF RESPONDENT* (*per cent*)

| In-Law relations | Under 12 Years | | 12 Years | | Total |
	Men ($n=33$)	Women ($n=22$)	Men ($n=12$)	Women ($n=21$)	($n=88$)
Good	24	27	25	33	27
Average	39	41	58	33	41
Strained	33	32	17	33	31
No contact	3	—	—	—	1
	99	100	100	99	100

* Mothers-in-law living in same communities or in others under two hours away by car (this includes four cases of recently deceased mothers-in-law).

TABLE 23

JOINT SOCIAL LIFE

Frequency of Joint Visits with
Another Couple (Non-Relatives)

	No.	Per Cent
Twice a week or oftener	10	17
Weekly	7	12
Once, twice or three times a month	17	29
Several times a year	5	9
Once or twice a year	4	7
Never	10	17
No information	5	9
TOTAL	58	100

TABLE 24a

JOINT SOCIAL LIFE, BY SEX AND AGE OF RESPONDENT

| | WIVES | | | | HUSBANDS | | | |
| | Age Under 30 Years | | Age 30 Years or Over | | Age Under 30 Years | | Age 30 Years or Over | |
Frequency of Contacts	No.	Per Cent	No.	Per Cent	No.	Per Cent	No.	Per Cent
Very frequent (twice a week or more)	7	18	2	10	7	25	2	7
Moderately frequent	23	61	12	60	19	68	16	53
Very infrequent or never (twice a year or less)	8	21	6	30	2	7	12	40
TOTAL	38	100	20	100	28	100	30	100

TABLE 24b

JOINT SOCIAL LIFE,
BY EDUCATION AND AGE OF RESPONDENT

	Per Cent with "Very Infrequent" or No Social Contacts
Young couples (both under 30 years of age)	
Both under 12 years' education (15 cases)	8
One or both high school graduates (15 cases)	13
Older couples (both 30 years of age or over)	
Both under 12 years' education (9 cases)	56
One or both high school graduates (11 cases)	9
Husband 30 years or older, wife under 30	
Both under 12 years' education (5 cases)	60
One or both high school graduates (5 cases)	40

TABLE 25a

SEPARATE SOCIAL LIFE WITH SAME-SEX FRIENDS, BY SEX AND EDUCATION OF RESPONDENT

	HUSBANDS				WIVES			
	Under 12 Years		12 Years		Under 12 Years		12 Years	
Frequency of Contacts	No.	Per Cent	No.	Per Cent	No.	Per Cent	No.	Per Cent
Twice a week or more	19	44	2	12	23	64	11	39
Weekly	11	25	5	29	3	8	6	21
1, 2, 3 times a month	7		4		6		7	
Several times a year	3 }	30	0 }	59	3 }	28	2 }	40
Never	3		6		1		2	
TOTAL	43	99	17	100	36	100	28	100

TABLE 25b

SEPARATE SOCIAL LIFE WITH SAME-SEX FRIENDS,
BY DURATION OF MARRIAGE

| | HUSBANDS | | | | WIVES | | | |
| | Married Under 7 Years | | Married 7 Years or Over | | Married Under 7 Years | | Married 7 Years or Over | |
Frequency of Contacts	No.	Per Cent	No.	Per Cent	No.	Per Cent	No.	Per Cent
Twice a week or more	9	39	12	32	14	48	20	57
Weekly	5	22	11	30	7	24	2	6
1, 2, 3 times a month	5 ⎫		6 ⎫		4 ⎫		9 ⎫	
Several times a year	1 ⎬	39	2 ⎬	38	3 ⎬	28	2 ⎬	37
Never	3 ⎭		6 ⎭		1 ⎭		2 ⎭	
TOTAL	23	100	37	100	29	100	35	100

TABLE 26

WIVES' EVENINGS AWAY FROM HOME, BY EDUCATION

	Under 12 Years		12 Years	
	No.	Per Cent	No.	Per Cent
Weekly or oftener	9	28	10	42
1, 2, 3 times per month	4	13	7	29
Several times a year	7	22	4	16
Never	12	37	3	13
TOTAL	32	100	24	100

TABLE 27

COMMENTS ON THE WILLIAMS' STORY, BY SEX AND EDUCATION OF RESPONDENT
(*Per cent of respondents with a specified comment*)

	WIVES		HUSBANDS		TOTAL	
	Under 12 Years ($n = 30$)	12 Years ($n = 17$)	Under 12 Years ($n = 31$)	12 Years ($n = 17$)	Under 12 Years ($n = 61$)	12 Years ($n = 34$)
Mr. Williams is right	50	29	65	41	57	35
Mrs. Williams is right	27	47	26	35	26	41
Others*	23	24	9	24	17	24
TOTAL	100	100	100	100	100	100

* About one-fifth of the respondents offered a variety of solutions without taking sides either with Mr. or with Mrs. Williams.

TABLE 28

PREFERRED ASSOCIATES IN LEISURE, BY SEX OF RESPONDENT *

| | WIVES | | HUSBANDS | |
	Enjoyed Activities Very Much (n = 1540)	Average Enjoyment (n = 1135)	Enjoyed Activities Very Much (n = 1420)	Average Enjoyment (n = 833)
Alone	16	11	14	8
Children	20	16	20	17
Spouse	30	31	25	32
Friends	17	21	21	23
Relatives	16	20	18	20
Neighbors	1	1	1	1
TOTAL	100	100	99	101

* Per cent of total number of associates.

TABLE 29

PREFERRED ASSOCIATES IN LEISURE,
BY DURATION OF MARRIAGE AND SEX OF RESPONDENT*

	Husbands				Wives			
	Married Under 7 Years		Married 7 Years or Over		Married Under 7 Years		Married 7 Years or Over	
	Enjoyed Very Much Activities (n = 541)	Average Enjoyment (n = 345)	Enjoyed Very Much Activities (n = 678)	Average Enjoyment (n = 494)	Enjoyed Very Much Activities (n = 635)	Average Enjoyment (n = 646)	Enjoyed Very Much Activities (n = 901)	Average Enjoyment (n = 641)
Alone	14	10	19	8	17	13	16	10
Children	19	13	26	19	20	15	20	18
Spouse	29	32	29	31	35	32	27	31
Friends	19	23	14	22	15	19	19	21
Relatives	19	21	12	19	13	21	16	18
Neighbors	0	—	0	1	0	0	2	2
Unspecified	—	—	0	—	0	—	0	—
TOTAL	100	99	100	100	100	100	100	100

* Per cent of total number of associates.

TABLE 30

PREFERRED ASSOCIATES IN MOST ENJOYABLE ACTIVITIES, BY SEX AND EDUCATION OF RESPONDENT

(specified associate as per cent of all associates)

	HUSBANDS	
	Under 12 Years ($n = 558$)	12 Years ($n = 427$)
Alone	15	13
Children	20	16
Wife	25	27
Friends	21	19
Relatives	19	19
Neighbors	0	2
Unspecified	0	3
TOTAL	100	99

	WIVES	
	Under 12 Years ($n = 555$)	12 Years ($n = 542$)
Alone	15	18
Children	21	17
Husband	26	35
Friends	19	15
Relatives	18	14
Neighbors	0	0
Unspecified	0	0
TOTAL	99	99

TABLE 31a

MARITAL HAPPINESS OF WIVES,
BY THEIR EDUCATION

	Under 12 Years		12 Years		Total	
	No.	Per Cent	No.	Per Cent	No.	Per Cent
Happy or very happy	6	18	10	40	16	28
Moderately happy	10	31	9	36	19	33
Unhappy or very unhappy	14	42	5	20	19	33
Inconclusive	3	9	1	4	4	7
TOTAL	33	100	25	100	58	101

TABLE 31b

MARITAL HAPPINESS OF HUSBANDS,
BY THEIR EDUCATION

	Under 12 Years		12 Years		Total	
	No.	Per Cent	No.	Per Cent	No.	Per Cent
Happy or very happy	11	28	8	44	19	33
Moderately happy	10	25	5	28	15	26
Unhappy or very unhappy	17	42	5	28	22	38
Inconclusive	2	5	—	—	2	3
TOTAL	40	100	18	100	58	100

BIBLIOGRAPHY

Axelrod, Morris, "Urban Structure and Social Participation," *American Sociological Review*, 21 (February 1956), 13-18.

Barber, Bernard, *Social Stratification*, New York: Harcourt, Brace, 1957.

———, "Social-Class Differences in Educational Life—Chances," *Teachers College Record*, 63 (November 1961), 102-113.

Barton, Allen H., and Paul F. Lazarsfeld, *Some Functions of Qualitative Analysis in Social Research*, Bureau of Applied Social Research, Columbia University Reprint, No. 181, n.d.

Bell, G. B., and H. E. Hall, "The Relationship Between Leadership and Empathy," *Journal of Abnormal and Social Psychology*, 49 (January 1954), 156-157.

Bell, Wendell, and Marion D. Boat, "Urban Neighborhoods and Informal Social Relations," *American Journal of Sociology*, 62 (January 1957), 391-399.

Berger, Bennett M., *Working-Class Suburb, A Study of Auto Workers in Suburbia*, Berkeley: University of California Press, 1960.

Bernard, Jessie, "An Instrument for the Measurement of Success in Marriage," Publications of the *American Sociological Society*, 27 (May 1933), 94-106.

Bernstein, Basil, "Some Sociological Determinants of Perception," *British Journal of Sociology*, 9 (June 1958), 159-174.

———, "Language and Social Class," *British Journal of Sociology*, 11 (September 1960), 271-276.

Bierstedt, Robert, "Power and Social Organization," in Robert Dubin, *Human Relations in Administration*, New York: Prentice-Hall, 1951, pp. 173-181.

Blood, Robert O., Jr., and Donald M. Wolfe, *Husbands and Wives*, Glencoe, Ill.: Free Press, 1960.

Bott, Elizabeth, "Urban Families, Conjugal Roles and Social Networks," *Human Relations*, 8 (1955), 345-384.

——, *Family and Social Network*, London: Tavistock Publications, 1957.

Bradburn, Norman M., and David Caplovitz, *Reports on Happiness*, Chicago: Aldine Publishing, 1965.

Brim, Orville G., Jr., *Education for Child Rearing*, New York: Russell Sage Foundation, 1959.

——, *et al.*, "Relations Between Family Problems," *Marriage and Family Living*, 23 (August 1961), 219-226.

Bronfenbrenner, Urie, "Socialization and Social Class Through Time and Space," in Eleanor E. Maccoby, Theodore M. Newcomb and Eugene L. Hartley, eds., *Readings in Social Psychology*, New York: Holt, Rinehart and Winston, 1958, pp. 400-425.

Burgess, Ernest W., and Leonard S. Cottrell, Jr., *Predicting Success and Failure in Marriage*, New York: Prentice-Hall, 1939.

——, and Harvey J. Locke, *The Family: From Institution to Companionship*, New York: American Book, 1953.

——, and Paul Wallin, *Engagement and Marriage*, Chicago: J. B. Lippincott, 1953.

Clarke, Alfred, "The Use of Leisure and Its Relation to Levels of Occupational Prestige," *American Sociological Review*, 21 (June 1956), 301-307.

Cottrell, Leonard S., Jr., and Rosalind F. Dymond, "The Empathic Responses: A Neglected Field for Research," *Psychiatry*, 12 (November 1949), 355-359.

Cuber, J. F., and W. F. Kenkel, *Social Stratification in the U.S.*, New York: Appleton-Century-Crofts, 1954, p. 249.

Davis, Kingsley, "The Sociology of Parent-Youth Conflict," *American Sociological Review*, 4 (August 1940), 523-535.

Denney, Reuel, and David Riesman, "Leisure in Urbanized America," in Paul K. Hatt and Albert J. Reiss, Jr., eds., *Reader in Urban Sociology*, Glencoe, Ill.: Free Press, 1951, p. 470.

Dobriner, William, *The Suburban Community*, New York: G. P. Putnam, 1958.

Dotson, Floyd, "Patterns of Voluntary Association," *American Sociological Review*, 16 (October 1951), 687-693.

Dubin, Robert, "Industrial Workers' Worlds," *Social Problems*, 3 (January 1956), 131-142.

Duvall, Evelyn Millis, "Conceptions of Parenthood," *American Journal of Sociology*, 52 (November 1946), 193-208.

———, *In-Laws, Pro and Con*, New York: Association Press, 1954.

Dyer, Everett D., "A Study of Role and Authority Patterns and Expectation in a Group of Urban Middle-Class Two-Income Families." Unpublished Ph.D. dissertation, University of Wisconsin, 1955.

———, "Parenthood as Crisis: A Re-Study," *Marriage and Family Living*, 25 (May 1963), 196-201.

Dymond, Rosalind F., "A Preliminary Investigation of the Relationship of Insight and Empathy," *Journal of Consulting Psychology*, 12 (July–August 1948), 228-233.

———, "The Relation of Accuracy of Perception of the Spouse and Marital Happiness," *The American Psychologist*, 8 (August 1953), 344.

Eisenstadt, S. N., *From Generation to Generation: Age Groups and Social Structure*, Glencoe, Ill.: Free Press, 1956.

Elder, Glen H., Jr., and Charles E. Bowerman, "Family Structure and Child Rearing Patterns: The Effect of Family Size and Sex Composition on Child-Rearing Practices," *American Sociological Review*, 28 (December 1963), 891-905.

Elder, Rachel Ann, "Traditional and Developmental Conceptions of Fatherhood," *Marriage and Family Living*, 11 (Summer 1949), 98-101.

Empey, La Mar T., "Social Class and Occupational Aspiration," *American Sociological Review*, 21 (December 1956), 703-709.

Feldman, Harold, "The Development of Husband-Wife Relationships," Department of Child Development and Family Relationship, New York State College of Home Economics, Cornell University. Mimeographed report, 1961.

———, "Development of Husband-Wife Relationship," Research Report, Department of Child Development and Family Relations, Cornell University, 1965 (an unpublished report).

Foote, Nelson N., and Leonard S. Cottrell, Jr., *Identity and Interpersonal Competence*, Chicago: University of Chicago Press, 1955.

Gage, N. L., and L. J. Cronbach, "Conceptual and Methodological Problems in Interpersonal Perception," *Psychological Review*, 62 (November 1955), 411-422.

Gans, Herbert J., The Urban Villagers, New York: The Free Press, 1962.

Glick, Paul C., *American Families*, New York: John Wiley, 1957.

———, and Hugh Carter, "Marriage Patterns and Educational Level," *American Sociological Review*, 23 (June 1958), 294-300.

Gold, Martin, and Carol Slater, "Office, Factory, Store and Family: A

Study of Integration Setting," *American Sociological Review*, 23 (February 1958), 64-74.

Goldhammer, Herbert, and Edward A. Shils, "Types of Power," in Robert Dubin, *Human Relations in Administration*, New York: Prentice-Hall, 1951, pp. 182-187.

Goode, William J., *After Divorce*, Glencoe, Ill.: Free Press, 1956.

――――, *Marital Satisfaction and Instability: A Cross-Cultural Class Analysis of Divorce Rates*, Bureau of Applied Social Research, Columbia University Reprint, No. 367, 1959.

――――, "The Theoretical Importance of Love," *American Sociological Review*, 24 (February 1959), 38-47.

――――, *World Revolution and Family Patterns*, Glencoe, Ill.: Free Press, 1963.

Gurin, Gerald, Joseph Veroff and Sheila Feld, *Americans View Their Mental Health*, New York: Basic Books, 1960.

Harper, Robert A., "Communication Problems in Marriage and Marriage Counseling," *Marriage and Family Living*, 20 (May 1958), 107-112.

Hartley, Ruth E., "Woman's Roles: How Girls See Them," *A.A.U.W. Journal*, 55 (May 1962), 212-216.

Hastorf, A. H., and I. E. Bender, "A Caution Respecting Measurement of Emphatic Ability," *Journal of Abnormal and Social Psychology*, 47, Supplement No. 2 (April 1952), 574-576.

Hauser, Philip M., "More from the Census of 1960," *Scientific American*, 207 (October 1962), 30-38.

Havighurst, Robert J., and Kenneth Feigenbaum, "Leisure and Life-Style," *American Journal of Sociology*, 64 (January 1959), 396-405.

Heer, David M., "Dominance and the Working Wife," *Social Forces*, 36 (May 1958), 341-347.

――――, "Husband and Wife Perception of Family Power Structure," *Marriage and Family Living*, 24 (February 1962), 65-67.

Herbst, P. G., "The Measurement of Family Relationships," *Human Relations*, 5 (February 1952), 3-5.

――――, in O. A. Oeser and F. E. Emery, *Social Structure and Personality in a Rural Community*, New York: Macmillan, 1954, pp. 118-130.

――――, in O. A. Oeser and S. B. Hammond, *Social Structure and Personality in a City*, New York: Macmillan, 1954, pp. 126-179.

Hill, Reuben, "Social Stresses in the Family," in Marvin B. Sussman, ed., *Sourcebook in Marriage and the Family*, Boston: Houghton Mifflin, 1963, pp. 303-314.

――――, J. Mayone Stycos and Kurt W. Back, *The Family and Popu-*

lation Control, Chapel Hill: University of North Carolina Press, 1959.

Hill, Reuben, *et al.*, "Intra-Family Communication and Fertility," *Rural Sociology*, 20 (September–December 1955), 258-271.

Hobart, Charles W., "Disagreement and Non-Empathy During Courtship," *Marriage and Family Living*, 18 (November 1956), 317-322.

Hoffman, Lois Wladis, "Effects of Employment of Mothers on Parental Power Relations and the Division of Household Tasks," *Marriage and Family Living*, 22 (February 1960), 27-35.

Hollingshead, August B., and Frederick C. Redlich, *Social Class and Mental Illness: A Community Study*, New York: John Wiley, 1958.

Homans, George C., *The Human Group*, New York: Harcourt, Brace, 1950.

———, "Social Behavior as Exchange," *American Journal of Sociology*, 63 (May 1958), 597-606.

Hunt, Morton M., *Her Infinite Variety*, New York: Harper and Row, 1962.

Hyman, Herbert H., *Interviewing in Social Research*, Chicago: University of Chicago Press, 1954.

———, *Political Socialization*, Glencoe, Ill.: Free Press, 1959, pp. 144-145.

Inkeles, Alex, "Industrial Man: The Relation of Status to Experience, Perception and Value," *American Journal of Sociology*, 66 (July 1960), 1-32.

Jourard, Sidney M., "A Study of Self-Disclosure," *Scientific American*, 198 (May 1958), 77-82.

———, "Self-Disclosure and Other Cathexes," *Journal of Abnormal and Social Psychology*, 59 (November 1959), 428-431.

———, and Murray J. Landsman, "Cognition, Cathexis, and the 'Dyadic Effect' in Self-disclosing Behavior," *Merrill-Palmer Quarterly of Behavior and Development*, 6 (1959-1960), 178-186.

———, and Paul Lasokow, "Some Factors in Self-Disclosure," *Journal of Abnormal and Social Psychology*, 56 (January 1958), 91-98.

Kahl, Joseph A., *The American Class Structure*, New York: Holt, Rinehart and Winston, 1957.

Karlsson, Georg, *Adaptability and Communication in Marriage: A Swedish Predictive Study of Marital Satisfaction*, Uppsala: Almqvist and Wiksells Boktryckeri, 1951.

Katz, Elihu, and Paul F. Lazarsfeld, *Personal Influence: The Part Played by People in the Flow of Mass Communication*, Glencoe, Ill.: Free Press, 1955.

Katz, Irwin, *et al.*, "Need Satisfaction, Perception, and Cooperative Interaction in Married Couples," *Marriage and Family Living*, 25 (May 1963), 209-214.

Kenkel, William F., "Influence Differentiation in Family Decision Making," *Sociology and Social Research*, 42 (September–October 1957), 21.

———, and D. K. Hoffman, "Real and Conceived Roles in Family Decision Making," *Marriage and Family Living*, 18 (November 1956), 311-316.

Kephart, William M., *The Family, Society and the Individual*, Boston: Houghton Mifflin, 1961, p. 618.

Kirkpatrick, Clifford, "Community of Interest and the Measurement of Marriage Adjustment," *The Family*, 18 (June 1937), 133-137.

———, *The Family as Process and Institution*, New York: Ronald Press, 1963.

———, and Charles W. Hobart, "Disagreement, Disagreement Estimate, and Non-Empathic Imputations for Intimacy Groups Varying from Favorite Date to Married," *American Sociological Review*, 19 (February 1954), 10-19.

Kluckhohn, Clyde, and Florence R. Kluckhohn, "American Culture: Generalized Orientations and Class Patterns," in *Conflicts of Power in Modern Culture*, Lyman Bryson et al., eds., Conference on Science, Philosophy and Religion, New York: Harper, 1947.

Knupfer, Genevieve, "Portrait of the Underdog," *Public Opinion Quarterly*, 11 (Spring 1947), 103-114.

Kohn, Melvin L., "Social Class and Parental Values," *American Journal of Sociology*, 64 (January 1959), 337-351.

———, "Social Class and Parental Authority," *American Sociological Review*, 24 (June 1959), 352-366.

———, "Social Class and Parent-Child Relationships: An Interpretation," *American Journal of Sociology*, 68 (January 1963), 471-480.

Komarovsky, Mirra, *The Unemployed Man and His Family*, New York: Dryden Press, 1940, pp. 17-22.

———, "Functional Analysis of Sex Roles," *American Sociological Review*, 15 (August 1950), 508-516.

———, *Women in the Modern World: Their Education and Their Dilemmas*, Boston: Little, Brown, 1953.

———, "Continuities in Family Research: A Case Study," *American Journal of Sociology*, 62 (July 1956), 42-47.

Kornhauser, Arthur, Robert Dubin and A. Ross, eds., *Industrial Conflict*, New York: McGraw-Hill, 1954.

Krutch, Joseph Wood, "Through Happiness With Slide Rule and Calipers," *Saturday Review* (November 2, 1963), 12-15.

Landis, Judson T., "Values and Limitations of Family Research Using

Student Subjects," *Marriage and Family Living*, 20 (February 1947), 100-105.

Landis, Judson T., and Mary G. Landis, *Building a Successful Marriage*, New York: Prentice-Hall, 1953.

Langner, Thomas S., and S. T. Michael, *Life Stress and Mental Health*, New York: Free Press of Glencoe, 1963.

Larrabee, Eric, and Rolf Meyersohn, eds., *Mass Leisure*, Glencoe, Ill.: Free Press, 1958.

LeMasters, E. E., "Parenthood as Crisis," *Marriage and Family Living*, 19 (November 1957), 352-355.

Lenski, Gerhard, *The Religious Factor*, Garden City, N.Y.: Doubleday, 1961.

Lewis, Claudia, *Children of Cumberland*, New York: Columbia University Press, 1946.

Lichter, Solomon, Elsie Rapien, Frances Seibert and Morris Sklansky, *The Drop-Outs*, New York: Free Press of Glencoe, 1962.

Litwak, Eugene, "Occupational Mobility and Extended Family Cohesion," *American Sociological Review*, 25 (February 1960), 9-20.

———, "Geographical Mobility and Extended Family Cohesion," *American Sociological Review*, 25 (June 1960), 385-394.

Locke, Harvey J., *et al.*, *The Family: Analysis of Dyadic Relations*, Abstracts of the meetings of the American Sociology Society, 1955.

Lyman, Elizabeth L., "Occupational Differences in the Value Attached to Work," *American Journal of Sociology*, 61 (September 1955), 138-144.

Lynd, Robert S., and Helen Merrell Lynd, *Middletown*, New York: Harcourt, Brace, 1929.

Mannheim, Karl, "The Problem of Generations," in Paul Kecskemeti, ed., *Essays on the Sociology of Knowledge*, New York: Oxford University Press, 1952.

Marcus, Peggy S., "A Study of In-Law Relationships of 79 Couples Who Have Been Married Between 2 and 11 Years." Unpublished Master's thesis, Cornell University, 1950.

Mayer, John E., "The Disclosure of Marital Problems," Institute of Welfare Research, Community Service Society of New York, 1966 (an unpublished report).

McKinley, Donald, *Social Class and Family Life*, New York: Free Press, 1964.

Merton, Robert K., *Social Theory and Social Structure*, Glencoe, Ill.: Free Press, 1957, pp. 161-195.

———, and Robert A. Nisbet, *Contemporary Social Problems*, New York: Harcourt, Brace and World, 1961.

Middleton, Russell, and Snell Putney, "Dominance in Decisions in the

Family: Race and Class Differences," *American Journal of Sociology*, 66 (May 1960), 605-609.

Miller, D. R., and G. E. Swanson, *The Changing American Parent*, New York: John Wiley, 1958.

Miller, S. M., and Frank Reisman, "The Working-Class Subculture, A New View," *Social Problems*, 9 (Summer 1961), 86-97.

Mogey, John M., *Family and Neighborhood, Two Studies in Oxford*, London: Oxford University Press, 1956.

Morgan, Edmund S., *The Puritan Family*, Boston: Boston Public Library, 1944.

Morse, Nancy C., and Robert S. Weiss, "The Function and Meaning of Work and the Job," *American Sociological Review*, 20 (April 1955), 191-198.

Newcomb, T. R., "Communicative Behavior," in T. R. Newcomb and R. Young, eds., *Approaches to the Study of Politics*, Evanston, Ill.: Northwestern University Press, 1958, pp. 244-265.

Oeser, O. A., and F. E. Emery, *Social Structure and Personality in a Rural Community*, New York: Macmillan, 1954.

Olsen, Marvin E., *Distribution of Responsibility Within the Family as Related to Social Stratification*, Grinnell, Iowa: Grinnell College, 1956-1957.

———, "Distribution of Family Responsibility and Social Stratification," *Marriage and Family Living*, 22 (February 1960), 60-65.

Ort, Robert S., "A Study of Role Conflicts as Related to Happiness in Marriage," *Journal of Abnormal and Social Psychology*, 45 (October 1950), 691-699.

Orzack, Louis H., "Work as a 'Central Life Interest' of Professionals," *Social Problems*, 7 (Fall 1959), 125-132.

Parad, Howard J., and Gerald Caplan, "A Framework for Studying Families in Crisis," in Marvin B. Sussman, ed., *Sourcebook in Marriage and the Family*, Boston: Houghton Mifflin, 1963.

Parsons, Talcott, "The Professions and Social Structure," *Social Forces*, 17 (May 1939), 457-466.

———, "The Social Structure of the Family," in Ruth Nanda Anshen, ed., *The Family: Its Function and Destiny*, New York: Harper, 1959, p. 209.

———, and Robert F. Bales, *Family Socialization and Interaction Process*, Glencoe, Ill.: Free Press, 1955.

Pineo, Peter C., "Disenchantment in the Later Years of Marriage," *Marriage and Family Living*, 23 (February 1961), 3-11.

Polansky, Norman A., "The Concept of Verbal Accessibility," *Smith College Studies in Social Work*, 36 (October 1965), 1-38.

Rabban, Meyer, "Sex-Role Identification in Young Children in Two

Diverse Social Groups," *Genetic Psychological Monograph*, 42 (August 1950), pp. 81-158.

Rainwater, Lee, "Marital Sexuality in Four Cultures of Poverty," *Journal of Marriage and the Family* (November 1964), 457-466.

———, Richard P. Coleman and Gerald Handel, *Workingman's Wife*, New York: Oceana Publications, 1959.

———, and Karol K. Weinstein, *And the Poor Get Children*, Chicago: Quadrangle Books, 1960.

Reisman, Leonard, "Class, Leisure and Social Participation," *American Sociological Review*, 19 (February 1954), 76-84.

Reiss, Paul J., "The Extended Kinship System: Correlates of and Attitudes on Frequency of Interaction," *Marriage and Family Living*, 24 (November 1962), 333-340.

Roth, Julius, and Robert F. Peck, "Social Class and Social Mobility Factors Related to Marital Adjustment," *American Sociological Review*, 16 (August 1951), 478-487.

Ruesh, Jurgen, and Kees Waldon, *Non Verbal Communication: Notes on the Visual Perception of Human Relations*, Berkeley: University of California Press, 1956.

Schatzman, Leonard, and Anselm Strauss, "Social Class and Modes of Communication," *American Journal of Sociology*, 60 (January 1955), 329-338.

Schorr, Alvin L., *Filial Responsibility in Modern American Family*, Washington, D.C.: U.S. Department of Health, Education and Welfare (Social Security Administration), 1960.

Scott, Greer, "Urbanism Reconsidered: A Comparative Study of Local Areas in a Metropolis," *American Sociological Review*, 21 (February 1956), 22.

Sears, Robert R., Eleanor E. Maccoby and Harry Levin, *Patterns of Childrearing*, Evanston, Ill.: Harper and Row, 1957.

Shostak, Arthur B., and William Gomberg, eds., *Blue-Collar World: Studies of the American Worker*, Englewood Cliffs, N.J.: Prentice-Hall, 1964.

Slater, Philip E., "Parental Role Differentiation," *American Journal of Sociology*, 67 (November 1961), 296-312.

Smardan, Lawrence Eugene, "An Exploratory Study of Communication." Unpublished Ph.D. dissertation, Cornell University, 1957.

Steiner, Ivan D. and John S. Dodge, "Interpersonal Perception and Role Structure as Determinants of Group and Individual Efficiency," *Human Relations*, 9 (November 1956), 467-481.

Stewart, Robert L., and Glenn M. Vernon, "Four Correlates of Empathy in the Dating Situation," *Sociology and Social Research*, 63 (March 1959), 279-285.

Stolz, Lois M., "Effects of Maternal Employment on Children: Evidence from Research," *Child Development*, 31 (December 1960), 749-782.

Straus, Murray A., "Conjugal Power Structure and Adolescent Personality," *Marriage and Family Living*, 24 (February 1962), 17-25.

———, "Communication, Creativity, and Social Class Differences in Family Responses to an Experimental Stimulated Crisis." A mimeographed report, 1964.

Strauss, Anselm L., "Strain and Harmony in American Japanese War-Bride Marriages," *Marriage and Family Living*, 16 (May 1954), 99-106.

Strodtbeck, Fred L., "Husband-Wife Interaction over Revealed Differences," *American Sociological Review*, 16 (August 1951), 468-473.

———, "The Family as a Three Person Group," *American Sociological Review*, 19 (February 1954), 23-29.

———, "Family Interaction, Values and Achievement," in D. C. McClelland *et al.*, *Talent and Society*, Princeton, N.J.: Van Nostrand, 1958, pp. 135-194.

Stryker, Sheldon, "Conditions of Accurate Role-Taking: A Test of Mead's Theory," in Arnold M. Rose, ed., *Human Behavior and Social Processes*, Boston: Houghton Mifflin, 1962, pp. 41-63.

Sussman, Marvin B., "The Help Pattern in Middle Class Family," *American Sociological Review*, 18 (February 1953), 18-28.

———, "The Isolated Nuclear Family: Fact or Fiction," *Social Problems*, 6 (Spring 1959), 333-340.

———, ed., *Sourcebook in Marriage and the Family*, Boston: Houghton Mifflin, 1963.

———, and Lee Burchinal, "Kin Family Network: Unheralded Structure in Current Conceptualization of Family Functioning," *Marriage and Family Living*, 24 (August 1962), 231-241.

———, and ———, "Parental Aid to Married Children: Implications for Family Functioning," *Marriage and Family Living*, 24 (November 1962), 320-332.

Terman, Lewis M., *et al.*, *Psychological Factors in Marital Happiness*, New York: McGraw-Hill, 1938.

Thomas, John L., *The American Catholic Family*, Englewood Cliffs, N.J.: Prentice-Hall, 1956.

Tilly, Charles, "Occupational Rank and Grade of Residences in a Metropolis," *American Journal of Sociology*, 67 (November 1961), 323-330.

Townsend, Peter, *The Family Life of Old People*, Glencoe, Ill.: Free Press, 1957.

Van Bortel, Dorothy Greey, "Home-Making: Concepts, Practices and Attributes in Two Social Classes." Unpublished Ph.D. dissertation, University of Chicago, 1954.

Van Bortel, Dorothy Greey, and Irma H. Gross, *A Comparison of Home Management in Two Socio-Economic Groups*, Michigan State College Agricultural Experiment Station, Bulletin 240, April 1954.

Vogel, Ezra F., and Norman W. Bell, "The Emotionally Disturbed Child as the Family Scapegoat," in Norman W. Bell and Ezra F. Vogel, eds., *A Modern Introduction to the Family*, Glencoe, Ill.: Free Press, 1960, pp. 389-390.

Waller, Willard, and Reuben Hill, *The Family*, New York: Dryden Press, 1951.

Wallin, Paul, "Sex Differences in Attitudes to In-Laws: A Test of a Theory," *American Journal of Sociology*, 59 (March 1954), 466-469.

Wesker, Arnold, *Roots*, Baltimore: Penguin Books, 1959, pp. 74-75.

West, James, *Plainville, U.S.A.*, New York: Columbia University Press, 1945.

White, Clyde R., "Social Class Differences in the Uses of Leisure," *American Journal of Sociology*, 61 (September 1955), 145-151.

White, Martha Sturm, "Social Class, Child Rearing Practices and Child Behavior," *American Sociological Review*, 22 (December 1957), 704-712.

Whyte, William H., Jr., "The Corporation and the Wife," *Fortune*, 44 (October 1951), 86 ff.

———, "The Wives of Management," *Fortune*, 44 (November 1951), 109 ff.

Williamson, Robert C., "Socio-Economic Factors in Marital Adjustment in an Urban Setting," *American Sociological Review*, 19 (April 1954), 213-216.

Wolfe, Donald M., "Power and Authority in the Family," in Robert F. Winch *et al.*, ed., *Selected Studies in Marriage and the Family*, New York: Holt, Rinehart and Winston, 1962, pp. 582-600.

Wolff, Kurt H., ed., *The Sociology of Georg Simmel*, Glencoe, Ill.: Free Press, 1950.

Woods, Frances Jerome, *The American Family System*, New York: Harper, 1959.

Young, Michael, and Peter Willmott, *Family and Kinship in East London*, Glencoe, Ill.: Free Press, 1957.

Index

ABOUT THE AUTHOR

MIRRA KOMAROVSKY is currently Professor and Chairman of the Department of Sociology at Barnard College, Columbia University. Before joining the Barnard faculty, she taught at Skidmore College and also did research at Yale University and at the International Institute of Social Research. She was President of the Eastern Sociological Society in 1954-1955. Dr. Komarovsky received her Ph.D. from Columbia University in 1940. In addition to numerous articles in professional journals, she is the author of *The Unemployed Man and His Family*, *Women in the Modern World: Their Education and Their Dilemmas*, coauthor of *Leisure: A Suburban Study*, and editor of *Common Frontiers of the Social Sciences*.

VINTAGE WORKS OF SCIENCE
AND PSYCHOLOGY